How to Use the Companion

The companion CD-ROM and the files included on it will run on all Windows platforms. System requirements for any of the software for this CD -ROM may vary widely. Please review all software readme files before installing software on your computer.

Please review the CD-ROM appendix for more information on the CD contents included with this book.

■ Minimum System Requirements

Computer: 386 IBM PC-compatible
Memory: 8 MB of RAM
Software: Windows 3.1, NT or 95
Hardware: 2X CD-ROM Drive

Doing Objects in Microsoft Visual Basic 5.0

Doing Objects in Microsoft Visual Basic 5.0

Deborah Kurata

Ziff-Davis Press
An imprint of Macmillan Computer Publishing USA
Emeryville, California

Publisher	Stacy Hiquet
Associate Publisher	Steven Sayre
Acquisitions Editor	Lysa Lewallen
Development Editor	Angela Allen
Copy Editor	Deborah Craig
Technical Reviewer	Joe Garrick
Proofreader	Pamela Vevea
Cover Illustration and Design	Regan Honda
Book Design	Laura Lamar/MAX, San Francisco
Screen Graphics Editor	P. Diamond
Technical Illustration	Sarah Ishida and Mina Reimer
Page Layout	Janet Piercy
Indexer	Valerie Robbins

Ziff-Davis Press, ZD Press, the Ziff-Davis Press logo are trademarks or registered trademarks of, and are licensed to Macmillan Computer Publishing USA by Ziff-Davis Publishing Company, New York, New York.

Ziff-Davis Press imprint books are produced on a Macintosh computer system with the following applications: FrameMaker®, Microsoft® Word, QuarkXPress®, Adobe Illustrator®, Adobe Photoshop®, Adobe Streamline™, MacLink®Plus, Aldus® FreeHand™, Collage Plus™.

Ziff-Davis Press, an imprint of
Macmillan Computer Publishing USA
5903 Christie Avenue
Emeryville, CA 94608

ISBN 1-56276-444-6

Manufactured in the United States of America
10 9 8 7 6 5 4 3 2

Dedicated to my children, Jessica and Krysta.
I hope to teach you that you can do and be anything, as my parents have taught me.

■ Contents at a Glance

■ Table of Contents

Part 3: Constructing an Application

Chapter 11: Building Classes: Additional Techniques   311

■ Acknowledgments

First I want to thank the people at Ziff-Davis Press who have worked hard to make this book happen. They took a risk allowing me to develop the original book, instead of doing just another user's guide. Specifically, I want to thank Lysa Lewallen, Angela Allen, and Deborah Craig for their help in creating the second edition of this book. Additionally, I want to thank Dan Appleman who introduced me to Ziff-Davis and provided moral support during the process.

Several software designers and developers have significantly shaped my view of software development and I want to take this time to thank them. Judy Young patiently taught me how to develop truly structured BASIC programs on a PDP-11 computer. I have continued to use many of the things I learned from her. Many years later, I worked with Carl Quinn, who is now at Borland, on the development of my first C++ application. Carl introduced me to concepts such as objects, methods, properties, inheritance, polymorphism, and object hierarchies. He hooked me on the object-oriented techniques that I was glad to brush the dust off when I started working with Visual Basic 4.0. Thanks to Bill Storage for helping me quickly make the jump from my C++ concepts to the object-oriented features of Visual Basic. His explanations saved me lots of trial and error!

I owe a lot of my ideas on user interface design to Alan Cooper. My first experience with Visual Basic was a project with Alan, who is sometimes called "the father of Visual Basic." He helped me to break the bounds of "it's always been done that way" and develop applications that were more user-friendly. Thanks for that, Alan, and your continued moral support.

There were many developers on the technical beta forum that provided technical help and friendly discussions of the topics. They include Karl Peterson (thanks for the virtual shoulder), Tim McBride, Chris Dias, Craig Goren, Gregg Irwin, Constance Petersen, Doug Marquardt, Zane Thomas, and Jonathan Wood. I thank you.

Thanks to the people who reviewed chapters in one form or another. For reviewing chapters in the first edition, thanks to L.J. Johnson, Glen Hamilton, Alan Cooper, W. Henry Lyne, Dean Fiala, Don Moonshine, Gary Khachadoorian, Richard Curzon, David Duncan, Cean Howman, Cary Ostrie, and Donald English. Your comments helped to shape the content of the book. And a special thanks to the technical editor for the first edition, Kathleen Joeris, who pushed me to fully research the design topics before I wrote about them. I thank you for your hard work and valuable comments. Thanks also to Dylan Kaufman for reviewing several chapters in the second edition.

For the technical editing of the second edition, thanks to Joe Garrick. His suggestions and comments kept me thinking and improved the technical details in the chapters. Adding the readme notes to the project files was his excellent idea. Thank you Joe.

Finally, I want to thank my wonderful support organization: my husband and partner, Jerry Kurata; our children, Jessica and Krysta; and my parents, Jerre and Virginia Cummings. They have supported me throughout this sometimes taxing, sometimes exhilarating adventure. I thank you for your patience and your understanding.

Deborah Kurata
February 1997

■ Introduction

There is a big step from throwing working code together to building complete applications. Too little has been discussed about how to take that step. When the idea first came along to write a Visual Basic book, I wanted to address this issue. I wanted to provide the Visual Basic programmer with pragmatic ways to design their applications, not as an afterthought, but as a preplanned activity. I wanted to present specific techniques for developing well-structured applications; applications where you can find the code you wrote last month and modify it without breaking other code. This is that book.

If you look at applications used in your company or in your home, you will find some of them look much better than others. The best ones are easy to look at, easy to work with, and easy to figure out. If you had the opportunity to look under the covers and see the inside of these applications, you would also find that some look much better than others. The best ones are easy to modify, easy to work with, and easy to figure out.

How can we make all of our programs look good on the inside and the outside? How can we design a better architecture and structure our Visual Basic applications? When I discovered the object-oriented features in Visual Basic I knew I had found the answer.

■ Why Do Objects?

Visual Basic is now in a similar place on the language life cycle as C was several years ago when C++ was emerging. The C programmers looked at the object-oriented features in C++ and wondered, "What are objects? When should they be used? Why do objects?"

Well, objects are simply the things involved in the application. The employees and time sheets in a time tracking system, the customers and invoices in a purchasing system, or the players, teams, and games in a baseball application.

As to the question of when objects should be used, I propose, with a tinge of skepticism, that they should always be used. Every part of every application could be done using objects. The business objects, such as the employees, time sheets, customers, and so on, can be implemented as objects. The implementation details, such as providing edit menu options, saving data to a file, and so on, can also be implemented as objects. How far you want to go with objects is a personal choice. However, I expect that as you use the object-oriented features of Visual Basic you will get hooked and you, too, will go all the way with objects!

There are many benefits to doing objects with Visual Basic, such as:

- Objects help you to think about an application in terms of real-world things, aiding in the design process.

- Objects define all of their data and their processing in one programming unit. This makes it much easier to find your code and to manage the complexities of software development. They also simplify multiple programmer development.

- Objects prepackage functionality that can be more easily reused throughout the enterprise. For example, you can develop an object for calculating the corporation's pricing model and reuse that functionality in any application needing it, including Excel!

- Objects allow you to participate in the excitement of ActiveX components. Using objects, you can build ActiveX EXEs and ActiveX DLLs to package functionality in a precompiled component. You can build your own ActiveX controls. You can even build ActiveX documents for displaying on Web pages.

This book clarifies and expands on these answers to help you understand when, how, and why to do objects.

■ Who Should Read This Book?

The first two parts of this book introduce object-oriented concepts and provide an in-depth description of designing an object-oriented application. This information is appropriate for all levels of Visual Basic developers. It is equally appropriate for managers, designers, technical writers, testers, and any other individuals interested in an overview of object-oriented design.

The third part of this book walks you through implementing an object-oriented application with Visual Basic. It provides detailed discussions and code examples. This part of the book assumes you are familiar with Visual Basic; that you know how to create forms and write code. If you have never used Visual Basic before, you will need to read an introductory text prior to working through this third part.

■ What Will This Book Tell Me?

This book is organized into three parts as follows:

Part 1: Preparing the Foundation

The chapters in Part 1 provide a foundation for object-oriented design by describing fundamental object-oriented concepts and the features of Visual Basic that support these concepts. This foundation includes a summary of the software development process. It presents information on preparing for an object-oriented design, including establishing the goals and requirements of the application.

Part 2: OOD: Designing the Framework

The second part of this book introduces the GUIDS methodology for object-oriented design (OOD). Taking a case study, it walks you through each step of the design.

- **Goal-centered design** focuses on the goals of the application to define the objects involved with the application. Techniques are presented to help you define the objects, their properties, and their methods.

- **User-interface design** describes the process of designing the user-view of the application. Tips are provided to help you develop a good user interface.

- **Implementation-centered design** looks at how the application will be implemented. Procedures for developing a polished object hierarchy are described. The three-tiered architecture is presented along with a discussion of how that architecture affects your design.

- **Data design** looks at the data in the application. Techniques are described for sorting through your data and defining how it will be accessed by the application. A general introduction to designing relational databases is also presented.

- **Strategies for construction** define the strategies you should consider prior to beginning the construction. Strategies such as buy or build, coding standards, and testing plans are discussed.

When you are finished, you will have an understanding of OOD basics.

Part 3: OOP: Constructing an Application

Part 3 details how to use the object-oriented features of Visual Basic.

- Chapter 10, "Building Your First Class," looks at how to build a class module and create objects from the class. It covers how to define constants and events in your classes and how to handle errors. In addition, it answers the top ten class questions.

- Chapter 11, "Building Classes: Additional Techniques," describes some advanced features such as using collections and saving objects to a file. It details how to define a class in a form. It then provides debugging tips and answers the top ten class techniques questions.

- Chapter 12, "Interfaces, Polymorphism, and Inheritance," describes how to define and implement multiple interfaces for your classes. By implementing an interface in several classes, you can leverage polymorphism to simplify your coding. Even though Visual Basic does not provide implementation inheritance, you can achieve implementation inheritance using interface inheritance and delegation, as shown in this chapter.

- Chapter 13, "Building ActiveX Components," provides a discussion of ActiveX. It details how to build ActiveX EXEs, ActiveX DLLs, ActiveX controls, and ActiveX documents. It also presents do's and don'ts when creating ActiveX components.

- Chapter 14, "Doing Database Objects," describes developing a database application with no code by using the data control. It then adds some code to the application to provide more flexibility and a more friendly user interface. Finally, it details developing a database application using the data access objects for a complete object-oriented approach to database accessing.

- Chapter 15, "Putting the Pieces Together," describes how to handle the details of a full-featured application such as using resource files, saving settings to the registry, logging events to the NT event log or any log file, using the Windows API, creating pop-up menus, creating What's This help, and adding icons for the application. It also provides an overview of building a large system from the components discussed in the prior chapters.

Each chapter provides extensive code examples to demonstrate the techniques. These code examples are provided on the enclosed CD-ROM as discussed in the Appendix.

■ What's New in the Second Edition?

The first edition of this book was written to provide a pragmatic approach to software design and showcase the object-oriented features in Visual Basic. This second edition continues with that goal, covering many of the new features of Visual Basic 5. The specific changes are as follows:

- Chapter 1, "Introduction to OO in VB," describes the object-oriented features of Visual Basic, many of which are new in Visual Basic 5. It includes a list of the new Visual Basic 5 features.

- Chapters 2 through 6 and Chapters 8 and 9 include minor wording changes, clarification, and new sections on documenting the design.

- Chapter 7, "Implementation-Centered Design," went through a major overhaul. When developing the first edition of the book, I was working with the beta version of Visual Basic which I could not, of course, use in projects for any of my clients. So it was not until after Visual Basic 4 was shipped that I was able to use it in a production environment. Since that time, I found many other techniques and tips for implementing component-based, object-oriented applications. The revisions in this chapter reflect that experience.

- Chapter 10, "Building Your First Class," includes new sections on defining constants with an enumeration and declaring and raising events. It also includes expanded information on error handling.

- Chapter 11, "Building Classes: Additional Techniques," includes new information on working with forms as classes. It also includes a new section on debugging techniques.

- Chapter 12, "Interfaces, Polymorphism, and Inheritance," is an entirely new chapter for new VB5 features.

- Chapter 13, "Building ActiveX Components," includes the new debugging techniques for ActiveX EXEs and ActiveX DLLs. It also includes entirely new sections on creating ActiveX controls and ActiveX documents.

- Chapter 14, "Doing Database Objects," includes major enhancements to the description of business objects, business object classes, and business object data transfer classes. It provides several alternatives for mapping objects to a relational database and when to use each alternative. This includes a discussion of ODBCDirect and OLE DB.

- Chapter 15, "Putting the Pieces Together," was reorganized with the focus on additional tools and techniques available in Visual Basic. New sections cover logging events to the NT event log or any log file, defining global objects, using the API with AddressOf and connecting forms to an object hierarchy.

Additional information about Visual Basic 5 and any corrections to material in this book can be found on the InStep Technologies Web site: http://www.insteptech.com.

■ How Do I Use This Book?

You can use this book to come up to speed quickly on the new features available in Visual Basic 5. Or, you can use this book to obtain a general overview of object-oriented concepts and how they apply to Visual Basic. You can also use this book as a tutorial, working through all of the examples and sample applications. It can be a reference to the object-oriented features in Visual Basic. You can use this book as it best suits your needs.

I have made every effort to describe the concepts presented in this book in a clear and concise fashion. I have tested the code examples using a beta version of Visual Basic, Enterprise Edition under Windows 95. If you have suggestions for improving the content of the book, or find something that is incorrect or unclear, I would like to hear from you. I can then incorporate your comments in future editions of this book. You can reach me via e-mail at deborahk@insteptech.com or you can write to me at:

Deborah Kurata
c/o Ziff-Davis Press
5903 Christie Ave.
Emeryville, CA 94608

1

Preparing the Foundation

- *What Is OO?*
- *Introduction to Object-Oriented Concepts*
- *The Basic Elements of an Object-Oriented System*
- *OO Features in Visual Basic*
- *New Visual Basic 5 Features*
- *Summary*
- *Additional Reading*
- *Think It Over*

1

Introduction to OO in VB

What difference is there, do you think, between those in Plato's cave who can only marvel at the shadows and images of various objects, provided they are content and don't know what they miss, and the philosopher who has emerged from the cave and sees the real things?

—Desiderius Erasmus (c. 1466–1536), Dutch humanist

Software development began in Plato's cave. Programmers used process charts and data flow diagrams to create the shadows and images of the real-world objects. Object-oriented methodologies have allowed us to emerge from the cave and model these objects as the real things. We can now design and develop software that is based on the objects themselves, not on their procedural shadows.

This chapter provides an introduction to the object-oriented (OO) concepts that are necessary to make full use of Visual Basic 5 and outlines the VB5 features that support these concepts. It then lists the many new VB5 features with references, where appropriate, to the chapter describing the new feature.

■ What Is OO?

The phrase "object-oriented," or OO, seems to be everywhere these days. It has been used to describe many things, such as user-friendly applications, window-based interfaces, application development environments, operating systems, database technologies, and component software strategies. The term "objects" has been equally prevalent—describing everything from business entities to Visual Basic controls and ActiveX components.

Object-oriented basically means looking at a problem in terms of the objects involved with that problem. Although this sounds techie, it is actually the way humans have looked at the world since long before the advent of computers.

Imagine early humans faced with the problem of getting enough food for their families. They didn't model the inputs and outputs of the hunting process. Rather, they focused on the objects involved and how to improve the interaction between the objects. They looked at the speed of the animals and how close they had to be to kill them; then designed and constructed a spear. They used an object-oriented approach to solving their problem.

Object-oriented concepts are used in many professions. For example, when designing an office, an architect thinks about working spaces, foundations, frameworks, and plumbing systems. These are the real-world objects. The architect does not concentrate on the process of pouring the foundation, hammering nails, or connecting the plumbing. These are lower-level procedures that are important, but are not applicable to the high-level design of an office building.

Business requirements can also be viewed in terms of objects. Defining how these objects relate provides a good model of the particular business area. But how do you recognize the objects? How can you design the objects to meet all of the defined requirements? How will the objects appear to the users? How will the objects be put together in Visual Basic to form an application? How will the data for the objects be stored?

Answering these questions may appear to be a daunting task. The list of requirements may seem unattainable and the user interface possibilities can seem infinite. It may not be obvious how to convert the objects into a design and the design to code. Deciding where to put code in a Visual Basic application and how to store application data can create turf wars. But the task is not difficult if you have a methodology for working through this process.

Keynote

This book introduces the GUIDS (pronounced "guides") methodology for object-oriented design (OOD). This methodology will guide you through the following:

- **G**oal-centered design

- **U**ser-interface design

- **I**mplementation-centered design

- **D**ata design

- **S**trategies for construction

OOD is followed by OOP, object-oriented programming. The design created using the GUIDS methodology is implemented. Visual Basic 5 provides many features for object-oriented development and can be used to implement an object-oriented design.

■ Introduction to Object-Oriented Concepts

Before diving into an object-oriented design, it is important to get your feet wet with basic object-oriented (OO) concepts. This introduction provides you with the background and terminology needed for understanding the OO literature, including some of the Visual Basic documentation. If you are already knowledgeable in OO, you may want to skip to the next section for an overview of how these concepts are supported in Visual Basic.

It's okay if you don't feel comfortable with all of this terminology right away. As you progress through this book you will see these object-oriented terms used in the design and again in implementation examples. Each time you see the terms used they will seem more familiar. Soon they will become a permanent part of your vocabulary.

What Are Objects?

Objects are things. People, companies, employees, time sheets, and ledger entries are all types of objects. In object-oriented terms, the word *object* is used to describe one specific thing, like Sam Smith the carpenter at 3322 Main Street and the May 15th time sheet for Jessica Jones.

Objects have an identity and this identity is defined with *properties*. Sam Smith has a name, occupation, and address. The time sheet has a time period and employee name. This is sometimes referred to as what the object *knows*. So the Sam Smith object knows its name, address, and occupation and the Time Sheet object knows its time period and employee name.

Objects also do things. Sam the carpenter builds buildings. The time sheet gets filled out, is validated, and submitted for payment. The things an object can do are called its *behaviors*.

Tech Note.   *In other object-oriented literature, different names may be used for the properties and behaviors. Properties are sometimes referred to as* resources, attributes, *or* private member variables. *Behaviors are called* services, operations, member functions, responsibilities, *or* methods.

If you want to form a mental picture of an object from an object-oriented point of view, it would look something like Figure 1.1. Each specific Time Sheet object is identified by the values of the properties shown at the center of the object. The behaviors are shown around the properties. This depiction indicates that the property values of an object should not be directly accessed by something outside of the object. For example, the time sheet hours should not be adjusted except through the "fill out" behavior and the employee name would not be retrieved except through the "get employee name" behavior.

Objects can be real-world things, such as the employee and time sheet examples just described. Objects can be conceptual things, such as an engineering process or payroll. These conceptual things are not tangible but they can have properties and behaviors. Objects can also be implementation-specific things, such as forms, modules, databases, windows, and controls. The same object-oriented concepts apply regardless of whether the object is based on the real world, on a concept, or on the implementation.

What Are Classes?

Humans like to classify things, to find similarities in things and to group them accordingly. Things with similar properties and behaviors are grouped together. In object-oriented terminology, the word *class* is used to refer to a group of similar objects.

Because Sam Smith and Jessica Jones both have a name, address, and occupation, and they both do work for the same company, they can be grouped together in an Employee class. Because Sam has construction license information and does carpentry work, he is also grouped into a Carpenter class with the other carpenters in the company. Jessica does programming and has a list of programming languages she uses, so she is grouped into a Programmer class with the other programmers.

Figure 1.1

The Time Sheet object
encapsulates the
properties within the
object and exposes them
through the behaviors.

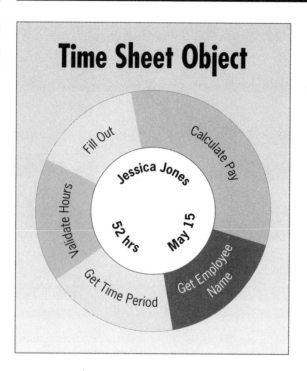

Keynote

The class provides a definition of the objects by specifying the properties and behaviors that each object in that class will have. This list of properties and behaviors is the class *interface*. To be in the Employee class, an object must have a name, address, and occupation property, and a "do work" behavior. Because Sam and Jessica meet these criteria, they belong to the Employee class. A specific object that belongs to a class is referred to as an *instance* of the class. Each instance of the class will have values for the defined set of properties and can perform the defined behaviors.

Classes are often described as cookie cutters. A class is a cookie cutter with defined size and shape properties. The objects are the cookies that are created from the cookie cutter class. Each cookie created from the class will have the size and shape properties. However, once the cookies are created from the class the size or shape of any cookie can be adjusted, so the value of the size and shape properties can be different for different objects from the class.

The Time Sheet class, shown in Figure 1.2, contains the definition of the behaviors (including the implementation) and the definition of the properties. Each object that is an instance of that class lists the behaviors and has specific values for each property. Figure 1.2 shows two Time Sheet objects created from the Time Sheet class: Jessica Jones's time sheet and Sam Smith's time sheet, both from May 15.

Figure 1.2

The Time Sheet class defines the properties and behaviors for each object from the class. The objects created from the Time Sheet class have values for the properties and can perform the behaviors.

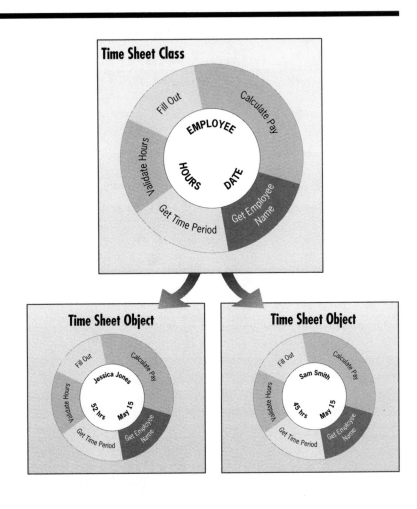

Keynote

A class itself does not have property values. Nor does it perform the class behaviors. Rather, the class defines the properties and contains the implementation of the behaviors that will be used by each object created from the class. These objects will have values for the properties and perform the behaviors. You do not eat the cookie cutter or fill out a Time Sheet class. Rather you eat each cookie and fill out each individual time sheet.

As a different example, the command button in the Visual Basic toolbox represents a CommandButton class. Each time you add a command button to a form in Visual Basic, you are creating an instance of that CommandButton class. The CommandButton class has specific defined behaviors, like

Move, and properties, like Name and Caption. The CommandButton class it-self does not have a value for the Name or Caption property. Nor does it move. Rather, it contains the implementation for the Name and Caption properties and Move behavior. The command button objects that you create as instances of that CommandButton class have values for the Name (cmdOK) and Caption ("OK") properties, and perform the Move behavior.

How Are Objects Related?

Objects are bound together by their relationships. There are three basic types of object relationships: subclasses, containers, and collaborators.

Subclasses: The "is a" Relationship

Objects in a class are sometimes subtypes, or *subclasses*, of objects from an-other class. This subclass relationship is very common. Biological objects are classified in a subclass hierarchy of kingdom, phylum, class, order, family, ge-nus, and species. For example, a mammal is a subclass of animals, a canine is a subclass of mammals, and a dog is a subclass of canines.

Subclass relationships are relatively easy to identify because the objects in these classes have an "is a" relationship. Each carpenter "is an" employee, each programmer "is an" employee. You can draw these relationships in a class hierarchy, as shown in Figure 1.3.

Figure 1.3

The class hierarchy model depicts the "is a" subclass relationship between the classes and objects from those classes.

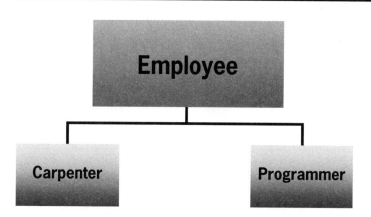

A class at the top of the hierarchy has behaviors and properties that are common to all subordinate classes. The classes lower in the hierarchy have specialized behaviors and properties. The Employee class has a generalized "do work" behavior and has name and address properties common to all em-ployees. The Carpenter class has a specialized "do hammering" behavior and a construction license property. The Programmer class has a specialized "do coding" behavior and a known programming languages property.

The objects that belong to the subordinate classes have the properties and behaviors of that subordinate class *and* the properties and behaviors of the classes above it in the hierarchy. In object-oriented terms, the object *inherits* the properties and behaviors of the higher-level classes. So the Jessica Jones instance of the Programmer class can do coding and knows which programming languages she has used. She also knows her name, address, and occupation and can do work for the company because she inherits these properties and behaviors from the Employee class.

Containers: The "has a" Relationship

Objects can contain or be composed of other objects. Everything from your car to the filing cabinet in your office is an example of a container object. Your car has an engine, tires, seats, and so on. A filing cabinet has a set of hanging folders, each hanging folder has a set of file folders, and each file folder has a set of papers.

The container relationships can be identified using the "has a" clause. For example, a company "has a" set of employees and an employee "has a" set of time sheets. Figure 1.4 illustrates this relationship.

Figure 1.4

The object hierarchy depicts the "has a" containment relationships between the objects.

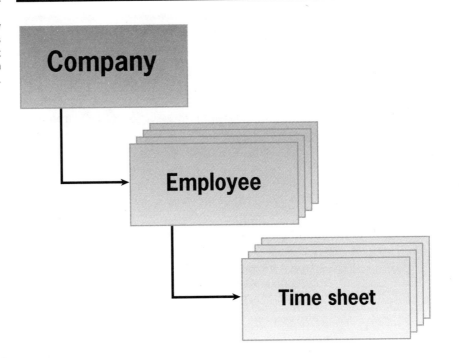

Objects at the top of the object hierarchy contain references to the objects below. The container objects know everything about themselves and the objects they contain. For example, the company object has company name and address properties. It contains a set of references to Employee objects that each have a name, address, occupation, and set of references to Time Sheet objects. Each of the Time Sheet objects has a time period and number of hours.

The forms in Visual Basic are another example of container objects. Each form contains a set of controls. The form knows about each control and each control is accessed through referencing the form, as in:

```
frmEmployee.txtName
```

The name of the form containing the control comes first, followed by the control name. This technique of referencing objects through their containers is used throughout Visual Basic. Using Figure 1.4 as an example, to retrieve the hours from one of Jessica Jones's time sheets, the syntax would be something like:

```
Company.Employee("Jessica Jones").TimeSheet("May 15").Hours
```

This syntax may seem somewhat complex at first, but it is basically an expanded use of the same syntax used in:

```
frmEmployee.txtName
```

Collaborators: The "uses" Relationship

In many cases, objects are not directly related to each other. You and your car, for example, are not related. Rather, you "use" your car to get where you need to go.

Collaborator relationships are identified with the "uses" clause. If an object needs to use another object for some purpose, it has a collaborator relationship. To establish this relationship, the object will contain a reference to the collaborator. The object will then access the public behaviors of the collaborator object to do what it needs. For example, a Time Sheet object may use a Calendar object or Printer object. The collaborator relationships are normally identified to ensure that all objects required by an object exist. If the Time Sheet object uses a Calendar object, a Calendar object must be defined in the application.

As another example, an employee data entry screen will use an Employee object. So the data entry screen form will contain a reference to the Employee object and can then use the properties and behaviors of the Employee object.

■ The Basic Elements of an Object-Oriented System

The four basic elements of an object-oriented system are abstraction, encapsulation, inheritance, and polymorphism. These are key requirements and are often used as evaluation criteria when defining whether a system is indeed object-oriented.

Abstraction: Focusing on What Is Important

Abstraction is a technique that we all use to manage the complexity of the information we collect every day. It allows us to recognize how things are similar and ignore how they are different, to think about the generalities and not specifics, and to see what things are without thinking about what makes them that way. You can abstract the important characteristics of an object at any given time and for any particular purpose and ignore all other aspects.

How you develop an abstraction depends on both its purpose and your perspective. For example, on a warm summer day I look at a tree and abstract it as a shade provider. My young daughter abstracts it as a place to climb. One tree, two different abstractions.

Abstraction is used to identify the objects involved with a particular application. In developing a payroll system, you would think about Jessica Jones and abstract her as an employee, thinking only about her salary and how she gets paid. When working on the company softball league application, you would abstract Jessica as a player and be more concerned with her position and batting average. One object, two completely different abstractions.

Keynote

Using abstraction, you can focus on the objects of an application and not on the implementation. This lets you think about what needs to be done and not how the computer will do it. It allows you to pull the design out from behind the technological wall of computer processing and bring it out to where the users can participate. The users, or subject matter experts, become key participants in the design process.

This seems so obvious, yet before current object-oriented methodologies existed, the user's participation all but stopped after the requirements definition phase and did not pick up again until the completion of the user-interface prototype. The design process, which had involved flow charting and data flow diagramming, was considered too technical and inundated with jargon. So the users were ignored throughout the design and then surprised with a prototype.

When object-oriented methodologies first appeared, the same was still true. Object-oriented techniques were for the academic crowd. The preferred object model diagramming techniques were complex and full of jargon and rules. Current object-oriented techniques, like the GUIDS methodology introduced in this book, use abstraction to provide an elegant yet simple and practical approach that keeps the users involved throughout the design process.

Encapsulation: Hiding Your Private Parts

In any organization there are independent units, usually called departments. The sales department gets the sales, the production department produces the item, the shipping department ships it, and so on. Each department is responsible for its own procedures and internal information. For example, the sales department has procedures for calling prospects, evaluating the opportunity, sending sales materials, following up with current customers, maintaining prospect information, and so on.

You could say the departments are *encapsulated* because the internal information (properties) and standard operating procedures (behaviors) are contained within the department. These are figuratively hidden from other departments except through defined interfaces. Anyone needing the department's procedures or information goes to that department to ask for it.

If a shipping clerk gets the name of a prospect, the clerk will want to use the "calling prospects" procedure; but the clerk knows better than to use that procedure directly. Rather, the clerk collaborates with the sales department by sending the name to them. The clerk knows that the calling prospects procedure is one of the department's functions. This concept is illustrated in Figure 1.5.

Figure 1.5

The shipping department uses the properties and behaviors of the sales department only through the sales department's defined interfaces.

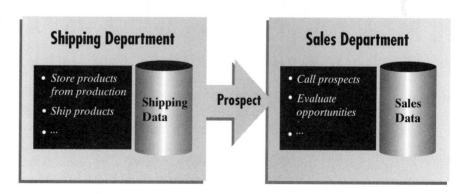

The same principles are used in object-oriented design to encapsulate each object's behaviors and properties. When an object needs to perform a procedure that is encapsulated in another class, the object does not perform the procedure directly. Rather, it collaborates with an object belonging to the other class to perform the procedure.

Keynote

The encapsulation aids in abstraction by hiding the internal implementation of an object within the class. An object can then be used without understanding how the object's class is implemented. So the shipping clerk can have the sales department perform the call to the prospect without knowing how the sales department actually handles the call.

You may already be using encapsulation, but referring to it as data hiding. By creating module-level variables and private routines within a module, you were encapsulating that data and those routines within the module.

Inheritance: Attaining Reuse

Things that are similar still have some differences and things that are different often have some similarities. For example, both Sam Smith and Jessica Jones work for the same company, so they can be classified as employees. Looking at their differences, Sam is a carpenter and Jessica is a programmer.

You could classify Sam as a carpenter and put all properties and behaviors for a carpenter employee into a Carpenter class. This class would include name, address, construction license information, and "do work" and "do hammering" behaviors. Likewise, you could classify Jessica as a programmer and put all properties and behaviors for a programmer employee into a Programmer class. This class would include name, address, known programming languages and "do work" and "do coding" behaviors. This duplicates the common employee information.

Keynote

You can remove the property and behavior redundancy and attain reuse by using *inheritance*. You can take the common employee properties and behaviors from the specialized classes and put them into a higher level Employee class. The objects that belong to the Programmer class or Carpenter class can then inherit the properties and behaviors of the Employee class. This "is a" relationship is depicted in Figure 1.3.

There are two basic types of inheritance: implementation and interface. *Implementation inheritance* provides for code reuse by generalizing common code in a parent class and then developing any specialized code in the subclasses. Any object belonging to the subclass automatically reuses all of the code for the behaviors and properties of the parent class.

If a new Project Manager class were added to the class hierarchy shown in Figure 1.3, objects of this class would automatically have all of the behaviors and properties defined for the parent Employee class. The Project Manager class would not need to include a name or address because that information is already taken care of in the Employee class. The request for the project manager to "do work" is automatically passed up to the parent class for processing.

Interface inheritance provides for reuse of an interface—that is, the set of properties and behaviors—but allows different implementations of those properties and behaviors. In the Employee class example, the

Employee class interface includes a "do work" behavior. By inheriting the interface and not the implementation of that interface, the Programmer and Carpenter classes can include the common behavior and yet provide different code for the behavior.

If a new Project Manager class were added, it could inherit the interface to ensure that it had the complete set of required properties and behaviors. It could then provide its own implementation of those properties and behaviors.

Keynote

Both implementation and interface inheritance are powerful tools and have a place in your developer's toolbox. Implementation inheritance provides for reuse of the interface and the associated code. Interface inheritance provides for reuse of the interface when the associated code would not be the same.

Visual Basic does not, however, provide implementation inheritance. You can achieve implementation inheritance by using interface inheritance and then *delegating*, or calling, the common code manually much like you call a subroutine. Although this process is somewhat tedious, it is the best we can do—at least for now.

Polymorphism: Same Behavior, Different Implementation

Two or more classes can have behaviors that are named the same and have the same basic purpose but different implementations. This is *polymorphism*. For example, a Carpenter class can have a "calculate pay" behavior and a Programmer class can have a "calculate pay" behavior. You can request the "calculate pay" behavior by an object from either class without knowing how either object plans to implement that request. Both the Carpenter class and the Programmer class have the "calculate pay" behavior, but the implementation of that behavior can be completely different.

You may recognize this description as similar to that defined for interface inheritance in the prior topic. You can use interface inheritance to ensure that like named properties and behaviors are defined in the classes. So interface inheritance aids polymorphism by enforcing the reuse of the property and behavior names.

The Move method in Visual Basic is an example of polymorphism. When the Move method is executed for a form object, the form knows how to move itself and all of its contents to the specified coordinates. When the Move method is executed for a button object, you do not expect the form to move. Rather, the button is moved to the correct location. The same named method provides polymorphic results.

Keynote

The benefit of polymorphism is that you don't need to know the class of the object to execute the polymorphic behavior. For example, you may have many classes in an application, each with its own "save" behavior. When the application is saved, each object knows the class it belongs to and automatically calls the correct class save routine.

■ OO Features in Visual Basic

Visual Basic 5 has many features that support an object-oriented design and implementation. These features are introduced in this section and demonstrated in detail in Part 3 of this book.

Defining a Class in a Class Module

Keynote

Class modules are a key object-oriented feature of Visual Basic. Class modules contain the definition for a class. You can define class properties with variables and Property procedures, and implement class behaviors with Sub and Function procedures in a class module. You can also define events and constants in the class module to completely encapsulate the code for the class. Class modules are demonstrated in Chapter 10, "Building Your First Class."

Providing Public Access with Property Procedures

Property procedures provide the public interface to the private properties in a class. With Property procedures you can set and get the value of an object's property or set a reference to an object. You can also define read-only properties for a class. Property procedures are illustrated in Chapter 10, "Building Your First Class."

Defining Polymorphic Methods

Methods are the Sub and Function procedures in a class that provide the implementation of the object behaviors. You can give these procedures any name; however, if you use the same name for similar properties and methods in different classes you can leverage polymorphism.

For example, you can create an Employee class that has a Save method and an Invoice class that has a Save method. Using the same name for both methods allows you to think about what the objects need to do without thinking about how they do it, or how they do it differently. Defining a method for a class is presented in Chapter 10, "Building Your First Class" and developing polymorphic methods is demonstrated in Chapter 12, "Interfaces, Polymorphism, and Inheritance."

Generating Events

In addition to properties and methods, you can define an event in a class. Events provide a simple mechanism for communication between components. For example, a form can notify another form when its contents are changed or an asynchronous process can provide notification when it is complete. Events are illustrated in Chapter 10, "Building Your First Class."

Encapsulating Class Constants

You cannot declare public constants in forms or class modules. Instead, you can define a public enumeration to provide a list of named long integer constants. These constants are great for exposing the list of errors that can be raised from the class and for providing named constants instead of magic numbers for parameters or return values of class properties and methods. There are enumeration examples in Chapter 10, "Building Your First Class."

Viewing a Class with the Object Browser

The Object Browser provides a list of all classes within the current project and the properties, methods, events, and constants for each class. You can use the Object Browser to quickly review the interface of a class or to navigate between the components of your project.

You can also use the Object Browser to list the classes contained in other libraries, such as VB itself, and in ActiveX components such as Microsoft Excel. This provides convenient online reference information. The Object Browser is described in Chapter 10, "Building Your First Class."

Creating Objects

You can create objects from the classes you have created or from any ActiveX component. The reference to the created object is stored in an object variable. The object variable is then used to set or retrieve the object's properties or invoke the object's methods. Creating objects from a class that you create is demonstrated in Chapter 10, "Building Your First Class." Chapter 13, "Building ActiveX Components," describes the process of creating objects from ActiveX components.

Using Forms as Objects

Many of the features provided for classes are available in forms as well. You can add public properties and methods to a form class defined in a form module. You can then create a form object from the form class, or Visual Basic will create the form object for you when the form is loaded. Chapter 11, "Building Classes: Additional Techniques," provides information on working with forms as objects.

Working with Sets of Objects

At times a class needs to reference a set of objects instead of a single object. For example, a Department class contains a set of references to all employees. This set is defined with a collection. Instead of exposing the details of the collection to the application, collections are frequently encapsulated in a class specifically developed to manage the collection, called a *collection class.* The details for creating and using a collection and developing a collection class are covered in Chapter 11, "Building Classes: Additional Techniques."

Defining Multiple Interfaces

Keynote

The properties and methods of a class define its default interface. If that interface contains many properties and methods, it may be easier to divide, or *factor,* the properties and methods into logical sets of functionality. Each set of functionality can be defined as an independent interface. You can then use a specific set of functionality by simply accessing the object through the associated interface.

For example, a Programmer class has properties and methods for generic employee functionality, for payroll functionality, and for task assignment functionality. These properties and methods could be factored into three separate interfaces. When you need to use the payroll functionality, you can use the Payroll interface so that only the properties and methods for payroll are exposed.

Interfaces also provide for reuse through interface inheritance. For example, the generic Employee interface could be reused in the Carpenter class. Using interface inheritance enforces like-named properties and methods and therefore promotes polymorphism.

Finally, interfaces provide a mechanism for adding a set of functionality to a class after the class has been developed. Adding a new interface instead of modifying an existing one ensures that existing applications that use objects from the class are not affected by the change. Interfaces are covered in Chapter 12, "Interfaces, Polymorphism, and Inheritance."

Exposing Objects with ActiveX Components

ActiveX describes a set of functionality that is the next generation of component-based software development technologies. The prior generation was called OLE. The new generation provides for the development of ActiveX controls, ActiveX servers, and ActiveX documents.

You can build ActiveX controls that add functionality to current controls, combine several existing controls, or provide an entirely new idiom. These controls can be used in any application that supports ActiveX controls (.ocx), including VB4, VB5, and Web pages. The process of creating ActiveX controls is outlined in Chapter 13, "Building ActiveX Components."

You can also build applications that expose their objects to other applications. These are the ActiveX EXE or ActiveX DLL components, also called ActiveX servers. For example, you could write a to do list ActiveX server and use objects from this server in a task assignment application and in a sales call follow-up application. Chapter 13, "Building ActiveX Components," details the process of creating an ActiveX EXE or ActiveX DLL.

Developing Web-Based Applications

To develop a simple Web-based application you could learn how to use HTML, Java, JavaScript, and so on. Or, you can simply use Visual Basic! You can create an ActiveX document with Visual Basic and display it as a Web page without knowing how to use any other Web development tool.

ActiveX documents are a special type of object that can be provided from an ActiveX document server. These documents can be displayed in any ActiveX document container, such as Microsoft Binder or Microsoft Internet Explorer. Chapter 13, "Building ActiveX Components," provides details about developing an ActiveX document.

Creating Client/Server Applications

Client/server technologies have helped businesses to fully realize their strategic advantage. The three-tiered client/server architecture is comprised of a network of distributed data sources for storing the corporate data, distributed processing servers for the business logic, and local user interface components. Now you can support all three tiers with Visual Basic.

**Enterprise
Edition**

The Enterprise Edition of Visual Basic provides the tools necessary to distribute components on a network including the Distributed Component Object Model (DCOM) and Remote Automation (RA). These tools allow a business to have ActiveX components containing the business logic distributed across several computers on the network.

Visual Basic provides high-performance remote data access for directly accessing remote data using Microsoft SQL Server or Oracle. These tools include a remote data control that can be bound to controls on a form, remote data objects that allow processing of records using Visual Basic code, and ODBCDirect to access remote data using the data access objects. Data access methodologies are described in Chapter 8, "Data Design," and demonstrated in Chapter 14, "Doing Database Objects."

■ New Visual Basic 5 Features

This section lists many of the new Visual Basic 5 features. Each feature is described and, where appropriate, there's a reference to the chapter in which it is introduced.

Major New Features: Speed and the Web

Visual Basic 5 provides several major new features:

- **Native compilation**. A Visual Basic application can be compiled to native code for faster execution. See Chapter 10, "Building Your First Class," for the details.

- **Display speed**. Improvements to the internal control handling provide faster display of Visual Basic screens.

- **Creating ActiveX controls**. You can now create your own ActiveX controls with Visual Basic. You can create a control and use it in any application that supports ActiveX controls, such as VB4, VB5, and Web pages. See Chapter 13, "Building ActiveX Components," for more information.

- **Creating ActiveX documents**. Visual Basic forms can be converted into ActiveX documents and displayed in an Internet browser window, so you can leverage your Visual Basic experience in the development of Internet or intranet applications. See Chapter 13, "Building ActiveX Components," for more information.

- **New Internet controls**. Internet Transfer, WebBrowser, and WinSock controls are provided for easy browsing, transferring files, and exchanging data with Web sites.

- **Web-based deployment**. The Setup Wizard now has features to support Web-based deployment of your components. See Chapter 13, "Building ActiveX Components," for the details.

New Object-Oriented Features: More Reasons to Go OO

Many new Visual Basic 5 features are specifically for the design and development of object-oriented applications:

- **Multiple interfaces**. You can define multiple interfaces for classes in your applications. Using multiple interfaces allows you to group the properties and methods of a class into functional units, reuse interfaces in other classes, and easily add functionality to a class after the class has been deployed. Chapter 12, "Interfaces, Polymorphism, and Inheritance," lists the benefits of multiple interfaces and describes how to create and use them.

- **Improved polymorphism**. To leverage polymorphism in VB4, you have to give up early binding. With VB5 you can use interfaces to attain early binding when using polymorphism. Chapter 12, "Interfaces, Polymorphism, and Inheritance," defines polymorphism and explains why and how you would use it.

- **Raising events**. Visual Basic forms and controls raise events and you can develop event procedures to respond to those events. With VB5, classes you create can raise their own events. Any class with a reference to an object from the class can then respond to the event. This feature provides an easier communication mechanism between components in an application, especially for asynchronous processing. See Chapter 10, "Building Your First Class," for more information on raising and responding to events.

- **Global constants**. You can now encapsulate public constants for a class within a class module using an enumeration. This approach is great for listing the error numbers raised by the class and for magic numbers required for modifying properties or calling methods in the class. See Chapter 10, "Building Your First Class," for more information on declaring and using an enumeration.

- **Improved Object Browser**. The biggest improvements to the Object Browser are the searching capabilities and the modeless window. Additional improvements make this an excellent tool for working with your objects and the objects from other applications. See Chapter 10, "Building Your First Class," for more information on using the Object Browser.

- **Improved debugging of classes**. If you have your Error Trapping set to Break in Class Module or Break on All Errors and generate an error, you can now press Alt+F8 to step into the error handler or Alt+F5 to continue. See Chapter 10, "Building Your First Class," for more information.

- **Class documentation**. You can develop documentation for a class using the new Procedure Attributes dialog box. See Chapter 10, "Building Your First Class," for more information on this dialog box.

- **Default property or method**. You can now identify a property or method of a class to be the default property or method. The default is the property or method that is assumed if you use the object variable with no property or method. For example, the Text property is the default property for text boxes, so you can use txtName instead of txtName.Text.

  Setting a default is particularly useful for the Item method in a collection class. See Chapter 11, "Building Classes: Additional Techniques," for an example of setting a default method.

- **For Each...Next syntax for collection classes**. If you create a private collection and expose it with a collection class in VB4, you can no longer use the For Each...Next syntax on the private collection. VB5 exposes the enumerator object to provide this feature. Chapter 11, "Building Classes: Additional Techniques," provides the details of this process.

- **Enhanced Property procedures**. Property procedures now allow variable arguments and typed optional arguments. This improves the performance and flexibility of Property procedures. See Chapter 14, "Doing Database Objects," for an example.

- **Global objects**. You can convert your function library or library of common routines into a class in an ActiveX component and define the class to be global. This feature allows developers to use the library of functions without declaring an object variable or creating an object. See Chapter 15, "Putting the Pieces Together," for more information on global objects.

- **Friend methods**. Classes in your ActiveX component can now communicate privately without exposing the classes to other applications. You can make this happen by using the Friend keyword to declare the procedure instead of using Public or Private. See Chapter 13, "Building ActiveX Components," for more information. Friend methods also provide a mechanism to pass user-defined types (UDTs) between classes as shown in Chapter 10, "Building Your First Class."

New ActiveX Features: OLE Gets Active

There are a few other new ActiveX features in addition to those already mentioned:

- **OLE renamed**. Many of the OLE features from VB4 are renamed to ActiveX in VB5. The OLE servers you created in VB4 are now ActiveX servers. See Chapter 13, "Building ActiveX Components," for more information.

- **Improved version compatibility.** Testing ActiveX components is easier with the new project compatibility option. Chapter 13 describes the new version compatibility settings.

- **Modeless dialog boxes in an ActiveX DLL**. ActiveX DLLs no longer have the modal dialog box restriction identified for VB4. See Chapter 13 for more information.

- **Multithreading**. ActiveX components support multithreading. Chapter 13 defines how the different types of components provide multithreading.

New IDE Features: Cool Tools Rule!

The Visual Basic 5 integrated development environment (IDE) provides many new productivity features and cool tools.

- **Wizards**. VB5 provides Wizards to maximize your productivity. The VB Application Wizard can complete the entire framework for your application, as shown in Chapter 6, "User-Interface Design." The VB Class Builder utility helps you to create your entire object model and then automatically generates the code for that object model. This process is outlined in Chapter 11, "Building Classes: Additional Techniques." Other Wizards build database maintenance screens, create ActiveX control property pages, convert VB forms to ActiveX documents, and much more.

- **Templates**. You can create any form, module, class module, or any other type of project component and copy it to a defined template directory. The project component will then appear in the Add dialog box, which makes it very easy to add the component to any project. See Chapter 7, "Implementation-Centered Design," for more information.

- **Add Related Documents**. You can add documentation or other support files directly into the project as related documents. You can also edit these files from within the IDE. This makes it easy to keep track of all of the associated documentation and support files required for a project. Chapter 10, "Building Your First Class," provides additional information on using this feature to document your classes.

- **Auto List Members**. Visual Basic knows the available properties and methods for every object. Wouldn't it be nice if it could just provide you with the list of valid properties and methods and let you select one? With VB5 it does. This is such a timesaving feature it is hard to imagine living without it.

- **Auto Quick Info**. This feature lists the syntax for a statement or function after you enter the statement or function name. This helps you enter the correct set of parameters. For parameters that require a constant, such as the Buttons parameter on the MessageBox, the constants are listed for your selection.

- **Drag and drop of code**. You can drag and drop code anywhere within the IDE.

- **Block and Unblock Comments**. Using this feature you can select a section of code and add or remove comment markers from each line in the selection.

- **Bookmarks**. You can set bookmarks in the code and return to the bookmark location. Chapter 11, "Building Classes: Additional Techniques," describes how to use bookmarks and explains how to add a shortcut key for bookmarks into the IDE.

- **MDI or SDI style interface**. Do you hate seeing your other windows through the VB IDE or do you love the way you can see your application with VB on top of it? With VB5 you can select a multiple-document interface (MDI) style or a single-document interface (SDI) style for the IDE.

- **Dockable windows**. You can dock any of the windows within the IDE to create the desired layout and Visual Basic will remember that layout.

- **Project workspace files**. When closing a project, Visual Basic stores the location and size of all open project windows, thereby saving your project workspace. When you reopen the project, the project workspace is restored and all windows are displayed in their last location and size.

- **Multiple Projects**. You can define multiple projects in a project group. You can then open the group and all of the projects in the group will be opened in the IDE. This is especially useful for debugging ActiveX components. See Chapter 13, "Building ActiveX Components," for more information.

- **Improved Project window**. With the new Project window, you can display all components of all projects in a project group, sort components by type, and access any project component, including additional files such as documentation or support files.

- **Multiple tabs on the toolbox**. You can add tabs to your toolbox so you can logically divide your toolbox into sets of tools. This is very helpful if you use a lot of third-party products or have developed many of your own controls.

- **Form Designer window**. The Form Designer window is a new window frame around your form. It separates the form displayed to the user from the window you use to create the form. Chapter 15, "Putting the Pieces Together," provides more information on the Form Designer window.

- **New Form Layout Window**. The new Form Layout window allows you to visually identify at design time the desired position for a form at run time. In prior versions of Visual Basic, the form would appear in the location defined when you edited the form, so if you moved the form in the IDE, the form would appear in a new location at run time. The Form Layout window allows you to place the form anywhere inside or outside the screen region independent of the location of the Form Designer window at design time. The Form Layout window comes with resolution guides to help you size or place windows for 640x480 or 800x600 resolutions. See Chapter 15, "Putting the Pieces Together," for more information on using the Form Layout window.

- **Improved Properties window**. The Properties window now has two tabs. The Alphabetical tab lists the properties in alphabetical order, as in prior versions of Visual Basic. The Categorized tab lists the properties by category. Using the categories is very helpful for setting groups of properties, such as the position properties. Chapter 14, "Doing Database Objects," describes how this feature makes it easier to set properties for bound controls.

  There's also a description of the currently selected property at the bottom of the Properties window. You can toggle display of this description by right-clicking on the Properties window and toggling the Description option.

- **Update Menu properties**. The menu options now appear in the Properties window so you can change the menu properties without using the Menu Editor. See Chapter 15, "Putting the Pieces Together," for more information on this feature.

- **Separate Project options**. The project options are now separated from the editing and environment options, making it easier to make appropriate option selections. See Chapter 10, "Building Your First Class," for a look at the new Project Options and Options dialog boxes.

- **Customizable Toolbar and Menu commands**. You can now customize your toolbar and menu commands. Chapter 11, "Building Classes: Additional Techniques," explains how.

- **Instant Watch**. When in break mode, you can view the value of any variable or expression by simply moving the cursor over the selection. See Chapter 11, "Building Classes: Additional Techniques," for more information.

- **Improved Immediate window**. With Visual Basic 5, you can call routines, execute code, or create objects from classes without first running and pausing the project. Simply type the statements into the Immediate window. See Chapter 11, "Building Classes: Additional Techniques," for an example.

- **Assert**. The Debug object has a new Assert method that checks the value of an expression and stops execution of the application at design time if that value is false. This allows you to verify the values of expressions when developing and debugging an application. See Chapter 11, "Building Classes: Additional Techniques," for an example of using Assert.

Other New Features: An Assortment of Enhancements

Here are some other new features that are important to mention:

- **ODBCDirect**. You can now access the RDO libraries through the DAO object model using ODBCDirect. See Chapter 8, "Data Design," and Chapter 14, "Doing Database Objects," for more information.

- **Access to the NT event log**. VB5 added several properties and methods to the App object to log application events to a log file or directly to the NT event log. Chapter 15, "Putting the Pieces Together," provides a sample Error class that logs events to the NT event log.

- **AddressOf**. Visual Basic can now pass a function pointer to an API call. See Chapter 15, "Putting the Pieces Together," for more information.

- **Typed optional arguments**. In VB4 optional arguments had to be Variants, but with VB5 they can be any data type. Using the specific data type for optional arguments can improve performance because typed arguments are faster to access than Variants.

- **OLE Drag and Drop**. When this feature is implemented in your application, the users can drag and drop text between controls and between controls and other applications such as Microsoft Word. See Chapter 15, "Putting the Pieces Together," for more information on this feature.

- **ToolTipText property**. A new ToolTipText property on many of the controls displays a ToolTip. See Chapter 15, "Putting the Pieces Together," for an example.

- **New form properties**. The new StartUpPosition property defines the startup location of a form at run time. There is also a new Moveable property that locks a window in place and prevents the user from moving it. Chapter 15, "Putting the Pieces Together," provides more information on these properties.

- **Defining a window owner**. A new parameter on the Show method for a form allows you to specify an owner form to establish a parent/child relationship between the owner form and the form being shown. This feature is described in Chapter 15, "Putting the Pieces Together."

**Enterprise
Edition**

- **DCOM**. In addition to Remote Automation provided in VB4, you can now remote your components using the distributed component object model (DCOM). See Chapter 13, "Building ActiveX Components," for more information.

**Enterprise
Edition**

There are several additional new Enterprise Edition features such as tools for debugging Transact-SQL and a built-in Repository. See Craig Goren's book, listed in the "Additional Reading" section at the end of this chapter, for information on the new Enterprise Edition features.

■ Summary

- Visual Basic provides many object-oriented features. To take full advantage of these new features, you need a basic understanding of the object-oriented concepts behind them.

- Object-oriented design involves the abstraction of the real world for a specific purpose. These abstractions define the objects for an application.

- Classes define the properties and behaviors for a set of objects.

- Defining the relationships between objects clarifies an understanding of the objects and how they interact. Objects can have subclass ("is a"), container ("has a"), and collaborator ("uses") relationships.

- Abstraction focuses on what is important for the application and not on the implementation. This approach allows you to design the application using the language of the business instead of using programming terminology.

- Encapsulation involves hiding the private properties and the implementation of the behaviors. The properties and behaviors are then accessed through a defined public interface.

- Inheritance provides a mechanism for attaining reuse by determining how objects are the same and how they are different. Visual Basic provides interface inheritance, but not implementation inheritance.

- Polymorphism allows public interfaces for objects that perform similar functions to have the same name but different implementations.

- The class modules are the key for implementing an object-oriented design. With class modules you can create abstractions of real-world objects, encapsulate the behaviors and properties within the module, develop polymorphic procedures, generate events, and define class constants.

- The Object Browser is a tool for displaying the classes in a library or project along with their properties, methods, events, and constants.

- You can define multiple interfaces for a class to divide the properties and methods of a class into sets of functionality, reuse the interface in other classes, and to simplify enhancements to the class.

- ActiveX components expose reusable objects that can be accessed from other applications without providing source code to those applications.

- You can develop Web-based applications using Visual Basic to create ActiveX documents.

- DCOM and Remote Automation support client/server development by allowing ActiveX components to be distributed across a network.

- Visual Basic 5 provides many new features for object-oriented design and development.

- The cool productivity tools provided in VB5 are enough of a reason to make the move to VB5.

■ Additional Reading

Booch, Grady. *Object-Oriented Analysis and Design with Applications (The Benjamin/Cummings Series in Object-Oriented Software Engineering)*. Redwood City, California: The Benjamin/Cummings Publishing Company, 1994.

  Booch provides an academic discussion of object-oriented design concepts. He then presents a specific notation and methodology for object-oriented design and applies them to several case studies implemented in Smalltalk, Object Pascal, C++, Lisp, and Ada.

Goren, Craig. *Visual Basic 5 Enterprise Development*. Indianapolis, Indiana: Que, 1997.

  This book describes the new Enterprise Edition features.

Kurata, Deborah. "Is VB an OOP Language?" *Visual Basic Programmer's Journal*, Vol. 5, No. 11, November 1995.

This article discusses the criteria for an object-oriented programming (OOP) language and evaluates whether Visual Basic meets the criteria. Even though the article is for Visual Basic 4.0, it provides OOP background information so you can participate in the continued debate.

Rumbaugh, James; Blaha, Michael; Premerlani, William; Eddy, Frederick; Lorensen, William. *Object-Oriented Modeling and Design*. Englewood Cliffs, New Jersey: Prentice Hall, 1991.

This book provides a thorough discussion of object-oriented concepts and object modeling. It then presents the Object Modeling Technique (OMT) as a methodology for software engineering. This book includes examples on implementing object-oriented techniques in C++, Ada, and Smalltalk.

Taylor, David. *Business Engineering with Object Technology*. Reading, Massachusetts: Addison-Wesley Publishing Company, 1995.

This book integrates business process re-engineering with object-oriented concepts. It provides a good, easy-to-understand overview of object technology and then presents an example of applying that technology to model a business.

Taylor, David. *Object-Oriented Technology: A Manager's Guide*. Reading, Massachusetts: Addison-Wesley Publishing Company, 1990.

Taylor provides a good description of object-oriented techniques from a manager's prospective. This book will help you understand why object-oriented software design and development are important in today's business environment.

Figure 1.1 in my book is similar to the view of an object that Taylor provides in his manager's guide. Figure 1.2 resembles Taylor's view of a class, which is also depicted in his guide.

■ Think It Over

To supplement and review the information in this chapter, try the following:

1. Next time you get into your car, think about object-oriented concepts.

    •   Notice that the gas pedal is an abstraction for the complex process of converting gasoline into forward motion.

    •   Think about how the objects that comprise the car are encapsulated. Look at the radio. It provides behaviors such as finding a station, playing music, increasing or decreasing the volume. The last selected volume and station are properties of the radio object. Identify other objects in the car and define the behaviors and properties of those objects.

- The brake has a push behavior, as does the gas pedal. What other polymorphisms can you find in the car?

- The car has many reusable components. That was the revolution that resulted in the Model T and most automobile manufacturing and repair since then. Think about the benefits of reusable components.

2. Look around you and think about other real-world objects and how they follow object-oriented principles.

3. Think about how you have done analysis and design of software in the past. Try visualizing one of your applications in terms of objects and classes.

2

The Software Development Process

"Going object-oriented" is not simply a matter of using C++, or object Pascal, or Smalltalk, or Eiffel or any other OO programming language. To get the benefit of an OO language—with all opportunities for improved code reuse, simpler code, and ease of extension—one must design a program that embodies an object-oriented philosophy.

In fact one should go OO all the way from analysis through various design levels, into implementation. When this is done in a project, it usually results in a more consistent model in all of the analysis, design, and implementation stages.

—N.A.B. Gray,
Programming with Class

This book goes all the way with OO. It presents an entire software development process based on object-oriented techniques. It casts the problem and solution in object-oriented terms. It allows the project team to collect requirements, perform the design, and implement the application using one set of object-oriented principles.

This chapter discusses the phases of the software development process and the benefits of using an object-oriented approach in that process. It then outlines a case study that will be used throughout the remainder of the book.

■ An Overview of the Software Development Process

Many different metaphors have been applied to the software development process and to software developers themselves. Some software developers liken themselves to artists. They creatively *craft* their code. Others prefer to think of themselves as authors as they *write* volumes of software. Another metaphor for the software development process is construction. Software developers call themselves engineers and these engineers *build* applications.

When starting with Visual Basic, it is easy to build an application by creating some forms and putting a little code here and a little code there. This is fine if you are creating a simple game for your kids, but if you are building something of any significant size, or if others will be working with you, you need a more formal process.

Imagine that you have decided to build a house, so you buy some wood and start to nail boards together. You may complete a house (or may not) and it may keep out the rain (or may not) and it may look okay (or it may not) but without a strong internal framework you would be worried about that first wind storm! What the house is missing is the architecture. It is the architecture that defines the internal structure and framework. The architecture also includes a design of the external, or user-view of what is to be built. If it's done well, the architecture provides a strong, goal-oriented design, ensuring that the construction reliably fulfills its original requirements.

By developing an architecture and using it as a blueprint for the construction, you minimize your risk of building something that is too difficult to complete, does not meet the intended requirements, is not user friendly, or looks ugly. This is just as true with software as it is with houses and office buildings.

Keynote

Building software, like building anything else, involves a basic set of overlapping and interrelated phases. All software development organizations have some process for the development of software. Some are *ad hoc* and depend on the development team. Others are complex, involving many steps and levels of approval. The majority fall somewhere in between. Generally, the software development process will, either formally or informally, include the following basic phases:

- Idea

- Requirements

- Plan and schedule

- Architecture

- Construction

- Inspection

Keynote

These phases of the software development process are illustrated in Figure 2.1. Notice that overlapping circles are used in this figure to depict the process. This is because the software development process is not a discrete set of steps with rigid boxes where you drop into the next phase like a waterfall, never able to return back up to a prior phase. Real software development projects are iterative. You work on each phase until it makes sense to move on to the next phase or circle back to a prior phase.

For example, you do not normally finish all of the requirements before beginning the architecture. You define some requirements and then begin to think about the design. As you design you may need to circle back and get clarification or refine some of the requirements.

It is very difficult to describe a process in a circular fashion, so methodologies are often discussed linearly even though they are executed more circuitously. With that said, a linear overview of each phase is provided in this section.

Keynote

The appropriate level of effort for the phases in your project will depend on the scope of the project. Remember, however, that small projects don't always stay that way. Designing small projects with the same care as large ones can pay off with a foundation that supports future enhancements. Otherwise, you could reach that dreaded process called redesign and find that you need to start the whole process over!

Beginning with an Idea

An idea arises from an observation, inspiration, experience, or a business problem. This idea is the concept or primary goal for the application. The time and resources required to construct something from the idea are then considered, thereby starting the planning and scheduling process.

For instance, one Saturday afternoon you get the idea to build a game program for your children. You decide to do it that particular afternoon. You've started the software development process.

Figure 2.1

The software development process is a set of interdependent and overlapping phases.

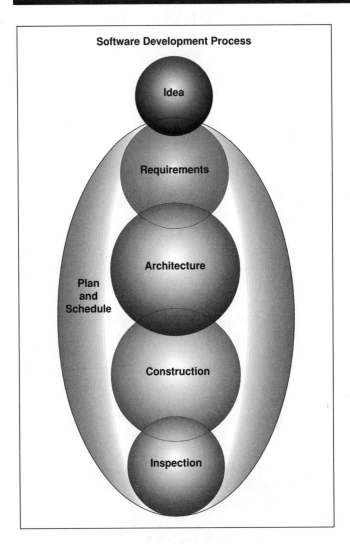

Here's a more complex example. At the office, you have been working with your sales department for weeks deciding whether to develop a new contact management system. You've done a cost/benefit analysis and given many talks on why the system will better aid the sales force in tracking contacts with their customers. The idea is finally approved along with your plan to make that idea a reality. Same phase, much different scope.

Establishing the Requirements

The requirements are generated from an examination of the idea. A project team is formed to set the scope of the project, define a feature list, specify the limitations and constraints, and prioritize the requirements.

Following the same examples presented above, you convert your game idea into requirements by deciding on the rules of the game and how many players it will allow. Establishing the requirements for the contact management system project necessitates forming a project team, interviewing users, performing a complete task analysis, and developing a detailed document of the precise requirements.

Planning and Scheduling the Project

The project plan defines how the project will be accomplished to meet the requirements defined in the requirements phase. A rough, high-level schedule for the project can then be estimated to put a time line on the plan.

Keynote

No one should be held to the high-level schedule created at this point in the project. It is important to develop this schedule because it provides a reality check to ensure that there is a balance between the features of the application and the imposed constraints, such as a required completion date. However, this schedule is based on guesses and not on the details of the project because these details are not yet developed at this stage.

In the examples, the plan and schedule for the game project may be as simple as deciding to do it now and to finish it before dinner. For the contact management system, the plan will include a strategy for completing the project. A high-level schedule will be estimated based on that plan. This schedule will be entered into project management software or recorded in a document and adjusted as necessary as the project continues.

Developing the Architecture

There is no one right way to design software, just as there is no one right way to design a house or office building. There are some requirements and the basic laws of physics and engineering, but there is much latitude within those restrictions. With almost limitless possibilities, how does an architect know where to begin or how to ensure that all aspects of the design are complete? That is where a methodology comes in handy. A methodology is not a cookbook where you follow some specific steps and have a design when you are finished. Rather, a methodology provides a path. As you proceed down that path, you use your experience and knowledge to create the design.

I have defined a methodology for designing an object-oriented architecture. It is called *GUIDS* (pronounced "guides") and is comprised of the following:

- **G**oal-centered design focuses on the goals that were identified during the requirements phase to develop the high-level design of the application. In this step, you work with the potential users of the application to define a set of real-world objects, including the properties and behaviors of those objects.

- **U**ser-interface design focuses on both the requirements and the specific goals of the application's users to define how the application will look and how the users will interact with the application.

- **I**mplementation-centered design details how the application will be structured and converts the objects from the Goal-centered design into classes.

- **D**ata design identifies how the data will be organized and accessed.

- **S**trategies for construction provide the approach that will be used in constructing the application. This includes programming standards and conventions, configuration management, testing methodologies, and an implementation plan and schedule.

In the architecture phase for the game example, you decide how the parts of the game will interact with each other and with the user interface. The contact management system, on the other hand, will require extensive meetings with the project team, days and days of thinking, and many pages of notes. The result will be a high-level design document.

Often a model or prototype is constructed to validate some of the design ideas. The extent of this model is dependent on the scope of the project. A sketch on a napkin at lunch might be enough for the game. Presentation of a user interface prototype and development of models for specific algorithms or programming techniques may be required for the contact management system.

Commencing the Construction

Finally, ground breaking! You use the architectural design developed in the architecture phase as a blueprint to build the application.

Looking again at the examples, for the game you could just sit down at the computer and start creating forms and code in Visual Basic. For the contact management system application, each programmer on the team is assigned a set of classes, given the architectural design, and can begin to create forms and develop code in Visual Basic to implement these classes.

Initiating the Inspection

After some of the construction is complete, the inspection process begins. The inspection can include code walk-throughs, unit testing, integration testing, and system testing. The purpose of the inspection is to identify bugs and other errors in the code as early as possible in the development process. This allows the bugs and errors to be corrected before they become major stumbling blocks to completing the application.

For the game, you pound out some code and give it a quick inspection. If anything isn't quite right, you can pull it apart and fix it. The contact management system requires a more intense build/inspect cycle with unit testing, integration testing, system testing, and so on. After the final inspection, the software is finished.

Maintaining the Application

Once the application is constructed, it will require maintenance. This maintenance may include bug fixes, enhancements, changes to the business rules, or any other revisions. These revisions will follow the same software development process defined earlier. The idea for a change is proposed, the requirements for the modification are defined, and the changes are planned, scheduled, architected, constructed, and retested.

■ The Benefits of Using an Object-Oriented Approach

There are many benefits of using an object-oriented approach to software design and implementation. Frequently, the benefits are described in vague terms. To make the benefits more concrete, let's examine common issues in the software development life cycle and review how an object-oriented approach can help address these issues.

Speaking the Same Language

How are your meetings with your users? Users are the experts in the business function and you are the expert in software design and construction. Why can't they just tell you what they want? Why are they instead telling you how many toolbar icons to put on the screen and how the Enter key should work? Does it ever seem that you just can't communicate with them?

Let's look at this problem from the user's viewpoint. The users are shown prototype after prototype and each time they are asked if it meets their requirements. Why is it a surprise that their biggest comment is that this button should be moved and that menu option renamed? But without the prototype, how can you discuss the user's requirements?

You need a common language to help you communicate. You need a language that will keep the user focused on the problem that the application should solve, not on the user interface of the application. With the object-oriented concept of abstraction you can discuss the high-level business issues without regard to implementation. Therefore, you can discuss the design in terms of the business and not the technology. You are no longer speaking a different language than your users!

Devising Real-World Models

Ever draw a flowchart? If you have ever taken a computer class you have probably created a procedural model of a software project in the form of a flowchart or data flow diagram, like the model shown in Figure 2.2. Drawing this type of flowchart or data flow diagram defined what a program would need to do, but it did not provide a model of the business. As businesses and the applications needed to support them become more and more complex, the procedural design model becomes too cumbersome and inflexible. Even minor changes to the business procedures can result in major changes to the flow.

Businesses tend to deal with things: customers, sales orders, and widgets. These things, or objects, have certain behaviors—customers place orders, sales orders need to be filled, and widgets need production. The objects also have properties—customers have addresses, sales orders have quantities and prices, and widgets have styles and colors.

The basic premise of an object-oriented approach is to model real-world things and real-world concepts. This approach keeps the real-world issues in focus and results in a design that forms a closer fit with the real world.

Figure 2.2

The procedural model used in structured design is too cumbersome and inflexible.

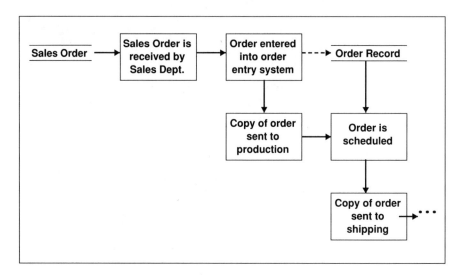

Estimating How Long It Will Take

You finally get some subject matter information from the user and obtain consensus on the project requirements. Now the project manager insists that you estimate how long it will take to develop this system. You look through your scribbled notes. In your head you are thinking "I have no idea" but your mouth says "six months," even though you know you have little to base the estimate on at this point in the project. But programmers are basically optimistic.

Keynote

At its best, software scheduling is a difficult process. At its worst, it is a meaningless guess or is based on an arbitrarily imposed deadline. It is impossible to look at a large system as a whole and establish a meaningful estimate of the work required. How can the project be broken down and estimated accurately? The object-oriented approach provides a way to abstract a project into classes that can be easily identified, understood, and reasonably estimated. These classes can be combined into interim deliverables. You can then use your past experience with similar components to set milestones and derive a more realistic schedule.

Justifying Time for Design

The project manager walks in and sees that you are not coding. He asks why you are scribbling notes and penciling cryptic diagrams when you should be at the keyboard. The schedule indicates that you should have the first module coded, but you have not yet begun.

You know you need to design the underlying structure for your application. But how do you get management to understand the importance of this architecture and put it on the schedule? How do you tell management that any time (and therefore money) saved by developing features quickly is lost later because of the complexity of working with code that has no underlying structure? How can you start building modules when you have no structure to attach them to? It would be like trying to put a tub into a second floor bathroom when the foundation had not yet been poured.

The GUIDS methodology for object-oriented design, introduced in this book, defines a clear set of steps for developing the architecture. Each step can be defined as a task on the schedule and will provide tangible results to show your progress. Using GUIDS will make it easier for you to define and schedule the architecture phase of your projects.

Preventing the Prototype Surprise

The users want to see how the whole system will look to make sure that they have communicated their requirements successfully, so you complete a prototype of the system. At the presentation of the prototype, the manager of the group expresses his appreciation. You've spent many late hours to get to this point, and are glad to hear the users are happy with it. The happiness turns sour, however, when the manager tells you how glad he is that you are almost finished. He has read about how easy Visual Basic is to use and just knew the project estimate you had given was bloated. The pressure is now on you to throw more code onto the prototype to complete the project.

For some insight here, let's look back on our construction metaphor. Would anyone ask a building contractor to take the architectural model and just tack a bit more plywood onto it to create an office building? Of course not! What would happen? A little wood could be tacked on here and there and things would be fine. Then a little more wood and it wouldn't take too long for the roof to wobble and the walls to fall in. Why? Because there is no internal structure to correctly hold the pieces together. The same will happen with the software. Some amount of code can be added to the prototype with no problem. As more and more code is added, however, it becomes increasingly difficult to modify and manage the routines. Soon it seems the code is falling in on you.

You need to explain to the users that they are looking at a prototype with nothing really holding it up, like a great facade on a sound stage. Why did they get misled? How do you get them to buy into the idea of waiting while you finish the architecture?

The GUIDS methodology presents ways to include the users throughout the architecture phase. Doing so allows them to learn more about the complexities of software development and the required processes. This helps you manage user expectations and prevents the prototype surprise.

Managing the Complexity of Programming

Now for the fun part. You get to write code.

You have it all in your head. You know exactly where everything is. You write more code. Things are starting to get messy. Weeks go by as you write more and more code. Now you can't remember which module has which routine. Modules are calling modules which are calling other modules. Something you added broke another routine. Now you are no longer confident that the next change will not break something else. The code is falling down around you and you start to wonder whether you need to redesign and start the coding over. But the deadline....

An object-oriented design manages the complexity of programming. It provides logic and order in the way the pieces of an application should be put together. A place for every routine and every routine in its place. This makes the development process more efficient because you know where code should be developed and what that code should do. There is much less redesigning and reworking of the code.

Keynote

Simplifying Multiprogrammer Development

Management is worried about meeting scheduling commitments, so more programmers have been added to the project. You ask yourself, "Which parts of this mess can be divided out and given to someone else? How will they know when to call which of my routines?" Maybe you can just give these additional programmers that dreaded piece called "reports." Nothing else seems easily separated from the whole.

You need a clean way to segment the application. To ensure effective use of multiple programmers, these segments must be independent so the programmers don't end up interfering with each other (and with you) as they develop their components. The application's internal structure needs walls between the components—walls with doors.

Keynote

Walls keep the segments from interfering with each other, while doors provide a mechanism for communication between the segments. The object-oriented design builds the walls by defining independent, encapsulated objects. These objects interact with other objects only through the public interfaces that are defined as the doors, thus simplifying multiple programmer development.

Adapting to Change

Ever have any requirements change during a project? Yesterday the vice president of sales met with Acme Widget Company, so the goal of your application was to manage the production of widgets. Today she met with ABC Paper Company, so now the goal of the application is to build a paper production management system.

Okay, maybe your requirements don't change that much, but I bet they do change. You are then asked to assess the scope of the change. How do you tell the difference between a minor change and a major one? How can you determine which routines or modules will be affected?

Any changes in requirements often result in large amounts of rework or attempts to adapt the code to do something for which it just wasn't designed. This would be easier if the design was defined more clearly and was therefore more adaptable.

The classes in an object-oriented design describe independent, well-defined components. Making those classes encapsulated keeps the implementation hidden from the rest of the system, so it is more flexible and can be adapted to change more easily.

Managing Special Orders

The vice president of sales is back. This time she wants you to implement one database structure for users who buy the single-user version of the product and a different database for the users who buy the multiuser version. You start thinking about the configuration nightmares of keeping two sets of code current.

Regardless of the client-specific change that is needed, you'd rather have one set of code. That code would have to be smart enough to include the correct routines based on those client-specific requirements. Using the architectural structure defined in the GUIDS methodology, you can make your application that smart and manage those special orders.

Preparing Interim Deliveries

The quality assurance/quality control group is starting to ask for completed pieces. You try to explain that nothing is really ready to be tested. You tell them they will get something as soon as the system is operational.

The documentation group files into your office next. They want some pieces that work so they can begin the online help and user documentation. They cannot wait until everything is finished before they start or they won't have the manuals ready in time for the first customer ship date.

The object-oriented approach allows you to build independent components that can be combined for an interim delivery. This allows you to deliver incremental components for independent testing and documentation.

Measuring Progress

The project manager comes in for a status check. You tell him the application is 80 percent complete. He shudders and asks why it has been 80 percent complete for three weeks. You tell him there were some other parts you had to build and those required additional changes to the system. As he goes back to update the schedule, he wonders which scheduled task should include the time required for these new parts. You guessed at the schedule and now it is coming back to haunt you. Your project plan was unable to anticipate all of the work that needed to be done.

The object-oriented approach of the GUIDS methodology allows you to define all of the components of your application and map these components to identifiable and measurable tasks on the schedule. You can then more accurately estimate the time required to develop each of these relatively small components and can more easily assess your progress.

Managing Maintenance

The application has finally shipped! Now you are assigned to a new project. Three months later your boss tells you that minor but critical maintenance must be done on your previous project. You look at the finished code and wonder whether you were really the person who wrote most of it. It is messy and difficult to follow.

The revisions are moving along slowly and you are getting frustrated. Because the code is so disorganized, you are far into the changes before you realize that this supposedly minor fix is going to be a major effort. You are lost in the details of the code. You make changes here and there, realizing that this means the entire application must be retested.

The classes in an object-oriented design describe independent, well-defined components. Encapsulating the classes keeps the implementation hidden from the rest of the system, so it is more flexible and can be adapted to change more easily. You can then make modifications with minimal effect on the entire system, simplifying the change and the retesting.

Reusing Components

Back on your current project, you find that you need to include a few features in your new application that you had developed in your old one. Instead of rewriting these, you decide to copy them to this project, but now you have two identical sets of code to maintain.

If the objects in an application are encapsulated, they can be purchased or built once and then reused in every application that needs them. The concept of reusable components is difficult for some programmers who like the "we invented it here" philosophy. These programmers like to know each detail of the implementation of each component. Often, however, knowing the details of each object comes at a very expensive price in terms of development time and money.

How quickly would an office building be developed if the builder built each subassembly from scratch at the building site? Trees would be converted to boards and trusses and steel would be converted into saws and hammers. This would add years and expense to the project. Instead, the builder buys prebuilt components such as the boards and trusses, reuses existing components like the saws and hammers, and builds what is necessary.

So, too, with the software developer. The components for the application are analyzed to determine which can be purchased, reused from internal component libraries, or built from scratch.

Keynote

With Visual Basic, you can create your own reusable components, called ActiveX components. In addition, there is a large third-party component vendor community providing all kinds of components. These include business objects such as accounting components, implementation objects such as spreadsheets, and database objects for manipulating data. Both the third-party and your own ActiveX components are object-oriented, making them easy to "glue" into your application. This can provide a significant time savings in getting an application operational.

As a simple example, say you need an application that will track the number of hours each day you work on different tasks and at the end of each month create an invoice. To minimize the development time for this application, you can look at existing components and how they could be used. You find you could use Microsoft Excel to create the time object and Microsoft Word to create the invoice object. You can then use Visual Basic to assemble the components into a complete application.

■ A Contact Management System Case Study

Descriptions of architecture and construction are quite vague and abstract if there are no examples to demonstrate how the concepts are applied. To help you understand how all of the pieces of a system are designed and implemented, one primary example is used throughout the remainder of this book.

This example will demonstrate how an idea can be converted into a plan of action and the plan can be followed through to the completion of an application. Here are the details of your mission.

- The vice president of sales and the sales force have been through the idea generation and evaluation process and have come up with several ideas for increasing sales. These ideas range from decreasing prices and improving marketing materials to developing a new contact management system.
- The last idea involves the technical staff. You are asked to develop the new contact management system.

If you are not involved in a business organization and cannot relate to this example, think of it in another way:

- You have a large number of clients (or customers) and need a method of tracking them. You have been through the idea generation and evaluation process and have come up with several ideas of how to better track your clients. These ideas range from a better business card file to a computerized contact management system.
- You decide to develop a contact management system. You then look at a plan of action and a schedule for moving forward with the idea.

■ Summary

- Construction is a fitting metaphor for software development. Software engineers create the architectural design and then use that design as a blueprint to build solid software.

- There are probably as many definitions of the "software development process" as there are places that develop software. Even so, the process normally includes the same basic phases: idea, requirements, plan and schedule, architecture, construction, and inspection.

- Projects begin with an idea of what is to be built. The idea may be your own or may come from someone else, such as a potential user of the application.

- Requirements analysis examines the idea to define the goals and requirements of what you are building. This ensures that you build the right features.

- The project plan defines how the project will be accomplished to meet the requirements and the schedule defines a time frame for the project.

- The GUIDS methodology provides a set of steps to help you design an object-oriented software architecture. The architecture is critical for constructing solid software.

- The construction phase converts the design into code. This is where the design is implemented.

- Inspections start early and continue through the construction process to help ensure that you are developing solid software.

- After the application is complete, maintenance activities can follow the same software development process.

- There are many benefits of using an object-oriented approach to software design and development. Abstracted objects provide a common language for the project team and a better model for the business. Encapsulation makes it simpler to define independent components that are easier to schedule, implement, test, modify, document, deliver, and maintain.

■ Additional Reading

Gray, N. A. B. *Programming with Class: A Practical Introduction to Object-Oriented Programming with C++*. New York: John Wiley & Sons, 1994.

This book provides a pragmatic approach to object-oriented design focusing on implementing the design in C++. The quote that appears at the beginning of this chapter can be found on page 35 of this edition.

Kurata, Deborah. "Ten Reasons to Go OO." *Visual Basic Programmer's Journal*, Vol. 6, No. 14, December 1996.

This is a Visual Basic 4 article, but it is still applicable to VB5. It provides ten reasons to help sell you and your management team into making the move to OO. It includes such reasons as "No More Kevorkian Applications" and "Leverage Legacy Code."

■ Think It Over

To supplement and review the information in this chapter, try the following:

1. Think about your last software development effort. Did it have a formal or informal development process? What steps did you follow in developing the project?

2. If you have worked at different companies or on several different projects, how were the development processes similar and different? What aspect of the development process made any project easier or harder than another?

3. Look at the phases for software development defined in this chapter. Did you go through each of these phases, formally or informally, in each of your projects? Were you satisfied with the results? Why or why not?

4. Review the common issues that arise during the software development cycle. Notice how these problems illustrate the benefits of the object-oriented approach to software development. How many of these issues have you experienced in your prior projects? How did you address these issues?

3

The Prerequisites of Design

First, you must understand the problem to be solved. The content of an object model is driven by relevance to the solution.

—James Rumbaugh *et al.*,
Object-Oriented Modeling and Design

Before beginning a design, you need to know what it is you are designing. You need to understand the problem or opportunity before you can begin to design a solution.

It all starts with an idea. A person in an organization has an idea for a better way to do things. Or you look at the marketplace and have an idea for a better software product. The idea becomes a goal and a project is born. To attain the goal, the project needs a team that is focused on achieving the goal. The project needs clear requirements, a well-devised plan, and a realistic schedule. Only then can you begin to design the object model that provides the solution.

This chapter focuses on the prerequisites of the design. It begins with techniques for getting ideas and turning those ideas into a project. It also describes how to perform a requirements analysis to set the goals and constraints of the project.

Finally, it outlines how to develop a project plan and a high-level schedule. After completing these prerequisites, you will be ready to begin the design.

■ Beginning with an Idea

I know you may be thinking: "A section on ideas? In a programming book?"

Well, every construction project begins with an idea. Someone sees a problem to be solved or discovers an opportunity to be exploited. The creativity process converts that problem or opportunity into ideas. After the ideas are explored, logic takes over to evaluate and validate the ideas. Cost/benefit and risk analyses are performed. A selected idea becomes the main goal for a project and the idea is on its way to becoming reality.

You can use the creative thinking techniques in this section to find that "big idea" for an application or simply to generate ideas for solving the daily problems you face. How could a particular set of information be presented to the user? What different user interface mechanisms could be employed? What algorithm can be used to accomplish a specific task? How do you get the code to do what you need it to do? What should you have for lunch?

Where Do Ideas Come From?

When presented with a problem or an opportunity, logical minds tend to look for the correct answer. Ideas should be the result of a logical thought process whereby any problem is solved using logic and hard work, right? If you think hard enough for long enough you'll figure out the solution, right? Not always.

Take the problem with earlier versions of Windows and the scripting languages that went with them. They were not easy enough to use. The logical answer was a tool to help the user build the scripts. Devise something that could construct If Then Else statements from selections in a list. Instead of using linear thinking to find this "logical" answer, someone applied creative thinking to the problem. The result was an idea significantly different and incredibly better: Ruby, the prototype to the visual component of what is now Visual Basic.

Keynote

Good ideas do not necessarily come when you are using logic to solve a problem. Rather, they come when you are being creative and illogical. Ideas are born from your imagination, experience, creativity, and inspiration.

Sometimes ideas seem to appear from nowhere. You are taking a shower and splash! An idea is floating around in your head. Many a time I have jumped out of the shower to write down a great idea for a specific routine or user-interface idiom. Although soggy, more often than not the ideas generated during these moments of inspiration were very useful.

Other times, ideas arise from your experience, grow out of adversity, or emerge from combining several thoughts in a unique manner. In a business environment, many ideas come from the people on the front lines. They are performing difficult tasks or procedures, keeping up with changes in the industry, tracking the competition, and hearing from customers. They use these sources for inspiration and can relate their ideas to a direct business need.

Inspiration is often thought to be spontaneous. You have a sudden burst of inspiration and an idea is miraculously revealed. There are, however, several ways to improve your creativity and increase the number of ideas you have. You can use the following techniques to find that big idea. You can also use them to generate ideas for daily problem solving throughout the software development process.

State the Question

Phrase the problem or opportunity in the form of a question. Rephrase the question and look at it again. "What can we do to increase sales?" could be rephrased as, "How can we improve the productivity of the sales force?" "What should this screen look like?" could be turned into, "How can the user best work with this information?" The way you phrase the question affects how you think about the question and therefore affects the kinds of ideas that are generated from it.

Look at all sides of that question. Turn the question inside out and upside down. Instead of asking "How can this be done better?" consider "How can this be done worse?" Play with your thoughts. Be illogical, be frivolous! Your answers may be silly, but they may also generate some more interesting and useful ideas.

Try Something Totally Different

Instead of looking in technical journals for ideas, try a toy catalog, or an architectural digest, or some fiction. Instead of taking yet another computer class, sign up for art or creative writing. Ideas often come from your experiences. Having different experiences allows you to take ideas from one area and adapt them to your current problem or opportunity.

Steve Jobs, one of the founders of Apple Computer, has stated that innovation results from connections of past experiences. Having different experiences allows you to look in different directions.

Visualize the Process

Form a mental model of the problem and walk through the model. Diagram the problem on paper. Seeing the problem more clearly may bring ideas into focus.

For example, you are searching for ways to improve an application that tracks contacts with prospective customers. You can imagine you are the salesperson and walk through the process of following up on a lead and contacting a prospective customer. Which steps are the most difficult and time consuming? How could these steps be improved? By visualizing the process you may visualize ideas.

Break the Bounds

Think beyond your current constraints. Look at possibilities beyond the obvious.

As a software developer, it is natural to look at all problems and opportunities and define an application as the solution. It is too easy to provide a standard answer to all problems such as "make that manual process better by automating it" or "make the software better by rewriting it." Think beyond that. Maybe the manual process just needs to be improved or thrown out all together. Maybe you just need to make a small user interface change in the software. Maybe doing nothing is the best approach.

Part of this technique involves questioning what has always been true. Why does the user need a Save button? Because that's how it has always been done! But...why? Why not automatically save unless specifically told not to? Don't let your presuppositions or defined "truths" limit your choices.

Talk to Someone

Explaining the issues to someone else often helps you think about them in simple terms. The person who is listening may ask questions that make you think about things differently. Whenever I am stuck on a problem, I talk to a colleague whose part of the conversation primarily consists of "but...why?" This type of questioning can really get your ideas flowing. Do this formally, or informally. Many great ideas have been recorded on napkins in restaurants and bars.

Brainstorm

Brainstorming is another good source of ideas. Get several people together (or use your imagination and be several different people) and let the creative process go. Look at the question from all points of view. Encourage participation from everyone. Let people suggest anything, without criticism. Even silly things can lead to important ideas.

Relax

Read a novel. Go for a walk. Take a nap. See a movie. Do anything but think about getting an idea. Something you see, hear, or feel may provide the spark you need. Or just the break and fresh start may give you a new perspective.

For example, you are again thinking about designing that contact management system. You give up for the evening and dial on to the Internet to check up on the latest sports scores and your stock quotes. Voilà, inspiration strikes. If the sales force could dial in to the system, they could manage their contacts when they are on the road and not have the burden of updating the system upon their return. Just letting your thoughts go will often lead to an idea.

Formalizing and Evaluating the Ideas

Roger von Oech, the author of *A Whack on the Side of the Head*, describes two phases for the development of new ideas: An imaginative phase that provides an opportunity to generate and play with ideas and a practical phase that allows you to evaluate and execute the ideas.

After you have all of those imaginative ideas, you'll need to move into the practical phase. However, you do *not* want to move into this phase too soon. When you have one idea, you are not yet ready to be logical because for any single problem there are many possible solutions. You should have at least three or four ideas before moving on to this phase.

The practical phase allows you to formalize and evaluate all of the ideas. This process is sometimes called a *feasibility study* or a *cost/benefit analysis*. Answering the following questions for each idea (and documenting the answers) will help you to formalize and evaluate the ideas.

Does the Idea Make Sense?

Because this is now the practical phase, the idea needs to define something that is logical, useful, realistic, and tangible. The idea needs to solve the defined problem. Throw out any ideas at this point that are ridiculous. If you completed the imaginative phase, most of these ridiculous ideas will have been stepping stones to more realistic ideas.

Formalize each idea by stating it clearly. Then evaluate each idea. Inspect it, dissect it, reconstitute it, turn it around, look at it from all sides, and try to apply it. Consider its usefulness and identify who will obtain value from it. Combine similar ideas as needed. Describe every idea in every detail. Write them down. This forces the ideas to become real.

An idea for a new user interface idiom may seem like a good idea at dinner after a few glasses of wine. However, it may not seem like a good idea after you clearly define the idea and outline exactly how the user would have to work with it.

Does It Fit with the Enterprise-Wide or Marketing Goals?

If you are in a business environment, the idea must fit into the organization's strategic plan. For entrepreneurs, it needs to fit into the company's marketing plans.

Because of the constant shortage of technical people, programmers are a critical resource in most organizations. When a company plans to allocate those programming resources, especially if it's for an extended time, the project must be in line with company goals.

If your company develops accounting systems, it may not be interested in an idea for a great audio clip library. That doesn't mean it is a bad idea. It just means you may need to find a different audience for the idea and a different path to fruition.

What Risks Are Involved?

Evaluate the business and technical risks of the idea. How feasible is the idea and what potential problems exist in implementing the idea in the organization and with current technology? What dependencies does this idea have on other external factors, such as third-party hardware or software products?

Suppose a mainframe accounts receivable system was recently replaced with a new system developed in Visual Basic. This project was high risk because it was the first major shift from the mainframe to client/server. Because that project was completed successfully, an idea for using the same approach to replace the accounts payable system has lower risk.

What Benefits Are Provided?

Look closely at each group of people that could potentially benefit from this idea and identify the benefits the group will receive. Include others that may indirectly benefit from the idea. The idea for a contact management system will help the sales force. The improved sales information will also help the department head and upper management, even though they will not be direct users of the application. Include the benefits provided to these individuals or groups as well.

As best as possible, quantify the benefits. How much money will the application save the company? How will productivity be improved? How many more sales will be made due to the better information? These benefit values will be estimates, but will provide enough information for a basic comparison against the cost estimates.

What Are the Projected Costs?

The projected costs define the financial impact of the idea. How much will the idea cost to implement? To calculate costs, you must define a high-level plan. Approximately how many people will be required to work on the project and for how long?

Defining the plan requires some definition of the project's requirements. This is where the idea phase overlaps the requirements phase, as shown earlier in Figure 2.1. A complete requirements analysis is not called for at this point, but you must have some idea of the requirements to estimate the cost of the project. Determining this cost is a complex issue; however, you just need a ballpark figure here.

Even though this estimate cannot be precise, this step is critical, especially when the ideas are reviewed and approved by someone else. How can a manager make a good choice between similar ideas without having some concept of the costs of those ideas for comparison with the benefits of those ideas?

Which Idea Is Best?

After you have answered these questions for each idea, you need to select the idea or set of ideas that best solves the problem or exploits the opportunity. Selecting the best idea or set of ideas often involves comparing the benefits of each idea with its cost and weighing in the expected risk. Do the benefits outweigh the costs? Is there an acceptable amount of risk? Is this idea attractive to the people that can benefit from it and to those who make the decisions?

In many medium to large organizations this cost/benefit analysis is crucial to prioritizing the work performed by the critical programming resources. Projects are selected or ignored based on the cost/benefit analysis.

■ Establishing the Requirements

Once an idea is selected, you need to make it happen. The first step in turning an idea into reality is to expand the idea into a set of specific requirements. These requirements define the project and set expectations for the users as well as the technical staff. Because this step provides the conceptual basis of the application, it is sometimes called the *conceptual design*.

Here's a construction example: Some executives have a great idea for solving their company's space shortage problem—a new office building. The executives meet with an architect and say, "We have a great idea. We'd like to build a new office building. We'd like a proposal from you for designing this building, including a plan, schedule, and cost." From this description, the building could be anything from a single-story structure with two offices to a 40-story office complex.

In this example, the architect began by working with the executives to define the project's requirements. The scope was defined (single building to house the entire organization), the needs were clarified (50 individual ergonomically designed offices, a loading dock, and so on), and the quality and technical specifications were identified (highest quality materials, meet state regulations, and so on). These requirements will form the basis of the building's architectural design.

Just as an architect works with executives to define their requirements, the software architect or analyst must collaborate with the prospective users to define their requirements. These project requirements are then defined and documented as a requirements specification, project analysis document, functional specification, or problem statement. Regardless of its name, this document forms the basis of the application's design.

Defining Goal-Centered Requirements

The common method of defining project requirements is with a *user-centered approach*. This approach involves asking the users what they need and designing the application to meet those stated needs. The primary problem with this approach is that most of the time the users don't really know what they want. They may know what they do and have some idea as to how the computer can make their job easier or more productive. But frequently, they don't know how the computer can really help them.

Sometimes users do not know the primary business goal being met by the tasks they are performing. They do the task this way because it always was done this way, so they think the computer should do it that way as well. However, the process may no longer make sense in an automated system.

The common illustration of this problem is the cook who always cuts the ends off of a roast before putting it in a large enough pan. When asked why she does it, she states that she has always done it this way because her mother had always done it that way. When her mother was asked why she had done it that way, she said "because my pan was too small."

Keynote

The goal-centered approach averts these problems by investigating further with the users to establish the true goals behind the defined needs. These goals are then used to morph the defined needs into project requirements that are better aligned with the user's true goals.

A simple example can illustrate this point. Say your users are salespeople who make calls to customers and prospects. As you are defining the requirements for a contact management system, the users state the requirement: "We need to automatically send e-mail to the accounting group if the contact name for a company has changed." By asking the user more questions about the need for that requirement, you find the true goal is to ensure that the contact name is updated in the accounting database. The goal-centered requirement can then be stated: "Keep the accounting data current with data obtained during sales calls." This allows more efficient solutions, such as automatically creating a transaction to update the accounting data when a customer contact name is changed.

The following steps can help you use the goal-centered approach to identify the project's requirements:

1. Create the project team.

2. Do your homework.

3. State the goals.

4. Set the scope.

5. Identify the needs.

6. Morph the needs into requirements.

7. Prioritize the requirements.

Keynote

As you walk through each of these steps, be sure the project team's thoughts and decisions are documented. The resulting requirements document will be the basis of the architectural design.

Creating the Project Team

The entire definition and direction of the project will come from the project team. Because it has such significant responsibility, the team must be carefully selected.

In a business environment, ideas for projects frequently come from or have an impact on the user organization. The team should include representatives from the user organizations because they are the ones that know the business. These subject matter experts are called *domain experts* because they are knowledgeable in the business area that will be affected by the application.

Entrepreneurial opportunities often stem from the entrepreneur's ideas. To define the project requirements in this situation, the entrepreneur functions as a subject matter expert or requests help from an external subject matter expert. The requirements can then come from these collaborators, who will be your domain experts.

When evaluating the original idea for the project, the groups of people who would potentially benefit from or be affected by the idea were identified. To guarantee that the project meets everyone's needs, representatives from each of these groups should participate in the project. Yet to get anything done, you cannot effectively work with that many people. You know the old saying "too many cooks spoil the broth." In software it is "too many designers spoil the design."

To include everyone but keep the team small enough to collaborate effectively, establish a full team with full representation. Then, define a core team to do the day-to-day work of the project. The core team should not include more than five or six people at a time. If the project is very large, it should be broken into smaller pieces with one small core team assigned to each piece.

In this respect, the project team is much like a sports team. The success of the season is dependent on all the members of the team. However, there are only a limited number of core players on the field at any one time. Using this technique prevents chaos on the field.

The Role of the Full Team

The full team serves as a steering and oversight committee. It includes representatives from all areas that are directly or indirectly affected by the project or have changes in responsibility due to the project. This team has regular status meetings and is responsible for ensuring that their department or other related individuals are kept informed of the project's status. Each team member has access to all project documentation and is asked to provide comments and suggestions.

Minimally, this team should have key members from the user organizations and the technical staff. In general, team members could come from any of the following areas:

- Current and prospective users
- Managers of affected user communities
- User's support staff
- Subject matter experts
- Software analysts, designers, and developers
- Software quality control/quality assurance staff
- Technical writers
- Technical support staff

Including representatives from these different groups allows collaboration among the participants and a view of the different perspectives. This blending of ideas leads to a better definition of the requirements of the project, which in turn leads to a solution that better meets the needs of all involved.

For some projects, you may be the only member of the official team. However, you will want to create an unofficial team with members from the user community, your domain experts. These will be the people you consult to define the requirements of the application. When you get to the technical portions of the project, you can add to your unofficial team by establishing a network of colleagues. You can also tap technical resources available through user groups, the Web, Internet newsgroups, or technical conferences.

Regardless of the team's size, several specific roles need to be filled. The project should have a record keeper, a project manager, a decision-maker, and an evangelist (even if you have to wear all four hats). The respective job descriptions are listed in the following table.

Team Member	Responsibilities
Record Keeper	Documents all of the information discussed by the team and maintains the formal project documents such as a requirements specification document, architectural design document, and so on.
Project Manager	Directs the project. Defines when to bring in which participants, listens well, watches carefully, knows how to get the participants to cooperate, works toward consensus wherever possible, and decides when to end each step.
Decision Maker	Provides the authority to make final decisions. Not all decisions made in a project can be done by consensus. There will be different points of view and disagreements on project details. This decision maker, who also could be the project manager, must be identified to make sure the team knows who has the final word.
Evangelist	Keeps the project in focus and moving forward. This is the domain expert or entrepreneur with the vision, with a clear idea of what the results of the project should accomplish. Although this person is not mandatory, most successful and enjoyable projects I have worked on have had an energetic evangelist who kept a clear project vision.

The Role of the Core Team

The core team is a subset of the full team that is responsible for doing the day-to-day work in the project. The members of this team work together to analyze and document the project requirements, design the architecture, build the application, and test and document it.

The members of the core team will change somewhat over the course of the project, depending on the skills required at each phase. For the development of the requirements and architecture, the core team should minimally include those who have the critical knowledge required for the project (domain experts from the user community), those who know how to convert that knowledge into analysis and design documents (technical experts), and the record keeper to document the results.

It is critical to select the right people for the core team. Select those from the user community who have the critical knowledge, can share that knowledge with someone else, and are motivated to participate in this process. Define a good mix of individuals. Include a few dreamers and a few pragmatists. The dreamers will help think of ideas when detailed problems arise and the pragmatists will help apply these ideas.

The leader of the core team must be a good listener and must be able to ask the right questions. This leader may be an experienced facilitator, the project manager, or the lead technical person. This decision will depend on the specific situation and experience of the team members.

Imagine yourself on the contact management system team. What role would you play?

Doing Your Homework

Remember the saying, "Be prepared"? Before you begin working with the team, you need to do your homework. If you are not adequately prepared, you may face the following scenario.

The project manager calls you to the first meeting of the project team. The users immediately start telling you about the problems they have and what keystrokes they need to solve these problems. They say, "If we could just press the F2 key and get the weekly reports without having to run these batch processes, our problems would be solved."

Without any background in the pertinent area of business and without a context for these problems, you are starting to feel like a peace-conference delegate who forgot his translators. So the other delegates try to express their complex ideas in the few simple words they know in your language. Something is definitely lost in the translation! How are you going to communicate with them to understand their vision?

Keynote

You need a common language. That common language must originate in the problem domain. The language must be that of the specific business area and *not* that of the computer. This means that you need to learn about the business area. You do not need to become an expert, but you need to learn the language enough to understand the problems the users face.

The preparation must begin well before the first meeting. Schedule some time to find out about the business area or user community that will be involved with the project. Take a user to lunch or sit next to a user for a few hours.

Ask questions, listen carefully to the answers, and restate the answers for confirmation. Scan the journals the domain experts read, review any current software the business area may be using, become familiar with their terminology and procedures. This will lay the groundwork for understanding the basic issues. Some companies have business analysts who are responsible for translating the users' words for the technical members of the team, and vice versa. Don't use their presence as an excuse to avoid learning about the business issues.

By preparing adequately, you establish a common language for communicating effectively with the domain experts throughout the project. You and the domain experts will better understand the problem. Together you will be able to define the requirements and propose solutions to meet those requirements. This common language and rapport you have established can help you keep learning about the business throughout the Goal-centered and User-interface design steps.

Stating the Goals

If you've done your homework, you have an understanding of the business environment within which the application is to be used. You can then work with the domain expert to clearly identify the business goals for the project.

Most projects have one primary goal and many secondary goals. The primary goal identifies the main objective of the application and often stems from the original project idea. The secondary goals provide additional information about the business and user needs that the application will meet.

For the case study defined in the prior chapter, let's define the primary goal of the contact management project.

Increase sales by providing a software system that helps the salespeople manage contacts with clients and prospects.

This goal identifies both the original business problem (the need to increase sales) and the project objective (providing a software system). Including the original problem in the goal helps keep you from losing sight of the project's original intentions.

The secondary goals include all of the other issues that the application should address. Secondary goals may include such things as improving efficiency, increasing customer satisfaction, providing better information to management, making the user more productive, and so on. The secondary goals for the example contact management system project are listed next.

- Provide a central repository for sales and customer information.
- Provide more timely contact information to management.
- Improve the salesperson's ability to track follow up tasks.
- Provide an effective interface that has minimal impact on the user while making the contact, especially with phone contacts when the user will be using the system during the call.

Setting the Scope

The next step is to set the scope of the project. The scope identifies and limits the business or functional areas affected by the application, called the *application domain*. Some amount of this definition was done previously to select the appropriate participants for the project team. At this step, these scope issues are more clearly established. If during this evaluation you find that additional user groups are affected, you can add representatives from those groups to the project team.

When establishing the application domain, evaluate how the application fits with other parts of the organization or other user activities, both computerized and manual. Look at how the application domain inter-operates with other products or other areas of the business, including existing legacy systems. Define the boundaries of the application. The interfaces between the application domain of this project and the existing systems need to be well defined to ensure that this piece will fit into the main system when this application is complete. Figure 3.1 depicts this concept.

The application domain for the contact management system is stated in the following list.

- The contact management system will support all salespersons in the sales department and provide summary reports to upper management.
- Only contact management functions will be included.

Keynote

When defining the application domain, keep the project goals in mind. Only those areas that are related to the goals should be included in this project. Be careful not to fall into the "something for everyone" trap (it slices, it dices…). A project that tries to do everything will be good at nothing. For example, the president of the company liked the idea of the new contact management system so much, he proposed including features to schedule the production process, track employee time sheets, and develop the stockholder's report. Bad idea. Keep these other areas out of this application domain.

Additional phases of this project or new related projects can be defined later to provide other features and meet the needs of other users.

Figure 3.1

How do the applications and other systems within the enterprise fit together?

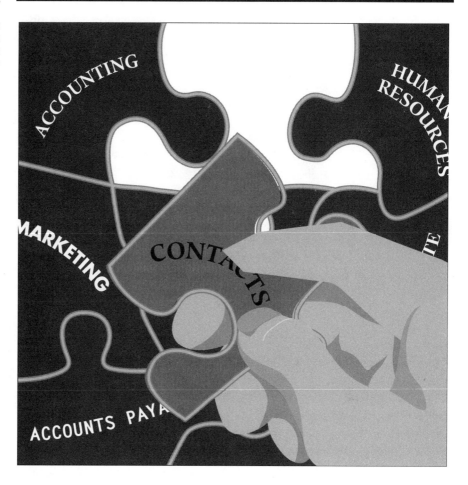

(I add a section to the back of my requirements specification documents entitled "Future Features" for out-of-scope ideas or features.) Managing single-focused projects and developing single-focused applications is easier than managing and developing applications that support a wide range of activities. The former is also less risky than the latter. Do you know of any system that tried to provide "something for everyone" that was ever actually finished?

If the example contact management system project is successful, the company may decide to identify another phase of the project to incorporate sales time reporting. Related projects could also be defined for order processing, sales commission tracking, and so on.

The point is, keep *this* project simple and limited to one focused purpose.

Identifying the Needs

The requirements identify what the application must do. These requirements are based on what the business needs to achieve and what the user needs to accomplish. To get a full picture of these needs, be sure to include quality standards and any predefined technical and marketing specifications.

Defining the Business Needs

The domain experts can best define the current business and user needs because they understand the nature of the business. By using the common language you learned during your preparation, you can ask these experts questions about the tasks they perform and you can understand their answers.

You can use the project goals as the launching point for the needs assessment. Get clarification on the goals. Look at what tasks the user currently accomplishes to meet the goals.

After you have an overview, you will want to get more detail on each task the user performs to currently meet those needs. This is called a *task analysis*. It involves working closely with the users to define the exact procedures and methods that are currently used to perform each task. Spend time with them as they perform their tasks. Ask the users to explain the procedures and demonstrate any software systems that they currently use. Listen carefully as they describe what they do and then ask probing questions.

When the task analysis is complete, you will have a basic understanding of what the user does to meet current business goals. This defines the business needs.

At the first meeting with the users in the example contact management system project, the core team developed the business needs assessment shown in the following list.

1. Keep the name, address, and phone number for every customer.

2. Keep the name, address, and phone number for every prospect.

3. Create a log entry for each contact made with a customer or prospect.

4. At the end of each week, summarize the log information.

5. Provide summary reports.

6. Maintain a list of required follow-up tasks.

This simplified example does not necessarily show all of the needs of a full-featured contact management system. For most medium-sized projects, there will be a dozen or more defined needs.

Specifying the Quality Standards

In addition to basic business needs, there are other factors that affect the requirements of the project. The quality standards provide some general statements about the overall required quality of the application. When defining quality standards, consider the following factors:

- Ease of use

- Conformity to established user interface conventions

- Maintainability

- Reliability

- Performance

- Acceptable defect level (bug count)

- Compatibility with other related systems

If you define quality standards at this point in the project, the entire design will incorporate quality considerations. If you don't state these standards, quality gets pushed back into the testing step. At that point, quality becomes solely a list of bugs instead of a primary project requirement.

The team defined the list of the quality standards for the contact management system, as shown here.

1. Easy to use
2. Easy to maintain
3. No "showstopper" bugs or crashes
4. Fast response time

Defining the Technical and Marketing Specifications

Every construction project must conform to some established parameters. Software construction is no different. The parameters for software construction could include the following:

- Minimal required hardware configuration

- Recommended hardware configuration

- Operating system(s)

- Network configuration

- Languages (if a particular programming language is required)

- Database (if a specific database or legacy system must be used)

- Portability

- Reusability

- Projected number of users

- Projected volume of data

- Security requirements

- Interfaces to other systems

- Current technical standards and programming conventions

- Projected technical support requirements

- Time to market

- Internationalization

Each of these items should be carefully considered and applicable items should be specified. The result is included in the requirements document.

The contact management system team specified the technical and marketing specifications shown next.

1. Run under the current Microsoft Windows operating system and support the associated hardware platform.
2. Follow naming and programming conventions.
3. Develop reusable components for future Windows projects.
4. Provide the application for the 1998 Sales Force kickoff meeting in February.
5. Display the screens in the local language for the sales staff in the U.S. and Europe.

Morphing the Needs into Requirements

After you identify the needs, you must convert them into project requirements based on the goals of the application. The statements change from "I need to do xyz" to "the project must provide xyz." An easy way to convert these needs into requirements is to directly map each need to a requirement. If the user must write down a customer's name, you could specify a requirement for entering the customer's name. If the user must create a log book entry for each phone call made, you could list "create a log book entry" as a requirement. But this does not provide an insightful list of requirements.

This direct way of mapping tasks to requirements can lead to something I call the *dishwasher principle*. To understand this concept, imagine that you are designing the first dishwasher and the following is the result of your task analysis:

1. The user picks up several dishes and sets them in a tub of water.

2. The user then scrubs each dish and places it in a holding area.

3. After scrubbing each dish in the set, the user rinses those dishes with clean water and places them in yet another holding area.

4. After all the dishes are washed, the user individually wipes each dish with a towel.

Imagine the dishwasher designed as a result of these "requirements"! Now try this. Instead of directly mapping the tasks, morph them into more generalized requirements such as: all dishes must be thoroughly cleaned, disinfected, rinsed, and dried. Morphing needs into requirements ensures that the requirements are goal-centered and opens up more options, giving you more flexibility to define a solution to meet the requirements.

Tech Note. *The dishwasher principle points out the reason behind the push for business process re-engineering. Instead of defining software systems that mirror the current business processes, re-engineering evaluates the business procedures and "re-engineers" them. Business policies and practices are often changed, processes are modified, and new responsibilities are established to make the most effective use of new technologies. Taking this wider view of the project can provide a much better solution, but can be time consuming and more risky. (See the "Additional Reading" section at the end of this chapter for references on business process re-engineering.)*

As you are morphing the needs into requirements, make sure that the requirement remains within the project goals. Keep each requirement as simple as possible. Will a programmer unfamiliar with the business issues be able to understand this requirement? If not, clarify any statement in question with further research before you proceed. (Put anything that veers from the project's goals or lies outside of the scope of this project onto the "Future Features" list.)

Ensure that each statement is presented as a requirement and not as a solution. For example, "We require a menu option to save customer record changes" sounds like a requirement. It even has the "require" word in it. But it is defining a solution, not a requirement. The real requirement may be to provide a mechanism for changing customer information.

As much as possible, make each requirement quantifiable. This provides a mechanism for measuring whether the requirement was met. This process is somewhat subjective. How does one define "simple" or "quick" or "easy"? You may need to modify some of the requirements to add measurement criteria. For example, convert the "easy to use" requirement into "passes usability testing."

Morphing the contact management system business needs, quality standards, and technical and marketing specifications into requirements produces the following list.

1. Maintain the customer list.

2. Maintain the prospect list.

3. Log contacts made with a customer or prospect.

4. Provide summary reports.

5. Manage follow-up tasks.

6. Provide an easy-to-learn user interface such that a new salesperson could learn how to log a contact within 30 minutes.

7. Display the Contact Management window in less than three seconds.

8. Display the screens in the local language for the sales staff in the U.S. and Europe.

9. Provide the application for the 1998 Sales Force kickoff meeting in February.

10. Run under Windows 95 and Windows NT 4.0.

11. Conform to the user interface conventions defined in *The Windows Interface Guidelines for Software Design* published by Microsoft Press.

12. Publish and follow coding standards for ease of maintainability.

13. Where feasible, develop reusable components for future Windows projects.

14. Trap all errors so the system continues reliably and log the errors to diagnose the problem.

15. Support the hardware configuration identified as the Windows 95 and Windows NT 4.0 recommended platforms.

Keynote

The key to morphing business needs into requirements is to understand the user's explanation of how a task is done and determine why the task is required. Then clearly state that requirement. Keep the goals of the project in mind to ensure that all requirements are focused on those goals. This will provide you with a requirements list that is general and open to many alternative solutions.

Prioritizing the Requirements

After you morph the needs into business requirements you must prioritize all of the requirements. Divide them into the categories: most important, relatively important, and nice to have.

Keynote

This prioritization is critical for evaluating solution alternatives and for designing the architecture. Many decisions must be made during the architecture and construction phases of the project. The team cannot accurately make the decisions without knowing the priority of the requirements. If you don't prioritize a potentially large list of requirements, the requirements can become unmanageable or even unattainable.

As a simple example, think about a grid on a form. The programmer can decide to use a third-party grid tool to provide a quick and easy solution, but this solution requires loading another third-party product and waiting for the grid to paint on the screen. Alternatively, the programmer can create an array of edit controls to ensure fast screen painting, but this will add over a week to the schedule, has a greater risk of bugs, and will be very difficult to maintain. Knowing the priorities of speed, reliability, memory usage, schedule, and maintainability will affect how this decision is made.

Every project involves trade-offs between the "big three" project parameters:

- Quality

- Schedule

- Features

Pick two. If the project requires high quality and a tight schedule, the features list will need to be a lower priority. If the project requires a large number of features and a tight schedule, quality will suffer. Any project can only have two of these as high priorities and the other one must be a lower priority. These two priorities should be clearly established at this time because they affect many design and implementation decisions.

In most programming situations, the precedence of one of these is fixed and unchangeable. You *must* have the new accounting system installed before the first quarter because the company needs the new standard accounting procedures. Or, you *must* provide specific "check list" features to compare your product with your competitors in product reviews. With a fixed parameter, you define that parameter as part of the project requirements and subordinate one (or both) of the others.

From a philosophical point of view, the project and resulting software should always be of the highest quality. However, in practice, quality is often traded for schedule or features. Ever had to add a feature to a project at the last minute when you knew there would not be sufficient time to test it? How many times has this had a large scheduling side effect or marketing ramification when the bugs from this last minute feature came to haunt the project? (For more information on the significance of quality, see Philip B. Crosby's book, *Quality Is Free*, listed in the "Additional Reading" section at the end of this chapter.)

■ Planning and Scheduling the Project

The project plan outlines how the project will proceed. It includes some basic decisions on how the project will be done, defines the tasks required to complete the project, and identifies the resource requirements for each task.

The schedule provides a time line for the plan. It defines milestones or checkpoints in the plan for the completion of tasks. Without a schedule, software gets the "soup syndrome." When is soup done? When you are hungry! Without a specified time for dinner, that soup will keep on cooking. Without a specific time frame for software, the application will keep changing, getting more and more features and tweaks.

During the construction of an office building, the plan and schedule ensure that all of the construction steps are performed in the correct order and all of the necessary resources are available when they are needed. The cement trucks must come first to pour the foundation, the foundation must be poured before the frame is completed, the frame must be in place before the roof is put on, and so on.

Goal-Centered Planning

The planning process begins when the team starts to identify strategies for meeting the requirements. These strategies could include choices such as purchasing a system, improving an existing system, enhancing a related system, developing a new system using Visual Basic, or developing a new system using another language. It could include deciding whether to use internal resources or consultants. These key decisions should be part of the project planning process.

After the strategies are defined, the specifics of the plan need to be outlined. This is when the team specifies the process and methodologies that will be used to complete the project. The key to developing a good project plan is to remain focused on the goal of the project. Each project strategy and task must be directed toward that goal.

The contact management system team carefully evaluated the requirements of the project to select an appropriate strategy. The team selected

Visual Basic 5 as the application development platform and devised the following plan:

---

1. Complete the architecture following the GUIDS methodology.

2. Develop a prototype of the user interface as soon as possible for early usability testing per the 30-minute learning requirement.

3. Develop a database prototype to ensure that the selected database engine can provide the three-second response rate required for the Contact Management window given the assumed user load and volume of data.

4. Design the architecture to provide as many reusable components as is practical given the requirements and schedule.

5. Following the architecture, divide the project into key deliverable groups, each with a clearly defined set of features and schedule.

6. Implement the project using object-oriented programming techniques.

7. Begin testing each deliverable group as it is completed.

Looking back at the requirements identified for the contact management system, you will notice that items 2, 3, and 4 are direct responses to specific requirements. Items 5, 6, and 7 are based on a key implementation strategy that is discussed in more detail in Chapter 9, "Strategies for Construction."

It is very important to document the plan and provide it to all members of the team. This ensures that all team members are aware of the process, goals, and direction of the project.

Project Scheduling

After the plan is established, the team can define a schedule for implementing the plan. This schedule details the tasks and projected times for the next step in the software development process, which is the architecture phase. In most cases, the team must also create a high-level schedule for the entire project.

Defining the Detailed Schedule for the Architecture

One of the key issues when defining the detailed schedule for the architecture is determining the availability of the core team members. If one key domain expert is required at the design meetings and this person is only available one afternoon a week, a two-week design task could turn into a 20-week task! I have found the best way to conduct the design is over a relatively short period of time, off-site if possible. This keeps the team focused on the issues and keeps the issues fresh in their minds.

To help you develop a schedule for an object-oriented architecture using the GUIDS methodology, consider the following:

- **G**oal-centered design requires one to two weeks of full-time, high-focused, intense discussion with the core design team. The record keeper may need to work overtime to make sure that the notes are kept up to date between meetings. This provides a current record and minimizes time spent re-discussing what had been decided in previous sessions.

- **U**ser-interface design requires another few weeks for a designer to sketch some original screens, and then a week or two to discuss and modify these sketches with the core team.

- **I**mplementation-centered design requires a few weeks for the software designers to define any implementation-specific features of the application. This will be reduced as libraries of reusable components are readily available from prior projects.

- **D**ata design requires a few weeks for the data designers to design and develop the data files and databases for the application.

- **S**trategies for construction includes a review of the design by the core team and additional meetings to discuss conventions, testing, documentation, and so on. Things like naming conventions and coding standards may require a significant amount of discussion for the first project, but very little in future projects because existing standards can be used.

- If the core team has the required resources and personnel, the time for user interface, implementation, and data design can overlap.

- Some strategy meetings may be required before completing the other steps of the design to establish strategies for making good design decisions.

- The core team may need additional time in the schedule to evaluate and learn new technologies.

- If the team consists of one person, the schedule must provide the time for these steps to be carried out sequentially, with sufficient time allocated to document the results of each step.

The amount of time your project will require will depend on the scope and availability of needed resources. The preceding information can provide some guidelines to help you build a detailed schedule for the architecture process.

Developing a High-Level Schedule for the Project

The high-level schedule is a rough approximation of the total project time. A more detailed schedule cannot be developed for the project at this point because the architecture is not done. Without the architecture, there is no clear design of what is to be built.

The high-level schedule normally includes all facets of the project: design, development, testing, documentation, training, customer support, and so on. As a very rough approximation, you can use the following estimates for the development of the high-level schedule:

- The GUIDS methodology requires about 30 percent of the overall project time.

- The construction process could be estimated at 40 percent of the overall project time.

- The inspection, which includes the testing and error correction process, comprises the remaining 30 percent of the project time.

- Alpha or beta releases are not included in the 30 percent. If the plan calls for alpha or beta testing, make sure to include time for the testing, for support of the testers, and for error correction.

- On average, one tester will be required for every 1.5 to 2 developers. The testers should begin development of testing strategies during the end of the design phase and should continue to be involved with the project through delivery.

- If testers are not available, developers will need to test each others' work. This will have an impact on the schedule because developers who are testing are not developing.

- On average, one technical writer will be required for every two developers. The technical writers should begin developing documentation and help system strategies during the end of the design phase and should continue to be involved with the project through delivery. Sometimes the technical writers are used as advocates for the users and are included on the project team throughout the design.

These are only rough estimates. Your mileage may vary depending on the complexity of the application and the experience of the designers, developers, and other members of the team.

You must be careful when developing this schedule. It is highly probable the end date of this high-level schedule will be set in stone in someone's mind—someone like your primary prospective user or upper management! This is a common problem with project scheduling. The project team is pushed for a schedule after the requirements analysis but before the architecture has detailed what needs to be built. The project team complies based on some rough estimates, comparisons to past projects, and a good deal of optimism.

The purpose of this high-level schedule is not to set a delivery date, but rather to set correct expectations on the relative size of the project. Is it a

Keynote

one-month, six-month, one-year, or five-year project? It is important for the team to provide this estimate to set the same expectation for all team members. If the schedule is estimated at one year and the users were expecting six months, it is better to find this out now. At this point, you can easily go back and review the requirements to determine what can be delayed until a later release to meet a six-month time frame.

Make sure that the high-level schedule is viewed as a general statement of project scope and not a commitment (unless, of course, meeting a specific schedule is a primary goal). Every time you say it or write it, refer to it as a "10-12 month project" and not as "released in the January/February time frame." Or you can use the delivery schedule technique Microsoft uses by vaguely saying "first quarter 1997."

Keeping the Goals in Focus

The key to developing a good project plan is to remain focused on the goals of the project. Having a plan that focuses on the project goals may seem obvious, but over the course of the project it is easy to lose this focus. The two primary distractions are new ideas and the project schedule itself.

Managing New Ideas

New ideas are normally a good thing. However, once a project is under way, new ideas can cause distractions that shift the focus away from the project's goals.

For example, the purpose of the project is to develop a contact management system. The team has created a plan for designing and developing that system. Part way through the development, you see an advertisement for a cool address book widget. It could be integrated into the system and would provide automatic phone dialing and all sorts of other neat features. Wouldn't it be fun to add that to the project?

You excitedly present your findings to the team and with all of these neat features, it is easy for the team to say "yes, looks cool!" So you order the product and start to look at it more carefully. If it is to be tightly integrated, some of the other screens will need to change to match the visual idioms used by the new product. The database will need to be modified to support the database used by this new product. Suddenly, the entire project is focused away from the goal of developing the contact management system and toward this fun little address book feature. Don't let this happen to your project.

It is very difficult to say "no," so don't. Instead say "later" and put it in the "Future Features" section of the design document. This may not make everyone happy, but it will keep the project on track. If the new idea is really too good to pass up, and actually does allow the application to better meet its goals, then do say "yes." But then carefully re-evaluate the project plan and schedule. The change will affect both, normally more significantly than originally anticipated.

Keynote

Keeping the Schedule in Perspective

Frequently, schedules are maintained and tracked using a project scheduling tool. These tools can shift the project focus from the project goal to the schedule. First of all, these scheduling products require so much effort on the part of the project manager, it's easy to get into a schedule mindset. With the manager in that mindset, it's easy to get focused on "how are you doing on the schedule?" instead of "how are you doing on the project?"

The scheduling tools also like to micro manage projects. These tools want to know exactly which hour of which day which person is working on which task. This may be suitable for a machine, but not for people. People don't usually start a task at a specific time, work uninterruptedly only on that task, and then finish.

A programmer starts a task, the phone rings, voices in the next cubicle cause a distraction that requires investigation, more work is done on the task, more thinking is needed so it's dropped and the next task is started. After a lunch break, the programmer resumes with the first task, realizes that it requires too much thought for right after lunch, goes back and works on the second task, and then goes to a meeting. The second day the programmer comes in wide awake and finishes the first task, except for one routine, and then completes the second task. You get the idea.

Now, when exactly did the first task start? When did it end? When did the second task start and end? Who really cares? The project management software does! So let's take two hours of every week in a status meeting figuring it out. Wrong!

Project management tools just cannot deal with this working style. They shouldn't have to. Project management software should be used for the schedules, not for micro managing a project. They should be used as support tools, not as the focus of the project.

If schedules are to mean anything, they have to mean target dates—milestones for primary components and interim release dates. Schedules should identify generally who was to do what and when. Schedules should not micro manage the programming staff and shift focus away from the project goals.

Keynote

Ten Myths of Project Planning and Scheduling

Project planning and scheduling always seem to be the most difficult tasks in software development. Here are ten myths of project planning and scheduling that identify some statements you may have heard and indicate why these statements are not true.

Some of these statements are applicable to the development of the high-level project plan while others apply more to specific detailed plans. As you work on detailed plans in later phases of your project, be sure to review these myths again.

Myth #1: We Have No Time to Design the Application

The corollary to this is: "We will save time and money if we jump right into the code." You may hear one or the other of these statements after discussing some generalities of what is to be programmed. The statement is then followed with the question, "So how long will this take?"

Starting a software development project and stating there is no time for a design is like stepping onto a train and stating you have no time to travel. Well, at this point, it's going to happen if you plan for it or not!

Keynote

Software cannot be developed without an architecture. The software needs an internal structure and a user interface. If there is no time allocated for the design in the schedule, it will be done while the coding is done. This has several negative consequences. First, the time estimates provided by the developers were most likely based on doing the coding, not on designing and coding. So the coding tasks will all overrun their scheduled times, often by a factor of two or more.

In addition, any time saved by skipping the architecture will be lost twice over with recoding and bug fixing. If the programmer does the design at the same time as the coding, there will not be an opportunity to think through the entire project, just the part that is being coded. So the programmer completes the first module and while working on the second realizes that changes need to be made to the first for the second module to work correctly. Where is the time savings here?

You will find that it actually takes less time to complete the project if you do it right. You may spend more time at the beginning analyzing the requirements, developing the architecture, and defining the quality standards. But you will spend less time in development and testing/debugging.

Do the architecture, following the GUIDS methodology, and do it with the quality standards in mind. You can't afford not to.

Myth #2: Scheduling Is Bogus

How many times have you heard a software developer say this (or at least suspect that they were thinking it)? There are many times in the midst of the estimation process or when a project is significantly behind schedule that I have agreed with this statement. But, it is a myth.

Programmers know that any project can fill any allocated amount of time. There is no way to know for certain how long something will take, and everything takes longer than you expect. With this knowledge it is easy to develop the attitude that scheduling is bogus.

You need to look at scheduling for what scheduling is. In *Webster's New World Dictionary*, scheduling is defined as "to plan for a certain amount of time." Programmers can plan for how long things are expected to take.

The problem is that once a schedule is defined, people reviewing the schedule forget that it represents the programmer's plans. It suddenly becomes the metric by which everything is measured. Everything from status reporting to MBOs (management by objectives) is tied to the schedule.

When you plan to go to the beach for two hours, you don't necessarily expect to run out of gas, run into friends, or stop for a snack. Your plan is not any less successful for doing these things, it just takes longer. Ensure that there is room in the plan (and the associated schedule) for changes throughout the process. As the team moves through the design process, the team will learn more about the project. The team members will think of additional things the project must include or find they don't need things they thought they did. As the team moves into the development, members may find additional modules that are needed or some that are not required.

Keep the schedule in perspective. Don't let it mean more than it should. Use the schedule as a time line for executing the project plan.

Myth #3: Estimates Are Certain

You can only estimate with certainty something you have already done, but then it takes zero time because you already have the code. If you haven't done it, you cannot estimate with certainty how long it will take.

Keynote

Estimates are just that—estimates. To add a set of estimates together to define a schedule makes the schedule bogus (see Myth #2). To help convert estimates to numbers on a schedule, define a risk factor for each estimate. Then add time to the estimate based on the risk. The risk factor should look at prior experience with the technique or technology, anticipated bug count, and the historical accuracy of the specific programmer's estimate.

For example, there may be two six-hour tasks on the schedule. One task is to display a form that was detailed in the user-interface design specification. Similar screens have been developed in five to six hours and the requirements are clear, so you have a high-level of confidence in the six-hour estimate.

A second task involves developing a database accessing routine that will use a new database accessing product. Similar routines have been created for many projects using different database accessing products and they have been completed in five to six hours, but no one has experience with this new database product. This task has higher risk, so the estimate may be increased to eight to ten hours.

Even though estimates cannot be certain, you can improve them by adding the risk factor and making room for some changes in the plan.

Myth #4: 8 Hours = 1 Day

A project manager asks a programmer how much time a specific task will require. The programmer responds with "80 hours." The project manager calculates 80 hours ÷ 8 hours per day = 10 days. That's two weeks. The project manager puts it on the schedule.

Two weeks later, the project manager brings in the tester and technical writer to review the new features the programmer has developed. The programmer looks surprised and says that only 50 percent of the work is done. The project manager is outraged. How can this be?

The programmer was estimating the amount of time required to do the task, not the amount of time on the calendar. What the project manager didn't realize was this programmer was still helping on the DOS products, was assigned to a committee for selecting a voice mail system, and was asked to sit in on code reviews for each of the other team members—not to mention responding to e-mail, spending time on the Internet, scheduled training courses, and attending meetings. The programmer had to spend many hours of overtime just to get 50 percent done in two weeks!

You can attack this problem from several different angles. You can schedule the resources at a reduced utilization (like 50 percent or 80 percent) to make sure the calendar time matches the work time available. This is often scary to do, because at 50-percent utilization the schedule doubles in calendar length. Suddenly this six-month project becomes a one-year project and the project manager is concerned that a project of that length will be seen as too costly and will be canceled.

From another angle, you can minimize the amount of work the programmers are doing that is not directed toward the goals of the project. How far you can go with this will depend on the work environment. If the project is a key goal of the company, some dedicated resources may be available. If other things are of an equal or greater priority than the project, this may not be an option. The worst choice is more overtime. Although this may help in the short term, it is not a viable long-term solution. It adversely affects both the team attitude and the quality of the software.

If you cannot get the end date in line with expectations and you cannot decrease the programmers' other responsibilities, it is time to call in a consultant. You pay consultants to stay focused on the project at hand.

Myth # 5: Keep Two Sets of Schedules

"But you don't know Pat. If you tell Pat the real deadline he'll miss it by two weeks." This is the essence of the common justification for Myth #5. To dispel it, all you have to do is keep everyone honest.

Some project management philosophies suggest that the manager develop one schedule for the programmers and define an expanded "hidden" schedule for upper management and customers. This basically involves lying to the programmers or managers about the true due date.

Now, the idea of adding time to the schedule because of anticipated problems makes sense. I used to add four to six weeks of what I called "clean up" at the end of each project. That was the time allocated for all of the things the programmers thought to do during the development but were not included on the schedule.

Every time I heard, "Won't it be cool if we also…," I would dutifully add it to the list of clean-up tasks. As the project progressed, we found many "must-do" tasks that were added to the project with no change in the overall schedule and many overruns of some scheduled tasks. By the end of the project, we had used all of the clean-up time on the must-do tasks so there was no remaining time for the extra things. However, we were within just a few days of our planned delivery date. The project was a success.

What doesn't make sense is hiding the true schedule from the programmer. How can intelligent decisions be made when the true date is not known? This is especially counterproductive toward the end of the project when decisions are made regarding how to handle bugs. How you fix a bug when you think the project needs to be done tomorrow may be entirely different from how you fix it when you know you have two weeks.

So, do one schedule. Add a filler task or fudge factor to be prepared for overrun. Make sure everyone knows there is only one schedule.

Myth #6: Pump Up the Pressure

The first mistake most new project managers make is to start putting pressure on the development team as soon as the project begins to fall behind. The team needs to work harder and longer. "Don't they realize how important this project is?"

The primary problem with this philosophy is that it takes the focus of the project away from the project goals and onto the schedule. Instead of thinking, "What do I have to do next?" and "How can I best implement this?" the programmer will be thinking, "What can I throw together the fastest?"

Which focus will give you the best code and which will give you the most bugs? Hurrying through the code does not finish the project faster. It just pushes the project delays into the testing phase.

Programmers (like anyone else) work better in a positive environment than in one full of blame, reprimand, and stress. They are most productive when enthusiastic, not pressured. To kindle the enthusiasm, focus on what was done, not on what was not done.

Provide motivation, not pressure. Instead of applying pressure, the project manager should be asking, "What can I do to keep the programmers productive and happy today?" Excuse them from status meetings, bring in a pizza, have a contest for fixing the most bugs. The project manager should begin every day by looking ahead at what needs to be done over the next several days. Looking ahead helps you foresee and avert potential roadblocks.

Creating an atmosphere of fun, keeping the programmers focused on the project goals, and doing some advanced planning are more effective ways for the project manager to motivate the team than imposing pressure tactics.

Myth #7: If the Project Is Behind, Add Programmers

This was the primary fallacy that was discussed in the book *The Mythical Man Month* by Frederick P. Brooks.

Keynote

Most projects can be cleanly divided into independent pieces and one or more pieces can be assigned to each programmer. You can also have some programmers in supporting roles to perform library and merging functions or to provide the interface to other organizations, such as documentation and testing. However, you reach a point where adding more programmers is less productive instead of more productive.

Let's look at a simple example of building a dog house. One person can build the dog house in four hours. Adding another person gets the job done in three hours because the second person can be preparing materials and holding boards. Adding a third person puts the job back to five hours because there are few additional benefits the person can provide yet there is much more discussion before each step.

If the project falls behind, look at why and fix the why. Don't just add resources.

Myth #8: If We Leave Chris Alone, It Will Get Done

Most every programming team has a Chris, a programmer who can walk on water. Chris is normally the person who has been there the longest and has worked with almost every line of the code (Chris may have even written all of it at least once).

Chris has a hard time getting anything done because everyone is always in Chris's office getting technical advice. The project manager believes that if Chris could just go off site for a few weeks, the project could get done.

This plan has several fatal flaws: First, if Chris is indeed the only one who knows all of the code, the other team members may become significantly less productive if Chris is not available. Who will they ask for advice?

Another flaw is that Chris remains the only one who knows the critical piece of code. What happens if Chris quits one day? The final flaw is that it will become more difficult to measure Chris's progress. The entire application could be held up waiting for something from Chris.

To prevent this problem, make sure that all of Chris's expertise is included in the architecture documents. That way, the other team members will be able to find the answers in the documents instead of depending on Chris for critical information. The project manager can then assign key pieces to programmers other than Chris, thereby preventing one programmer from being responsible for all key pieces. This trains the other team members in the project and creates a much stronger team, not to mention the attitude improvements!

Myth #9: Interim Releases Are a Waste of Time

Programmers often think interim releases require too much work and are not worth the trouble. *Au contraire*!

Establishing interim releases during the construction phase ensures that every two weeks or so the pieces of the project can be put together. By defining the releases to be goal-oriented, you keep the project focused on the goal for each interim milestone. This provides a good project check point and a test of how done the project is.

"Done" is one of the most misused words in project scheduling. What does that word mean, anyway? Have you finished the design? The entry of the code? The syntax checking? Or have you really finished every detail from the keyboard equivalents to the technical documentation to the lowest level algorithms? Having interim releases provides a method of determining how "done" everything is.

This interim release can be provided to the staff for documentation, usability, and testing. Having access to the release gives them a chance to review the software early on in the process so they have the opportunity to make suggestions that can be used to improve the product.

This is also an excellent opportunity to get the bug counts down to a reasonable level, preventing the bugs from delaying the final release. The project manager can provide additional motivation to the programmers by requiring that each programmer's critical bug count is zero before moving on to the next task.

These interim releases are also a good time to recheck the schedule. Maybe some yet-to-be-developed features can be thrown out at this point to ensure the product is released on schedule.

Interim releases provide benefits that significantly outweigh the amount of time required to create them.

Myth # 10: We'll Catch Up

How many times have you heard something like "we need to get back on schedule" or "we need to catch up"? These are invalid statements. Rarely is a deadline so critical that it should become the focus of the project. Focusing on meeting the schedule instead of meeting the project's goals can lead to poorly designed and sloppy code.

If the schedule is slipping, the reasons for the slippage should be determined. The remaining tasks should then be reviewed based on the results of the determination and a new schedule should be developed. If the completion date cannot be changed, tasks should be removed from the schedule. If the tasks cannot change, the dates should be adjusted for the remaining tasks. There is no "catching up."

Keynote

■ Summary

- Before you begin the design of an application, there are several prerequisites. You need to have an idea of what to build, the requirements for what you are going to build, and the plan and schedule for building it.

- You can use idea generation techniques to answer the big question, "What should I build?" You can also use these techniques to solve the daily questions, such as "How should I implement this?" or "How should this screen look?"

- To design solid software, you need a solid set of requirements based firmly on the business and user goals.

- The domain experts are the best source of information about the pertinent business area (application domain). The domain experts can help you to understand the language of the business, refine the project goals, set the project scope, and define the business and user needs.

- The defined needs are often stated as solutions, not as problems, or are too vague or too detailed. You can morph the defined needs into requirements for clarity and flexibility in defining solutions.

- Prioritizing the requirements keeps them manageable. Be sure to consider the "big three" parameters: quality, features, and schedule.

- Documenting the requirements, including quality standards and technical and marketing specifications, ensures that all members of the team know these requirements.

- Planning and scheduling are essential to ensuring that a project actually happens. The project plan provides the map for getting from the requirements through the architecture, construction, and inspection to the completed application. The project schedule provides the time line for executing this plan.

- By avoiding the ten myths of project planning and scheduling, you will be able to create a comprehensive project plan and reasonable project schedule.

■ Additional Reading

Brooks, Frederick P., Jr. *The Mythical Man Month: Essays on Software Engineering*. Reading, Mass.: Addison-Wesley, 1975.
　　This is the classic book about considering the human element in project planning and scheduling.

Crosby, Philip B. *Quality Is Free*: *The Art of Making Quality Certain*, New York: McGraw-Hill, 1979.

The premise of this book suggests that if you do it right the first time, the time and money you save in not needing to fix things or redo them pays for the extra time required to do it right.

DeMarco, Tom, and Timothy Lister. *Peopleware: Productive Projects and Teams*. New York: Dorset House, 1987.

This book is a series of easy-to-read essays full of aphorisms such as "Quality is free, but only to those who are willing to pay heavily for it."

Donovan, John. *Business Re-Engineering with Technology : An Implementation Guide*. Cambridge: Cambridge Technology Group, Inc, 1993.

This book details the process of re-engineering a corporation using specific clients as examples. It includes a detailed discussion of the benefits of using a client/server architecture and how to implement such an architecture in an organization.

Hammer, Michael & James Champy. *Reengineering the Corporation : A Manifesto for Business Revolution*. New York: HarperCollins, 1993.

Hammer and Champy provide a detailed description of what corporations should do to meet the changing needs of today's business environment. They suggest taking a problem (move faster from point A to point B) and moving beyond the logical solution (design a faster airplane) to more creative solutions (develop a Star Trek-like transporter).

McConnell, Steve. *Rapid Development: Taming Wild Software Schedules*. Redmond, WA: Microsoft Press, 1996.

This book discusses techniques for rapid development. It covers topics such as lifecycle planning, estimation, scheduling, and teamwork.

Rumbaugh, James; Blaha, Michael; Premerlani, William; Eddy, Frederick; Lorensen, William. *Object-Oriented Modeling and Design*. Englewood Cliffs, New Jersey: Prentice-Hall, 1991.

The quote that appears at the beginning of this chapter is on page 46 of this edition.

Taylor, David. *Business Engineering with Object Technology*. Reading, Massachusetts: Addison-Wesley Publishing Company, 1995.

This book integrates business process re-engineering with object-oriented concepts. It provides a good, easy-to-understand overview of object technology and then presents an example of applying that technology to model a business. The example walks you through creating a project team, setting the project scope, defining the requirements using scenarios, and designing an application.

von Oech, Roger. *A Whack on the Side of the Head*. New York: Warner Books, 1990.

This book is very thought-provoking and easy to read. It encourages you to unlock your mind and open up to new ideas and inspiration.

The Windows Interface Guidelines for Software Design. Redmond, Washington: Microsoft Press, 1995.

This book is the definitive guide to user interface elements and standards.

■ Think It Over

To supplement and review the information in this chapter, try the following:

1. Think of a problem, any problem. How about something someone mentioned to you at work, or something you noticed around the house today?

2. Think of the logical solution to the problem. This would be the "obvious" answer.

3. Now think of four imaginative ideas for solving the problem. (If you cannot think of at least three ideas, use the steps provided in the section "Where Do Ideas Come From?" earlier in the chapter.)

4. Now take the ideas you've just defined and formalize and evaluate them by answering the evaluation questions in this chapter. Based on the evaluation, select one of the ideas as a project.

5. Identify the people you will need on your project team.

6. Define the goals and set the scope of your project.

7. Define some probable needs relating to your project and morph these needs into project requirements.

8. Identify the quality, technical, and marketing requirements for your project.

9. Define a plan and schedule for accomplishing your project.

10. Look at the myths of project planning and scheduling. How many of these myths have you heard spoken as truths? How have these myths affected projects you have worked on?

- *The GUIDS Methodology*
- *Summary*
- *Think It Over*

The GUIDS Methodology for Object-Oriented Architecture

If you have built castles in the air, your work need not be lost; that

is where they should be. Now put the foundations under them.

—Henry David Thoreau (1817–62),
U.S. philosopher, author, naturalist

Ideas and requirements create "castles in the air." These mental images of an application provide the vision of what is to be built. Once you have these mental images (and the supporting documentation), you have the prerequisites for defining "the foundations under them." You define these foundations by designing the application architecture. This architecture is the external design and internal framework of your application. It describes how the application should look and provides a blueprint of how the application should be constructed.

This chapter describes the GUIDS methodology for object-oriented design (OOD). The remaining chapters in Part 2 will guide you through each step of the GUIDS methodology using the case study introduced in Chapter 2, "The Software Development Process." The resulting application design will be implemented using Visual Basic 5 in Part 3 of this book.

■ The GUIDS Methodology

Object-oriented design involves organizing the software architecture into independent components called *objects*. Hence the name "object-oriented." Objects represent the real-world entities, such as employees and time sheets, that are needed to meet the goals of the application. Objects can also be implementation-based components that are needed to construct the application, such as windows and databases. Using an object-oriented approach results in a design that resembles the real world rather than an artificial computer process.

A good methodology can help you through the object-oriented design by clearly defining a set of steps and the tasks that must be accomplished at each step. This helps you work through the design in a logical manner. It keeps you focused on the primary goals you are trying to accomplish. It guides you through the abstract design process to prepare for the concrete construction phase.

Keynote

However, a methodology cannot be used as a cookbook. You cannot blindly follow the set of steps and expect a complete object-oriented design to appear. You need to apply your experience and knowledge with the background and experience of the other team members to create this design. Designing is not a mechanical process, rather it is a human one.

Object-oriented design techniques and programming languages originated from academics. Many books on OO reflect this heritage and are theoretical and complex. Visual Basic developers need something more pragmatic, more applicable to the business problems or application opportunities they are facing. With that objective in mind, I defined a practical set of steps for designing object-oriented applications, which I described briefly in

Chapter 2. I call it the GUIDS ("guides") methodology. GUIDS is comprised of the following high-level steps:

- **G**oal-centered design
- **U**ser-interface design
- **I**mplementation-centered design
- **D**ata design
- **S**trategies for construction

These steps are shown in Figure 4.1 as processes within the architecture phase. Modeling, though not a step in the architecture, can be incorporated into the design steps, as shown in the figure.

Figure 4.1

GUIDS methodology for developing an object-oriented design.

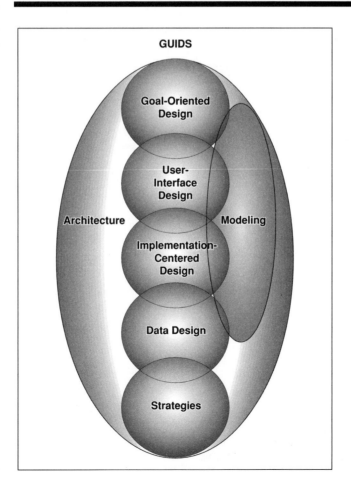

The GUIDS methodology provides an incremental and iterative approach to object-oriented software design. Figure 4.1 illustrates this by using circles instead of waterfall steps that prevent any return to the prior step, and overlapping areas instead of discrete boxes with well-defined beginnings and endings. As you go through each step in the process, you become more knowledgeable about the application. You may discover new objects or new roles for objects. You may find that your assumptions in prior steps are flawed. You will circle back as needed, altering and refining your design until it meets the requirements.

The architecture or design document details the design. The design can then be converted to tasks on a schedule, assigned to one or more programmers, and coded and tested.

Goal-Centered Design

Goal-centered design defines the objects needed to meet the goals and requirements previously specified in the requirements prerequisite. You and the subject matter experts on the project team can work together to describe these objects and what each object can do to meet the requirements of the application. All of this information is specified in the architecture or design document.

For example, in designing an employee time tracking application, your team could identify an Employee object and a Time Sheet object. The team can then define the things the objects must do. The Employee object will need to "set hourly rate" and the Time Sheet object will "fill out," "validate hours," and "calculate pay."

User-Interface Design

User-interface design examines how the user will view and communicate with the application. The project team uses the requirements and information collected during the Goal-centered design to design a user interface that meets the goals of the business and of the user. You illustrate and record the look and feel of the application in a User-interface design document.

In the employee time tracking example, the user interface may include a screen to review or update employee information, a screen to enter or edit time sheet information, and a report selection screen to define management reporting information.

During the User-interface design process, you may create a prototype to test some of the user interface mechanisms. You can create this prototype on paper, with a visual presentation product such as Microsoft PowerPoint, or with Visual Basic. The User-interface design document consists of drawings or screen shots from the prototype and written descriptions of the components of the screens.

Implementation-Centered Design

Implementation-centered design defines the system architecture and internal framework of the application and the components and classes that are the building blocks of the application. The classes are defined from the objects identified in the Goal-centered design. The properties and methods for these classes are detailed. Key procedures, business logic, and algorithms are also defined in this step. This design is documented in a design document.

For the employee time tracking example, the Implementation-centered design would define the Employee and Time Sheet classes, including the properties and methods for those classes. The algorithms used to calculate pay, including all of the tax and benefit calculations, would be included in the design document.

Data Design

Data design involves reviewing the data associated with each class and defining how that data will be stored. Depending on the requirements of the application, data can be stored in a file, in a database, in internal memory, or in the registry (an alternative for the initialization, or .ini, files).

The data for the employee time tracking example includes the employee name and address and the hours worked each day. This information will be stored in a database. Application-specific information such as the last location of the Employee window would be stored in the registry.

Strategies for Construction

Strategies for construction define the approach that will be taken during the implementation (coding). These strategies include the following:

- Buy versus build

- Conventions and standards

- Configuration management/source code control

- Inspection and testing procedures

- Implementation planning and scheduling

By defining these strategies before you begin constructing your application, you will have a more effective development process. You can build the unique components and buy the others. You can develop source code that is easier to manage, maintain, and test.

Integrating Modeling into the Process

Although modeling is not a step in the GUIDS process, it can be included in the design steps to test the design. Define the user interface first, and then test it with a prototype. Define the system architecture first, and then test it with a prototype. Define the database first, and then test performance with a prototype. Design the algorithms first, and then test them with a prototype.

With Visual Basic, it is easy to do rapid application development (RAD). RAD allows you to quickly develop an application by iteratively developing the features of the application. Too often, however, the "rapid" part of RAD skips over the design. This increases the number of iterations required to complete the application and decreases the quality of the resulting application.

The GUIDS provides a methodology for an iterative design that can be used with RAD. The modeling aspects of GUIDS provide the first iterations of the application. The interim releases described in Chapter 9, "Strategies for Construction," also support the RAD process.

Make sure you do not use the model or prototype as a replacement for any step in the design. Doing so shifts the focus from the design process to the model itself. For example, the users get so focused on a prototype they cannot see the forest for the trees. Or put another way, they cannot see the application through the interface.

■ Summary

- The GUIDS methodology provides a pragmatic, object-oriented approach to the development of software architecture. Using this methodology will allow you to systematically work through the software design process.

- The Goal-centered design involves using the goals and requirements you specified in the requirements prerequisite to describe the real-world objects for the application.

- The User-interface design combines the business requirements with the users' needs to design a user interface that meets the goals of both the business and the users.

- The Implementation-centered design defines the system architecture and converts the real-world objects into classes that can be implemented. The defined relationships between the classes provide the structure upon which the application will be built.

- The Data design reviews the data for the application and identifies how it should be managed. This data may reside in a file, in a database, in memory, or in the registry.

- The Strategies for construction include buy versus build decisions, conventions, configuration management, testing, and an implementation plan and schedule.

- Document the design along the way. This design defines the architecture that is the blueprint for the implementation phase.

■ Think It Over

To supplement and review the information in this chapter, think about the following:

1. How is the GUIDS methodology similar to how you have developed software in the past? How is it different?

2. Think about how the GUIDS methodology could be applied when designing a real-world object. For example, if you were designing a new type of car, how would each of the following steps come into play?

   - **Goal-centered design**: What objects are there? Engine, steering, air conditioning, radio, seats, and so on.

   - **User-interface design**: How should it look to the user? Placement of controls, color, texture, and so on.

   - **Implementation-centered design**: How can this be built to meet the standards for emissions and miles per gallon defined during the requirements? Design the framework holding the components together, define how the power gets to the wheels, and so on.

   - **Data design**: How will it remember the last radio station or seat position?

   - **Strategies for construction**: Which components should be bought instead of built? What quality control processes should be put in place? When should the first unit come off the assembly line?

5

Goal-Centered Design

*Abstraction is the selective examination of certain aspects of a prob-
lem. The goal of abstraction is to isolate those aspects that are important for some purpose and suppress those aspects that are
unimportant. Abstractions must always be for some purpose, because the purpose determines what is and is not important. Many
different abstractions for the same thing are possible, depending on
the purpose for which they are made.*

—James Rumbaugh, *et al.*,
Object-Oriented Modeling and Design

Simply said, abstraction lets you focus on the role that each object plays within the application. For example, developing a payroll system you would think about Jessica Jones as an employee, concentrating on her salary and how she gets paid. When working on the company softball league application you would consider Jessica as a player and be more concerned with her position and batting average. One object but two different goals leads to two completely different abstractions.

The abstractions are represented by specific objects involved with the application, such as an Employee object or Player object. To ensure that the abstractions and the defined objects are appropriate, the purpose of the abstraction needs to be clear. This purpose is identified by the goals and requirements of the application defined in the requirements phase as a prerequisite to this design step.

This chapter demonstrates how to use the goals and requirements of the project to form the abstractions and define the objects. It describes a simple technique for documenting the objects, their properties, behaviors, and interactions. The result of this process is a set of *candidate objects* (suggestions based on the real-world view of the application) that are ready for the transformation to classes.

■ What Is Goal-Centered Design?

Goal-centered design, highlighted in Figure 5.1, is the first step in the GUIDS methodology for object-oriented architecture. The focus of the Goal-centered design is to examine the goals and requirements of the application and develop the appropriate abstractions. These will be the real-world objects in the application.

This step is called goal-centered because the goals are key in defining the appropriate abstractions, which lead to the appropriate objects. If you are developing a contact management system, you would form an abstraction for the customers as contacts. You would not be concerned with abstractions for payroll because that is not within the goals of the project. Because this step is not concerned with the physical implementation details at this point, this step is sometimes called the *logical design*.

During the Goal-centered design, the project team analyzes the goals and requirements and forms abstractions to design the objects involved in the application domain. This design involves the following tasks:

1. Describe the objects.

2. Model the relationships between the objects.

3. Validate the objects using scenarios.

Figure 5.1

Goal-centered design defines the application objects and their relationships.

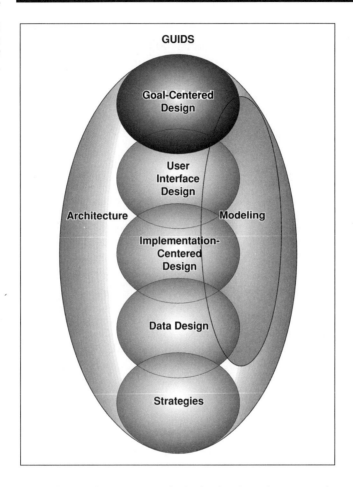

It is very important to include the domain experts (potential users or subject matter specialists) on the project team for this step. These domain experts have an in-depth knowledge of the application domain and are best suited to developing the appropriate abstractions and identifying the appropriate objects. However, it is important to walk these domain experts through the process without distracting them with object-oriented concepts. Talk to them in the language of the business you learned in the requirements phase.

As you work through this process, be sure to document the analysis so none of the team's great abstractions are lost. When this step is complete, your document will fully describe the candidate objects in the application. These objects may be combined, split, or modified later, during the Implementation-centered design.

Keynote

■ Preparing for Goal-Centered Design

Before you can guide the project team through the Goal-centered design process, *you* need to understand how to describe the objects. This section will provide you with the object definition basics you need to get the team started and keep them on course. If you are already familiar with these object-oriented concepts, jump to the next section and begin walking the team through the design process.

Describing the objects for a project involves:

1. Identifying the objects

2. Defining the behaviors of those objects

3. Listing the properties of those objects

Even though these items are listed and commonly discussed as a set of discrete tasks, they seldom are executed that way. You think of objects as you think about what needs to be done. Thinking about one object's properties helps you to think of other objects. For that reason, the discussion with the team combines these tasks into one task: describing the objects. But for a technical understanding, each one is discussed separately in the following sections.

Tech Note.   *Objects can also have events, which are basically notification messages an object can broadcast. The project team may define an event at this point in the design. If so, it can be added to the documentation of the object. In most cases, however, events are an implementation issue more than a part of the object definition.*

Identifying the Objects

Identifying the objects for an application is not a clear cut task. There is no one correct object representation for any given application, no set of steps that will lead you to the correct set of objects. Ask five kindergartners to draw a house and you will get five different abstractions of a house. Ask five designers to define the objects for an application and you will get five different abstractions of that application.

You do not need to be concerned about identifying the correct set of objects, only a set that clearly defines the application. The identified objects are simply candidate objects. They will be simplified, discarded, combined, or enhanced during the later steps of the design.

To be called an object, a thing must have a role in the application. It must have things it can do (behaviors) and/or things that it knows (properties). The easiest first attempt at object definition is to use the nouns specified in the goals and requirements. Whether a specific noun is an object depends upon the context. For example, a requirement to track employee

Keynote

time includes the nouns "employee" and "time," which would both be candidate objects for the application. An employee will be an object in an employee time tracking system, but may only be a property of a Person object in a loan processing application.

Defining the Behaviors

The behaviors identify what an object can do, how it can act or react. As the team identifies objects, the behaviors of those objects can be defined. The behaviors can include operations the object performs, data manipulation the object requires, support functions the object provides, or interactions the object allows.

Look at the verbs in the requirements to define possible behaviors. Think about the role the object plays within the context of the project. An Employee object in an employee time tracking system will have behaviors such as "set hourly rate" and a Time sheet object will "fill out," "validate the hours," and "calculate pay."

When defining behaviors for objects, remember that objects can be intelligent. They can do more things than their "real-world" counterparts. For example, a Time sheet object can total itself. Keep the behaviors in line with the real-world object, however. For example, a Time sheet object should not create invoices. Define behaviors that are applicable to the object to ensure that the object encapsulates all of the required functionality.

Listing the Properties

The properties are the data associated with the object. These properties identify what the object knows. To define the properties, the team should consider the data that will need to be tracked for the object. Also consider the data needed by other objects in the application. This should provide the list of properties.

The properties include basic information about the object, such as the name for an employee. They can also include application state information, such as the last report type selected. (But you may not discover needed state values until the Implementation-centered design later in the process.)

■ Describing the Objects

Now that you know how to identify objects, define their behaviors, and list their properties, you are ready to work with the team to describe the real-world objects involved with the application. So, you could start this step by describing to your team how objects are encapsulated abstractions in the application domain. The team needs to define these objects and create an object hierarchy to show the subclassing, composition, and collaborator relationships. Then the properties and methods need to be factored into multiple interfaces, and polymorphic methods need to be identified along with the delegation mechanisms. Whoa! As the other team members look at each other with blank faces, you are not making much progress!

Keynote

The team members don't need to know they are doing object-oriented design. You do not need to explain the intricacies of identifying well-defined objects, classes, properties, and methods. You need to get back to speaking their language, which you learned in the requirements step. By asking the right questions, you can help the team formulate the abstractions and discuss the information necessary to fully describe the objects without the team members knowing they are performing an object-oriented design.

I taught an algebra class at a community college that was primarily for math-avoidance students. When we got to word problems, the resounding consensus was they could not do word problems. So I began with the following: "You go to the mall and see this great shirt. It is priced at $40 and marked 25 percent off. How much is it?" They laughed at such a simple question and provided the answer. I then told them they had successfully solved a word problem! Try this technique with your team.

Starting with the Goals

So, let's begin again. Start the Goal-centered design process by taking the team back through the goals that were specified in the requirements phase. Examine each noun in the context of the application (you may want to start with an obvious noun to get things rolling). Begin asking questions:

- What is it?

- What does it do?

- What information does it need or have?

- What does it do with that information?

Keynote

Be sure to keep this process high-level. This step in the design should be concerned with what needs to be done by the application, not how it is done. Don't let the team get bogged down in details and don't let the developers in the group start to discuss how any of these objects could or could not be implemented. Implementation issues have no place in this discussion. If desired, you can note any issues that come up and save them for the Implementation-centered design phase.

Let's look again at the contact management system example. The contact management system project team started by examining the primary goal of the application:

Increase sales by providing a software system that aids the salespeople in managing contacts with clients and prospects.

This was written on the white board to ensure that the abstractions were based on this goal.

Picking out some key nouns from the goal statement provided four candidate objects: salespeople, contacts, clients, and prospects. Because the goal is centered around the salesperson, the SalesPerson object will be considered first.

- **What is it?** It will be called SalesPerson and it represents the person responsible for making the contacts.

- **What does it do?** It creates and maintains information for customers and prospects and it creates contact and follow up entries.

- **What information does it need or have?** It needs all of the contact information for each of its customers and prospects and contact and follow up entries.

- **What does it do with that information?** It defines it originally and then reviews it as needed.

Documenting the Objects

As you work with the team to define the objects, you will want to begin documenting them. This records the team's findings and ideas. It provides the team with a richer understanding of the objects that have been identified. One way to document the objects is to use 4×6 index cards. On each card write the object name, its role, its set of behaviors, and its properties.

Tech Note. *The idea of using index cards for object-oriented design was originally proposed by Kent Beck and Ward Cunningham (see the "Additional Reading" section later in this chapter for the reference). They called them Class-Responsibility-Collaboration (CRC) cards. These cards contained the class name, responsibilities of an instance of the class, and a list of the classes that collaborate with this class. In this step in the design, a similar card format can be used to define the objects, their behaviors, and properties. This provides an effective method of documenting the objects.*

The index card for the SalesPerson object designed for the contact management system is shown in Figure 5.2.

Figure 5.2

The SalesPerson object
card for the contact
management system
describes the object and
lists its behaviors
and properties.

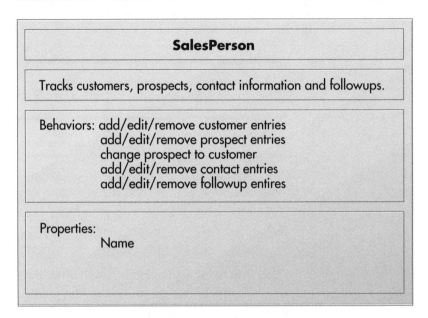

SalesPerson

Tracks customers, prospects, contact information and followups.

Behaviors: add/edit/remove customer entries
add/edit/remove prospect entries
change prospect to customer
add/edit/remove contact entries
add/edit/remove followup entires

Properties:
Name

Using actual index cards has many benefits. Recording the object on the card makes the object tangible. It gives it life, but not permanence. Different members of the team can create cards concurrently. The index cards are portable. As you meet with the team, you can take the objects with you. They are always there for reference or refinement.

I have seen computer versions of these cards, which I feel detract from their usefulness. Although the computer can provide linking to more details and to later parts of the design, it prevents the cards from being used as a team design tool. The computer tools assume the designer will work independently to identify the objects and enter the information onto the computer, discouraging interactive use by the team. These products often produce nice reports and can provide a benefit in formalizing the cards as part of the design documentation *after* the design process is complete.

Examining the Requirements

After working through the project goals, the team can examine the requirements to find more objects. The same questions used during the examination of the goals can be asked of the nouns in the requirements. During this process, the team can determine if any additional objects are needed or if behaviors or properties of objects need to be enhanced or modified.

In the contact management system example, the five feature-related requirements were:

---

1. Maintain the customer list.
2. Maintain the prospect list.
3. Log contacts made with a customer or prospect.
4. Provide summary reports.
5. Manage follow-up tasks.

The nouns in these requirements suggest another candidate object: follow-ups.

- **What is it?** It will be called FollowUpItem and it represents an individual follow-up entry. Its purpose is to provide each follow-up item in a to do list for the salesperson.

- **What does it do?** It tracks the things that a salesperson needs to do, specifically the follow-ups that were promised. This includes things such as "I will mail that to you today" and "I will call you back next week."

- **What information does it need or have?** The FollowUpItem object will need to know the date and time the entry was created, when it should be done, an item's priority, and a description summarizing what needs to be done.

- **What does it do with that information?** It will need to store it and retrieve it.

Figure 5.3 shows the card for the FollowUpItem object, including the behaviors and properties.

For completeness, the cards for the other objects in the contact management system are shown in Figures 5.4 through 5.6.

There is no one right way to define the objects for a project. Take your best shot. You can make adjustments and refinements as you continue through the design process. By answering the questions defined in this section as you work through the project requirements, you should have a very good starting set of candidate objects.

Keynote

■ Modeling the Relationships

Modeling the relationships between the objects clarifies each object's role and helps to point out similarities and differences between objects. After the objects have been defined, establish the relationships between them by asking the following questions:

Figure 5.3

The FollowUpItem object card for the contact management system identifies information for a generic to do list.

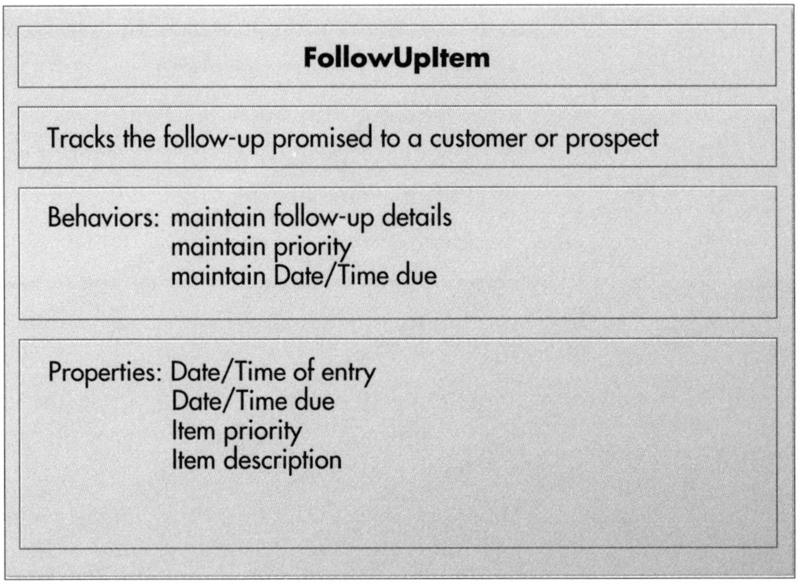

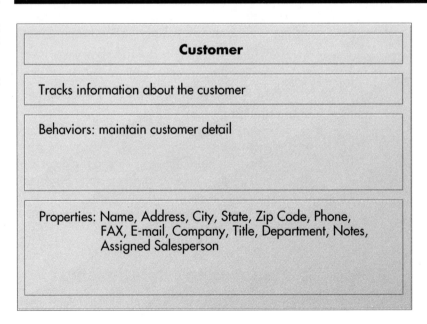

FollowUpItem

Tracks the follow-up promised to a customer or prospect

Behaviors: maintain follow-up details
maintain priority
maintain Date/Time due

Properties: Date/Time of entry
Date/Time due
Item priority
Item description

Figure 5.4

The Customer object card for the contact management system specifies general information about a customer.

Customer

Tracks information about the customer

Behaviors: maintain customer detail

Properties: Name, Address, City, State, Zip Code, Phone,
FAX, E-mail, Company, Title, Department, Notes,
Assigned Salesperson

Figure 5.5

Notice the similarities between the Prospect object card, shown here, and the Customer object card.

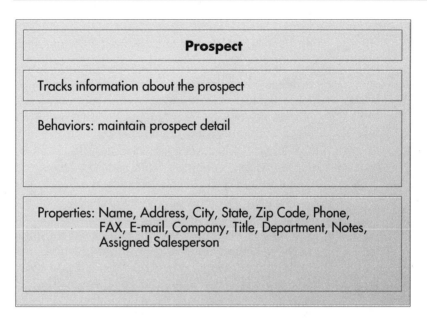

Prospect

Tracks information about the prospect

Behaviors: maintain prospect detail

Properties: Name, Address, City, State, Zip Code, Phone, FAX, E-mail, Company, Title, Department, Notes, Assigned Salesperson

Figure 5.6

The ContactEntry object card for the contact management system identifies the information required to log a contact.

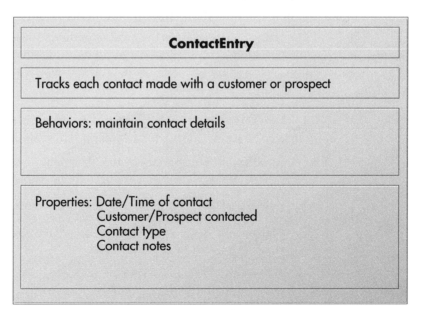

ContactEntry

Tracks each contact made with a customer or prospect

Behaviors: maintain contact details

Properties: Date/Time of contact
          Customer/Prospect contacted
          Contact type
          Contact notes

- Does an object belong to another object? (An employee "has a" time sheet)

- Is an object a kind of another object? (A carpenter "is an" employee)

- Does an object use another object? (A time sheet "uses a" calendar)

To define the relationships, start by laying the object cards on the table. Arrange them to visually place together related objects. You can then document an object's relationships on the back of the index card for the object. Repeat this process for other types of relationships. The result of your work will be a set of object models.

You can also develop object models using automated tools, such as Rational Software Corporation's Rational Rose object-oriented analysis and design tool. This tool can help you document the objects and model the relationships between the objects. It then automatically generates the code for the classes in the model. If the actual implementation later strays from the design or if you want an object model of an existing system, this tool will also reverse engineer the object model. I have not yet had an opportunity to use the version of Rational Rose that supports VB5, but the demos (included on the CD-ROM) are impressive. This tool could be very useful, especially when you're developing large systems for which a stack of index cards may be too large to manage effectively. (See http://www.rational.com for more information.)

Containers—The "has a" Relationship

The "has a" relationship is the most important of the three relationships for creating a model of the entire application. It identifies containers or composition objects. Have the team consider which objects are parts of other objects and which objects belong to other objects. Again, keep the project goal in mind as you define these relationships.

For example, the "has a" relationships for the contact management system are shown in Figure 5.7. Each object is described next:

- **SalesPerson**. The primary goal of the application is support of the Sales-Person, so this is the primary object in the application.

- **ContactEntry**. The SalesPerson object has many contacts with customers and prospects. This is represented with a set of ContactEntry objects (shown with two boxes). Each ContactEntry object "has a" customer or prospect defined for the contact.

- **FollowUpItem**. The SalesPerson object has many follow-up items. This is represented with a set of FollowUpItem objects.

- **Customer**. The SalesPerson object has a set of Customer objects that it is responsible for contacting.

Figure 5.7

The object model for the
contact management
system illustrates the
"has a" relationships
between the objects.

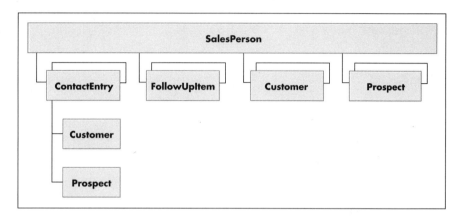

- **Prospect**. The SalesPerson object has a set of Prospect objects that it has been assigned.

As you can see from Figure 5.7, the entire contact management system is based on the SalesPerson object. This sales-centric view matches the primary goal, which is to support the salesperson. This example illustrates the importance of correctly defining the goal and using the goal as the basis of this design step.

Subclasses—The "is a" Relationship

The "is a" relationship helps the team identify similarities and differences between objects. The team should look for objects that have similar behaviors and properties to find these types of relationships.

When two or more objects have similar behaviors and properties, the similarities can be removed from the individual objects and added to a new object that will become the parent of the other objects. The original objects will then contain only the specialized properties and behaviors unique to the particular object. This helps the team clarify the related objects.

In looking for "is a" relationships, the contact management system project team noticed that there were many similarities in the Customer and Prospect objects as shown in Figures 5.4 and 5.5. Studying those objects, the team identified a general Person object that could have the behaviors and properties that are similar to both the Customer and Prospect. The prospect "is a" Person and the customer "is a" Person, as shown in Figure 5.8.

Notice the difference between the two object models. The "has a" relationships are drawn as sets of stacked boxes. The "is a" relationships are drawn as a hierarchy, like an organization chart.

This object model
presents the "is a"
relationships in the
contact management
system.

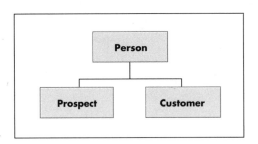

Collaboration—The "uses a" Relationship

The "uses a" relationship identifies the behaviors that an object needs from other objects. Evaluating this type of relationship ensures that the objects have all of the behaviors that are required by other objects. You can draw these collaborator relationships or just list them on the back of the object card.

In the contact management system, the FollowUpItem object could "use a" Calendar object to view the follow-up items in a calendar format. This was beyond the requirements of the application, and was not included in the design of the contact management system.

■ Validating the Objects Using Scenarios

To complete the Goal-centered design, the team should look back at the goals and requirements of the application and document several scenarios, or use-cases. Each scenario lists the set of steps needed to meet a requirement of the application.

As you begin this process, it sometimes helps to define several user profiles. What types of users will be using the application? Alan Cooper recommends giving each profile a name: Vic the VP who has trouble with computers or Sal the busy salesperson. (See "Additional Reading" at the end of this chapter for information on Cooper's book.) This approach helps the project team think about the users of the system and provides a context for the usage scenarios.

For example, the team for the contact management system identified eight scenarios. One of them outlined the process of calling a current customer, as shown on the next page.

Identify scenarios that closely mimic the way the tasks are really performed. This should include interrupting a specific set of steps to do another task. For example, as the user is reviewing a report, a phone call comes in.

Keynote

1. Salesperson begins a new contact entry.

2. Salesperson finds the desired customer from a list of the salesperson's customers.

3. Salesperson views the customer's phone number.

4. Salesperson makes the call. (Future feature: Call will be placed automatically.)

5. As conversation proceeds, SalesPerson enters notes about this call.

6. Call ends.

7. Contact entry is complete.

Or, as the user is entering information about a meeting, a manager comes in and requests a report. You should include scenarios for these types of cases.

The team can play out the defined scenarios with the object cards that were created for the application to determine whether there are any missing or incorrect behaviors or properties. Any missing functionality can easily be added or modified during this validation process.

Your team could have fun with this by asking members of the team to role play with the objects. Hand out the object cards to different people on the team. You can use sheets of paper to "store" each object's properties. You could then literally walk through the scenarios using the team members as the objects.

The contact management system team decided to do this. Members of the team volunteered to be each of the objects. The team ran through the defined scenarios. In one scenario, the team found that an e-mail address property was needed for the Customer object to support the e-mail contact type.

■ Documenting the Goal-Centered Design

The result of the Goal-centered design step is normally a design document. If you compose a document describing the design details you can pass the design on to all members of the full project team. The design document also provides a historical perspective on the application for future maintenance activities.

The Goal-centered design document should contain the following:

- **Description of the project goals.** Listing the primary and secondary goals in this design document ensures that they are kept in focus when the design is reviewed.

- **List of project requirements.** This list was generated during the prerequisites to this phase. It is included here to make sure that the design meets these requirements.

- **Definition of objects.** The information on the object cards should be included in this document for long term maintenance. (It's hard to put index cards into SourceSafe!)

- **Object model.** The document should include the drawings of the "has a," "is a," and "uses a" relationships.

- **Scenarios.** Document the defined user profiles and scenarios. The scenarios will be used again during the User-interface design and to validate the Implementation-centered design. They can also be used as the basis of the "how to" help topics and for test suites.

After you finish the design and move into development, you may find that items in your Goal-centered design document are no longer correct. You then have two choices: update the document or don't update the document. In most cases, you don't need to keep the Goal-centered design document up to date because the document is simply the starting point for the Implementation-centered design. In contrast, the Implementation-centered design document, described in Chapter 7, should be updated to reflect the changes to the project.

■ Summary

- The focus of the Goal-centered design is to examine the goals and requirements of the application and develop the appropriate abstractions. These abstractions help clarify the problem, identify the candidate objects and their relationships, and lay the framework for the design and implementation.

- Include the domain experts (potential users and subject matter specialists) in this step. They have the background and knowledge needed to develop the abstractions and describe the objects.

- Prepare for the Goal-centered design step by learning how to identify objects and define their properties and behaviors.

- Use your knowledge of object-oriented concepts to guide the team through the process of identifying and describing the application objects. The team does not need to know the details of object-oriented design.

- For each object, answer the following questions: "What is it?", "What does it do?", "What information does it need or have?", and "What does it do with that information?"

- Keep the Goal-centered design focused on the objects and not the implementation of the objects.

- Document each object, its role in the application, its behaviors and its properties. Index cards provide a simple, team-oriented, easy-to-use, and portable method for creating this documentation.

- Define the "has a," "is a," and "uses a" relationships between the objects.

- Draw object models to clarify the relationships between the objects.

- By defining all of the objects, their behaviors, their properties, and their relationships, your team has defined the application. The behaviors are the features of the application; the properties are the data; and the relationships provide the structure of the application, which connects the objects.

- Develop scenarios from the project's requirements and validate the design using those scenarios.

- Develop a formal document for the Goal-centered design to share with the project team and to provide a historical background for the application.

■ Additional Reading

Beck, Kent and Cunningham, Ward. "A Laboratory for Teaching Object-Oriented Thinking." *SIGPLAN Notices*, Vol. 24, October 1989.

This article introduced the CRC cards that have become popular in object-oriented design.

Booch, Grady. *Object-Oriented Analysis and Design with Applications (The Benjamin/Cummings Series in Object-Oriented Software Engineering)*. Redwood City, California: The Benjamin/Cummings Publishing Company, 1994.

Booch provides a more academic discussion of object-oriented design concepts. He then presents a specific notation and methodology for object-oriented design and applies them to several case studies implemented in Smalltalk, Object Pascal, C++, Lisp, and Ada.

Coad, Peter; North, David; Mayfield, Mark. *Object Models: Strategies, Patterns, and Applications*. Englewood Cliffs, New Jersey: Prentice-Hall, 1995.

This book walks you through an object-oriented design of five applications. It includes identifying the goal-centered and implementation-centered objects, selecting appropriate design patterns, and defining scenarios.

Cooper, Alan. *About Face: The Essentials of User Interface Design*. IDG Publishing Company, 1995.

About Face is an outstanding guide to putting the right face on your software, written by Alan Cooper, the "father of Visual Basic." Cooper's practical suggestions, thought-provoking insights, and anecdotal style make *About Face* a must-read book for anyone involved with application design.

Dollard-Joeris, Kathleen. "Designing Objects for VB 4.0." *Visual Basic Programmer's Journal*, Vol. 5, No.12, December 1995.

This article walks you through a design using CRC cards and demonstrates how to implement the design using VB4.

Gray, N.A.B. *Programming with Class: A Practical Introduction to Object-Oriented Programming with C++.* New York: John Wiley & Sons, 1994.

Although this book focuses on developing C++ applications, it supplies a pragmatic approach to object-oriented design. Its example Space Invaders game provides insights into defining classes and implementing them in several OO languages (not including Visual Basic).

Rumbaugh, James; Blaha, Michael; Premerlani, William; Eddy, Frederick; Lorensen, William. *Object-Oriented Modeling and Design.* Englewood Cliffs, New Jersey: Prentice-Hall, 1991.

This book provides a thorough discussion of object-oriented concepts and object modeling. It then presents the Object Modeling Technique (OMT) as a methodology for software engineering. This book includes examples on implementing object-oriented techniques in C++, Ada, and Smalltalk.

The quote that appears at the beginning of this chapter is on page 16 of this edition.

Taylor, David. *Business Engineering with Object Technology.* Reading, Massachusetts: Addison-Wesley Publishing Company, 1995.

This book integrates business process re-engineering with object-oriented concepts. It provides a good, easy-to-understand overview of object technology and then presents an example of applying that technology to model a business, including development of the CRC cards for each object in the model.

Wirfs-Brock, Rebecca; Wilkerson, Brian; Wiener, Lauren. *Designing Object-Oriented Software.* Englewood Cliffs, New Jersey: Prentice-Hall, 1990.

This book contains a thorough explanation of CRC cards and their use.

■ Think It Over

To supplement and review the information in this chapter, think about the following:

1. Think about the objects associated with driving your car. Using one index card for each object, list the role of the object, the behaviors, and the properties. For example, the Radio object plays music and provides news. It has channel and volume properties.

2. Think about how those car objects relate to each other. Draw some object models.

3. Think about a prior application you have developed. Describe the objects for that application. Looking at the application from this object-oriented perspective, would you have done anything differently in designing the application?

4. The salespeople in the contact management system example also want an appointment book that shows follow-up information in a calendar format. Think through how this additional requirement affects the object model.

User-Interface Design

Contrary to what you might suspect, few users are consciously aware of their goals..... While it is the user's job to focus on tasks, the designer's job is to look beyond the task to identify the user's goals. Therein lies the key to creating the most effective software solutions.

—Alan Cooper, *About Face:*
The Essentials of User Interface Design

Software development would be so easy if the users could just tell you what they want. Then you could go back to your office and, without further interruption, code it and deliver the completed application to them. It would be exactly what they had asked for. They'd love it, and you would all live happily ever after. Well, life doesn't work that way and neither does software development.

Users cannot tell you what they want. Yes, they can tell you what they do and what they think a software application should do, but they cannot tell you what they really want. Have you ever delivered an application that followed a defined specification only to hear, "That wasn't exactly what I was looking for," from the users?

This chapter describes how to determine the users' goals and tailor the user interface to meet those goals while also meeting the goals and requirements of the application. By considering both sets of goals you can design a more effective user interface.

■ What Is a "Good" User-Interface Design?

The U in the GUIDS methodology is for User-interface design, shown highlighted in Figure 6.1. The User-interface design defines how the application will look and how it will interact with the user.

I attended a conference recently and one of the speakers noted that users may spend more time with your application than they do eating, sleeping, or being with their kids! Think about that. What a responsibility that puts on you as the user-interface designer! You could be the cause of eight hours a day of frustration "fighting" with your interface or you could significantly increase your users' daily productivity. The difference in the two extremes is the quality of the design. So what makes one interface "good" and another one "bad"?

One answer to this question leads back to the goals and requirements of the project. A user interface that allows the users to easily perform their daily tasks and accomplish the business needs will be a "good" interface. A user interface that distracts the users with excess information, hides functionality, or in any other way detracts from the users' ability to accomplish their tasks will be considered a "bad" interface, or at best a "difficult" interface.

Another answer to the "good" versus "bad" user-interface design question comes from determining the individual's personal goals. Software is used by flesh and blood people who have needs. They need to feel empowered, they want to get their job done efficiently and successfully, they need a sense of security that what they are doing is right, and they need to feel that they are in control.

Figure 6.1

User-interface design
defines the look and feel
of the application.

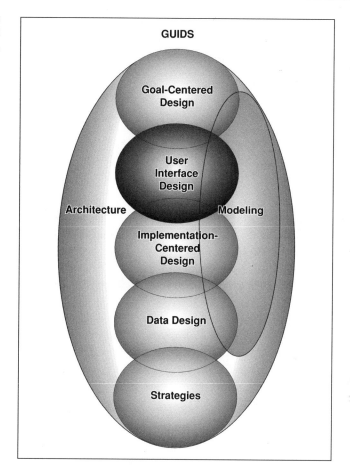

The User-interface design step in the GUIDS methodology uses a goal-directed design process. This process combines the project goals and requirements with the users' goals to create an effective user-interface design. By following this process and observing basic user-interface design principles, you can define a "good" user interface.

■ Creating a Goal-Directed Design

I borrowed the name of this section from Alan Cooper's *About Face* book because "goal-directed" so perfectly describes the process needed for designing a "good" user interface. A goal-directed design remains focused both on the project's goals and requirements and on the users' goals. The tasks needed to perform a goal-directed design are

1. Identify the users' goals.

2. Define the features of the application.

3. Provide a mental model.

4. Lay out the features.

5. Select an interface style.

6. Lay out the screens.

7. Add some flair.

The goal-directed design process can be done iteratively. If the application is large, you may want to design the user interface details of the primary screens at this point. After implementing these primary screens you will return here and polish the details of the secondary screens. Regardless of how you iterate through the process, be sure to keep the goals in focus.

Keynote

It is sometimes tempting to skip right from the list of features to creating the user interface prototype. The visual part of the application is often the most fun and elicits the most excitement from the user community. It may even have been what you were asked to do: "This is the list of features we want, do a prototype." But you cannot design a good user interface without first understanding both the project requirements and the users' goals.

Identifying the Users' Goals

The goal-directed design process begins with an analysis of the users' goals. These may not be the same as the goals and requirements of the application. For example, the primary goal of an application may be to track contacts with customers. The primary goal of the user may be to not sound stupid on the telephone.

In the requirements phase, you worked closely with the users to understand their tasks and convert them into project goals and requirements. The task of defining the users' goals is much harder. While discussing the goals of the project, the users will tell you the kinds of things they do. They will not tell you how they are constantly interrupted by their boss who is checking on their status. They will not tell you how stressed they feel every time they have to use a software product. They will not tell you how frustrated they are when they just cannot get software to do what they want.

You frequently have to infer the users' goals from their comments and questions and from your observations of them. Alan Cooper listed some common user goals in *About Face:*

- Not looking stupid

- Not making any big mistakes

- Getting an adequate amount of work done

- Having fun (or at least not being too bored!)

In the contact management system example, the team identified several key user goals.

---

1. Users do not want to sound stupid on the phone when talking to customers or prospects.

2. Users want to sound impressive on the phone by recalling personal details about a customer or contact.

3. Users do not want to feel like jerks because a promised follow-up was forgotten.

4. Users want the software to function in an environment of constant interruptions.

5. Users do not want to announce to the entire office (with a loud beep) when they have made a mistake.

With these user goals, and the goals and requirements specified for the project, you are ready to define the application features.

Defining the Features

The next task in the goal-centered design process is to establish the application features. This features list summarizes all of the things the application must do from the perspective of the user. To define these features, start with the requirements specified in the requirements phase. Include any new functionality identified during the Goal-centered design.

Keynote

It is very important to define the features in terms of the user, not in the terms of the computer tasks. For example, the user will "add an address to an address book," not "create reference records." You can see this incorrect mapping of computer tasks to user interface components in much of the legacy software that used the add, update, delete, and review computer processes as menu options. The users' goal was to review the customer's address information, to add it if it was not there, and to update it if it was in error. By defining separate "add," "update," "delete," and "review" features instead of a "maintain customer information" feature, the software focused on the computer tasks instead of on the users' goals.

After the list of features is defined in user terms, the project team can logically organize the features of the application. This will provide the framework for the user interface. The project team can evaluate each feature against the project and user goals to determine which are the primary or key features and which are secondary features. Think of this process as a triage for your features. The most critical features should get designed first and should be the primary focus of your application. The less critical features get designed afterward and should be molded to fit around the primary features. Everything within the user interface should be designed to fit together to meet the primary goals of the application and the users.

Let's go back to the contact management system example. For a review, here are the requirements of the contact management system that affect the user interface:

1. Maintain the customer list.

2. Maintain the prospect list.

3. Log contacts made with a customer or prospect.

4. Provide summary reports.

5. Manage follow-up tasks.

6. Provide an easy-to-learn user interface such that a new salesperson could learn how to log a contact within 30 minutes.

7. Conform to the user interface conventions defined in *The Windows Interface Guidelines for Software Design* published by Microsoft Press.

The contact management system project team examined these requirements and reviewed the objects defined for the application. The features were listed and triaged as follows.

Contact Management System Critical Features:

1. *Provide quick entry of contact information.* If the salesperson can quickly enter the contact information while on the phone, the information can be collected at the source instead of at some later date. This helps to ensure that the information is more accurate and up to date. This must not interfere with the sales call.

2. *Allow quick entry of data for new customers and prospects.* When the salesperson is receiving a call from a new customer or prospect, allow rapid entry of information for that customer or prospect. This must not interfere with the sales call.

3. *Allow quick lookup of data for existing customers and prospects.* This allows the salesperson to quickly find the customer or prospect when receiving or making a call.

4. *Provide quick access to the follow-up list.* The follow-up list will track the salesperson's to do list. The salesperson should be able to easily add or check on to do list items.

   Contact Management System Secondary Features:

1. *Provide reports on demand.* At any time, the user should be able to generate the necessary reports.

2. *Supply follow-up reminders.* The user should be reminded of required follow-ups. Because this is a secondary feature, these reminders should *never* interfere with the primary features.

By documenting the primary and secondary features as just shown, you are outlining the basics of your user interface. Start your user interface document with the results of your triage.

Providing a Mental Model

For an application to make sense to the users, it should provide a mental model, a way to think about the application in terms of something the user is familiar with. For example, Microsoft Word provides a piece of paper you can type on, matching the mental model of paper in a typewriter. Microsoft Excel presents an on-screen spreadsheet, mapping to the mental model of the paper-based spreadsheets.

If you provide a good mental model, the user can intuitively apply familiar knowledge to something unfamiliar. When a computer neophyte uses Microsoft Word, the neophyte normally recognizes the mental model and begins to type.

After you have a clear idea of the primary and secondary features of the application and before you start to lay out these features into a user interface, give some thought to the mental model that makes sense with your application. This does not have to be a physical metaphor, but rather a cohesive vision for viewing your application. You can then emphasize this mental model in designing the layout of the screens.

Don't go overboard with this model. The system should not be designed around a metaphor. The mental model should provide a way for users to think about the application and provide a common vocabulary; it should not become the focus of the user-interface design.

You could develop a metaphor for the contact management system to reflect the current manual tasks the user performs. The salespeople currently have a log book to track all incoming and outgoing calls. They have an address book or card file with the names and addresses of each customer and prospect. Usually, they also have some type of to do list to track what sales literature needs to be sent out and to whom.

Instead of this metaphor, consider a mental model of a hyper-index card that displays needed information and has links that let you quickly access related information. The contact and customer information can both be displayed on the main screen so you can see the customer's phone number as you are making the contact. To find more information on the customer, you can link directly to the Address Book entry for that customer. This shifts the design from a stylish metaphor to a more productive mental model.

Laying Out the Features

Ever been in an emergency room? You will notice that everything the staff needs most often and most quickly is right where it is needed. The bed is right in the center, the lights are easily reached and positioned, the gloves are close at hand, and the oxygen is attached to the wall just above the patient's head. All of the things that are less critical, used less frequently, or are dangerous are out of the way. The X-ray machines are in another room, the mixtures to build casts are tucked away in the drawers, and the scalpels are locked in a cabinet.

Keynote

This is how a good user-interface design should be put together. All of the features needed to perform the primary tasks should be close at hand and everything else should be out of the way. The primary features should stand out. The secondary features should be easy to get to, but tucked neatly away in a menu.

It is important to look at each feature of the application carefully and fit it into the user interface based on how frequently the user will need to access it. The primary features should be available on the main screens in your application. Provide quick access to them with toolbar icons or a pop-up menu that appears when you right-click. Add them to the most logical place in the application's menu. Be sure to define keyboard equivalents as well.

All secondary features should be available from menu options. Even though they are secondary features, they should not be hidden. How often have you been frustrated by knowing that you could do something with an application yet not being able to find where to do it? You may want to provide access to subordinate features using buttons from the primary screens, but don't make this the only way to get to those features. All nontrivial features should be available from the menu.

Name the screens and menu options based on the users' goals, not on the tasks the computer needs to perform. For example, instead of "Create Inventory Transactions" the user can "Receive Goods." This allows the user to intuitively recognize the options that should be used from the mental model instead of the user documentation.

Examining the results of the Goal-centered design, you might find it logical to lay out the features of the user interface by object. One screen for the Employee object, one for the Department object, and so on. Even though these objects provide the best way for the computer to work, they may not match how the user works. For example, an employee time tracking system may have an Employee and a Time Sheet object. The design could define an Employee window and a Time Review window, but the users may always want to see both at the same time. So the employee information could be provided on one part of the screen with a scrollable grid or other mechanism on another part of the screen to show the times the employee worked each day.

The contact management system project team decided to have one main window in the application called the Contact Management window. An Address Book window and To Do List window will handle the other primary features. The contact management system menu options were defined:

Menu	Option	Description
File	New	Creates a new contact file
	Open…	Opens an existing contact file
	Save	Saves the current changes
	Save As…	Saves to a new contact file
	Print…	Prints selected information
	Print Preview	Displays a preview of what the information will look like when printed
	Exit	Exits the application
Edit	Cut	Cuts the selected text
	Copy	Copies the selected text
	Paste	Pastes the selected text
View	Address Book	Displays the address book
	To Do List	Displays the to do list
Help	Help Topics	Displays the Help Topics property sheet
	About Contact Manager…	Displays an About box

This first definition of menu options may be rough, but it gives the team a starting point for the remainder of the user-interface design.

Selecting an Interface Style

After defining the primary forms and menus, you need to select the basic style of your interface. You can determine whether to implement the design with a single-document interface (SDI) or a multiple-document interface (MDI). The "document" terminology is a little misleading. An application may work with customers and employees, not documents. In this context, the term *document* refers to the views that the application manipulates. For example, an application that provides multiple customer windows for viewing several customers simultaneously will be implemented as an MDI application.

You may also want to define an explorer-style interface for some forms. In addition, you need to decide which of the forms in your application will be shown as modal or modeless.

Displaying Single Forms with the Single-Document Interface (SDI)

If your application has one primary form, or a set of very independent forms, with optional support forms, the application may be best implemented with a single-document interface. This is the case with the contact management system, as shown in Figure 6.2.

Figure 6.2

A single-document interface (SDI) application can have the menu and toolbar attached to the form.

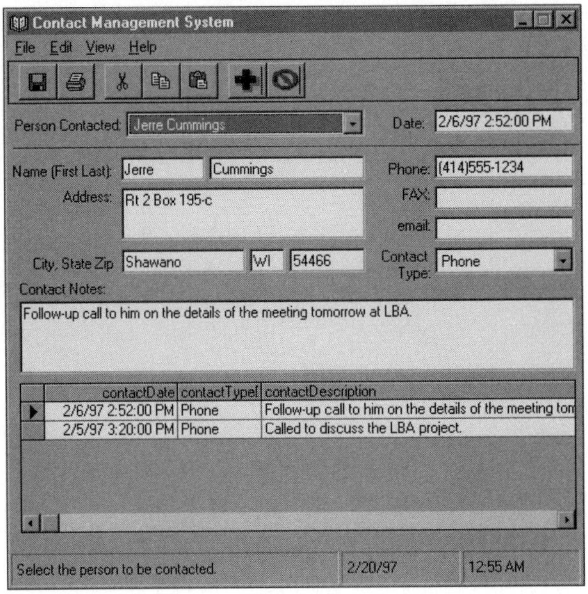

A form that uses SDI can have its own menu, toolbar, and status bar. Using SDI can provide a very user-friendly interface when the application has a primary focus. However, if there are many independent forms, each with its own menu, toolbar, and so on, SDI may not be the best choice. The different menus and toolbars may be confusing for the user.

Displaying a Work Space Using the Multiple-Document Interface (MDI)

The multiple-document interface is significantly different from SDI. An MDI application has an MDI parent form, as shown in Figure 6.3. This MDI parent provides a work space for the user. It normally includes the menu bar, toolbar, and status bar. The central part of the form, called the *client area*, cannot contain any controls. Rather, it provides the open space for multiple forms in the application, called *child forms*. If a child form has its own menu, the menu in the parent form is replaced with the child form's menu when the child form is active. The child form cannot display its own menu.

Figure 6.3

A multiple-document interface (MDI) application has multiple forms within a single container form.

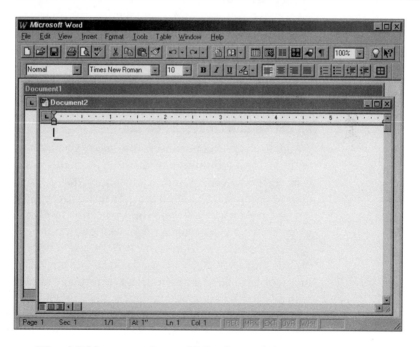

The child forms can be multiple views of the same data, such as a spreadsheet view and a graph view of the same sales information. In this case, two different forms would be designed and developed for the two different views. The child forms can also be similar views of different data, such as an employee application that allows simultaneous viewing of multiple employees.

In this case, only one form needs to be designed and developed. Multiple instances of that form can be displayed when the application is executed.

I have also used MDI for applications with multiple independent forms, even if the project required only one view of each form. For example, an application that displayed a single inventory form or single purchase order entry form could be MDI. Even though there is no "multiple document" view for this type of application, using MDI provides a user-friendly desktop with a common menu, toolbar, and status bar. All features of the application fit neatly within this desktop.

Displaying a Navigation Window Using the Explorer-Style Interface

The third common interface option is an explorer-style interface. This interface resembles Windows Explorer, as shown in Figure 6.4. The left side of the window displays a hierarchical view and the right side displays appropriate information based on the selection on the left side of the window. This type of interface is best when users need to navigate through a large number of documents or display information that is hierarchical in nature.

Before you select this type of interface, make sure that it will meet the user's goals. I have seen applications that provide explorer-style interfaces because the data was hierarchical in the developer's eyes. The users, however, could not easily navigate through the information in this fashion because they saw the data in terms of the tasks they performed on the data, not the hierarchical relationship of the data.

Modal Versus Modeless Forms

Modal forms prevent the user from accessing any other application feature until the form is dismissed by the user. Normally modal forms have two buttons, such as OK and Cancel, or just one OK button. The application will stop all processing and wait until the user responds to the modal form. Modal forms are best used when you want the application to wait for a user selection—for example, when displaying a Login window or a Printer Options dialog box.

You can use *modeless* forms in conjunction with other forms. They allow the user to shift the focus between the form and any other modeless form. The primary forms in an SDI application are normally modeless so the user can work with any combination of them open. All MDI child windows must be modeless.

Be careful not to overuse modal forms. Modal forms can be very frustrating for the user. Imagine running an application with a modal form that requires you to enter 50 fields. Half way through entering the data you need to look up something for one of the fields. Because the form is modal, you can only select OK or Cancel. You don't want to Cancel and lose your work, but you can't select OK either because it validates the fields and doesn't permit saving half the fields as empty. (Too many required fields is

Figure 6.4

The explorer-style interface, as shown here with Windows Explorer, provides a hierarchical view of information.

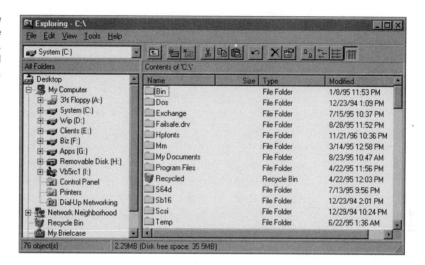

also frustrating for the user, but that is another story.) Modeless forms are often more practical because they match with the *ad hoc* way information is accessed in the real world.

The contact management system project team selected an SDI interface to keep the focus of the interface on the primary Contact Management window. The Address Book and To Do List windows will be modeless forms brought up from the Contact Management window. This will allow the user to work with any combination of these forms.

Laying Out the Screens

When designing a building, an architect does not need to invent every element of the design. Rather, the architect uses existing elements—such as windows, doors, walls, and hallways—and combines them in different ways to create new styles and new designs.

The same is true when designing a user interface. There are many standard design elements available for designing Windows applications. When designing your screens, you can work with the standard elements, purchase third-party controls, define your own elements, or combine these elements into a new interface mechanism. The new mechanism could become a new standard element, as tabbed dialogs have become. And with Visual Basic 5 it is now easy to create your own custom controls (called ActiveX controls).

Tech Note. *Keep the number of different ActiveX controls in a project to a minimum to better manage memory and speed and provide a consistent look and feel for the user. For example, select one grid control and use it wherever a grid is required. Don't use a different vendor's grid on each form.*

Keynote

In designing the layout of the screen, it is important to keep focused on the requirements of the application. Apply appropriate emphasis and balance to the elements. The parts of the screen the user will interact with the most should be readily available and at the beginning of the tab order. Sets of related information should be visually grouped to help the user find and work with the information. The screen should not be crowded or difficult to read. The layout should be orderly and efficient and the tab order should be set to match the layout. This helps the user quickly find what is needed and ignore what is less critical.

Designing screens is a fun task for a team meeting. You can gather the team members and just dive into this process using the white board or paper flip charts. Start with the application's primary screens, and then move on to the secondary screens. Alternatively, you can assign the screens to team members and have them present the screens to the team for feedback.

Some of the screens will require a significant amount of work and re-work to get the layout just right. *The Windows Interface Guidelines for Software Design*, mentioned in the "Additional Reading" section at the end of this chapter, provides some specific guidelines to help you with the screen design details.

Adding Flair

After you have done the basic design, add a little flair, but not too much flair. This helps keep the application visually interesting and is especially important if the user must look at the screen all day every day. Begin by adding icons to the buttons. Alan Cooper calls these "buttcons." These are visually appealing and allows more visual users to quickly identify the buttons by their icon instead of the text.

Add icons to symbolize each object in the application, and then use the icon whenever referring to the object. This could be in the upper-left corner of each screen for the object, in every list that contains this object (especially when grouped with other types of objects), in the menu, and anywhere else you refer to the object.

You can use simple colored lines to provide detail and separate different parts of the screen. Just as a car looks more polished with the detail lines, the application can look more polished as well. Use these lines to replace frames within frames to avoid clutter.

You can also add unobtrusive background bitmaps to the design to make the screens visually appealing. A few things to watch out for: Don't use too much color or too many graphics, and leave plenty of white (or gray) space for readability.

If time and budget allows, it is beneficial to have a graphic designer or user-interface design expert review the user interface. This person could then add the necessary flair to make the application look interesting and feel comfortable.

■ Observing Basic User-Interface Principles

Following these basic principles will help you design a user interface that will meet the most common user goals.

Keeping It Simple

As you work through the features of the application, adding them to the user interface, be sure to keep the primary features simple, even if it means making the secondary features more complex. Don't sacrifice simplicity in the features used the most by extending them to include the secondary features.

For example, the Contact Management window could be changed to a tabbed dialog that would allow access to the contact entries, address book, or to do list. This complicates the Contact Management window and prevents the user from looking at the address book information and the Contact Management window at the same time.

When things do need to become more complex, help the user manage the complexity using a technique called *progressive disclosure*. Progressive disclosure involves organizing or limiting what the users see to what is applicable at any one time. For a simple example, when no contact entry is selected, there is nothing to delete so the Delete button would be disabled.

Keeping the primary features as simple as possible helps the users complete their primary tasks more efficiently and effectively.

Providing Answers, Not Questions

When discussing user interface alternatives, it is often easiest for the design team to skip making decisions by stating, "Let the user decide." Parts of the application then become a series of questions or option settings that allow users to make their decisions. Although this approach makes it look as though the team is providing the users with flexibility, in many cases it just confuses them and demonstrates the team's inability to make decisions.

For example, the contact management system project team cannot decide whether to use a spreadsheet format or dialog boxes to input contact information. The team considers letting the user decide. So when the user starts the application for the first time (or worse, during installation), a question is asked: "Enter contact data in spreadsheet format or with a dialog box?" Well, the user has no clue at this point what the implications of either answer could be. The user is thinking: "If it is in spreadsheet format, does that mean I enter the data like in Excel?," "What does 'with a dialog box' mean?," "If I answer, is it permanent or can it be changed?"

Instead of providing these types of questions, which generate more questions in the users' minds, provide an answer. Think through the options and give them one data entry mechanism. If the user really needs to have a choice, pick one choice for a default and let the user change it if desired. That way, the users can use the application without ever knowing they have a choice, but can find the choice if they need it.

The same thinking should apply to the questions asked in the data entry screens. Ensure that the questions are meaningful. Wherever possible, provide a default answer and allow the user to change the default. For example, when users create a new contact entry in the Contact Management window, the application can set a default value for the current date. This decreases the time required to create a new log entry.

As another example, one programmer I worked with started her network-based executive information system by asking the user what drive letter to attach to. I suggested that the application could figure this out, display it in the status bar, and allow the user to change it (if they even knew what it was). She looked at me with a horrified expression and said, "But they need to set it specifically for their system so they don't use one intended for something else." Think about the user, not the computer; provide answers, not questions.

Making It Flexible

Users do not always do what you expect them to. That does not mean they are wrong, it just means they are human. The computer should not be forcing the user down a path and scream "wrong answer" every time the user moves outside of that path. There should be no right or wrong way to use the application.

Today's Windows environment allows the user to work with the software more productively, yet also more unpredictably. Consider this scenario: While the user is updating an Address Book record, the boss comes in and requests a status report, so the user selects report generation. How irritating for the user if the application responds with the message box "Table is locked." The software has just embarrassed the user in front of the boss. Now the user has no clue what is wrong or how to fix it and the boss is starting to wonder whether the application is meeting its advertised objectives.

The work day is full of interruptions and unanticipated requests. The software should give users the flexibility to move between tasks and between steps within a single task without generating obtuse error messages. It should

Keynote

provide multiple navigational methods so users can easily move between different operations. Make sure that the software can handle the different tasks the user must accomplish.

Remember the scenarios the team identified for the application in the Goal-centered design? Ensure that the scenarios include random, but valid, use of the features such as the scenario described earlier. Provide for interruptions and backtracking within a set of functional steps. Giving the application this flexibility makes it better able to fit with how the users normally accomplish their tasks.

Making It Forgiving

A valid concern of software developers is the accuracy of the data maintained by the application. Sometimes developers take this to mean that each field needs to be carefully controlled and the user needs to verify every action to guarantee that it is correct before doing it.

Let's look again at the contact management system application design. Suppose, while the user is entering new contact information for one call, another call comes in and the user wants to create another new record without finishing the first. Imagine the user's frustration if the software comes back with the message "Contact person Address field cannot be blank."

So the user rushes to fill in the address of the prior contact and then tries to create the other new record (all the while trying to carry on a conversation with the new caller). The software responds with another message box stating: "Contact Person Type must be numeric."

In anger the user clicks on the Delete button, but because the addition was never finalized the software responds with "Contact person not found."

By this time the user is furious and turns off the computer. So, the application's high standards for keeping the data absolutely accurate prevent the user from getting the job done. There are cases where careful validation is absolutely necessary. If performing calculations for a nuclear power plant you want to ensure that data is valid!

Keynote

In most cases, the application can be more forgiving. If the user does not fill in all of the data entry fields, it should still be an acceptable entry. If an action could cause some other side effects, make the consequences of the action visible and reversible. The user can then see the error and have an easy way to correct it. For example, validation errors can be displayed in red or in a panel on the screen without interrupting the user's flow and without affecting whether the record can be saved.

In deciding on the appropriate level of validation and appropriate number of required fields, it helps to think about the database as a repository for information instead of a set of valid records. It is simply a place where the user can store data. The fact that a record is or is not valid can instead be a flag in the record. For example, a mortgage certificate requires a large amount of data to be a valid certificate. The user should be able to save the information entered for the certificate at any point without worrying about completing all fields. This gives the user the flexibility to enter some information now and the rest later, which may be required if the paperwork used for the data entry is not complete. When all necessary fields are entered, the certificate becomes valid.

You can minimize the chances of some data validation errors by using combo boxes or radio buttons instead of requiring entry of a value. For example, instead of requiring entry of "T" or "F," use radio buttons. Then you don't need to validate the entry and present message boxes when the response is "wrong."

If you do have to provide a message box, supply information that is helpful to the user. Identify the problem and point out how it can be solved. Don't display messages that are technical and meaningless to the user. For example, you could change "Fatal Error in File Indexing Mechanism" to "The contact person you entered already exists…." If technical information about an error is required, add error information to a log file.

Design your validation to meet the true goals of the users. Minimize the possibility for error. When the users do make an unexpected entry, provide a clear way to correct the problem. Let the application be more forgiving.

Making It Remember

Computers are good at remembering things. If data is written to a permanent storage device, the computer will remember it. Applications should use the "memory" of the computer to make the users more efficient and effective.

Have you ever used a dialog box to find a file in a specific path, and then gone back to the dialog box a moment later to find another file in that path? Did the application remember the original path you selected or did it return to some useless default? It's frustrating defining the entire path again.

Here are some things your application should remember:

- **Last opened files**. The last few opened files, usually four, are often listed in the File menu for the application. This provides a quick method for the user to select and open a file without remembering where that file is located or what it is called. Depending on the application and user's requirements, you may even want to open the last opened file automatically when the application starts.

- **Location of windows**. Normally, a user will work with an application in a similar way from day to day. Every day a user will open your application and move the windows to the desired locations. Instead, the application could remember the previous locations and by default bring the windows up in those locations.

- **Sort selections**. If the user selects a specific sort, filter, or other arrangement of data, the application should remember this. When the user accesses this data again, the same arrangement of data should be used.

By letting the application use some of the computer's "memory" you can significantly add to the user's productivity.

Making It Believe the User

Applications frequently don't believe the user. Imagine this: You ask your secretary to file a stack of letters and your secretary asks, "Do you really want to save these?" Of course you wanted to save them or you would not have asked to have them filed! Then you spend an hour with the design team discussing changes to the specifications. At the end of the meeting, the team asks: "Do you really need to keep all of these changes?" As you walk out the door at the end of the day, the security guard stops you and asks "Do you really want to exit?" You can see how ridiculous this is, but applications do it all of the time!

In many applications, the user makes changes and is then asked: "Data changed, do you want to save?" Well, the user wouldn't have changed the data if it wasn't to be saved! The application should make it visually clear what has been changed, automatically save it (believing the user meant to make the changes), and allow an undo if it is not to be changed. The application should believe the user.

Making It Fit In

Ever seen a room that, although elegant, was not designed to facilitate comfort or good conversation? You walk into one of these rooms, afraid of breaking something. These rooms make you feel uncomfortable. So too, with software that is not correctly designed for the environment in which it is run. For the users to feel comfortable with your application, it must fit appropriately into the environment. When you're developing a Windows application, it is important the application fits into the guidelines of a Windows application.

I have heard DOS programmers say that they don't want their existing customers to relearn their product, so they are using the same user interface and are simply "porting" to Windows. The users of these applications hate them. Why did those users want a Windows product? It's because they have Microsoft Office and other Windows applications. The DOS-turned-Windows application uses the F1 key to bring up the customer window. F1 has always brought up the customer window in the DOS product. Now the user presses F1 to get help (as in the Microsoft Office products they have) and the customer window comes up. Ugh!

Keynote

The application must adapt to the capabilities and expectations of the target platform. Microsoft has pressed this issue by stating that a product cannot get the Windows 95 logo unless it conforms to the basic Windows 95 guidelines. So it is even more important to ensure that your application fits in to the Windows environment.

Starting Off Right

After you have identified and designed the components of the user interface, look carefully at the user's first introduction to your application. Decide how the application will present itself to the user. If there is one primary feature of the application, make that the default starting place for the user. Instead of starting with a blank work space, fill the work space with the tools needed to perform the primary task.

If there are several common tasks, start with a Welcome screen. You may have seen these screens in products such as Microsoft PowerPoint, as shown in Figure 6.5. The Welcome screen appears when you open the application, provides you with a list of the most common choices, and gives you a hint as to the best place to start. Many of these screens also have a "don't show me this again" check box so the user can turn this screen off when they no longer need the assistance it provides.

Figure 6.5

Displaying a Welcome screen gives the user a place to start.

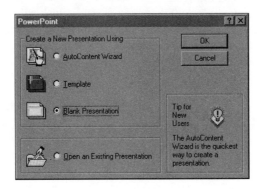

Welcome windows prevent the "empty page syndrome," where the user stares at an empty page, not knowing where to begin. They are like the receptionist for a large office building. Without one, a user could wander around a long time. With a friendly receptionist, the user will feel welcome and will be efficiently shown where to go.

■ Validating the User-Interface Design

When learning to read and write, my daughter would draw all of the letters of the alphabet on a page, and then ask, "Is that right?" After you have drawn the user interface for your application, how do you know if it is "right"? There are several ways the team can validate the functionality and usability of the design. They can use the scenarios documented in the Goal-centered design step to walk through the user interface, create a prototype to review the look and feel of the design and test the usability informally, or formally with a usability testing lab.

Validating Features

The project team should ensure that there is a user interface component for each feature being implemented. What good is a really neat address book feature if there is no user interface component for accessing the feature?

The team can perform this validation using the scenarios documented in the Goal-centered design step. Look again at the primary tasks and walk through how the user would accomplish the task with your current design. Make sure the primary features really shine and the secondary features are easy to find and provide the needed functionality.

Stepping through the scenarios with the user interface also helps the team determine the number of user actions needed to meet the requirements of the application. For example, five user actions required to perform a task that will be done 100 times a day will not be satisfactory, so the team may need to make some changes to the user interface design.

Creating a Prototype

To help with the user interface validation, the team may want to develop a prototype. Prototypes are nice. They are easy to do with Visual Basic and they provide something the team and the users can really try out to get a feel for the application.

User interface prototypes should include the menu, toolbar, and primary screens in the application, with only enough code to navigate between the menu, toolbar, and screens. You can create test data, or even hard code it in the application, to demonstrate how data will be displayed.

Visual Basic 5 comes with a new Application Wizard that makes it easier to create prototypes. This Wizard generates the basic framework of a fully functional application, including a main window with associated menu, toolbar, and status bar. You can select an MDI, SDI, or explorer-style interface. The Wizard also allows you to select a splash screen, login form, data entry forms, or any other form templates you may have defined. Once the Wizard creates the application, you can add forms and controls to complete your prototype.

To run the Application Wizard, follow these steps:

1. Launch Visual Basic.

2. Select VB Application Wizard from the New tab of the New Project dialog box (see Figure 6.6).

   If the New Project dialog box did not appear when you launched Visual Basic, choose New from the File menu to display it.

Figure 6.6

The New Project dialog box allows you to create a project and define the type of application, or access the VB Application Wizard to create the basic framework of an application.

3. Click on the Open button on the New Project dialog box.

4. Answer the questions presented on the screens of the Wizard.

5. When you've entered all necessary information, click on the Finish button. The application will be generated right before your eyes.

6. Add forms and controls to complete your prototype.

Keynote

You should not use prototyping as a substitute for the User-interface design step, but rather as a validation of the design. When developing a prototype, focus can shift from the goals of the user—and even the goals of the application—to the fun and excitement of getting some screens working. As you finish the prototype, remember that this is not the application! Don't stop the design because the users like what they see. Rather, continue with the design to ensure that the façade created with the prototype can become a solid application.

Validating Usability

Usability testing involves reviewing the user interface with a set of potential users in a controlled environment. This process has become quite popular, but is often misused. In many cases, it is included as part of the software testing, after the majority of the application is developed. By this time large amounts of code have been written and the project is probably behind schedule. Help text and user documentation have been written, and no one wants to make any changes. So the results of the usability testing are used to identify where in the help or user documentation things need to be better explained. That is not the purpose of usability testing.

Keynote

By using the prototype developed at this step, usability testers can walk through the application and identify problem areas early enough to change them. This testing can define how well your design works and how well the mental model translates to the tasks needing to be accomplished. This process will review the screens for consistency and conceptual integrity. It will guarantee that similar user interface mechanisms are used for similar tasks and that each screen does not have its own unique set of user interface idioms to learn. It will verify that the application does not "feel" different as the user moves from screen to screen.

■ Documenting the User-Interface Design

The result of the User-interface design step is normally a design document and the prototype. This document collects the pictures and descriptions of the screens. It is also a good mechanism for beginning to collect business rules because the screens themselves bring out ideas. For example, a user sees a screen and comments that the price shown on the screen must not be greater than the price shown on the prior screen.

The User-interface design document should contain the following:

- **List of user goals.** Listing the goals in this design document ensures that they are kept in focus when reviewing the design.

- **List of application features.** This list is included to document the feature list. It should read something like a marketing list in that it is user-oriented and not computer-oriented.

- **Screen shots and notes.** Using the prototype, screens can be copied and pasted into this document. Below each screen you can add a written description and notes on the operation of the screen. It is much easier for reviewers to put notes on these pages than on the screens of the prototype!

- **Scenarios.** Optionally, you could repeat the scenarios here with the specific steps for using the user interface to perform a task.

With a user-interface design in hand, and your object model on the wall, you are ready to get technical and start looking at the implementation details of the application.

■ Summary

- The User-interface design defines how the application will look and how it will interact with the users.

- Identify the users' goals to determine what the users personally want from the application. The users' goals may not be the same as the project's goals and requirements, which identify what the business wants from the application.

- Use the project's requirements, the object model, and users' goals to define the features required for the application.

- Triage the features into primary and secondary features. The primary features should be designed first and the secondary features should be designed around them.

- Provide a mental model of the application that allows the users to relate more easily to the application features.

- Ensure that the primary features of the application are easy to access and the secondary features are easy to find.

- Select an SDI or MDI interface style and employ the new explorer-style interface where appropriate.

- Design the screens based on the users' goals and the project's requirements, and add flair to keep the screens interesting.

- When appropriate, define your own user interface mechanisms, either as new components or as combinations of existing components. It's easy to create your own custom controls, called ActiveX controls, in Visual Basic.

- Follow the basic user interface principles to ensure that the screens are simple, easy to use, flexible, forgiving, and appropriate.

- Validate the user interface by walking through the scenarios.

- Use a prototype for validation and usability testing.

- Develop a formal document for the User-interface design to share with the project team and to provide a definition of the user interface of the application.

■ Additional Reading

Cooper, Alan. *About Face: The Essentials of User Interface Design.* IDG Publishing Company, 1995.

 About Face is an outstanding guide to putting the right face on your software, written by Alan Cooper, the "father of Visual Basic." Cooper's practical suggestions, thought-provoking insights, and anecdotal style make *About Face* a must-read book for anyone involved with user-interface design. I highly recommend this book as an extension of the information provided in this chapter. The quote at the beginning of this chapter is on page 11 of this book.

Cooper, Alan. "The Perils of Prototyping," *Visual Basic Programmer's Journal,* Vol. 4, No. 6, August/September 1994.

 This article provides a case for using paper and a pencil instead of a programming tool for the high-level design of the user interface for an application.

Kurata, Deborah, "Make the Most of MDI," *Visual Basic Programmer's Journal,* Vol. 4, No. 6, August/September 1994.

 This article discusses the multiple-document interface (MDI) and how to implement it in an application. Although the article was written for Visual Basic 3.0, some of the techniques are similar for Visual Basic 5.

Laurel, Brenda. *The Art of Human-Computer Interface Design.* Reading, Massachusetts: Addison-Wesley, 1990.

 This is a compilation of articles on user-interface design.

The Windows Interface Guidelines for Software Design. Redmond, Washington: Microsoft Press, 1995.

 This guide describes design principles and methodologies within the context of Windows 95. It provides very specific user interface details. You should read this book if you plan to use the Windows 95 logo on any developed application.

Norman, Donald A. *The Design of Everyday Things.* New York: Double-day, 1990.

This book has great insights into the design of common things you use. It does not specifically focus on software design, but provides information applicable to designing in general.

■ Think It Over

To supplement and review the information in this chapter, think about the following:

1. Think about some of the applications you use. Which are easy to use? Why? Which are frustrating or difficult to use? Why?

2. Review the list of principles for creating a good user interface and think about an application you use, such as Microsoft Word. Which features in the application meet these guidelines and which do not? How does this affect the usability of the application?

3. Add the design of an Appointment Book feature to the contact management system application. Define how this feature would fit into the application. Draw the layout of the screen.

4. Use the VB Application Wizard to get started on the prototype of the contact management system or another application. Then add other forms and controls to complete the prototype. No need to add code yet.

7

Implementation-Centered Design

...As a simple example a clock, whose architecture consists of the face, the hands, and the winding knob. When a child has learned this architecture, he can tell time as easily from a wristwatch as from a church tower. The implementation, however, and its realization, describe what goes on inside the case—powering by any of many mechanisms and accuracy control by any of many.

—Frederick P. Brooks, Jr.,
The Mythical Man-Month

It's time to shift the focus of the design from the users' perspective of the clock face, hands, and winding knob and concentrate on what's inside the case—on what will make the clock tick. The Implementation-centered design describes what will go on inside the application—behind the user's interface.

The structure of the inside of an application is described by a system architecture. This chapter presents several system architectures and criteria for selecting an architecture for your application. It walks you through the process of defining the components appropriate for the selected architecture and shows you how to design the internal framework for each component. It then describes how to design the set of classes that form the building blocks of each component.

The resulting design can be validated using walk-throughs and prototypes and documented in an implementation specification document. With a good internal architecture, framework, and design, applications and associated components are easier to build, maintain, and enhance.

■ What Is Implementation-Centered Design?

The Implementation-centered design is the third step of the GUIDS methodology, highlighted in Figure 7.1. It provides the blueprints for an application. Just as the blueprints of a building show the high-level view and then detailed component views, the blueprints of an application include a high-level view of the system architecture and a detailed view for each component required for that architecture. The component views detail the framework of the component and describe the building blocks that will be used to build the component. The Implementation-centered design prepares the architectural plans for the construction phase. Because this step of the design maps to physical modules in an application, this step is sometimes called *physical design*.

During the Goal-centered design and User-interface design steps, the team included both technical staff and users or domain experts. The Implementation-centered design requires thorough technical knowledge, so is best performed by the technical staff working closely with the nontechnical members of the team only when questions arise from the existing design documents. The technical staff converts the user view of the application into a technical design that is ready for implementation.

The tasks involved in the Implementation-centered design are

1. Define the system architecture.

2. Design the components.

3. Design the classes.

4. Consider implementation issues.

5. Validate the design.

Figure 7.1

Implementation-centered
design defines the
architecture, framework,
and building blocks
of the application.

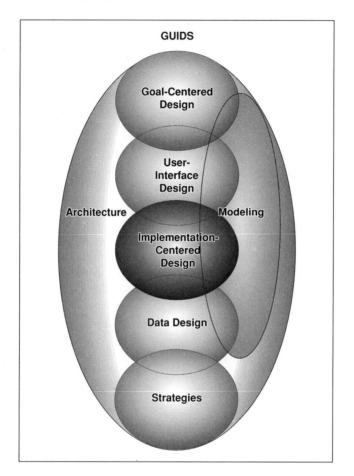

There are general implementation issues to consider when developing the Implementation-centered design. This includes performance, resource and security considerations; modeling dynamic object states using state transition diagrams; and evaluating existing design patterns. This chapter includes an overview of these issues to provide a general introduction to each topic and to explain how it can affect the Implementation-centered design. This overview is not meant to be a detailed presentation of these topics. For more information, consult the "Additional Reading" section at the end of this chapter.

■ Preparing for Implementation-Centered Design

In the old days of PC programming, applications were designed for single users. They resided on individual end-user computers and were run by one person at a time from those computers. Life was simpler then. With today's advances in component architecture, client/server technologies, the Internet, intranets, and distributed object computing, the choices are expanding. And more choices bring the need for more decisions.

Consider a corporate information management application. The project team can decide to put logical components where they make sense. The user interface can be local at the user's desktop in Wisconsin, the address book component can reside on the network in Los Angeles, and scheduling software can reside on the R&D machine in Washington. The data for the address book can reside on the corporate mainframe in Chicago and the data for scheduling conference rooms can reside on the local data server. Figure 7.2 shows how these components are distributed.

Figure 7.2

Developing an application as a set of discreet components provides flexibility in deploying the components where they make the most sense.

Even if an application doesn't require distributed components, it can be designed with a component-based system architecture and implemented as one or more individual components for use on single systems. This allows the application to gain the benefits of components, such as better encapsulation and easier maintenance and enhancements.

As you can imagine, defining a component-based architecture can have a profound effect on the design of the application. And when some of the components will be distributed, there are more factors to consider in the design. This section reviews several common system architectures to provide you with some basic options before you begin the Implementation-centered design.

Monolithic Architecture

Monolithic is the term used to describe the single-user, local-system architecture. The application is developed as one primary executable, installed on individual computers, and executed by a single user on that computer. This architectural style is quite common for single-focused, single-user applications. For example, a personal checkbook balancing program could be installed on a user's computer, the data could be stored on that computer, and the application could be used on a single-user basis.

The primary benefit of this type of architecture is in its simplicity. There is one project to develop and one executable to manage. However, in a multiprogrammer development effort, that is not always an advantage. What if the application later needs to support multiple types of databases? If no thought had been given to separating database logic from the rest of the application, the entire application may need to be changed. And what if this checkbook balancing program includes a tax module that has to be updated every year? If the application had a monolithic architecture, users would have to replace the entire application instead of simply downloading a small revised component.

Tech Note.   *This is not to say that single-user, local-system applications are poorly designed. On the contrary, many developers building single-user, local-system applications use a structured approach to the development that closely resembles the three-tiered architecture approach described in this section. As you work through the process later in this chapter, you may recognize that you already use many of the techniques described here.*

File Server Architecture

As soon as business enterprises began to distribute PCs throughout the organization, there arose a need to share information between those PCs. So the local PCs were connected to a network with file servers. The Microsoft Access databases were then moved from the local PCs to the file servers to store the shared data. The local PCs could map the file server drive as a local drive and treat it as an extension of the local PC.

This type of architecture allows users to share information. If one user changes a customer's address, that change is available to anyone else who needs that information. With a file server architecture there is still just one project to develop and one executable to manage. However, system administrators have the large task of distributing software updates to each PC on the system. Every time a new version of a product is released, the system administrator needs to ensure that the new version is installed on each user's PC.

As these systems expand, there are often problems with scalability, security, performance, and data locking issues. File servers work fine when there are a small number of database requests, but they can get bogged down quickly as the number of concurrent users starts to increase.

Two-Tiered Client/Server Architecture

Database products such as Microsoft SQL Server and Oracle provide scalable, high-performance database management systems specifically designed for a distributed client/server architecture. Applications on the user's computer (the client tier) access the database on a shared computer (the server tier) through a data server interface such as ODBC.

Tech Note.   *ODBC (Open Database Connectivity) defines a standard interface used in data servers for accessing databases. You need to install the appropriate ODBC driver for the particular database product you are using.*

An application can access a database through the ODBC driver in several different ways:

- **Through a data control.** This is the simplest, but least powerful of the approaches. In this approach, a data control on a form is bound to the desired set of records in a database. The simplicity of this approach makes it ideal for prototyping, but can make database intensive applications inefficient and limited in functionality.

- **Through the Data Access Objects (DAO) object model.** The DAO provides an object model for accessing data in Microsoft Access and other databases. DAO 3.5 is the newest version and is supported in Visual Basic 5. This new version of DAO provides access to distributed database servers, such as Microsoft SQL Server and Oracle, through ODBC-Direct. ODBCDirect provides a direct path to the ODBC (and remote databases) without going through the Jet engine.

**Enterprise
Edition**

- **Through the Remote Data Objects (RDO) object model.** If you have the Enterprise Edition of Visual Basic, you can use RDO to access a remote database. RDO provides a thin, object-oriented layer over the ODBC that is similar to the DAO model but provides many additional ODBC features such as high-speed local cursors and event-driven operations.

- **Directly, using an application programming interface (API).** This technique requires handling the database accessing yourself using a set of external DLLs and, optionally, an object model provided by the database product. This approach is often complex, but gives you the best performance and access to all of the features of the database product.

Most Internet and intranet applications have also been developed using a two-tiered client/server architecture. The users use a Web browser such as Internet Explorer (IE) or Netscape Navigator as the user interface on the first tier. The server on the second tier provides the Web pages and the database functionality on a server.

This type of architecture allows users to share information in a faster and more manageable way. It does not, however, provide an easy mechanism for sharing components or applications.

Three-Tiered Client/Server Architecture

The three-tiered architecture has been hailed as the solution that allows businesses to realize their full strategic advantage. It provides for a network of distributed data sources, distributed processing servers, and local user interface components. This approach has become the choice for distributed client/server computing because of its flexibility and interoperability with existing legacy systems.

The three-tiered architecture is comprised of three logical categories, or *tiers*, as shown in Figure 7.3. The user interface tier supports user services, the server tier supports business services, and the data tier provides data services. Hence this architecture is sometimes referred to as the *services model*.

Figure 7.3

Three-tiered architecture separates the components of the application so they can be better managed and optionally distributed.

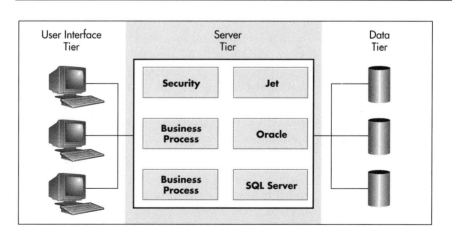

Keynote

Each tier is comprised of one or more *components*. The components required for each of the three logical tiers can all reside on one computer or can be distributed across any number of networked computers. An *application* then becomes the combination of components across the three tiers. Life is just not simple anymore!

A three-tiered architecture has many advantages:

- It enables both purchased and prebuilt components to be assembled into an application.

- It supports distributed functionality on a heterogeneous network. Tasks can be executed at specific locations for improved performance, administration, and maintenance.

- It simplifies the replacement of components. A user interface, server, or database component can be replaced with minimal impact on the overall system.

- It encapsulates business processes into a separate tier for better approval, control, maintenance, and reusability.

- It provides a convenient migration path from legacy systems to new technologies. Current components can be rearranged into this architecture and then upgraded as opportunities allow.

- New Internet and intranet technologies, such as Internet Explorer 3.0, allow for application-based and Internet/intranet-based user interfaces that reuse the same user interface, server, and database tier components.

The three tiers are described in the following paragraphs.

User Interface Tier

The user interface tier includes the components of the application that will interface directly with the user, along with any associated support components. These components are responsible for presenting information to the user and allowing the user to navigate through, enter, and edit the information.

The user interface components are implemented on the local users' computers. If the user interface was provided on any other computer, the interface would appear on that computer, rather than the users'!

Tech Note. *If application components will be distributed on remote systems, it is important not to put message boxes or other user interface mechanism in any of the distributed components. Any message box or user interface mechanism included in the distributed component will appear on the remote system, possibly blocking the user interface component and preventing the application from continuing.*

Server Tier

The server tier provides the business logic and other services the application performs. It also handles the interaction between the user interface and the data, insulating the user from the complexities of data access. Components in this tier can be implemented on the local computer or distributed to other systems on the network.

**Enterprise
Edition**

Keynote

Tech Note. *To use Remote Automation or the Distributed Component Object Model (DCOM) to communicate with code components distributed across a network, you must have the Enterprise Edition of Visual Basic.*

Regardless of the expected location of the components, local or distributed, the source code for those components is the same. So components can be developed and run locally and distributed across a network later, with no changes to the source code. This provides for simplified testing and greater flexibility.

If the server component is expected to be on a different computer from the user interface component, however, you do need to consider performance issues. Code components on a remote computer are separate executables. When the first object is requested from the component, the executable must be started. As we all know, launching executables is a very slow process. If all objects requested from the component are later released, the executable will automatically terminate. When another object is later requested from the component, the component must start up again. This can greatly affect the performance of the application.

To improve performance, consider including a *pool manager* component in the server tier. A pool manager can keep a pool of objects from a code component and allocate the objects to applications as they are needed. When the application is finished with the object, it is returned to the pool. Keeping a pool of objects ensures that the component executable remains loaded, eliminating the time required to launch it.

Tech Note. *You can use existing products such as the Microsoft Transaction Server to provide pool management services, or you can create your own pool manager. For more information on pool managers, check out the pool manager source code in the samples directory, the Application Performance Explorer (APE) utility from Microsoft, or Craig Goren's book* Visual Basic 5 Enterprise Development. *An APE document and Goren's book are referenced in the "Additional Reading" section at the end of this chapter.*

Data Tier

The data tier can include any new database, existing legacy databases, or an entire set of databases on heterogeneous systems. The database can be installed on the local PC, but is implemented more frequently on a separate data server on the network using a distributed database product, such as those defined in the section "Two-Tiered Client/Server Architecture" earlier in this chapter.

■ Defining the System Architecture

Now that you are familiar with some system architectures, you can define which architecture will work best for your application. When defining the architecture, keep in mind the project goals and system requirements. Don't design an Empire State Building architecture for a Tree House application.

Then system architecture is comprised of both a physical architecture and a logical architecture. Whether you define the physical or the logical architecture first will depend on your environment and your project. If the requirements or constraints require a specific hardware solution, you should first define the physical architecture. If the hardware system will be designed specifically for the application, it makes more sense to define the logical architecture first.

Physical Architecture

The physical architecture defines how the application will be distributed across one or more physical computer systems. Will the entire application be run on each user's computer, or will some components run on shared systems? Because the answers to these questions define how the application will be deployed, the physical architecture is sometimes referred to as the *deployment model*.

Selecting the physical architecture may be easy—it may have been defined in the requirements. For example, one of the project requirements is to develop an address book application that uses the client database on a computer in Chicago. The application should be provided to everyone in the company, but with security features based on business rules centrally located in Los Angeles. This would require a three-tiered physical architecture to access all of the required systems.

The selection process can be influenced by more than just the technical requirements. Factors such as corporate culture, available funds for computers, existing network connectivity, and company experience with distributed components can all impact the decision.

The selection process is also affected by the database product selected for the application. Even though the data design is not done at this point, you do need to review the requirements of the application to determine which database product to use, if any. The Microsoft Access database product is inexpensive because it is provided with Visual Basic and has no license fee, but it limits the physical architecture to monolithic or file server architectures. Using a product such as Microsoft SQL Server or Oracle is much more expensive but provides more choices for a physical architecture.

Tech Note. *You can use Microsoft Access on a remote system if you write an ActiveX component on that remote system that handles the database operations. This technique is detailed in Anthony Sneed's article listed in the "Additional Reading" section later in this chapter.*

Scalability is a factor here as well because the physical architecture of the first deployment of the application may not be the long-term architecture. For example, suppose an application is deployed first in one department with a Microsoft Access database on a single file server. If the deployment is successful, the application will be moved to SQL Server and introduced to other users throughout the company and the world. Knowing about the possibility of a second deployment when designing the first will simplify the eventual migration.

The contact management system team defined a physical file server architecture for the first deployment of the application. This decision was based on two criteria: the desire to use Microsoft Access as the database product and the need to leverage existing hardware. Future deployment may involve a move to SQL Server and off-loading of primary processing to server computers, but that will depend on the success of the initial roll out.

Logical Architecture

Keynote

The logical architecture defines how the application will be divided into components, regardless of the physical distribution of those components. Because this is not dependent on physical limitations, I recommend using a three-tiered approach for the logical architecture of any medium to large applications.

To support this type of architecture, you can design your application to separate the user interface from the business rules from the database accessing. This approach simplifies the development of the application and future maintenance and enhancements.

For example, because the user interface component is separate from the rest of the application, one developer can be assigned to build the user interface. This makes it easier to assign a good user interface programmer to that component and helps to ensure that the user interface is consistent throughout the application.

A three-tiered approach also allows you to add user interface components without major changes to the application. For example, after successful deployment of a large application, the users request an additional user interface component that allows Web-based access to information managed by the application. Using a three-tiered approach to the original design allows the new Web pages to reuse the existing server and database tier components, greatly simplifying the enhancement effort.

As another example, consider a personal checkbook balancing program application. If the business rules for the tax module were in a separate component it would be easier to provide an update to that component on a yearly basis.

The contact management system team decided to take a three-tiered approach to the logical architecture of the application. The user interface components will be separate from the business components and separate from the data access components.

■ Designing the Components

After you have defined the high-level architecture, you need to design the components that make up each logical tier of the architecture. A *component* is a logical set of code developed for one primary purpose. A component can be a separately compiled unit of code, such as an ActiveX component, or a logical set of code within an application.

The common components for each tier of a three-tiered architecture are described in the topics which follow. Each description includes tips and techniques for designing the components.

User Interface Tier Components

The user interface tier, as it's name implies, presents the user interface of the application. The primary component of the user interface tier is the user interface itself—the forms that make up the application. The ActiveX controls used to build the forms are also user interface tier components. Additional components in this tier can include code components to encapsulate standard user interface behavior or to communication with the server tier.

Application Forms

The forms that comprise the user interface of the application were defined during the User-interface design phase. You may have developed a portion of this component already as part of the prototyping process. If there are any open or unresolved user interface design issues, you should resolve them at this step in the design.

Application Controls

The forms defined for the application can contain intrinsic controls—that is, the controls that come within Visual Basic—and ActiveX controls. You should define the set of ActiveX controls to be used in the application if you did not define them during the User-interface design step. (See "Buy Versus Build" in Chapter 9, "Strategies for Construction," for guidelines on selecting third-party products.) These controls are additional components in the user-interface tier.

Keynote

If you plan to build ActiveX controls as part of the project, you should design each control individually following the GUIDS methodology. Define the goal for the control and define the objects that the control needs to manipulate, if any. For example, grid controls manipulate column objects. Then design the user interface either as a new element, a combination of existing controls, or a combination of the two. Next perform the Implementation-centered design and determine the UserControl, Form, and Class modules required for the control. Look at how the control will maintain its property data. Finally, define the strategies for constructing the control. Will it be part of a single project or developed as a general-purpose control? How will it be tested and documented? And so on.

Application Code

For forms to have behavior, they must have some code responding to events such as Load or Click. But adding too much code to the forms makes the user interface fat and sluggish. Because the user interface is the component the user will see and interact with, you should try to keep the user interface thin and swift.

Tech Note.   *As code is added to a form, a form module gets larger. Larger form modules load more slowly than smaller form modules.*

Keynote

Instead of defining a lot of code to be implemented within the form, define the minimal amount of code to make the forms respond to the user and call other components for all other processing. For example, a support component for the main form can provide the code for the Edit menu cut, copy, and paste options. The user interface simply responds to the menu event and delegates the processing to the support component.

As another example, your company can define a component that provides standard user interface mechanisms in all applications (or at least throughout a single application). This could include code to automatically select text when a text box receives focus, to boldface changed text, and to validate data in a control when the control loses focus. This component can then be called from the forms, keeping the forms thin. Then if the users later request that all 150 forms in your application be modified to set changed text to blue instead of bold, only one line of code in one component need be modified.

You may also want to include components in this tier to provide the communication between the user interface tier and the server tier. For example, to minimize network traffic, address book information from a server tier on a network is provided to the user interface tier in one large array. A communication component on the user interface tier can convert the array elements into logical object properties. This keeps the user interface component thin and simple and encapsulates the array processing in the communication component. From some points of view, this communication component would not be considered a user interface component, but rather a server tier component implemented on the same computer as the user interface component. Regardless of the tier distinction, the important point is to ensure that these types of components are defined, if needed.

As part of the User-interface design, the contact management system team defined a main form (Contact Management window) and two primary support forms (Address Book and To Do List windows). As part of this step, the team decided to develop a window support class to handle standard windows processing, such as the Edit menu options.

Server Tier Components

The server tier provides the business services. For many applications, business services are the primary function and, as you would expect, comprise the majority of the code. This includes code for the business rules and the communication between the user interface tier and the data tier. Additional components in this tier could include support components and a pool manager component (see "Preparing for Implementation-Centered Design" earlier in this chapter for a discussion of pool managers).

During the Goal-centered design, the project team described candidate objects based on the real-world application domain. Those candidate objects identified the real-world things in the application and defined the properties and behaviors of those things. The relationships between the candidate objects were defined and illustrated with object models. These object models describe the business services and provide the first cut of the design for the primary server tier component. For review, the object models originally defined for the contact management system example during the Goal-centered design are shown in Figures 7.4 and 7.5.

In this Implementation-centered design step, you scrutinize the candidate objects in the object models, clarifying or eliminating irrelevant or vague objects. You add objects required for implementation. You convert the hierarchy of candidate objects into a hierarchy of classes that can be implemented. You perform this conversion as follows:

- Break it up.

- Define the top-level class.

- Evaluate candidate objects.

Figure 7.4

This object model defines the "has a" containment relationships for the candidate objects.

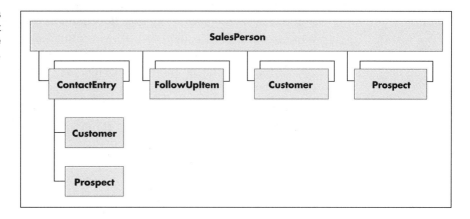

Figure 7.5

This object model describes the "is a" subclassing relationships and illustrates similarities among the candidate objects.

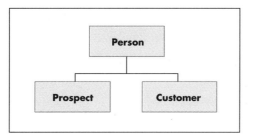

- Generalize classes for reuse.

- Add collection classes.

- Consider data transfer.

- Flatten the hierarchy.

- Convert subclass relationships.

Each of these steps is described in detail in the following sections, using the contact management system example to illustrate the step.

Breaking it Up

The first step is to determine whether the hierarchy of candidate objects should be divided into multiple components. This decision is normally based on encapsulation, changeability, and the size and potential reuse of the components.

If an object model for a component contains hierarchies of objects for separate and distinct functionality, you can divide the component into separate components, each with responsibility for one primary function. For example, if the contact management system object model included a set of objects for payroll and production, it would be better to separate those sets of objects into independent components that are designed separately.

If some of the features of the component are more changeable than others, the features that are more changeable may be segregated from those that are not. This simplifies the replacement of components as business requirements change. For example, if the SalesPerson component in the contact management system included calculations for bonuses that were different each year, you could segregate the bonus calculation component into its own replaceable component.

Defining the Top-Level Class

Frequently, each component has one topmost class. By convention, this class is called the Application class. Having one topmost object can provide simplified access to the component. It can also provide a single entry point to all subordinate classes in the hierarchy.

The contact management system project team defined one topmost class for the component: the SalesPerson class. The team decided to leave the name SalesPerson instead of renaming it to Application to keep the focus of the application on the salesperson functions.

Evaluating Candidate Objects

Work down the hierarchy from the topmost class to examine every object in the object model and determine whether it should be defined as a class in the application. If so, give the class a name. Make sure that the name is specific and reflects the role of the class in the application. For example, an Entry class in the contact management system would be too generic and misleading. A better name would be ContactEntry.

Generalizing Classes for Reuse

Keynote

Look at the defined classes and determine whether any class could be generalized and used by other applications. Defining generic components promotes the reuse of components and simplifies future projects. This was the case with FollowUpItem class. Instead of having a very specific class to track follow-up of sales calls, you could have a more generic class to track any type of tasks in a to do list. Since the name reflects the generic description, you could change the name FollowUpItem to Task, for managing the set of tasks.

Adding Collection Classes

Objects depicted with two offset boxes, such as ContactEntry shown in Figure 7.4, represent a set of objects, called a *collection*. For example, the

SalesPerson class will not track one contact entry, but rather an entire collection of contact entries. Each collection in the object model will normally require two classes: one for the collection and one for the object itself. By convention, the name of the collection class is the plural of the object.

For the contact management system, the Task set of objects requires a Task class describing a single to do list item and a Tasks collection class tracking the set of to do list items.

Considering Data Transfer

Even though Data design is not performed until the next step of the design process, to complete the Implementation-centered design you need to give some consideration to the data. This overlap in design phases is depicted in Figure 7.1 as the area between the Implementation-centered design and the Data design. If the application will include a database, the application will need to transfer data from the database through the business rules in the server tier to the user interface when data is requested, and back again when data is saved.

Depending on the data transfer technique(s) selected, you may need additional classes in the object model. These classes are sometimes called *business object data transfer (BODT) classes*. Some choices for data transfer are

Keynote

- **Data control.** This is a control that is added to a form and tied to a specific set of records in a database. Other controls on the form, such as text boxes and grids, can be tied to the data control. Data is automatically transferred from the database to the user interface when data is requested and from the user interface to the database when data is saved. As is apparent, this is not a three-tiered approach because the server tier is ignored. However, it does provide a simple way to transfer data between the user interface and the database. This technique is demonstrated in Chapter 14, "Doing Database Objects."

- **Collection.** A collection is a convenient way to track a set of objects. But when you are working with databases, a collection may not be the most practical approach. A collection class in the server tier would need to obtain the specific set of records from the database, assign the data for each record to properties of an object, and put the object into a collection in the server tier. When the user interface needs a particular record, it can then request the associated object from the collection.

  Depending on the number of records in the recordset, this technique can be very inefficient. Imagine a customer table with 10,000 records. An application moves through each record, creates an object, transfers the data from the record to the object properties, adds the object to the collection, and repeats this 10,000 times. Five minutes later, the processing is complete! (Okay, that may be an exaggeration, but you get the point.)

A collection is a good technique for data transfer if the number of records is small or if you're working with data files. For example, all of the line items on an invoice could be retrieved from the database and kept in a collection. A simple example of using a collection to track data from a file is presented in Chapter 11, "Building Classes: Additional Techniques."

- **Recordset.** A recordset is a set of data retrieved from a database. If an application uses a collection to track a set of objects, the data must be copied from the recordset to the object properties as described earlier. Alternatively, the application could use the recordset itself as the collection of data. This saves the time and memory required to copy the data into the collection.

  The server tier can then manage the recordset. When the user interface requests a particular record, the record can be located within the recordset and returned to the user interface. This approach will be demonstrated in Chapter 14, "Doing Database Objects."

- **Array.** Data in a recordset can be copied into a two-dimensional array in the server tier. This array can then be passed from the server tier directly to the user interface tier. In this situation, there would be no need for a class for the object on the server tier with properties and methods. Nor would there be any need for a collection class. Rather, a class on the server tier would be responsible for accessing the recordset to fill the array and passing the array, or a single array element, to the user interface. With this technique, you may want to add a class to the user interface tier to handle the transfer of the array and the transformation of the array elements into object properties. This topic is discussed further under "User Interface Tier Components" earlier in the chapter.

To demonstrate several of these techniques, the contact management system will use a different technique for each component. This may not be desired in a real application where you would want some consistency in the approach.

The contact management system team decided to use a data control as the means of data transfer for the contact management data. This will simplify the code required to keep the text boxes and other controls on the form in synch with the grid on the form. A ContactEntries class will manage the recordset bound to the data control. Because this recordset can include both contact entry information and associated customer or prospect information, individual Customer and Prospect objects are not required.

For the address book data, the team will use the recordset data transfer approach. This prevents the performance hit of using a collection, yet provides more flexibility than the data control approach. Customer and Prospect classes will be defined to manage information about each address book entry and Customers and Prospects classes will manage the recordsets.

The to do list data will be stored in a file instead of a database. This allows the component to be easily reused in any application. The collection class data transfer approach will be used. The Task class will manage each to do list entry and the Tasks class will manage the collection of tasks.

Flattening the Hierarchy

It is difficult to navigate a deep hierarchy, one that has many levels. The application needs to go through each level to access a property of the lower-level objects. Deep hierarchies also make reuse more difficult because objects have references to all lower-level objects. If your hierarchy is deep, consider moving some objects up to a higher level. Consider a hierarchy of Company, Employees, and Goals. The company has a collection of employees and each employee has a collection of goals, as shown in Figure 7.6. The code to reference the description of the second goal for the first employee would be something like:

```
Company.Employees.Item(1).Goals.Item(2).Description.
```

Although this syntax may not yet look familiar (and isn't optimized), it is definitely not trivial. Also, to reuse the Employees and Employee class in a payroll application, the Goals and Goal classes would need to come along. Instead, the Goals and Goal classes can be moved up in the hierarchy as shown in Figure 7.7. This flattened hierarchy makes it easier to access each object and to reuse the classes.

Converting Subclass Relationships

You will need to convert any subclass ("is a") relationships defined for objects in the prior design steps during the Implementation-centered design. Depending on the classes involved, there are several options for converting a subclass relationship:

- **One class.** If the differences between the subclass objects are minimal, generalize all of the subclassed objects to the same class with a "type" property to identify the different types of these objects. You could do this in the contact management system example by generalizing the Customer and Prospect objects into a Person object with a Type property that identifies whether the person is a current customer or a prospect.

- **Separate classes.** If the differences between the subclass objects are substantial, generalize each set of subclassed objects into separate classes and repeat any common code in those classes. In the contact management system example, if the properties and behaviors for the prospects were significantly different from the properties and behaviors for the customers, separate Prospect and Customer classes would be appropriate.

Figure 7.6

A hierarchy with many levels makes sense in some situations, but it can add unnecessary complexity and limit reuse.

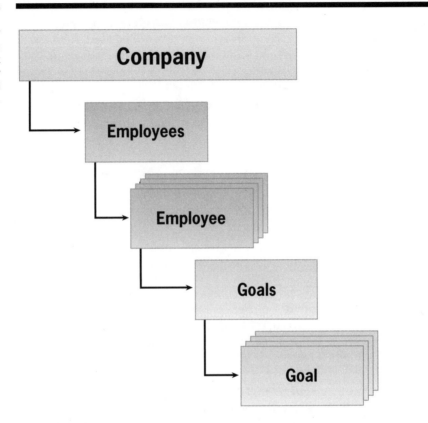

- **Delegation.** If the differences and the amount of common code are both significant, define a parent class and a class for each subordinate. The parent class will include the common code and the subordinate classes will contain the unique code. In Visual Basic 5, the subordinate classes do not automatically inherit the behavior of the parent class. Instead, the subordinate classes must implement the interface (properties and methods) defined in the parent class and then delegate to the parent class by calling its matching property or method.

Tech Note.   *This type of process is called* interface inheritance *because the subordinate classes inherit the interface of the parent class. This technique is demonstrated in Chapter 12, "Interfaces, Polymorphism, and Inheritance."*

Figure 7.7

Flattening the hierarchy can simplify the design and increase reuse in many situations where the objects are not tightly coupled.

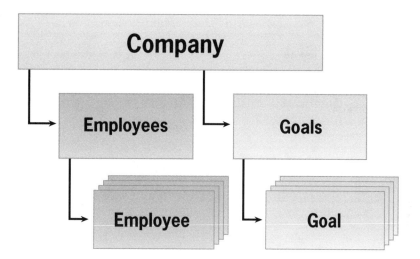

The subclass relationship defined for the contact management system is shown in Figure 7.5. The Person object is the parent and the Prospect and Customer objects are the subtyped, subordinate objects. The Person class could include the code for the common properties and methods. The Customer and Prospect classes could then implement the interface of the Person class (that is, include the declarations for the Property, Sub, and Function procedures) and delegate to the Person class, as shown in Figure 7.8.

Figure 7.8

To implement subclass relationships, delegate from the subordinate classes to the parent class.

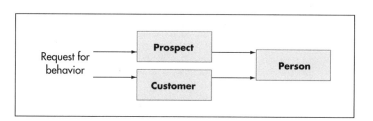

The contact management system team evaluated the defined subclass relationship and found that the differences between the Customer and Prospect objects were minimal. So they combined the objects into one Person class. This removes the Customers, Customer, Prospects, and Prospect objects from the object model and replaces them with Persons and Person.

After the entire process was complete, the contact management system team candidate object model was converted into the implementation object model shown in Figure 7.9 and documented in Table 7.1.

Figure 7.9

The candidate object model from the Goal-centered design is converted into an implementation model during the Implementation-centered design. This is the resulting implementation model for the contact management system.

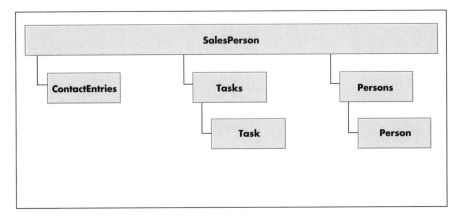

Table 7.1

The classes defined for the Contact Management System are described here.

CLASS	DESCRIPTION
SalesPerson	Defines information for the specific salesperson using the application. This is the topmost class in the object model.
ContactEntries	Manages the recordset containing the contact entries for the salesperson.
Tasks	Defines a collection of follow-up items or other tasks that the salesperson needs to track. Note that this class was renamed from FollowUpItems to allow more generic functionality.
Task	Defines an individual task on the to do list.
Persons	Manages the recordset containing the contact persons for the salesperson, both current customers and prospects.
Person	Defines an individual person to be contacted. This could be a current customer or a prospective customer.

Data Tier

The data tier provides the database services. These services are normally provided by the database product such as Microsoft Access, Microsoft SQL Server, or Oracle. No additional components are normally required for this tier. However, Microsoft SQL Server 6.5 can make calls to ActiveX components, so it is possible to define components which will be called from this tier.

For example, you could write a component to generate e-mail messages automatically. When specific data is changed in a database, a letter can be sent out to confirm the change or notify other users of the change. Another example is a component to access the Web to determine the current conversion factor for foreign currencies. When the database needs to calculate a total for an invoice, it can call the component to convert all currency transactions to one common currency.

Additional Components

The preceding topics have identified common types of components for each of the three tiers. There may be additional components needed by an application, such as application startup code, generic components that are reused in many applications, or implementation-specific components. Some of the possible additional components are described in the topics that follow.

The Sub Main ( ) Procedure

In Visual Basic, an application can be started by loading a specified form or by executing Sub Main, a Sub procedure named Main in a standard module. Which startup method you use is defined using a project property called Startup Object.

The Sub Main routine will execute the startup code for the application. Depending on the application, this may be trivial or it may be very complex. If the startup process is relatively complex, you should develop a flowchart like the one shown in Figure 7.10. This flowchart, and associated descriptive text, should be included in the detailed design document.

In addition to the processing shown in Figure 7.10, Sub Main can include other functionality such as checking for a previous instance of the application, displaying a login screen, and opening required databases or data files. The functionality needed in your application will depend on the project and environment requirements.

Keynote

You can add a Sub Main procedure to the user interface tier in an application. Using a Sub Main procedure instead of a form to start the application is both faster and more flexible. It can be faster because the standard module can be kept smaller so as to require less time to load than a form. It is more flexible because it allows the application to perform validation and other processing prior to loading the first form.

You can add a Sub Main procedure to the server tier in any separately compiled server component. In Visual Basic 4.0, this Sub Main procedure is required in any separately compiled component. In Visual Basic 5, this procedure is only required if the component needs to perform operations on startup of the component.

Figure 7.10

A flowchart can be used to illustrate the flow of complex procedures, such as the processing required when an application is started.

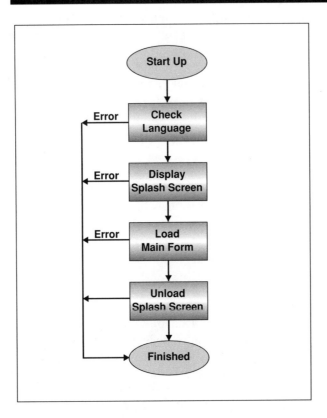

Continuing with the contact management system example, the technical staff designed the Sub Main routine as shown in Figure 7.10. The application will determine the user's selected language and display a splash screen in that language. A main form will then be loaded and the splash screen will be unloaded.

Generic Components

Most applications will need routines to handle files or databases, display an About box, or manipulate strings. Instead of designing and creating these routines for each application, you can design and develop them once and put them into generic support modules. These generic modules become prefabricated building blocks that you can add to any project.

Here are some common components and the types of routines which might be included in the modules:

- **Window class**. Provides for general window processing. This could include properties beyond those provided by the form, such as an OnTop property. It can also include routines for handling the Edit menu options, generic data validation, and so on. This component would normally appear in the user interface tier.

- **Error class**. Manages common error handling code and writing of errors to a log file.

- **String class**. Supplies additional string handling such as conversion or validation.

- **File class**. Includes routines to open, read, write, and close files.

- **Database class**. Provides routines to access databases. This component makes it easier to modify or replace the database with minimal impact on the application or use more than one type of database in a single application at the same time. This component would normally appear in the server tier.

- **Splash screen**. Provides an initial startup screen for the application.

- **About box**. Provides a dialog box that displays information about the application and the available system resources.

- **Login screen**. Provides for entry of a user ID and password and logs into the network.

Keynote

As you design these generic components, make sure that they are general and encapsulated. This will make it easier to reuse them. You can save these components to a Visual Basic Template subdirectory (for example, \VB\ Template\Classes) and the component will appear in the appropriate Add dialog box, as shown in Figure 7.11. This makes it easy to add the component to any project. If the template directory is defined on a shared file server, the entire department can share these generic components.

Implementation-Based Components

Additional components may need to be identified based on implementation requirements. These components have no real-world counterpart and exist for the sole purpose of the implementation. They can make the implementation simpler, more flexible, or more formal.

To identify the implementation-based components your application may require, consider each of the following issues:

- **Do any of your components have complex interactions with other components?** If so, you may want a component to manage the interactions. For example, an application that handles mail routing may need a routing component to coordinate the interaction of other components. Although "routing" is not in itself an object, a class can be defined to encapsulate the routing processing.

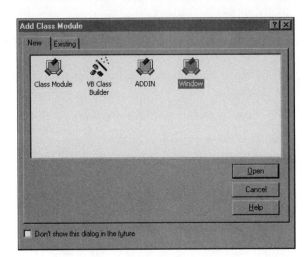

Figure 7.11

When Window.cls is placed in the Classes template directory, it appears in the Add Class Module dialog box and can easily be added to any project. Visual Basic also provides several templates, such as the ADDIN class template.

- **Does your application need to include legacy non-object-oriented code?** If so, you may want a component that handles all interaction with the non-object-oriented code. This type of component is called a *wrapper* because it wraps itself around the legacy code and handles all interactions with that piece of code using properties and methods. If the legacy code is ever modified or rewritten, only the one wrapper component will need to be modified. This is a good way to add object-oriented features to legacy applications.

■ Designing the Classes

Classes are comprised of properties and methods. The *properties* define the attributes for all objects created from the class. The *methods* are the implementation of the objects' behaviors. The properties and methods together define the *default interface* of the class. Classes can also have *events*. Events define the signals the object can generate. To design a class, you define the properties, identify and design the methods, and define the events.

The classes that were defined from real-world objects have a description of the properties and behaviors resulting from the Goal-centered design. Those object properties and behaviors are revisited and refined in this step.

For any new classes you have identified in this Implementation-centered design, you must identify the properties and methods. For all classes, you can define events if required for the implementation.

You may find that some classes have properties and no methods. This is common for the lowest level business objects that are responsible for the object's data. Other classes have methods but no properties. These are often called *function servers* or *stateless servers* because they only provide functions and don't keep any state properties. Function servers are especially useful in classes that will be managed with a pool manager. Objects from these classes can then be added to a pool, allocated to clients as needed, returned to the pool when no longer needed, and reused without regard for maintaining state information. See the section "Three-Tiered Client/Server Architecture" earlier in this chapter for more information on pool managers.

Defining the Properties

The *properties* for a class are the attributes or data for each object in the class. For each property, you need to define a name, data type, scope, description, and required validation. The results should be documented in the design document.

Think carefully about the name for each property. The same property name should be clearly understandable and used for the same attribute regardless of the class it is in. For example, in Visual Basic a control has a Caption property. A form also has a Caption property. Using one property name in both cases makes it easier to work with the classes.

In the contact management system example, the Person class will require a last name property, a first name property, and so on. Table 7.2 lists the properties defined for the Person class.

Each instance of a class will have a value for each of the defined properties. For example, one instance of the Person class could have a value of "Jessica" in the FirstName property and a value of "Jones" in the LastName property. Another instance could have different values for each property.

In addition to standard data types such as strings and integers, properties can include references to objects. If a class "has an" object within it, the class is a container and has a reference to the object as one of its properties.

In the contact management system example, the SalesPerson class "has a" list of all contacts made by the salesperson, all tasks on the salesperson's to do list, and a list of all persons assigned to the salesperson. Table 7.3 lists the properties for this SalesPerson class.

In most cases, you will implement the properties as private variables which are not accessible to any procedures outside of the class. For a class to be useful, however, there must be a way to access the property values for a specific object. This access is provided by public Property procedures.

Table 7.2

Properties of the
Person Class

PROPERTY NAME	DATA TYPE	SCOPE	DESCRIPTION
LastName	String	Public	Last name
FirstName	String	Public	First name
Name	String	Public	Concatenation of first name, a space, and last name
Address	String	Public	Address
City	String	Public	City
State	String	Public	State; should be two uppercase letters
ZipCode	String	Public	Zip code
Company	String	Public	Company
Title	String	Public	Title
Department	String	Public	Department name
Phone	String	Public	Phone number
FAX	String	Public	Fax number
Email	String	Public	E-mail address
PersonType	Integer	Public	Type of person: customer or prospect
Notes	String	Public	Notes about this person

Table 7.3

Properties of the
SalesPerson Class

PROPERTY NAME	DATA TYPE	SCOPE	DESCRIPTION
UserID	Long	Public, read-only	SalesPerson's user ID
ContactEntries	CContactEntries Object	Public, read-only	Manages the contact entries defined by this salesperson
Tasks	CTasks Object	Public, read-only	Manages the set of tasks for this salesperson
Persons	CPersons Object	Public, read-only	Manages the set of persons assigned to the SalesPerson

Property procedures were new in Visual Basic 4.0. They are used to get and set the values of the properties in a class. If you have ever written a procedure to set or retrieve the value of a module-level variable, you have written your own property procedure. If you have ever wanted to be able to access form-level variables in a form from outside of the form, you have wanted Property procedures.

A property that has a public Property procedure is said to be *exposed* to the other parts of the application. Every property of the class that needs to be exposed for read access will need a Property Get procedure. Every property of the class that is to be exposed for write access will need a Property Let (for non-object variables) or Property Set (for objects). For the Person class from the contact management system example, the Property Get Last-Name procedure returns the value of the private property variable and the Property Let LastName procedure assign the person's last name to the private property variable.

A public Property procedure in a public class is exposed both to the other parts of the application *and* to any other application. To expose a Property procedure in a public class to other parts of the application yet keep the Property procedure private from any other application, define the scope of the Property procedure using the Friend keyword instead of Public.

Tech Note.   *Variables cannot have Friend scope; only Sub, Function, and Property procedures can use the Friend keyword.*

Defining the Methods

Methods are the implementation of the objects' behaviors. They are the Sub and Function procedures that will be created in the application. You should define and document the list of methods for a class and decide which methods will be public and exposed to other applications and which should be private.

A public Sub or Function procedure in a public class is exposed both to the other parts of the application *and* to any other application. To expose a Sub or Function procedure in a public class to other parts of the application yet keep the Sub or Function private from any other application, define the scope using the Friend keyword instead of Public.

Document the list of methods for each class with a one- or two-line description. The calling convention (procedure name and parameters) for all public and friend methods should be clearly documented to ensure that the default interface for the class is well defined and can easily be used throughout the application. This is especially critical in multiprogrammer environments. Private methods do not generally require as much detail.

In most cases the documented class description, property list, and method list (with calling conventions for public methods) provide enough information for a programmer to implement a class. If there are portions of the application that are complex or computationally intensive, a low-level design may be needed. This low-level design is normally only done for key processes; all other procedure details are left to the construction phase of the project. The low-level design can include flowcharts, pseudo code, which is an English-like description of the required processing, or both. Totaling invoices and calculating heat transfer rates are examples of processes warranting low-level design as part of this step.

Depending on the type of calculation or process, the low-level design may require additional information from the users or subject matter experts. Reviewing how the calculations are performed manually will give you insight into how they must be done electronically.

Defining Interfaces

The properties and methods for a class define the default interface of the class. If your project team is developing a large application with many components, it may be desirable to define a standard set of properties and methods for use in every class or form or in a specific set of classes and forms. These definitions will assist in developing efficient code and maintaining consistency. Each programmer is then responsible for ensuring that each class (or form) does indeed include each standard property and method. Then a new developer comes along and needs to determine which standard properties and methods need to be included in a particular type of class. In Visual Basic 4.0 there is no easy way to do this beyond accurate documentation.

Keynote

Visual Basic 5 has a way to help. With VB5 you can define a set of related properties and methods as an *interface*. A class or a form can then implement this interface, thereby requiring that all properties and methods in the interface be implemented in the class or form. This guarantees that no standard properties or methods are missing from the class or form.

Tech Note. *Using an interface also provides for* polymorphism. *Polymorphism allows a routine to call a property or method on an object without knowing the type of object. Polymorphism was available in Visual Basic 4.0, but because the object type was not known most polymorphic calls were late bound. Using an interface provides for early binding. This technique is demonstrated in Chapter 12, "Interfaces, Polymorphism, and Inheritance."*

To define potential interfaces for an application, look through the list of properties and methods for the classes you have defined. Are there properties and methods included in several classes that could be defined as an interface? A Data interface could define query and save methods and a flag indicating that data is changed. A File interface could define read and write methods. An Address interface could define properties for street address,

Keynote

city, state, and zip code. This process of defining which properties and methods should be put into which interface is called *factoring*.

When defining the interface, be sure to select a logical set of related properties and methods that will not change. Once an interface is implemented in a component, the interface can not be changed. Think of this as a contract between the interface and all of the components that use the interface. Any code within a property or method of the interface can change, but the definition of the property or method (that is, the name and parameter list) cannot be changed without breaking the component implementing it.

If the contact management system team had decided to retain the subclass relationship between Person, Customer, and Prospect shown in Figure 7.5, this relationship could be implemented using an interface. A Person interface would be defined to include the common properties and methods for Customer and Prospect classes. The default interface for the Customer and Prospect classes would then include the unique properties and methods for customers or prospects.

Classes with multiple interfaces are frequently shown with lollipops, as in Figure 7.12. Each lollipop defines one interface for a class. The top lollipop in the figure defines the default interface—that is, the interface defined by the class's properties and methods. The bottom lollipop depicts the Person interface.

Figure 7.12

The properties and methods for a class can be factored into logical sets of functionality and encapsulated into interfaces.

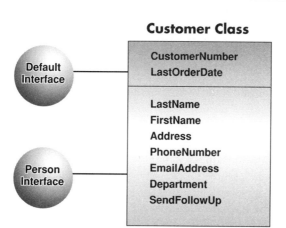

Defining Events

In prior versions of Visual Basic, all events were predefined. Forms had Load events, buttons had Click events, and classes had Initialize events. With Visual Basic 5, you can now define your own events for classes and forms.

Suppose you want a class to do some background processing and notify the application when the processing is complete, or a primary form needs to notify a secondary form when data on the primary form is changed. Events make this easy.

You should define the events you want for the classes and forms in this step. Some common events are a Notify event for completion of processing, a Change event for when a change in one component requires a response in another component, or a StatusChange event to keep a component informed of the status of another component.

The contact management system team decided to have the software provide notification whenever a task on the to do list was due. The team defined an Alarm event for the Task class that will be generated when the task is due.

■ Considering Implementation Issues

There is more to implementation than just building the components. You must consider several other factors which are described in the topics which follow.

Performance Requirements

What type of performance requirements does the application have? Where is that performance most critical: application startup, queries, response to form interactions? Different implementation strategies affect performance in different ways.

You should define and evaluate performance requirements before beginning to construct the application. During this Implementation-centered design step, you can develop prototypes to test selected architectures, database access strategies, and remote components to ensure that they will perform as expected.

Too often performance is ignored until the first delivery milestone. If the application does not perform within the requirements, you may simply have to tune the application or data design. Or, there may be a more serious design flaw that requires a major effort to re-architect the application. Performance testing now instead of later ensures that performance does not become an issue.

Enterprise Edition

If you have the Enterprise Edition of Visual Basic, you have the Application Performance Explorer (APE) utility developed by Microsoft. If you don't have the Enterprise Edition, you can download the APE from Microsoft's Web page. See "Additional Reading" at the end of this chapter for the URL. The APE utility provides features for performance testing and tuning distributed applications. Microsoft provides the source code for APE, which was written in Visual Basic, so you can modify it or use the code as an example.

Resource Constraints

What resource constraints does the system have? Will the application need to be optimized for memory usage instead of performance? What about network constraints?

Different implementation strategies also affect resource utilization in different ways. With today's cheap memory and storage capacities, this has become less of a problem. But if your application will need to be deployed on computers with 8 megabytes of memory and 640x480 monitors, you need to consider resources now and not during deployment. Network bandwidth can also be a major concern if you are deploying components across a network.

Security Requirements

What are the security requirements of the application? To answer this question you may need to answer several others questions first:

* Will the database need to be secured? If so, how?

* Will the application need to be secured? If it will have a login screen, how will the IDs and passwords be maintained?

* Would the Windows NT security features alone meet the security requirements? Are there Windows 95 systems to be supported as well?

* Do all users have access to all screens, or are some features of the application limited to a certain set of users?

* Do some users have read-only access to screens while others have read-write access?

* How will ActiveX components be secured against improper access?

Defining the appropriate security mechanisms during this design phase can simplify the implementation of the security plan. For example, you can design the user-interface components such that access to screens is checked and only the appropriate read-only or read-write access is provided. Implementing this type of feature from the original design is much easier than retrofitting it after the application is developed.

Designing Dynamic States Using State Transition Diagrams

Does your application, or the objects in the application, have complex dynamic states? Do the objects change their behavior based on the value of their properties? If so, the states should be identified and clearly documented.

An object model, such as the one shown in Figure 7.9 shows the static relationship between the objects in a set of classes. The object model does not illustrate the objects' dynamic behaviors. In many cases, the dynamic behavior of an object can easily be implemented based on the description of the procedures for the class. In other situations, the dynamic behavior is more complex and needs to be precisely designed. One way to model dynamic behaviors is with state transition diagrams, also called state machines.

What Are State Machines?

Many real-world objects have *states* or specific clearly defined conditions. Consider your dishwasher. It has an "empty" state, a "holding dirty dishes" state, an "is running" state, and a "clean, needs emptying" state. In addition, these objects have *events* that cause changes or transitions in the state. Dishes are put into the dishwasher, causing the transition between the "empty" state and the "holding dirty dishes" state. The "pushing the start button" event causes the transition between the "holding dirty dishes" state and the "is running" state.

A state machine can be illustrated in a state transition diagram using circles to represent the states and arrows to show the transition events between the states. As a simple example, the state transition diagram for the dishwasher is shown in Figure 7.13.

Figure 7.13

This state transition diagram depicts the dishwasher states and the events that cause transitions between those states.

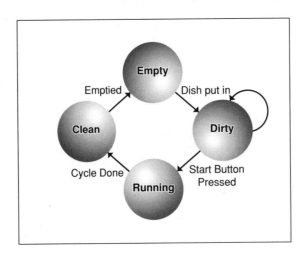

Using State Machines

So, you are not developing a dishwasher control application. What use are states in Visual Basic applications? Visual Basic is based on an event-driven paradigm. Everything that happens in a Visual Basic application is done through the generation and processing of events. The events and the application states can be represented with a state machine.

Let's look at an overly simplified—yet more relevant—example. An application has a Print option that displays a Print dialog box. The Print dialog box contains some selection controls and OK and Cancel buttons. The application has two primary events that can occur: Button_Clicked on the OK button or Button_Clicked on the Cancel button. The application has three states: Print dialog box not shown, Print dialog box shown, and printing. This is illustrated with the state transition diagram in Figure 7.14.

Figure 7.14

This simple state transition diagram shows the states for a printing application.

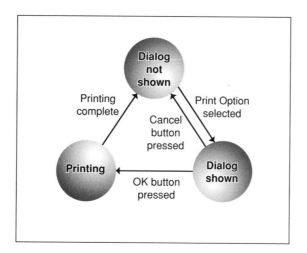

Examples of the types of processing best represented with a state machine are as follows:

- **Field validation**. Valid and invalid states can be defined with transitions based on focus or change events in the application.

- **Long tasks**. Instead of using DoEvents throughout the application, divide long tasks into states with transitions between the states. Printing, repaginating, and major database manipulation routines fit into this category.

- **Automatic saving**. New, displayed, and edited states can be defined with change, move, and button click events providing the transitions between these states. An example of this is described next.

The contact management system project team decided to use a state machine for automatic saving of address book information. (The address book was the user interface for the Person class.) The state machine defined for this feature is illustrated in Figure 7.15.

Figure 7.15

This state transition diagram illustrates the complexity involved in automatic saving of changes.

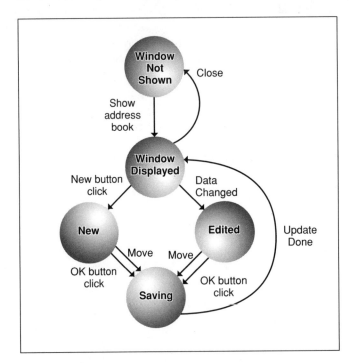

The states are as follows:

- **Not Shown**. The address book window is not shown.

- **Displayed**. The address book is shown.

- **New**. A new address book entry was requested. Note that changes made when in this state will not cause a transition to the Edited state because the new entry has not yet been saved.

- **Edited**. The current address book entry has been changed since the last time it was saved.

- **Saving**. The address book data is currently being saved. This is a defined state because other parts of the application, such as the error handling, will need to know this state.

The transitions are as follows:

- **Show Address Book**. The user requested the Address Book option. Changes the state to Displayed.

- **New Button Click**. The user clicked the New button to create a new address book entry. Changes the state to New.

- **Data Changed**. The user changed something in the current address book entry. Changes the state to Edited.

- **OK Button Click**. The user clicked the OK button to save the new or edited information. Changes the state to Saving. The routine that changes to the Saving state will evaluate the current state to determine whether a new entry is to be created or a current entry is to be updated.

- **Move**. The user moved to another record. This automatically saves the current record before moving to the other record. Changes to the Saving state.

- **Update Done**. The updating process is complete and the record returns to the Displayed state.

- **Close**. The user selected to close the address book. Changes the state to Not Shown.

Defining the states with a State Transition Diagram makes it easier to understand and implement the dynamic states of the application. See Dan Appleman's article referenced in the "Additional Reading" section at the end of this chapter for details on implementing state machines.

Evaluating Existing Design Patterns

Can existing design patterns be reused? One of the key benefits of an object-oriented system is the reusability of components. A Person class can be reused within any application requiring personal information such as name and address. Recently, the search for reusable components has moved up the software development process to the design itself. In addition to reusing implemented object-based components you can reuse object-oriented designs. You can reuse both the user-interface design and the design of the classes and their interactions.

As more and more systems have been modeled using object-oriented techniques, some class design patterns have been identified and documented (see the "Additional Reading" section at the end of this chapter). Studying these patterns provides you with standard design components that could take years to accumulate through your own design experiences.

A design pattern is comprised of a set of classes that communicate with each other to provide a specific type of functionality. These classes can then be applied to specific application requirements. For example, a State pattern provides a generic class design for implementing an object that alters its behavior when its state is changed. This pattern can be used to implement drawing tools, data validation, or network connection activities that change behavior based on the object's state. For more information, see *Design Patterns: Elements of Reusable Object-Oriented Software*, listed in the "Additional Reading" section at the end of this chapter.

As you design object-oriented systems, you can use existing design patterns and establish your own patterns. By identifying and documenting reusable design elements you can become a more productive designer and can share your expertise with others.

■ Validating the Implementation-Centered Design

Defining the implementation object model is an iterative process. You design some classes and try validating the classes. If any components are missing, if the object model is too vague, or if the classes are too cumbersome, you need to iterate back through the steps in this chapter again. When you have a clear object model with well-defined classes and you can successfully work through the scenarios for the application, you can consider your design "complete."

Revisiting Your Scenarios

In Goal-centered design, the project team defined scenarios to validate the object model for the application. In this step, those scenarios are used again to validate the final application design. Just as architects can walk clients through the design for a building, the technical staff can walk through the Implementation-centered design. This guarantees that all needed functionality can be accomplished efficiently.

Ensuring Complete Collaboration

Collaborators were identified for the real-world objects in the Goal-centered design. These collaborators defined the public methods that each object needed to use from other objects. Review the collaborators to ensure that all needed public methods are defined and well documented.

Creating a Prototype

Prototyping can refine the team's understanding of a specific design issue. It can ensure that a set of classes will be feasible to implement. If you plan to prototype your design at this point, you may want to jump ahead to the first two chapters of Part 3, "OOP: Constructing an Application." These chapters describe how to implement classes in Visual Basic.

■ Documenting the Implementation-Centered Design

The result of the Implementation-centered design step is normally a design document. This document provides the blueprints for the developers who will construct the application.

The Implementation-centered design document should contain the following:

- **Description of the system architecture.** Describe both the physical and logical architecture.

- **Component design.** Include the set of object models and associated descriptions for each component required for the application.

- **Definition of classes.** List the properties, methods, interfaces, and events for each class in each component.

- **Implementation issues.** Describe resolutions to the implementation issues.

- **Scenarios.** Document the results of the validation against the scenarios defined in the Goal-centered design.

■ Summary

- The focus of the Implementation-centered design is to convert the logical design defined during the prior steps into a physical design that is ready for implementation.

- Distributed computing has many strategic advantages in a corporate environment. Using a three-tiered architecture, applications can be divided into logical components that support the user interface, business processes, and data access.

- Begin the Implementation-centered design by defining the high-level view of the system architecture and identifying the components required for that architecture.

- Review the object model defined during the Goal-centered design and divide it into manageable components.

- Most components will have a single top-level class that will control access to the remainder of the component.

- Evaluate the candidate objects in the object model from the Goal-centered design step to determine the classes required for the application.

- Generalize classes or components where appropriate to make them reusable in other applications.

- Consider data transfer strategies and add appropriate data interface, conversion, or translation classes to the model.

- Flatten the object model when possible to simplify access to the lower level objects.

- Convert subclass relationships to a single class, individual classes for each subclass, or to an interface and subclasses that implement the interface.

- Define the properties, methods, interfaces, and events for the classes that make up each component.

- Consider implementation issues such as performance, resource constraints, and security.

- Validate the design with the original scenarios from the Goal-centered design.

- The Implementation-centered design document provides the blueprint for the construction of the application.

■ Additional Reading

Appleman, Dan. "Design True Event-Driven Code," *Visual Basic Programmer's Journal*, August/September 1994.

This article provides a clear example of developing a state machine with Visual Basic. Even though the example was done in Visual Basic 3.0, the basic philosophy is the same.

Betz, Mark. "InterOperable Objects," *Dr. Dobb's Journal*, October 1994.

The primary focus of this article is distributed object computing, and why this is important to today's businesses. It then introduces all of the key players and models in distributed computing, including CORBA, COM, and SOM.

Booch, Grady. *Object-Oriented Analysis and Design With Applications (The Benjamin/Cummings Series in Object-Oriented Software Engineering)*. Redwood City, California: The Benjamin/Cummings Publishing Company, 1994.

Booch provides an academic discussion of object-oriented design concepts. He then presents a specific notation and methodology for object-oriented design and applies them to several case studies implemented in Smalltalk, Object Pascal, C++, Lisp, and Ada.

Brooks, Frederick P., Jr. *Mythical Man Month: Essays on Software Engineering*. Reading, Massachusetts: Addison-Wesley Publishing, 1975.

This is the classic book about considering the human element in project planning and scheduling. The quote that appears at the beginning of this chapter is from this book.

Coad, Peter; North, David; Mayfield, Mark. *Object Models: Strategies, Patterns, and Applications*. Englewood Cliffs, New Jersey: Prentice-Hall, 1995.

This book walks you through an object-oriented design of five applications. It includes identifying the goal-centered and implementation-centered objects, selecting appropriate design patterns, and defining scenarios.

Donovan, John. *Business Re-Engineering with Technology: An Implementation Guide*. Cambridge: Cambridge Technology Group, Inc. 1993.

This book details the process of re-engineering a corporation using specific clients as examples. It includes a detailed discussion of the benefits of a client/server architecture and describes how to implement such an architecture in an organization.

Gamma, Erich; Helm, Richard; Johnson, Ralph; Vlissides, John. *Design Patterns: Elements of Reusable Object-Oriented Software*. Reading, Massachusetts: Addison-Wesley Publishing, 1995.

This book caused a large commotion in the object-oriented design community by offering a published set of very specific, reusable design patterns. These patterns are fundamental designs that can be applied to many different types of applications. It is like having an experienced OO software designer at your fingertips. Although the book was not written for Visual Basic, many of these designs can be implemented in Visual Basic. Using these patterns provides a base from which you can build your own set of reusable designs.

It is also interesting to note that this "gang of four" recommends "Favor object composition over class inheritance" in object-oriented design. This is in line with Visual Basic's use of object compositions (containers) and interface inheritance instead of class inheritance. (But it would be nice to have the choice!)

Goren, Craig. *Visual Basic 5 Enterprise Development*. Indianapolis, IN: Que, 1997.

This book focuses on advanced topics specific to the enterprise developer. Among other things, it covers ActiveX technologies, remote automation, DCOM, and the Microsoft Transaction Server.

Gray, N.A. B., *Programming with Class: A Practical Introduction to Object-Oriented Programming with C++*. New York: John Wiley & Sons, 1994.

Although this book focuses on developing C++ applications, it also provides a pragmatic approach to object-oriented design. Its example Space Invaders game provides insights into defining classes and implementing them in several OO languages (not in Visual Basic).

McConnell, Steve, *Code Complete: A Practical Handbook of Software Construction*. Redmond, Washington: Microsoft Press, 1993.

The primary focus of this book is on software construction. It includes details on designing routines, pseudo coding, and flowcharting that are applicable for this chapter.

"The Microsoft Object Technology Strategy." Microsoft Corporation, 1994.

This white paper describes Microsoft's Component Object Model (COM) and details Microsoft's strategy for object technologies. This paper provides a detailed, albeit biased discussion of COM and how the Microsoft object technology can be used to solve real business problems.

Rumbaugh, James; Blaha, Michael; Premerlani, William; Eddy, Frederick; Lorensen, William. *Object-Oriented Modeling and Design*. Englewood Cliffs, New Jersey: Prentice-Hall, 1991.

This book provides a thorough discussion of object-oriented concepts and object modeling. It then presents the Object Modeling Technique (OMT) as a methodology for software engineering. This book includes examples on implementing object-oriented techniques in C++, Ada, and Smalltalk.

Sneed, Anthony. "Create a Poor Man's SQL Server," *Visual Basic Programmer's Journal*, Vol. 6, No. 13, November 1996.

This article details a technique for creating an ActiveX component to off load Jet processing onto a remote computer. The result is a poor man's SQL server.

"A User's Guide To The Application Performance Explorer" at http://www.microsoft.com/vbasic/download/usingape.htm

This paper describes several models for distributed applications that are support by Microsoft's Application Performance Explorer (APE). It also includes instructions for using the APE utility for performance tuning.

■ Think It Over

To supplement and review the information in this chapter, think about the following:

1. How do you think distributed computing will affect how we develop software in the future?

2. In the Goal-centered design, you thought through how to add an appointment book object to the contact management system. That object was tied to the task list but shown in a calendar format. Now think through how this affects the Implementation-centered design.

3. Consider the benefits of interfaces. Look back at a prior project and how you could have defined some standard interfaces for the project.

4. Classes and forms can now generate programmer-defined events. Look back at a prior project and think about where you could have used an event.

5. Think through the high-level states for the radio in your car. Draw a state transition diagram for the radio.

6. Design patterns provide some standard components for the design. What are the benefits you could gain from collecting and reusing design patterns?

Data Design

The object-oriented paradigm is versatile. It not only provides a sound basis for designing systems and programming code but can also be used to design databases.

—James Rumbaugh *et al.*,
Object-Oriented Modeling and Design

Every nontrivial application works with some data. It may be business-related information such as customer name, employee hours worked, or invoice amount. The application may need values supplied from another system, like stock quotes or currency exchange rates. Some type of temporary data, such as object state information or intermediate calculations, may be required. The application may need configuration related information, such as the last four files the user accessed or the last user-selected window locations.

Regardless of the type of information or what your application does with it, the data needs to be designed in a logical manner so it can be easily manipulated. The application may want to add new data, review or edit existing data, or present the data in reports. A good design will make accessing the data easier.

This chapter describes the types of data you may need in your application and outlines how to design the interface between the application and that data. Because Visual Basic comes with the Microsoft Jet relational database engine, we'll take a brief look at designing relational databases. Finally, this chapter presents common data access architectures to help you evaluate the effects of your architecture on your data and application design.

■ What Is Data Design?

The D in the GUIDS methodology is for Data design, shown highlighted in Figure 8.1. The data required by the application was identified as object properties and data access strategies were defined in prior steps of the design. This step involves logically organizing that data and designing how the application will interface with that data.

The two primary questions you need to answer during the Data design are:

- How will the data be stored?

- How will the application interface with that data?

As you find the answers to these questions, be sure to document your results in a data design document. This ensures that the data design and data access mechanisms are well-defined both for yourself and anyone else working on the application now and in the future.

■ Sorting through the Data

When organizing the pile of papers on your desk, you sort through the papers and store each one somewhere. The papers you want to read through are stored in your in-box in a random (or sequential) order. Papers to be kept with related papers will be stored in a filing cabinet by some type of key

Figure 8.1

Data design organizes
and manages the
data for efficient
data manipulation.

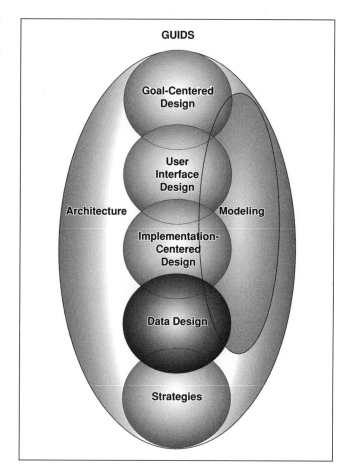

("project notes" or "time sheets," for example). Papers to be submitted to
management are put in your out-box. Those temporary notes you need while
you are working will be scattered about.

You begin designing your data using the same approach. You sort
through each data element defined for your application and decide how it
will be stored. The primary choices for data storage are

- Data file

- Database

- Registry

- Internal structures

Your application may use any number of these storage mechanisms for its data. To help you determine how your data should be stored, each of these mechanisms is discussed in the sections that follow and illustrated using the data for the contact management system example.

For review, the data defined for each class of the contact management system was as follows:

- **SalesPerson class.** User ID.

- **Person class.** Last name, first name, address, city, state, zip code, company, title, department, phone number, FAX number, e-mail address, person type, and notes.

- **ContactEntries class**. Person contacted, date/time of contact, contact type, and contact notes.

- **Task class.** Date/time due, task priority, and task description.

- **Other.** Last accessed contacts file and last position of primary window.

■ Storing Data Efficiently in a Data File

A *data file* is a stream of data stored in one physical file. The file can be accessed sequentially, reading character by character or line by line. If the data is stored in the file in multiple repeating groups, called *records,* you can access the data randomly by record number. To achieve the most control over the data, you can use binary files to store and retrieve information.

When to Use a Data File

Data files are the best choice for data elements in the following situations:

- **The application data must make efficient use of disk space.** Databases are normally created with a large minimum size, so even if there are only a few data elements the database size may be over 130KB. If disk space is an issue, or if only a few fields need to be stored, a data file is an efficient solution.

- **The application must be distributed as efficiently as possible.** Databases require a set of additional (large) components. If you need an efficient distribution of your application, you may not want the additional size and extra files required by a database. For example, if you are developing a shareware application that must be downloaded from an online service, you will want to store your data in a data file.

- **The data is already in a data file**. Your application may need to process data that is provided in a data file. For example, information from a hardware device is output into a data file and must be read by your application.

- **The data needs to be imported to or parsed by another application**. If another application will need to read and process the data, you may need to use a data file. For example, a set of financial information that is to be imported into Excel could be in a sequential data file. Files that will be uploaded to a central computer may need to be in a data file that can be parsed by the central computer.

- **The data needs to be viewed in a text editor**. Lines of information can be written to a sequential data file and viewed using a text editor. For example, if your application creates an error log or transaction log that is to be viewed by a text editor, a sequential data file is a good choice.

After heated discussions, the contact management system project team decided that the salespeople will keep their to do lists on their local PCs in a binary data file. This makes it easier for them to take the to do list on the road and kept the data private.

Interfacing with a Data File

The mechanism used to interface your application with a data file depends on how the data file will be used. Regardless of your approach, you will want to define some specific routines to handle your file processing.

If the primary data required and manipulated by the application is in the data file, the most common approach is to retrieve the data from the file(s) at the start of the application. This data is then stored in internal structures, such as collections or user-defined types (UDTs). At the end of the application (or during save operations), this data can be written back to the file(s). At this step in the design process, you may want to define the structure of the UDTs or the index and key for the collections. This is especially important in projects with multiple programmers to ensure that all modules are working with the same data structures.

Using this approach, your file processing routines will need to open the file to read it, read the data from the file into the internal structures, and close the file. When the data is saved, the routines will need to open the data for write access, write the data from the internal structures to the file, and close the file. You could implement this by defining a File class with methods to handle the open and close and a property for the open file number. Each class in the application could contain a method to read/write the object's data. This implementation is detailed in Chapter 11, "Building Classes: Additional Techniques."

If the data files are used for support functions, such as storing configuration information, you may not need to store the information from the file in the application. Rather, you can open the file, perform the required operation on the file (such as writing the error log entry), and then close the file.

Because the processing for this file management may be very specific, the open, data operation, and close may be in one method. If this same processing is more generic and used for several types of log files, for example, then a more generic class with specific methods may be appropriate.

■ Using a Database for Flexibility

One way to store data for an object-oriented system is an object database. An object database management system (ODBMS) allows storage and retrieval of complete objects. ODBMS products are becoming more well known and several ODBMS vendors now provide tools to integrate their products with Visual Basic. One such product is Poet ODBMS from Poet Software. (See http://www.poet.com for more information.) Watch for more information on ODBMS products and tools in the near future.

The most common method for storing data is a *relational* database. A relational database management system (RDBMS) stores data as related sets of *tables*. A table is a logical grouping of related data elements that are stored in a row and column format, like a spreadsheet. There is one row for each record and one column for each field in the table. For example, in an employee table there would be fields for name, address, phone, and occupation. Each record would represent one employee. Jessica Jones would be one record and Sam Smith would be another record. Each record has independent values for the fields.

As you can see, this matches closely with the object-oriented design. Generally, the data for one class can be stored together in one table (or set of normalized tables). Each object of that class has a record in the table(s). The properties for each object are the fields in that record.

When to Use a Database

Relational databases are the best choice for data in the following situations:

- **The data is to be used in ad hoc reports**. Several report generation packages—such as Crystal Reports, which comes with Visual Basic, or ReportSmith—will read information stored in a database and generate ad hoc reports. Using a database and a reporting package provides flexible retrieval of information and relieves you from having to develop a large amount of code to generate reports.

- **The data will be queried in an ad hoc fashion**. A database has the flexibility to collect information in many different ways. For example, the database can easily provide the answers to queries such as "which customers from the mid-western region have not been contacted within the last 30 days?"

- **The data needs to be shared by other applications or multiple users**.
  Most database products, including Microsoft Access, provide facilities
  for sharing information, such as security, locking, and integrity checking.
  If the data is to be shared with other users or other applications, the data
  should be stored in a database. For example, an application creating customer data used by several users in the sales department is best implemented using a database.

- **The data is already in a database**. Your application may need to process
  data currently stored in a database. For example, the current customer
  data may already be on a centralized server.

The downside of a database is the required overhead, both in space and
performance. For example, if your application uses the Microsoft Access database, you must deliver it with several large components. This overhead is
acceptable when data is a primary purpose of your application. It will probably not be acceptable if you are storing just a few data elements.

Reviewing the data for the contact management system, a database was
chosen for salesperson, contact person, and contact entry data because this
data will be stored on a file server and accessed by multiple concurrent users.
The salespeople will access their own data, but the sales management will
want summary reports of all contact information.

Interfacing with a Database

Visual Basic provides three primary techniques for interfacing the application with a database: the Data control, Data Access Objects (DAO), and
data access APIs. You can use the Data control or DAO to go through the
Microsoft Jet database engine directly to Microsoft Access. Or, you can use
them to go through Jet and through the Open Database Connectivity
(ODBC) drivers to a remote database such as Microsoft SQL Server or Oracle. An additional alternative available with DAO 3.5, which is provided with
Visual Basic 5, is to use the Data control or DAO to go through the Remote
Data Objects (RDO) libraries using ODBCDirect and through the ODBC
to a remote database.

The Enterprise Edition of Visual Basic supplies two additional options:
the Remote Data control (RDC) and Remote Data Objects (RDO). RDO
provides a thin layer over the ODBC for access to remote databases such as
Microsoft SQL Server and Oracle.

EE

**Enterprise
Edition**

These techniques are shown in Figure 8.2 and described in the following
paragraphs.

Another technique for interfacing an application with a database is Active Data Objects (ADO). ADO provides a data model for accessing OLE
DB data sources. OLE DB is a new specification for a common interface to

Figure 8.2

Visual Basic provides
many choices for
transferring data between
the user interface tier
and the data tier.

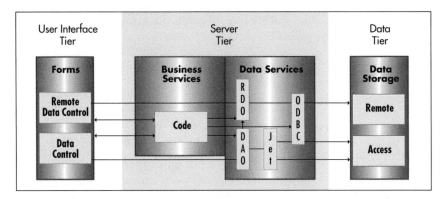

many different types of data sources on different types of systems. OLE DB allows seamless integration of data from the mainframe, UNIX servers, and Windows workstations. Although the ODBC works primarily with relational data, OLE DB provides for alternative data architectures. As of this writing, ADO was not provided as part of Visual Basic 5 and is therefore not shown in Figure 8.2. For more information on ADO, see the Roger Jennings' article referenced in the "Additional Reading" section at the end of this chapter.

Binding the UI to the Database Using the Data Control

The simplest approach to interfacing with the database is to use the data control. The data control is a tool in the Visual Basic toolbox that can be added to any form. It provides a link from the form in the user interface (UI) tier of the application to the database. By specifying database information in the data control properties, the data control is bound to a specific set of data from the database, called a *recordset*. That recordset is part of the DAO.

Data-aware controls, such as text boxes and list boxes, can be bound to individual fields in the data control's recordset. The user of the application can access records in the database using the visual interface of the data control and the fields in the record will automatically appear in the bound controls. The data control handles all inserts, updates, and deletions automatically. This connection is shown in Figure 8.2 as a line between the data control in the user interface tier through the DAO.

The advantage of using the data control and bound controls is that it is easy and requires very little coding (or none at all). This approach is excellent for developing prototypes because it's quick. Improvements to the performance and flexibility of the data control and bound controls in Visual Basic make this a valid option for straightforward production-level systems as well.

The downside of this approach is that it ties the user interface directly to the database. This makes it more difficult to modify the database because changes in the database may need to be reflected in all of the forms that contain a data control tied to that database. In addition, no business servers can be accessed to perform validation or conversion.

The contact management system team decided to use the data control for the contact entry data to minimize the amount of coding required to keep the data entry fields and the grid on the Contact Management window in synch. The implementation of this technique is detailed in Chapter 14, "Doing Database Objects."

Interfacing with the Data Access Objects (DAO)

A more difficult, but more flexible approach to interfacing your application with a database is to use the Data Access Objects (DAO) directly. The DAO object model provides an object-oriented interface to the Microsoft Jet database engine. You can use the objects and collections in the DAO object model to work directly with the transactions, tables, records, fields, or queries in the database. The Jet engine handles the mechanics of accessing the data from the data storage area. This process is shown with the arrow coming from the Code box through the DAO through Jet in Figure 8.2.

The direct link between the Jet engine and the physical data storage shown in Figure 8.2 is for data stored in a database supported by the Jet engine, such as Microsoft Access. Other types of databases are supported through an additional layer called the Open Database Connectivity (ODBC) layer. This layer provides access to remote databases such as Microsoft SQL Server and Oracle. In the figure, this is depicted with the line between Jet and the ODBC.

Going through the DAO and through Jet and then through the ODBC is a long way to go to retrieve data from remote databases, especially considering the size of Jet. Visual Basic 5 with DAO 3.5 provides a new interface from the DAO through RDO to the ODBC for faster and more full-featured access to remote databases. This interface, called ODBCDirect, is shown in Figure 8.2 with the arrow from the DAO through RDO through the ODBC.

The advantage of using the DAO approach is its flexibility and expanded functionality. Features are provided to create or modify any database component. You can work with data generically instead of by matching field names to user interface controls. The disadvantage of this approach is the large amount of coding required compared with using the data control and bound controls.

In the contact management system example, DAO was selected as the technique of choice for accessing Person information from the database. The code required to implement this technique is demonstrated in Chapter 14, "Doing Database Objects."

Keynote

Using a Data Access Application Programming Interface (API)

For optimal performance with a specific database product, you can directly access the database engine using the data access application programming interface (API) that is appropriate for the database. You can use the Open Database Connectivity (ODBC) API to access any ODBC-complaint database.

The advantages of this approach are optimization and completeness. Each API will be optimized for accessing all of the functionality available for a specific database. The disadvantage of this system is its direct tie to a specific database. If a different database needs to be supported, an entirely different API may be required. (This effect can be minimized if the application creates wrapper methods around the database API calls.)

With the new remote access objects and the improved performance, this option is no longer necessary in many cases.

Enterprise Edition

Binding the UI to the Database Using the Remote Data Control (RDC)

The Enterprise Edition of Visual Basic provides the remote data control (RDC). This control allows connections to remote ODBC data sources through RDO. Like the data control, the RDC can be used to bind controls to fields in a result set. The remote data control automatically handles inserts, updates, and deletions. The pros and cons of this approach are the same as those for the data control described earlier.

Enterprise Edition

Interfacing with the Remote Data Objects (RDO)

The Enterprise Edition of Visual Basic provides Remote Data Objects (RDO) as an alternative to DAO when working with remote databases such as SQL Server and Oracle. The RDO accesses external ODBC sources, bypassing the Jet database engine. Because the RDO provides a thin layer over the ODBC, it is significantly faster than going through the DAO and Jet engine when accessing remote databases. The RDO differs from the DAO with ODBCDirect in that it is an entirely different object model. It also provides additional features not available in the DAO such as event notification. See the *Guide to Building Client/Server Applications with Visual Basic* document that comes with the Enterprise Edition of Visual Basic for more information.

■ Registering Configuration Data in the Registry

The Windows *Registry* is a single, system-wide file that is maintained by Windows 95 and Windows NT for storing configuration information. The registry provides an alternative to the Config.sys, System.ini, Win.ini, and other .ini files used in prior versions of Windows.

The registry provides a better and more standard place for configuration information. It provides the user with one location for all configuration information instead of many application-specific files. The registry can be secured, can support individual entries for multiple users (so it can be on a network), and can be administered remotely. It cannot be inadvertently edited with a text editor.

When to Use the Registry

You can use the Windows Registry for the following types of information:

- **Application status information**. To help users, your application should remember its state when the user exits and return to that state when the user runs the application again. This state would include things such as the window positions and the last opened files.

- **User-defined preferences**. If your application allows user-defined preferences, you could store them in the registry. For example, your application may allow the user to turn off the Welcome screen. You could store a flag for this in the registry.

Keynote

Any type of information you may have put it into an initialization (.ini) file, you can now store in the registry. This is not to say that .ini files are no longer used. Some information may still be easier to store in an application-specific .ini file than in the registry. This is especially true when the user may want to copy the information between systems such as an office workstation and a laptop.

Interfacing with the Registry

There are two methods for accessing data in the Windows registry. You can use the registry functions provided in Visual Basic or you can access the registry directly using API calls.

Although they are easy to use, the registry functions are limited. All settings are written to the registry entry HKEY_CURRENT_USER\Software\VB and VBA Program Settings*appName**section**key*, where *appName*, *section*, and *key* are the only values that you can define using the registry function parameters.

Using the API to access the Windows Registry is much more flexible. You can define any registry entries. However, this approach is also more complex because you need to navigate the registry on your own. This is not an easy task, unless you are familiar with the hierarchical design of the registry. For more information on using the API to access the registry, see the "Additional Reading" section at the end of this chapter.

The contact management system team decided to store the last accessed contacts file and the last position of the primary window in the registry using the registry functions provided by Visual Basic. The implementation of this strategy is presented in Chapter 15, "Putting the Pieces Together."

■ Permanent and Temporary Internal Data

There are two types of internal data: permanent and temporary. Permanent data is obtained from an external source (file, database, registry), stored internally during application execution, and then stored back into the external source. Most applications that process files use internal permanent data storage. The file is opened, the data is read into some variables, and the file is closed.

Temporary data is easy to recognize because it does not exist outside of the application. If the data is not stored anywhere, it is internal temporary data. Variables for intermediate calculations or strings and internal state information are examples of temporary data.

Real-time applications make extensive use of internal temporary data. The state information common in a real-time application has no relevance once the application has terminated. For example, a stock ticker server application would receive update messages from a host system and would receive request messages from a client application. The content of these messages would need to be stored internally, but is not needed after the application terminates.

Regardless of the type, permanent or temporary, internal data is stored in variables or arrays. These variables and arrays can be given a logical structure by using user-defined types (UDTs) or objects and collections.

Interfacing with Internal Data

Interfacing with internal data is dependent on the data scope. Data scope identifies which parts of the application can read and write a particular data element.

Keynote

Internal data elements defined to be global, or public, will be available to any part of the application. Any routine can access or modify global data elements. This makes global values convenient, but dangerous. You can think of global data as a billboard along the freeway. If I want to meet you for lunch, I could write the place and time as a global value on a billboard. When you go by the billboard, you don't know for certain that what you see on that billboard is what I wrote. I may not have written anything yet. Or, someone else could have drawn a 1 in front of the 1 o'clock in the message so you show up at 11 when I did not expect you until 1.

Module-level data elements are private to the module in which they are defined. No other module in the application can read or modify the value directly. If the data element is a property of an object, Property procedures can be defined to provide read-only or read/write access to the value and still keep the data element private. You can think of a module-level data element as a note on your refrigerator. No one from the outside can see or modify the note, unless you specifically let them in.

Procedure-level data elements are local to the specific routine in which they are defined. Their values exist only when the routine is executing.

Procedure-level data elements are primarily used for temporary data, such as the interim value in a calculation and loop counters.

■ Designing a Relational Database

Because the relational model is the most common data storage mechanism for Visual Basic applications, it seems appropriate to include a section on designing the layout of a relational database. A relational database arranges data based on its relationship to other data in the database. It divides the data into logical homogeneous units and uses simple identifiers to define the relationships between the units. For example, all customer data is in one unit and all invoice data is in another unit. Storing a customer ID with each invoice establishes the relationship between the invoice and the associated customer. This arrangement is independent of the physical storage of the data.

To design a relational database that is flexible, yet efficient, follow these steps:

- Define a table for each of the application's objects that have database data.

- Define the primary key for each table.

- Normalize the data.

- Tune for performance.

Defining the Tables

In many relational database design methodologies, the first step is to identify the entities involved with the database and to develop an entity model. An entity is an object that has associated data, such as departments and employees. The entity model shows the relationships between these entities. Using object-oriented techniques and the GUIDS methodology, you've already defined the objects. Now you can take the objects and develop an entity model, as shown in Figure 8.3.

The SalesPerson entity in Figure 8.3 is responsible for one or more contact persons and has one or more contact entries. Each contact entry is for one and only one contact person, but each contact person can have any number of contact entries. Notice how similar this model is to the class model shown in Figure 7.9. Each object in the object model that has database properties is shown in this entity model. You can then follow the steps for normalization to improve this design.

Figure 8.3

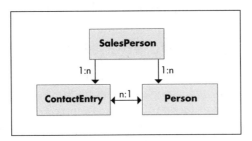

The entity model for the contact management system depicts the relationship between the SalesPerson, ContactEntry, and Person data.

Defining the Primary Key

A *primary key* is a unique identifier assigned to each record in a table. It is used to uniquely identify the record and connect related data in different tables to this record. For example, each record in the Person table will have an assigned person ID as the key. Each contact entry in the ContactEntry table has a person associated with it, so a person ID is stored in each ContactEntry record. This person ID can be used to find all contact entries for a particular person.

Keynote

An important point here is to ensure the defined keys are meaningless. For example, the person's name should not be a key. If the name was used as a key, it would take up more space than a numeric key, and it would run the risk of needing correction. If there were 30 different contact entries for Jessica Jones and she married Sam Smith (and she decided to change her name), every one of the 30 records would need to be updated to Jessica Smith. Instead, a unique, meaningless number should be assigned to each record and used as the key, such as a counter or identity column.

A manager at a utility company told me they had once used the customer's phone number as the primary key in many of their critical databases. If a customer's phone number changed, the keys could not be changed so a new record had to be created. The technical staff had to develop many additional program features to allow the creation of these new records and copying of historical information from one record to another. You could avoid this by using meaningless keys.

The Normalization Process

Once you have the tables and keys, you need to perform something called *normalization*. Normalization involves following a set of rules to remove redundancy and inconsistencies in the database. This results in a more flexible (and semantically correct) database structure. Normalization involves the following:

- **Ensure that there is no repeating information**. For example, the contact management system currently assumes that a contact is made with only one contact person. If a future request required tracking of all of the people in a conference call or at a meeting, the ContactEntry table could be modified to allow a list of contact persons for any one contact entry. This, however, would be a repeating group. Instead of adding some arbitrary number of repetitious fields in the database for each person, you should move the repeating information to a separate table. In this case, you can define an additional contact entry person table with records for each person involved with a specific contact entry.

- **Ensure that all data in a table is related to the table key**. For example, the ContactEntry table has a key that uniquely identifies each contact entry record. That contact entry record would not include the salesperson's commission rate because that does not relate to the key of the table.

- **Ensure that all data in a table is independent and has no unnecessary relationships**. No data in the table should depend on other data in the table. Some data designers generalize this to mean no calculated fields, but actually this has a much broader implication for no redundancy. For example, with the new contact entry person records, each record would contain the key to the person table identifying the person contacted and the key to the contact entry table identifying the associated contact. The salesperson's ID does not need to be in the contact entry person's table because that data element is not independent. It is already defined in the relationship between the contact entry and the salesperson's record.

Tech Note.   *From an academic perspective, normalization has three basic forms:*

- *First Normal Form. A table is in first normal form if all of the data elements are atomic. That is, the data elements are in a simple, tabular structure and there are no repeating groups.*

- *Second Normal Form. A table is in second normal form if it is in first normal form and every data element in the record is dependent on the record's key.*

- *Third Normal Form. A table is in third normal form if it is in second normal form and all of the fields in the table are mutually independent.*

Other normal forms that deal primarily with compound keys have been defined. In most cases, getting to the third normal form is sufficient. See the "Additional Reading" section at the end of this chapter for references to additional information on this topic.

One benefit of normalization is flexibility. What if a company had repeating location address groups and then needed another location? (As many times as the users tell you they will *never* need another one, you can be guaranteed there will be another one!) You would need to add the new location fields to the department table and modify the software to handle the new fields. If these locations were in a separate table, adding a new location would simply involve adding a new record to the table. No software changes would be required.

Tuning for Performance

With normalized tables comes the need to perform *joins*. Joins refer to the combination of records based on a defined matching field. For example, the SalesPerson and ContactEntry tables could be joined on the salesperson ID to find all of the contacts made by a specific salesperson. As you may guess, performing joins requires some processing time. Performing very complex multi-joins requires noticeable processing time. For this reason, you may want to develop a database prototype to get a feel for the performance of your database design.

Keynote

The primary goal in creating a database prototype is to determine performance for some of the data accessing that will be done in the final application. If the application will retrieve data from the server, the prototype should access the server. If the application will join six related tables, the prototype should perform this join. If the database will normally have ten concurrent users, the prototype should be tested with that number of users. To ensure that the information gleaned from your prototype is accurate, you should create enough fake data to fill the database to its expected size.

After developing this prototype, you may find a particular, frequently used join is too slow. To improve the performance, you can consider adding additional indexes or denormalizing the table. This may involve adding calculated or redundant fields in the record, breaking the normalization rules.

■ Common Data Access Architectures

As part of the Data design for a specific application, it is important to look at the organization's data access architecture. This answers such questions as "how will the data for this application fit into the current data processing architecture?" and "is the data needed for this application already available?"

There are several common data configurations:

- **Local Configuration.** Data is local to the user's computer.

- **Network Configuration.** Data is available on a network.

- **Data Server Configuration.** Data is accessed through a data server application.

- **Data Snapshot Configuration.** A snapshot of the data is downloaded and accessed.

The configuration for your application's data may fit one of these common architectures, it may be a combination of several configurations, or it may be unique. Reviewing the data architecture that is applicable to your application helps to identify additional considerations for your Data design.

Local Data Configuration

The local data configuration is the simplest architecture, as shown in Figure 8.4. If your application is to be installed on individual computers with data local to the computer, it uses this type of configuration.

Figure 8.4

In a local data configuration, all data is accessed on the local hard drive.

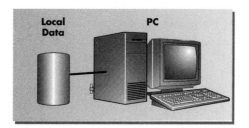

With this type of data configuration, there are no concerns for network support or multiple users accessing the data. The data can be in data files or in a database. The type of file or database is less important, since it will not need to be shared. Microsoft Access may be a good database choice here because support for Access is integrated into Visual Basic.

Networked Data Configuration

The networked data configuration has a database on a network drive that is shared between the users, as shown in Figure 8.5. This is often called a file server configuration. Each PC on the network can access its own local files and can access the database on the file server.

This configuration is commonly used for small workgroup applications where the shared data is stored on the file server. For example, the PCs in the sales department are networked and share a central database of contact information. As another example, the contact management system development team can use this configuration for source code control whereby the project resides on the server and each developer checks files out for editing.

Figure 8.5

In a networked configuration, data can be accessed locally or from a shared network drive.

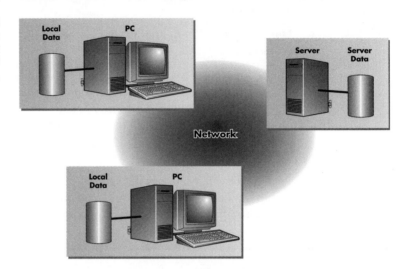

When using a network configuration, you need to consider the issues of nctwork support and multiple users accessing the data. You will want to select a database that provides the needed locking, data integrity, security, and so on. Microsoft Access is still a good choice in this situation. However, if there are over 40 or so users concurrently accessing the data, you may want to consider the next configuration.

Data Server Configuration

The data server configuration is a type of client/server approach. In this configuration, there is a separately running data server application that retrieves the data from the database. Your (client) application does not retrieve the data from the database but rather requests information from this data server, as shown in Figure 8.6.

An application can directly access local data, but to access information on the server, the client application on the PC must request the desired data from the data server application. The data ordering and filtering is done on the server and only the required data is transferred down the network back to the local client application.

Alternatively, the application can use the remote data control or remote data access objects to access the remote data. The functionality of the data server application is then provided by the remote data objects.

Because all data requests are through the data server application, the physical data design is completely hidden from the client application. The data could be stored anywhere in any format and the client application would not

Figure 8.6

The data server
configuration allows client
applications to request
data services.

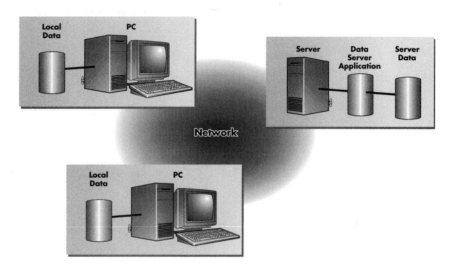

need to know. The data format could also change without affecting the client application. That is why this type of configuration is becoming very popular.

Tech Note.   *The data server application can also support triggers. These are procedures stored on the server that are executed by the server when specific actions occur. Triggers can perform data validation before an insert, check for referential integrity issues on a delete, or verify valid edits before an update.*

The data server configuration is best suited for any data access intensive application, any application with distributed databases, or any application in which the structure of the database must be kept separate from the access to the data. Microsoft SQL Server and Oracle are examples of products that support this type of configuration.

Data Snapshot Configuration

Snapshots are copies of data at one particular point in time. The data snapshot configuration involves periodically taking a snapshot of data from another computer and storing it either locally or on a network, as shown in Figure 8.7.

At periodic intervals, a snapshot of the data from the host computer is downloaded to a server file. Each PC on the network can then access this data without the network traffic to the host computer. This configuration can be combined with the data server configuration so the snapshot data can be retrieved through a data server.

This configuration is best suited for situations where the data for the application is read only, does not need to be current, and comes from a high-traffic

Figure 8.7

In a data snapshot configuration, a read-only copy of the data can be accessed. This copy is normally refreshed from the host database on a regular basis.

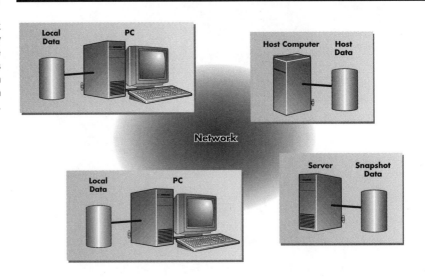

mainframe or other computer. This scenario is most common in decision support applications where the user works with corporate data to make operating decisions or review past performance.

When using this type of architecture, you may need to develop a support application that periodically retrieves the data from the host computer and transfers it into a database for use in the primary application.

Additional Considerations

As part of the Data design, consider the following:

- **DBA.** Is there a database administrator (DBA) responsible for the database you plan to use or need to modify? If so, that person or group of people need to be involved early in the Data design process.

- **Database tool.** Different database tools provide different features. Select the tool that best meets the goals for the application.

- **Volume/size of the data.** A data accessing architecture that works well with small amounts of data may not work as well when the volume of data gets very large.

- **Data integrity.** You need to consider the issue of data integrity to ensure that the correct level of integrity can be achieved with the architecture and database tool.

- **Security.** Database tools often provide additional levels of security beyond that provided with the network.

- **Network traffic.** If a network is very busy, the data configuration must be such that only the required data is transferred down the network.

- **Performance.** The data architecture in concert with the defined data design can have a significant impact on the performance of the data accessing.

Understanding the expected data architecture and the impact of these issues will help you to make intelligent data design decisions.

■ Documenting the Data Design

The result of the Data design step is normally a design document. This document provides information on the data fields, tables, schema, and other data structures used in the application.

The data design document should contain the following:

- **High-level data design.** This should discuss when and where data files, databases, the registry, and other data accessing will occur. It should also discuss what database product will be used, if any.

- **Database design.** If a database will be used, this section lists each field in each table of the database. It should include the entity model or relationship diagram.

- **Stored procedures/triggers.** If the selected database product supports stored procedures or triggers, they should be defined in this document.

- **File formats.** If custom files will be used, document the internal format of these files including access and locking strategies if the files will be shared over the network.

- **Configuration Settings.** Document the names of keys, subkeys, values, and data types of registry settings or the structure of .ini files or custom configuration files.

■ Summary

- Data design defines the data used by your application and how the application will interface with that data.

- Begin the Data design by reviewing the data required for the classes in the application and deciding how each will be stored: in a data file, a database, the registry, and/or internally.

- Select to store data in data files when the data needs to be imported from or exported to another system, when a text file is desired, or when the speed or overhead of a database does not meet the requirements of the application.

- Select to store data in a database when the data must be accessed by multiple users or ad hoc queries or reports are needed.

- The registry is a configuration file that can be used to store application configuration and state information.

- Internal data is the data stored within the application. That data can be stored in simple variables, user-defined types (UDTs), or in an object or a collection.

- Designing a relational database requires examining the relationships between data and making trade-offs between a normalized design and performance.

- The data access architecture your application must support affects the design of the data.

- The Data design document provides details on the data and how it will be stored.

■ Additional Reading

Appleman, Daniel. *Dan Appleman's Visual Basic 5.0 Guide to the Win32 API*. Emeryville, California: Ziff-Davis Press, 1997.

This book is an excellent source of information on accessing the Windows Application Programming Interface (API). It is listed as additional reading for this chapter because it provides detailed information on using the API to access the Windows Registry.

Codd, E.F. *The Relational Model for Database Management, Version 2*. Reading, Massachusetts: Addison-Wesley Publishing Co., 1990.

E.F. Codd invented the relational model. He describes it fully in this book.

Jennings, Roger. "Activate Data Objects with OLE DB," *Visual Basic Programmer's Journal*, December 1996

This article quotes Microsoft to say, "Over time, all our products will standardize on ADO and OLE DB." It then describes the OLE DB object model and how it compares to DAO and RDO.

Jennings, Roger. *Database Developer's Guide with Visual Basic 5.* Indianapolis, Indiana: Sams Publishing, July 1997.

    This book is a complete reference on how to access data using Visual Basic 5.

Jennings, Roger. "Scaling Visual Basic 4.0 to the Enterprise," *Visual Basic Programmer's Journal*, October 1995.

    This article discusses how to use Visual Basic 4.0 to build scalable client/server applications. It also includes an example of using API functions to access the registry.

Vaughn, William R. *The Hitchhiker's Guide to Visual Basic & SQL Server, Fourth Edition.* Redmond, Washington: Microsoft Press, 1996.

    This book provides details on accessing remote data from Visual Basic including DAO, RDO, RDC, and the ODBC. Packed with sample code, this book provides must-read information when doing client/server applications.

■ Think It Over

To supplement and review the information in this chapter, think about the following:

1. In your last application, how did you design and store the data?

2. Think about the benefits of storing data in a file versus storing the data in a database. When would you use a database or a file?

3. Review the different types of data architectures. Think of an example of when each one could be used in a corporate environment.

4. In the Implementation-centered design, you thought through how to add an appointment book feature to the contact management system. Now think through how this feature affects the Data design.

Strategies for Construction

Therefore, we may reasonably conclude that no matter how sophisticated the design method, no matter how well-founded its theoretical basis, we cannot ignore the practical aspects of designing systems for the real world. This means that we must consider sound management practices with regard to such issues as resource allocation, milestones, configuration management, and version control. To the technologist, these are intensely dull topics; to the professional software engineer, these are realities that must be faced if one wants to be successful in building complex software systems.

—Grady Booch,
Object-Oriented Design with Applications

There is more to developing software than just designing and coding! There is project management, scheduling, configuration management, testing, documentation, testing, maintenance, testing, and version control. (And did I mention testing?) Defining strategies for these activities before beginning to build the application makes the entire application development process more efficient and easier to manage.

This chapter defines some strategies for making buy versus build decisions, defining coding and naming conventions, implementing configuration management and source code control, developing the required user documentation, and devising a development plan. And let's not forget a testing plan.

■ What Strategies?

The final step in the design process is the definition of strategies for construction. Strategies is the S in GUIDS, shown highlighted in Figure 9.1. Defining these strategies prior to the construction phase will help make the construction process more efficient. To stress this point, let's look at a scenario.

The software construction is well underway and an experienced VB developer, Lee, is added to your three-person development team. Lee soon finds that the team has developed its own version of the corporate login screen instead of reusing the component developed for another project. Now the code that could have simply been reused must be completed, debugged, and tested.

Lee has spent much more time than anticipated coming up to speed on the rest of the code. There are few comments and little consistency in coding techniques. Lee is spending a lot of time just figuring out which modules perform which operations and which classes are used for what. Some simple headers on the classes and on each module would have made the code so much easier to understand. Defining a set of coding standards and requiring all of the developers on the team to follow these standards would have made it easier and more efficient for other people working on the code both now and during the maintenance phase.

Lee also noticed that in some code modules the number of contacts variable is *iNumContacts*, in others it is *nContacts*, in others it is *contacts*, in others it is just *i*. In other places, the *contacts* variable is a string and is used for the contact description, other places the contact description is *sContactDescription*, and in still other places it is just *temp*. This confusion (and the possible bugs it could cause as Lee starts to modify this code) could have been avoided simply by defining some naming conventions.

Lee retrieves some code from the server computer and begins making major modifications on several modules. A day later, one of the other developers fixes a bug reported in one of those modules and returns the fixed module to the server. A few days later, Lee copies the modified modules back to

Figure 9.1

Strategies for
construction is the last
step in the GUIDS
methodology.

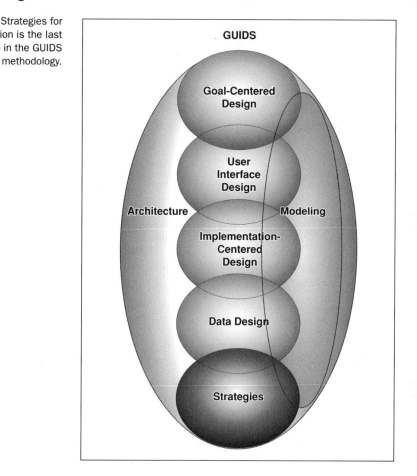

the server. Suddenly, the bug that was fixed surprisingly reappears! "How
could this happen?" management asks. A simple configuration management
plan with version control will prevent these types of problems.

The software is finally finished, only two weeks behind schedule. But it
has not been tested. Because the required deadline cannot be pushed back,
the testing phase is compressed from the originally scheduled four weeks to
only two weeks. Major bugs are found in every module. Some of the modules
were done months ago, and the developer does not even remember how it
was supposed to work. It is soon clear that the deadline will be missed, and
by a large amount. Putting a testing plan in place before the development begins would ensure that it is an integral part of the development process, not
just an afterthought. Testing early makes the testing more efficient and
catches the bugs before they affect the delivery of the application.

Too much of the software was not finished until the last moment, so the documentation staff has not had much to work with. Each module was done to about 80 percent and then the developers moved on to the next module. That way, the module could be checked off as *basically* done on schedule. So now the documentation staff has only two weeks to work with the barely operational software to complete the documentation. There is no way to develop good documentation plus help system content for such a large project that quickly. The entire documentation process could be more efficient if it, too, were defined well before beginning development.

All of these scenarios point to the need to have a good construction plan that includes all of these strategies:

- **Buy versus build**. Which components of the design should be purchased or reused from other projects and which should be constructed?

- **Coding standards**. What standards should be followed in coding the application to make it easier to work with and maintain?

- **Naming conventions**. What naming conventions should be used for clarity and consistency?

- **Configuration management/source code control**. How will the source code be managed and controlled?

- **Inspection and testing procedures**. What testing methodology will be used and how will bugs/change requests be managed?

- **Documentation and help systems**. What type of help system and documentation is needed?

- **Implementation plan and schedule**. How will the implementation be executed, how long will it take, and how will it be deployed?

This chapter provides an overview of each strategy and its effect on the software construction.

■ Buy Versus Build

With the advent of component-based software development and the Visual Basic support of third-party controls, the buy versus build decision takes on a whole new meaning. Instead of deciding whether to buy or build an entire application, you can elect to buy some components of the application and build others. You can also readily reuse internally developed components throughout the organization.

How do you decide what to build and what to buy? The following guidelines will help you to make those decisions.

What's Out There?

To make the buy versus build decisions intelligently, you need to be aware of the available third-party products. One way to do that is by subscribing to a Visual Basic magazine, such as the *Visual Basic Programmer's Journal*. These magazines frequently have sections that announce new products and provide product comparisons. The advertisements provide an overview of the types of products available and supply a phone number for more information.

Another place to look for products is an online service such as CompuServe or the Internet. Third-party vendors often supply demonstration versions of their products that you can download. You may also find many ingenious shareware products.

Finding internally developed components is often harder because there are no advertisements to review or marketing materials to obtain. To make use of these components a feasible option, there must be a mechanism for announcing these components, providing documentation for them, storing them somewhere, and maintaining them throughout the enterprise.

What Do I Need?

Look back at your design with some knowledge of third-party products and available existing components. Do you need to manipulate and display data in a spreadsheet format? Do you need to provide a full-featured text editor? If so, buying a third-party product is much easier than building your own. Do you need to display that company login screen? Why rewrite it when you can simply plug in an existing component?

The parts of an application you should consider purchasing include the following:

- **Database engine**. You can use the Jet engine provided with Visual Basic or purchase another engine such as Oracle to manage the data for your application.

- **Report writer**. You can write reports using Crystal Reports, which comes with Visual Basic. Or you can purchase products such as Borland's ReportSmith or Microsoft Access, which has a nice report writer.

- **Multimedia support**. Manipulating audio, video, and graphics can be much easier using third-party tools.

- **Graph generators**. There are several products for displaying graphs in your application.

- **Communications**. There are products that provide many different types of communications, including FAX support.

- **Spreadsheets and grids**. There are several spreadsheet and grid controls available for Visual Basic in addition to the grid controls that are provided. Or you can include Excel spreadsheets in your application.

- **Accounting functionality**. Instead of developing your own accounting system, you can use any one of several third-party products that can be included in a Visual Basic application.

Components frequently developed and reused in house include the following:

- **Login screen**. It helps both the users and the developer to have one login screen used for every application that needs one.

- **ActiveX controls**. Standard controls can be created for entry of address information, entry and formatting of pricing information, or other common user-interface functionality required for the business.

- **Business objects**. This would include standard components for business-related activities such as creating journal entries or calculating profit margins.

How Flexible Is It?

Many third-party products and internally developed components are very flexible and can be used in a variety of situations. Others are more focused on a specific task. For products in the second category, look at how closely the features of the product match what you need. In some cases, programming workarounds for third-party products or internal components that don't do exactly what you need cost more in terms of programming and testing hours than just building it over for your exact needs.

Purchased products that come with source code can be very flexible, because you can change them as needed. On the other hand, this source code gives your technical team more code to maintain and test.

What Is the Risk?

Evaluating the risk of internally developed components can be difficult and often includes some level of politics. Is it possible that you will not be able to finish your application because you are waiting for some changes another department needs to make to a reused component?

It is also important to evaluate the risk of purchasing components. Basing your mission critical project on a really neat shareware product may not be a good idea, even with the source code. Look at the reputation of the third-party vendor. Do they have a support line? What do you do if the product does not work or if you have questions?

Keynote

To make the decision to buy or build, weigh the cost of the third-party product against the cost of developing the component. Take into consideration the time it will take to learn and implement the third-party product and some measure of the risk of using the third-party vendor. In some situations, third-party products are a great benefit; in other situations, it is easiest to do the work yourself.

Aiding Productivity with Developer Tools

In addition to the buy versus build decision for application components, you will want to research available developer productivity tools. When selecting tools, use the same parameters defined earlier. Evaluate the expense of the tool, including the time to learn to use it properly, against the productivity benefits to determine whether the tool is worth having.

With Visual Basic's extensibility model, you can create your own developer tools as well. These tools, called *add-ins*, are ActiveX components that connect to the Visual Basic IDE. You can create tools to develop your own shortcuts, automate repetitive tasks, or perform complex operations. You can also create your own Wizards using the extensibility model or the new VB Wizard Manager.

Don't forget to check out the tools provided with Visual Basic (found in the \Tools directory of your Visual Basic CD-ROM). For example, the Visual Basic Code Profiler tool analyzes your application and aids in evaluating performance. It helps you identify how frequently different parts of the application are accessed and how long it takes to execute sets of code.

■ Coding Standards

Coding standards are guidelines for how the code for a project is actually written. They define things like program structure, variable scoping, syntax standards, error handling, and commenting. If you define coding standards before beginning to write code, the code will be more standardized between team members, simplifying the development and maintenance activities.

This section provides some suggested coding standards. You can use these as a starting point to discuss this topic and mold these suggestions to the specific goals and requirements of your project. Select a set of standards that is workable for you and the development team.

Why Have Coding Standards?

I have frequently seen messages on CompuServe or newsgroups saying essentially, "Visual Basic is no good. I cannot find any of my code!" Well, it is not the tool, but the coding standards used (or not used) that make it easy or hard to find your code.

Coding standards are sometimes ridiculed by developers who think that what they write should be obvious to everyone, and if it is not obvious it shouldn't be touched! However, good structure and appropriate commenting can provide an outline for the code. This makes it easy to scan the code to find a particular procedure or code segment. These factors benefit both the original developer and new developers who must work on this code.

Here is a list of some good reasons for coding standards:

Keynote

- It helps you manage the complexity of the software and keeps your code organized so it is easy to find things.

- It provides a consistent look to easily read and understand the code. Any developer familiar with the standards will be able to pick up any piece of the code and understand the basic conventions used. This is helpful when you do code walk-throughs, when your testing team does code reviews, and for multiple developer projects.

- It ensures a smooth transition to the maintenance activities, especially if those activities will be provided by someone else.

If that did not convince you, set your stopwatch and look at this poorly written routine:

```
Function myFunc(temp As String, i As Integer)
Select Case i
Case 1
Dim y
y = "Yes " + temp
myFunc = y
Case 2
Dim n
n = "No " + temp
myFunc = n
Case 3
Dim b
b = "Close " + temp
myFunc = b
End Select
End Function
```

How long did it take you to get a general idea on the purpose of this code? This routine will be improved over the next several sections. The resulting code is provided in the section "Naming Conventions" later in this chapter.

What Kind of Standards?

As with most things in life, standards should be defined in moderation: not too little, not too much. It is very important to define standards that can be followed. Standards that are too restrictive or too lenient are ignored, defeating the purpose of establishing them in the first place.

Some of the kinds of standards that should be defined are listed here and discussed in the paragraphs that follow:

- Commenting

- Basic code structure

- Variable scope

- Syntax standards

- Error handling

Commenting for Clarity

Commenting is something most developers hate only more than writing documentation. I once knew a developer who always swore he would go back to put in the comments. But then it was a major task and seemed too overwhelming, so there were very few comments in his work.

It does not have to be that bad. Adding comments is like pulling weeds in the yard; if you pull a few every couple of days, it is not a major task and it keeps the yard well maintained. If you wait for two months, you have a major task and the yard is such a mess, it may be better to start over than attempt to maintain it. (How many routines or entire projects have you had like that?)

Keynote

I have heard more than one developer state the following reason for not commenting: The code speaks for itself. Some developers feel that the comments could be incorrect and mislead developers who read them. This reasoning is totally bogus and illustrates the misconception of commenting code. Comments are not supposed to provide a "play-by-play" description to go with every line of the code. The code itself does that. Rather, the comments are there to provide an outline of the code and to describe the purpose of the code. The comments should answer "what?" and "why?" but not "how?"

If you comment as you code, the comments will be correct and will be there to help you remember the purpose of the routine. By making it a policy to change the comments when the code changes as well, you'll keep the comments up to date.

Some developers write the comments before they code using the comments as pseudo code or program design language (PDL) for the routine. Using comments in this manner is described in detail in *Code Complete,* which is referenced in the "Additional Reading" section at the end of this chapter.

Defining some commenting standards as part of the overall software development strategies provides direction and consistency in how to document the code. It also ensures that it gets done.

The Overview Description

This description provides an overview of the project. I find this description is most easily and clearly done with the object model that was shown in Figure 7.9. The module names could be added to the figure to easily identify the files that relate to the different objects in the object model.

Another option is to write a general description in one of the primary modules of an application such as the main module or Application class. The written description could include an overview of the purpose of the application. It would also include the names of any databases accessed or other additional files required for the project. Some of this information would be in the design documents, but when you add an overview to the code itself, it is easier to find and maintain this information.

Module Comments

All modules (forms, standard modules, classes, and so on) should begin with a brief comment describing the general purpose of the module and any revisions made to the module. For example:

```
' Class Name:   CScore
' Author:       Deborah Kurata, InStep Technologies
' Date:         2/1/97
' Description:  Score the on-line test
'
' Revisions:
' 2/08/97  D. Kurata Modified the routine to include a
'          notification message as per PCR #12
```

Routine Comments

All routines (subroutines, functions, and Property procedures) should begin with a brief comment describing the functional characteristics of the routine (what it does) and mentioning the parameters passed to or returned from the routine.

This description should not describe the implementation details (how it does it) because these often change over time, resulting in unnecessary comment maintenance work or, worse, erroneous comments. The code itself and any necessary local comments will describe the implementation.

For example, a comment, as shown here, is added to the poorly written code you saw earlier. With the new comment, at least you have a better idea of the purpose of this routine.

```
' Prepares a notification message
' Parameters:
'   temp        name of the user
'   i           status of the response
' Returns:
'   string      notification message
Function myFunc(temp as string, i as integer)
```

Body Comments

Too many comments in the body of the module can detract from instead of improve readability. Usually, in your coding standards you will want to limit body comments to descriptions of more complex processing and again provide information on "what?" or "why?," not on "how?"

Variable Comments

Some coding standards call for every nontrivial variable to have an inline comment. Depending on the maintenance needs of your project, this may be required. Normally, I prefer to have clear naming conventions instead. If the variable name is clear, there is no need for the comment, nor is it necessary to keep referring back to the comment when reading the code. More on naming conventions in the next section.

Giving the Routines Some Structure

Look again at the poorly written code shown in the "Why Have Coding Standards?" section. A little hard to read, isn't it? That is the extreme case, but it emphasizes the need to consistently provide some structure to your code. There are several things you can do to give your applications some structure.

Indenting for Better Structure

Try indenting for easier reading.

```
Function myFunc(temp As String, i As Integer)
    Select Case i
        Case 1
            Dim y
            y = "Yes " + temp
            myFunc = y
        Case 2
            Dim n
            n = "No " + temp
            myFunc = n
        Case 3
            Dim b
            b = "Close " + temp
            myFunc = b
    End Select
End Function
```

The only difference in the two examples is the indenting. By giving the application some structure, you have developed a module that is significantly easier to read.

Declaring Variables First

You may also want to place all declares at the top. With Visual Basic, you can insert your variable declarations anywhere you want, as in the preceding coding example. However, it's easier to find the declarations if they are all at the top of the module.

```
Function myFunc(temp As String, i As Integer)
Dim y
Dim n
Dim b
    Select Case i
       Case 1
          y = "Yes " + temp
          myFunc = y
       Case 2
          n = "No " + temp
          myFunc = n
       Case 3
          b = "Close " + temp
          myFunc = b
    End Select
End Function
```

Putting them at the top also makes it easier to determine when variables can be reused within a module. It is easy to see from the preceding code that one string could be used for all of the cases. This greatly simplifies the code.

```
Function myFunc(temp As String, i As Integer)
Dim s
    Select Case i
       Case 1
          s = "Yes " + temp
          myFunc = s
       Case 2
          s = "No " + temp
          myFunc = s
       Case 3
          s = "Close " + temp
          myFunc = s
    End Select
End Function
```

Compare this again with the code example in the "Why Have Coding Standards?" section. Which would you rather read?

One Routine, One Purpose

This standard is as old as modular programming, but it is as important today as it was back then. Each routine should have one and only one purpose. The trick to making this plan work is to name and comment the routine first. The name and one- or two-line comment should state the one purpose of the routine. The code can then be written to meet that purpose.

A related standard is to keep the routines small. Most routines should not exceed the amount of code you can view on the screen at one time. In the past many routines had to be much larger to implement large case statements. In many situations, that is no longer required because of the capabilities of classes. Often the existence of a large case statement in the code is an indication that a polymorphic method may be needed or the classes are not clearly defined.

One Exit Point

This is another holdover from the modular programming days. There should be one exit point from a routine. The sister statement to this is to have only one entry point into a routine. With Visual Basic, it is not possible to go to the middle of another routine.

Having one exit point makes it easier to debug a routine because it always starts at the top and ends at the bottom. This means there are no Exit Sub or Exit Function statements within the body of the routine. Don't be afraid to use a GoTo statement to jump to a label at the end of the routine if necessary, although too many GoTos is normally an indication of poor coding techniques.

The one big exception to the one exit point rule is for error handling. If you use the On Error GoTo type of error trap, as described in "Error Handling" later in this chapter, you will need an Exit statement immediately before the error handler so the error handler is not executed when no error occurs.

A similar standard is to only assign the value of a function at the end of the function. In the poorly coded example in this chapter, the *myFunc* string is assigned in each Case statement. Instead, the statement can reside at the end of the function. This ensures that a value will be returned, even if the execution falls through the Case statement.

```
Function myFunc(temp As String, i As Integer)
Dim s
   Select Case i
     Case 1
        s = "Yes " + temp
     Case 2
        s = "No " + temp
     Case 3
        s = "Close " + temp
   End Select

   myFunc = s
End Function
```

Notice also how much smaller this routine is getting from the original code in the "Why Have Coding Standards?" section.

Ordering the Routines

To help you or other developers find the code in a module, you may want to define a standard routine order. I like to order my routines as follows:

- Property procedures (in alphabetical order), with Get/Let or Get/Set pairs together

- Initialize and Terminate event procedures

- Public Sub and Function procedures (in alphabetical order)

- Private Sub and Function procedures (in alphabetical order)

You and your team may select a different order. The important point is to have a standard order defined for all developers on the project.

Minimizing the Variable Scope

Scope is the word used to describe the extent to which a variable can be seen in an application. If a variable is accessible to all routines in a project, it has a global or public scope. If it can only be accessed by routines in a module, it has module-level scope. If only the routine can access the variable, it has local scope. It is best to use the smallest scope possible for a variable.

Local Variables: Temporary Scraps

Local variables are declared within the body of a routine and are only accessible from that routine. For example, if you need a loop counter that is only used in a routine, the variable should be of local scope. Unless the variable is declared to be Static, the value of the variable will be destroyed (or for objects, the reference will be released) when the routine is terminated by an End Function, End Property, or End Sub statement.

You can think of a local variable as a temporary scrap of paper with a personal reminder. You use it until you are finished with it and then discard it.

Module-Level Variables: Notes on Your Refrigerator

Module-level variables are declared in the Declarations section of a module and are private to the module in which they are declared. No other module in the application can read or modify the value directly. If the variable must be accessed from outside of the module, Property procedures can be defined to provide read-only or read/write access to the value and still keep the variable private to the module.

You can think of a module-level variable as a note on your refrigerator. No one from the outside can see or modify the note, unless you specifically let them in to change it.

Module-level variables exist from the time the module is initialized until the time that module is terminated. For standard modules, this initialization occurs when the application starts and the module-level variables will retain their values until the application terminates.

For classes, the module-level variables are private to each instance of the class. This means that the values for one object from the class are independent and private from another object from that class. The values are initialized when an object is initialized and terminated when the object terminates.

For forms, the module-level variables are private to each instance of the form. This means the same thing as it does for class modules. The form module is not terminated until all references to the form are set to Nothing. Even when a form is unloaded, the form module is not terminated so any module-level variables will persist.

Public Variables: Billboards on the Freeway

Public, or global, variables can make it extremely difficult to understand the logic of an application. They also adversely affect the reuse and maintenance of your code. If you create a class that needs a public variable, that class cannot just be plugged into another application. The public variables need to be found and copied over to the new routine as well.

You can think of public variables as billboards along the freeway. If I want to meet you for lunch, I could write the place and time as a public variable on the billboard. When you go by the billboard, however, you don't know for certain that what you see on that billboard is what I had written. I may not have written anything yet. Or someone else could have drawn a 1 in front of the 1 o'clock in the message so you show up at 11 when I did not expect you until 1. Or someone could have destroyed the message completely.

There are many alternatives to public variables. If a subroutine or function needs access to a variable from another routine, it could be passed in as a parameter instead of converted to a public variable. If a variable is needed in several places in the application, it should be of module-level scope with access to it provided with a Property procedure. Public variables should only be used if there is no other choice to meet the requirements of the application.

Setting Syntax Standards

Syntax standards make the application code more consistent and ensure that the Microsoft recommended syntax standards are defined for all of the developers on the project.

Here are some sample syntax standards you could include in your standards:

- **Use a "." operator between a form and a control.** In Visual Basic 3.0, the recommended approach was to use form!control. With later versions, the recommended syntax is form.control. The "!" implies a collection look-up and is therefore slower than the "." operator.

- **Don't use magic numbers.** Magic numbers are those numbers in the code that have some magical meaning only to the person who put them there. Instead of using magic numbers and attempting to remember them, you can use the constants provided by Visual Basic or create your own constants. For example, instead of using Screen.Mousepointer = 11, use Screen.Mousepointer = vbHourglass. Another example is the Case 1, Case 2, and Case 3 structure shown in the code provided in the "Why Have Coding Standards?" section and improved with constants in the code following this bulleted list. Constants instead of magic numbers are especially useful for control array index values, help context ID numbers, and error code numbers. You'll see more examples of this in Chapter 10, "Building Your First Class."

- **If you have a Case statement, include a Case Else.** Many uncaught bugs are introduced into code because a Case statement variable is not what is expected. Without a Case Else statement, no code is executed so no problem is defined. Using a Case Else ensures that there is a default case, even if it simply displays an error message or logs an error message to an error log file.

- **Use the line continuation character for long lines.** Some standards actually set a maximum, such as 70. This ensures that most lines will fit in the code window.

- **Don't put multiple statements on one line.** It makes the code harder to read and can make it difficult to find some errors. For example, any single term statement such as "Beep" will be seen as a label if it is on a line with another statement as follows:

```
Beep : x=5
```

This statement will not perform the Beep because Beep is seen as the line label instead of the Beep statement.

- **Explicitly state the data types of variables.** You should explicitly state the data type of a variable. If you don't, Visual Basic assumes a Variant data type and you may not get the results you are expecting. In addition, provide the return data type for all Function and Property Get procedures. In the example shown at the end of this topic, the "As String" was added to the function definition. This will ensure that a string instead of a Variant is returned from the function.

- **Don't put multiple declarations on one line**. This is the cause of many variable typing problems. For example:

```
Dim y, n, b As String
```

This line appears to be declaring three strings. In actuality, it is declaring two Variants (y and n) and a string (b).

- **Explicitly state the scope**. When declaring a module-level variable or a routine, explicitly state whether the variable or routine is public or private. For routines you can also select Friend as the scope. Friend implies that the routine can be accessed from any code within the application, but not from outside of the application. This is useful when creating ActiveX components. See Chapter 13, "Building ActiveX Components," for more information.

Note that Private and Public keywords can not be used for local variables. All local variables are private to the local routine. The Friend keyword can only be used on routines, not on any variables.

- **Always use "&" when concatenating strings and "+" when working with numerical values.** Visual Basic has many features for automatically converting data types. To ensure that you are performing the operation you think you are performing, always use the appropriate operator. For example, when concatenating strings, use the concatenation operator (&) instead of the numeric addition operator (+).

Tech Note.   *Using + or & has a unique effect when working with Nulls. If you add a Null to an expression using a +, the value of the expression will be Null. If you concatenate a Null onto an expression using a &, the value of the expression will remain unchanged.*

The results of all of these syntax changes in the revised routine are shown here:

```
Private Const scrCorrect = 1
Private Const scrIncorrect = 2
Private Const scrAlmost = 3

Public Function myFunc(temp As String, _
                       i As Integer) As String
Dim s As String

    Select Case i
        Case scrCorrect
            s = "Yes " & temp
        Case scrIncorrect
            s = "No " & temp
        Case scrAlmost
            s = "Close " & temp
```

```
        Case Else
            s = " "
        End Select

        myFunc = s
End Function
```

Error Handling

Keynote

Like comments, error handling is sometimes seen as something added after the code is done. But as with comments, it is much better to add the error handling as you are writing the code that can generate the error instead of waiting until sometime called "later" to do it.

A coding standard for error handling, should include three steps:

- Check for the error.

- Handle the error.

- Proceed appropriately.

Defining a standard for each step ensures that errors are handled appropriately.

Checking for the Error

There is no global error trapping built into Visual Basic, so each procedure should trap its own errors. There are several ways to trap errors:

- **On Error Go To <*label*>.** If a trappable error occurs in a procedure after this error trap is in effect, this statement will cause execution to go to the defined label in the procedure. Normally, this goes to a label at the end of the procedure defined specifically for error handling. This technique keeps the main processing of the procedure free of the additional code required to handle the errors.

- **On Error Resume Next.** If a trappable error occurs in a procedure after this error trap is in effect, this statement will cause execution to return to the next line after the line generating the error. The code to handle the error can then immediately follow the line that would cause the error. This strategy is useful if errors could occur in several places in the procedure and the error handling needs to respond accordingly.

- **Perform validation.** Sometimes errors in the application do not cause a trappable error. For example, no error will occur if the user enters today as a delivery date when a business rule stated that the delivery date must be the first business day after today's date. Rather, the application can perform validation to make sure this business rule is met.

- **Assert** *<expression>*. The Assert method is new to Visual Basic 5. It causes an application in the development environment to stop execution if a specific condition is false. For example, an Assert could be used to ensure that a variable used in a Select Case statement is an expected value. If this assertion is false, the application will stop. Assertions are ignored in a compiled application, so this technique aids with debugging, but is not a solution for trapping errors in a final application.

Tech Note. *If a procedure generates a trappable error and has no error trap, the error will automatically be raised to the procedure that called it. If that procedure has no error trap, the error will again be raised to the next level. If no error trap is found at the top level, the application will generate an untrapped error and terminate.*

Handling the Error

Once an error is trapped it needs to be handled—that is, appropriate processing needs to occur to deal with the error. There are several possibilities for handling an error:

- **Fix it and try again**. Code in the error handler can correct the error (or ask the user to correct the error) and retry the operation with a Resume statement. For example, if a file open operation generates an error because a file is not found, the error handling routine could create the file and then resume to open the file. This is not always possible.

- **Deal with it and continue**. Code in the error handler can attempt to correct the problem or decide to ignore it and continue with a Resume Next statement. For example, when reaching the end of a file an EOF error occurs. The application is expecting the error, so it can set a flag to denote a completed process and resume on the next statement to continue the application.

- **Raise an error**. Sometimes an error handler cannot know what to do with an error, or it can attempt to correct the problem but fail, or there is a validation error that must be reported to the user. In these cases, the error handler can raise the error to the routine that called it. That routine should then have code to check for the error and handle it appropriately.

- **Set an error return value and exit**. Instead of raising an error, a procedure can trap an error, set the return value of the procedure to that error, and exit the procedure. This requires that all procedures be functions because they have to have return values. Any other values to be returned from the function would need to be passed to the function as part of the parameter list. Note that this strategy won't work for errors in Property procedures.

In any of these cases, it may be useful to log the errors to an error log. This lets you track the exact specifications of the error without relying on a user to write down the information in a message box.

Tech Note. *Visual Basic 5 provides an easy way to log information to the Windows NT event log or to a log file. See Chapter 15, "Putting the Pieces Together," for more information.*

Proceeding Appropriately

Upon return from a procedure that had an error, the calling routine needs to proceed appropriately. This step is often missed in an application, especially if error routines are simply cut and pasted instead of evaluated and implemented. As an example, imagine an application that loses a database connection, generates a fatal error, and then continues as if nothing were wrong. That application will then proceed to generate more errors as it continues to attempt data manipulation.

To perform this step, each call to a procedure needs to be evaluated to respond appropriately to any errors that occur in the called procedure. How this is done depends on how the error was handled. Errors raised from procedures need to be trapped like any other trappable error. If the error is instead provided as the return value from the procedure, this return value needs to be checked. Any errors need to be handled as defined in the prior section "Handling the Error."

It is a good idea to create a ShutDown or Abort type method in your application that will perform a controlled application shutdown should a fatal error occur. This method could include processes such as rolling back transactions, shutting database connections, and so on. This method can be called whenever a fatal error occurs in the application.

■ Naming Conventions

Naming conventions provide readable, memorable, and unambiguous names to help developers (especially in multiple-developer projects) read and maintain an application. There is not one "correct" or "standard" naming convention for use with Visual Basic. But it is important to have an easy-to-use convention. You can use the following suggestions as a starting point to help you define the conventions appropriate for your project and project team.

Good Name/Bad Name

There are good names and there are bad names in applications. Can you tell what the following variables are for? *iCustomerType, j, fBalanceOnTheAcctForCurrentMonth.* Can you tell which one you are apt to misspell frequently?

Here are some general guidelines on naming:

- **Not too short**. The name *j* says nothing to the developer reading the code. Unless they are simple loop counter variables obvious in the code, names should be more descriptive.

- **Not too long**. Long names are hard to remember and are easy to mistype. If you set the Require Variable Declaration option in Visual Basic (Tools|Options), the system will catch your variable misspellings, but why go through the hassle?

- **Says something**. The name should be readable and should say what it is. *iCustomerType* says it is an integer customer type, no comment needed! One additional suggestion is to use *bIs* as the prefix for Booleans. For example, *bIsValid* or *bIsCanceled*. This results in easy-to-read statements such as

```
If bIsCanceled then iValue = 7
```

- **Consistent**. A name that is used in several places in the code, each time with a different meaning, raises many possibilities for error. Variables meaning the same thing but with different names in different routines are also likely to give rise to errors.

So let's revisit that piece of code we have been working on, replacing the function and variable names to follow basic naming conventions.

```
Private Const scrCorrect = 1
Private Const scrIncorrect = 2
Private Const scrAlmost = 3

' Prepares a notification message
' Parameters:
'    sUserName       Name of user
'    iStatus         Status of the response
' Returns:
'    string          Notification message
Public Function myFunc(sUserName As String, _
                       iStatus As Integer) As String
Dim sReply As String

   Select Case iStatus
      Case scrCorrect
         sReply = "Yes " & sUserName
      Case scrIncorrect
         sReply = "No " & sUserName
      Case scrAlmost
         sReply = "Close " & sUserName
      Case Else
         sReply = " "
   End Select
```

```
    Notify = sReply
End Function
```

Compare this code to the original code at the beginning of this chapter. Notice how the readability is significantly improved by the use of a few basic conventions.

Object Naming

Table 9.1 lists some object name prefixes similar to those found in the *Visual Basic 5.0 Programmer's Guide*. Object naming conventions make it easier to recognize which object was used.

Table 9.1

Object Naming
Conventions

PREFIX	CONTROL TYPE DESCRIPTION	EXAMPLE
chk	Check box	chkReadOnly
col	Collection	colPersons
cbo	Combo box	cboTasks
cmd	Command button	cmdOK
dlg	Common dialog	dlgFile
ctl	Control (used when the specific control type is unknown)	ctl
dat	Data control	datTask
db	Database	dbContact
dir	Directory list box	dirSource
drv	Drive list box	drvTarget
fil	File list box	filSource
frm	Form	frmToDo
fra	Frame	fraOptions
grd	Grid	grdItems
hsb	Horizontal scroll bar	hsbScroll
img	Image	imgIcon
lbl	Label	lblName

Table 9.1 (Continued)

Object Naming
Conventions

PREFIX	CONTROL TYPE DESCRIPTION	EXAMPLE
lin	Line	linBlue
lst	List box	lstCompanies
mnu	Menu	mnuFileOpen
out	Outline	outTasks
opt	Option button	optYes
pic	Picture box	picBackground
pnl	3-D panel	pnlGroup
rs	Recordset	rsPerson
shp	Shape	shpCircle
spn	Spin control	spnAge
txt	Text box	txtName
tmr	Timer	tmrAlarm
vsb	Vertical scroll bar	vsbPage

For new objects not listed in this table, define a unique three-character prefix. However, it is more important to be clear than to stick to three characters.

Some standards suggest that derivative controls, such as an enhanced list box, should have an extended prefix so there is no confusion about what control is really being used. For example, a control instance created from the Visual Basic Pro 3-D Frame could use a prefix of fra3d (the standard fra for Frame plus 3d to represent 3-D).

In practice, it may be easier to keep the standard name than to define a new one for derivative controls. Often during the course of a project a specific control is changed numerous times. For example, a project is started using a standard combo box. An extended combo box is available from vendor X that provides new features, so the project is modified to use that combo box. A problem is then found with vendor X's combo box that prevents the project from going into testing. So the vendor X combo box is replaced with one from vendor Y. It is much easier to keep the prefix as "cbo" instead of changing it each time the vendor changes.

Some of these naming conventions may work for you and your team and some may not. Whatever conventions you decide to use, you should use them consistently.

Tech Note. *You should define the names of your controls as your create them. If you begin to add code for the control and then define the name, the code will no longer be associated with the control.*

Menu Naming

One method of naming menus and menu options is to use the mnu prefix with the menu abbreviation and then the menu option name. This is shown in the Menu Handler Name column of Table 9.2.

Table 9.2

Menu Naming
Conventions

MENU CAPTION SEQUENCE	MENU HANDLER NAME	CONTROL ARRAY NAME
Help | Contents	mnuHelpContents	mnuHelp(mainHelpContentsOption)
File | Open	mnuFileOpen	mnuFile(mainFileOpenOption)
Format | Character	mnuFormatCharacter	mnuFormat(mainFormatChrOption)
File | Send | Fax	mnuFileSendFax	mnuFileSend(mainFileSendFaxOption)
File | Send | E-mail	mnuFileSendEmail	mnuFileSend(mainFileSendEmailOption)

An alternative option is to define all of the menu options for a menu as one control array. This is shown in the Control Array Name column of Table 9.2. I prefer this approach because it puts all of the code for one menu in one routine. Notice in Table 9.2 that the index values for the control array are defined as constants instead of the magic numbers. This allows you to change the index value (which you may have to do if a menu option is added or deleted) without changing all references to that menu option and makes the code easier to read.

Even though there are two common naming conventions for menu options, your team should select one method and stick with it.

Module Naming

The naming convention for a module depends on the type of module. Standard modules have a prefix of "M"—for example, MMain. Class modules should be prefixed with a "C" and then the name of the class—for example, CPerson. Class modules used as the definition of an interface should be prefixed with an "I" and then the name of the interface. For example, an interface that provided all of the data accessing services may be called IData.

To follow the object and module naming conventions, a form name should be defined with an "F" prefix and the form object should have the three-character object name "frm." Because Visual Basic automatically creates the form object variable from the form name, it is standard to use the "frm" prefix for the form. So a form with name, address, and phone information could be called frmPerson.

The remainder of the module name should clearly define the purpose of the module. In many cases, this is the name of the object. For example, CPerson is the name of the class for the Person objects. The names for the modules should have been defined during the design phase.

For ActiveX components, these naming conventions are even more important. Because other applications will reference these components, the names must be relatively obvious and unique.

Routine Naming

Routine naming depends on the type of routine:

- The standard event procedures are automatically named with <object>_<verb> syntax, such as Class_Terminate or txtName_Click. You may want to follow that standard in defining your own events as verbs.

- The public Property procedures will be the public interface to the properties for the class. They should be named with a logical property name, without a prefix or suffix. For example, Visual Basic controls provide properties such as Top and Caption. Your properties could be named Address, DateofBirth, and so on. Notice that these names are normally nouns.

- The public subroutine and functions will be the public interface to the methods for the class. They should also be named with a logical action name, without a prefix or suffix, following a <verb><object> syntax. For example, Visual Basic controls provide methods such as Move, Add, and SetFocus. Your methods could be named Display, WriteFile, and so on. Notice that these names are normally verbs.

- Private subroutines and methods frequently follow a <verb><object> syntax, as in OpenFile or CalcPay.

Variable Naming

Variable naming conventions are often the most difficult to define. It seems to be a very individual choice, with developers adamant about using their own convention and not someone else's. Defining a compromise and following one set of standards makes it easier for others working on the project and taking on the maintenance activities.

One common approach to variable naming is based on Hungarian naming conventions frequently used in C. This includes a prefix and body. The prefix should describe the scope and data type of the variable. The body should use mixed case for easy reading and should be as long as needed to describe the purpose of the variable—or example, bIsDirty and m_sUserName. Table 9.3 lists commonly used variable prefixes. Defining a standard set of prefixes improves the naming of variables in the application.

Table 9.3

Commonly Used
Variable Prefixes

PREFIX	SCOPE DESCRIPTION
g_	Global or public
m_	Module-level
mw_	Module-level object variable declared WithEvents
	Local (no additional prefix)
a	Array
b	Boolean
byt	Byte
cur	Currency – 64 bits
dt	Date+Time
dbl	Double – 64-bit signed quantity
err	Error
f	Float/Single – 32-bit signed floating point
i	Integer
l	Long – 32-bit signed quantity
s	String
v	Variant
udt	User-defined type

Hungarian is valuable in Visual Basic just as it is in C because the variable name itself does not provide standard (and valuable) information about what a variable is used for or where it is accessible. For example, *iSend* (which might be a count of the number of messages sent), *bSend* (which might be a Boolean defining the success of the last Send operation), and *curSend* (which might be an amount of money sent) all succinctly tell a developer something very different. This information is fundamentally lost when the name is reduced down to *Send*.

Keeping the scope name in the variable name also helps ensure that you work with the variable correctly. With the data type coercion done in Visual Basic, you could get unexpected results if you do not watch your variable types.

Keynote

Use Option Explicit to force proper variable declaration. The time lost trying to track down bugs caused by typos (*aPersonTmp* versus *sPersonTmp* versus *sPersonTemp*) far outweighs the time needed to declare variables. See Chapter 10, "Building Your First Class," for more information on setting Option Explicit.

Constant Naming

Constants follow the same basic naming conventions as variables. However, each constant in a component should have a three- or four-letter prefix identifying the name of the component. This minimizes the chance of a conflict with constants in other components used in an application.

For example:

```
' Define priority values for the task component
Public Enum taskPriority
    taskEmpty
    taskUrgent
    taskHigh
    taskMedium
    taskLow
End Enum
```

Tech Note. *Enumerations are new in Visual Basic 5 and are provided to define logical sets of integer constants. Public enumerations in a component are available to the client applications that reference the component. See Chapter 10, "Building Your First Class" for a more complete example of enumerations.*

■ Configuration Management/Source Code Control

Configuration management and source code control are basically two different names for managing source code. This includes tracking the changes made to the code to ensure that changes are not lost, making check points of the application at certain points in time, and assigning and tracking application version information. Configuration management is sometimes allocated to the maintenance activities, following implementation. However, a good configuration management plan defined prior to the construction will help you track the changes made during the construction phase and make it easier to merge code from multiple developers.

Check Out Time

The first step in defining a management plan for the source code is to define a check in/check out process. This ensures that only one developer is working on a particular module. There are several options for how this process is defined.

The Chief Surgeon

Consider the role of the chief surgeon in a medical procedure. All other members of the team are support members, even if they are critical to the success of the operation. A source code check in/check out plan can be modeled the same way. One member of the team can be assigned the role of the lead or chief developer. This person would be responsible for checking out components of the application to the other members of the team and checking pieces back in.

I have had success with this manual process on two- or three-person development teams. It does, however, take a great deal of time on the part of the lead developer to make sure the code is checked out properly and is correctly merged back with the other parts of the application upon check in. Then the merged code needs to be given back to all members of the team.

The Librarian

Instead of being managed by a key developer, the check in process can be managed by a support person on the team—basically a librarian responsible for checking modules in and out. The downside of this approach is that in most cases, this person would not have the skills to merge any required changes or notice technical errors in the code being checked in.

Let the Computer Do It

Many software products provide check in/check out functionality. Several have features specifically for Visual Basic.

The Enterprise Edition of Visual Basic comes with SourceSafe, a version control system. SourceSafe provides the following features:

Enterprise Edition

- Checking in out of files, adding comments if desired to define why the files were checked out.

- Optional limitation of only one person checking out a file at one time. This prevents two people from accidentally modifying the same code.

- Tracking files that are in multiple projects, simplifying the maintenance of reusable classes and forms.

- Tracking of all changes made to the files and reporting of this information.

- Backtracking to review or create a prior version of the application.

The software products all require some amount of management by a person, but this approach is much more efficient and more robust than manually tracking checked in and checked out modules.

Managing Change Requests

When the check in and check out process is in place, the next step in defining a configuration management plan is to define how change requests will be managed. The amount of formal procedure here depends on the size of the project and the number of developers on the team.

I once worked on a project where I did all of the development for a particular client. I would provide a delivery, he would look at it and verbally describe what he wanted changed. I would take notes, go through and implement all of the requests, and provide another delivery two weeks later. Very simple process for a very small team.

If there are multiple reviewers or multiple developers, this process is not sufficient. Many companies use a more formal Product Change Request (PCR) system. Anyone requesting a change and any errors the testers find are written onto PCR forms (either paper or online). Each form includes a description of the problem, how to reproduce it, its criticality, and other related information. The project team then reviews the PCRs and defines a status and priority for the changes. Some are marked as nonproblems, others as later enhancements, and some as bugs.

When the team decides which PCRs should be done they are each assigned to a developer. The developer checks the required files out, makes the changes, and then checks the files back in. The changes then need to be tested and deployed.

■ Inspection and Testing Procedures

Keynote

The primary theme in this testing section is from Steve Maguire's *Debugging the Development Process*. He stated: "Don't fix bugs later; fix them now." With that in mind, it is important to define a testing strategy that starts now, not later. This section recommends a specific set of steps to follow, but you can adjust the process to fit into your organization and project requirements.

Writing Bug-Free Code

Writing bug-free code is the ultimate in fixing bugs now instead of later. The bugs are fixed by correctly developing the code the first time, so no bug reports need to be submitted, tracked, or retested. The code is just right.

Some primary things you can do to aim for bug-free code are

- **Complete the design process.** Many reported bugs are not really bugs at all but are rather open design issues peeking out of the code.

- **Follow the design.** If changes need to be made to the design, make the changes to the design and then follow the design.

- **Develop error handlers throughout the code.** Define a strategy and methodology for error handling in your application and use it throughout the application.

- **Don't leave parts unfinished.** These unfinished parts will show up later as missing features. If you must leave something undone, mark it clearly. I use "@@@." Then you can search for the marks as part of your testing process. If you put the "@@@" in without a comment mark in front of it, it will ensure the application does not compile until the routine is finished.

By following these suggestions, you can improve the quality of your code.

Testing As You Go

As you finish parts of an application, you should test it. Not someone else, but *you*. Not later, but now. Taking a few minutes to test and debug each component of the code now, when you are most familiar with it, will minimize the number of times you need to come back to this code, refamiliarize yourself with it, and change it.

If you are waiting for a key component from someone else, just create a stub. A *stub* is a piece of code that has the correct interface but no internals. For example, if you need the CalculatePay routine in order to test your routine, create a temporary CalculatePay stub routine so you can test your application.

Keynote

I like to use the "F8 test" when testing my own code. This test involves stepping through the module or component line by line using the F8 key. This lets you see exactly which events are firing when and which lines of code are running. Especially when I was first learning Visual Basic, I found many places where unexpected code was executing because unexpected events were generated. The F8 test helped me find where the code was not executing as I had planned. This test is similar to the old-fashioned verbal walk-through of the procedural code.

Another way to do this type of testing is with a checklist. Create a standard checklist of the things to be tested, such as bounds checking and data validation, and mark them off when they are complete. You can combine the F8 test and the checklist for greater coverage.

When you find bugs during this process you should fix them now, not later. Think of the time savings here! No one will need to find the bug and write it on a PCR. No one will need to track the PCR. The entire team will not need to discuss it and assign it. You will not have to go back to a module you may not have seen for awhile, get reacquainted, make the change, and check in the module. The testers will not need to retest the module. Add this up and any time you use now to perform this test and fix the bugs will be much less than finding the bug later!

A Sight for Someone Else's Eyes

After you have finished your testing, you should submit the module or component to someone else for testing. This is often called *unit testing* because it is testing one specific unit of the code.

The unit testing can be done by anyone, but *not* by you. In some projects I worked on, we exchanged units between the developers. In other projects, the documentation personnel filled that role.

Alternatively, you could perform a code walk-through on the component. This involves discussing how the code works with another developer or group of developers. Although it's time consuming, this process not only improves the quality of the component, it also helps the less senior developers improve their programming skills.

The testing at this point is still preliminary, prior to any official code check in or testing process. Therefore, no PCRs need to be written at this stage. The bugs can simply be listed and provided to the developer.

Bugs found during this process should be fixed now, not later. Remember that time savings we were talking about? After you fix these bugs and retest, the module is ready to be officially checked in. You no longer "own" this module.

If you want to force yourself (or the others on the team) to do this testing, make this step required before work on the next unit can begin. Developers who want to start that next new challenge will get right on those outstanding bugs!

Over the Wall: Performing the Integration Test

When all of the code for a deliverable has been developed, it is time for a component test, often called an *integration test*. This test involves doing a build of all of the code in the deliverable and testing the resulting software. The person performing the merge (chief developer or librarian) normally does just a cursory feature test. The code is then "passed over the wall" to the testing personnel (or whomever is testing the application).

The testing personnel use the test plans they have been working on to test the component. This testing is frequently a feature or scenario test (gleaned from the scenarios defined during the Goal-centered design) ensuring that the features of the application are operational.

At this point, the PCR process starts. Any bugs found are reported on PCRs and assigned through the process described a moment ago. All critical bugs should then be assigned and corrected immediately. This prevents the critical problem from becoming an even more critical problem at the end of the project. All other bugs should be fixed at some defined time. Some companies define a bug count maximum. For example, if 200 bugs are found, all new development stops until those bugs are eradicated .

This is especially important when developing components that will be shared or used by others. Bugs in these routines will show up in many places and in unexpected routines.

Testing the Entire System

The final internal test is a *system test*. All of the pieces of the application are together and all of the critical bugs are corrected. Every feature is retested, using selected portions of the test plans.

It is during this test that all versions of the application are made and tested (if multiple languages are supported, for example). The application should also be tested on all expected platforms (both Windows NT and Windows 95, for example).

■ Documentation and Help Systems

Most applications need some type of documentation or help system to aid the user in using the application. The documentation and help system appropriate for a specific application should be determined prior to the construction phase. This allows the documentation staff to prepare the design and begin work early in the process.

Defining the Documentation

Documentation comes in many forms. Because this is a book about program design and development, it will not cover all of the options for defining documentation. The point is, the design of the documentation should be an integral part of the overall software development process. This ensures that the documentation is not an afterthought.

Designing the Help System

The design of the help system, on the other hand, normally affects the programming team. The developers need to tie the help system context IDs to the correct location in the application.

There are two methods for displaying help. There is the standard F1 key to display context-sensitive help on a screen. There is also the "What's This" type of help that displays field level help. The implementation of these two methods is demonstrated in Chapter 15, "Putting the Pieces Together."

Be sure to include the help system in the test plan for the application. Help won't be much help to the user if it does not bring up the correct help topic for each field or if it includes missing or inaccurate information.

■ Implementation Plan and Schedule

The implementation plan is the key strategy for the construction. It defines how the application will be built and delivered.

One way to design an implementation plan is to define interim deliveries. The project design has already divided the project into logical components. Now these components can be grouped together to form logical deliveries.

Following the concept of Rapid Application Development (RAD), each delivery should be about two to four weeks apart. This will help you decide how many components should be included in each delivery. The most difficult or risky components should be scheduled first. This will guarantee that there is plenty of time to finish them. Defining these interim deliveries will result in a schedule for the project.

As all of the modules for a delivery are complete, the set is made into an executable. The executable is provided to the testers for the integration testing and to the documentation staff so they can develop the documentation for the provided features.

There are many benefits to producing interim deliveries:

- The testing staff gets a logical piece relatively early in the project, not the entire thing at the end.

- The documentation staff gets the software early in the project so the documentation has a better chance of keeping up with the development, instead of having to catch up after all of the software is complete.

- Any major design errors or omissions will become apparent early enough that they can be corrected.

■ Summary

- The buy versus build strategy helps you define which components of the application should be bought (or reused) and which should be built.

- Coding standards make the application easier to read and ensure that all developers on the team are following the best coding techniques.

- Naming conventions provide consistency in the application, improving its readability and maintainability.

- Configuration management manages changes to the source code. It tracks what was changed and by whom.

- The key to a good testing strategy is to fix the bugs now, not later.

- Include strategies for the documentation and help system so these can be started early in the process.

- Define an implementation plan and schedule based on interim deliverables.

■ Additional Reading

Booch, Grady. *Object-Oriented Analysis and Design with Applications (The Benjamin/Cummings Series in Object-Oriented Software Engineering)*. Redwood City, California: The Benjamin/Cummings Publishing Company, 1994.

Booch provides an academic discussion of object-oriented design concepts, including information on the software development process.

Kurata, Jerry. "Devise a Configuration Management Plan," *Visual Basic Programmer's Journal*. Vol. 5, No 7, July 1995.

This article provides some tips for managing the source code for your Visual Basic applications. It suggests methods to prevent overwriting changes and to track code in multiple developer projects.

Maguire, Steve. *Debugging the Development Process: Practical Strategies for Staying Focused, Hitting Ship Dates, and Building Solid Teams*. Redmond, Washington: Microsoft Press, 1994.

If every developer could have only two books, I would recommend this one and *Code Complete*, listed shortly. This book focuses on what every member of the development team can do to make high-quality software ship on time. This book's anecdotal style, clear key points, and highlights section make it very easy and enjoyable to read.

Maguire, Steve. *Writing Solid Code: Microsoft's Techniques for Developing Bug-Free C Programs*. Redmond, Washington: Microsoft Press, 1993.

The subtitle explains what this book is all about. Most of the information in the book is excellent, and relevant to Visual Basic developers. But all of the examples are in C, so if you are not familiar with C you may miss some of the key points.

McCarthy, Jim. *Dynamics of Software Development*. Redmond, Washington: Microsoft Press, 1995.

You may have heard Jim McCarthy's excellent presentation: "The 21 Rules of Thumb for Shipping Great Software on Time" at functions such as VBITS. These rules have been expanded to 54 in this interesting and enjoyable book.

McConnell, Steve. *Code Complete: A Practical Handbook of Software Construction*. Redmond, Washington: Microsoft Press, 1993.

This book contains chapters such as "The Power of Data Names," "Characteristics of High-Quality Routines," and "Managing Construction." It is highly recommended reading for every developer.

■ Think It Over

To supplement and review the information in this chapter, think about the following:

1. In your prior projects, how did you decide which components to buy and which third-party products to use? Did you regret any of your choices? Why or why not?

2. Have you used any defined coding standards in your prior projects? Think about how coding standards could help you maintain your own code.

3. What naming conventions do you use? Think about how a consistent naming convention could help you maintain your code.

4. Have you used a configuration management tool? If so, did it meet your needs? If not, think about the times you wished you had one!

5. How do you currently test your applications? Do you follow a process that is similar to or different from the one recommended here?

6. What types of documentation are normally included with your application? Would it make the life of the documentation staff easier if you got them operational components sooner?

7. Have you ever provided interim deliverables? If so, were they successful? If you have not done interim deliverables, would you consider trying them? Why or why not?

Constructing an Application

10

Building Your First Class

The right tool for the right job.

—Anonymous

Before beginning construction, a builder must know which tools are appropriate and understand how to use those tools. You would not find a professional builder using a wrench as a hammer or a table saw to cut down trees. So too in programming. You would not use an integer to store a string or use the help compiler to compile your program logic.

As a Visual Basic developer, you have already mastered the basic tools. You know how and when to use forms and code modules. Visual Basic 4.0 introduced a major new tool: *class modules*. With class modules you can incorporate more formal object-oriented programming techniques in the development of your applications. The construction set provided in Visual Basic 5 adds many new gizmos to this class module tool, such as programmer-defined events and interfaces.

To make full use of these new VB5 features, you need a firm understanding of class modules. This chapter presents the basics you need to harness the power of classes. It begins with a review of the class terminology that was presented in Chapter 1, "Introduction to OO in VB," and then demonstrates how to build a class in a class module and how to create objects from the class. It then illustrates how to enhance the class using enumerations, error handling, and programmer-defined events. Several new Visual Basic 5 features will be introduced and described along the way. When you finish this chapter, you will have a basic understanding of classes and the Visual Basic tools for building and using them.

■ What Is a Class?

At a very general level, a *class* describes a group of similar objects. All employees at a company are objects of an Employee class. All time sheets for those employees are objects of a Time Sheet class. Each individual object in the class is called an *instance* of the class. Jessica Jones is an instance of the Employee class and her May 15th time sheet is an instance of the Time Sheet class.

The class defines the properties and behaviors of all the objects in the group. In object-oriented terminology, the class defines the *properties* and *methods* for all objects created, or instantiated from the class. The Employee class might have Name and Address properties and a "do work" method. The Time Sheet class might have Date and Hours properties and a "calculate pay" method.

Classes can also have *events*. An event is a message that an object can broadcast. Events are normally used when an object wants to notify other objects of an action so the other objects can react appropriately. For example, the Time Sheet class may have a "pay calculated" event it will raise when it is finished calculating the pay. Another object can respond to this event and begin generating the pay checks.

Keynote

Visual Basic has always used classes. For example, the text box in the Visual Basic toolbox is the visual representation of a TextBox class, complete with properties, methods, and events. When you select the TextBox control from the toolbox and add it to a form, you are creating an instance of the TextBox class and defining the text box object's Top, Left, Width, and Height properties based on the location of the text box on the form. When the end user types in the text box, the text box generates a Change event and your form will react to that event if you have code in the Change event procedure for the text box. The forms you have created are also classes. When you load a form you are creating an instance of that form's class.

Visual Basic allows you to define your own classes with their associated properties, methods, and events. You define your own classes by inserting class modules into your project. You define the properties by declaring module-level variables and writing code for Property procedures. To define the methods, you insert Sub and Function procedures in the class module. You define the events by declaring event variables, and then raising those events where appropriate in a procedure in the class module.

Tech Note. *A form module can also contain the definition of a class. As a friend of mine says, "Remember, a form is a class, although it takes a slightly different form." I believe the pun is intended. You should use a form instead of a class module for the definition of the class if the primary purpose of the class is to provide a user interface. For example, you could develop a standard class to present a login screen in a form instead of a class module. Chapter 11, "Building Classes: Additional Techniques," explains how a class defined in a form behaves differently from a class defined in a class module and provides a login screen example.*

Keynote

The set of properties and methods for a class define the class *interface*. Because a class module contains the properties and methods, it encapsulates all of the information for the class. When you want to use an object anywhere in an application, you create the object from the class and then use the interface to communicate with the object without concern for how the interface is implemented. You set the properties of the object by using the properties in the class interface. You run code from the class for an object by calling the methods in the class interface.

Tech Note. *The properties and methods are part of the* incoming *interface of the class. They provide a mechanism for other parts of the application to use an object from the class. Events are part of the* outgoing *interface of the class because events are sent out from the object and handled by another part of the application. Events are not considered part of the standard interface of a class.*

Provided that the interface of the class does not change, the class can be modified at any time without affecting how the object is used. For example,

Keynote

the code in the CalculatePay method can be changed without affecting how an object from the class is used. This makes the code easier to develop, test, and maintain.

When you construct an application, it is important to define the pertinent set of classes and appropriate properties, methods, and events for each class. This ensures that the correct set of information is encapsulated in each class, making it easier to work with and maintain the class. How do you define that set of classes and their appropriate interfaces? That was the purpose of the object-oriented design described in the previous chapters of this book.

■ Creating a Class

Creating a class in Visual Basic involves inserting a class module into your project and then adding code to that module. This section details the steps for creating a class. A simple Task class example will help you visualize these steps. This sample class tracks the priority, description, and time due for one task.

This is a very simple (and not incredibly useful) class. Likewise, your first programming task was probably not a 100,000-line mission critical system but rather something smaller, like an application that displayed "Hello World." Starting with a simple class lets you focus on understanding the basic tools and techniques before building a large and complex system.

This same Task class example will be used and enhanced throughout this chapter as well as Chapter 11, "Building Classes: Additional Techniques," and Chapter 13, "Building ActiveX Components," so be sure to save your work along the way if you want to work through these chapters.

What Will This Cover?

This section will cover the following key Visual Basic techniques:

- Using class modules

- Defining properties with Property procedures

- Displaying the Code window in Full Module View or Procedure View

- Using private variables and Property procedures versus public variables

- Passing parameters ByVal or ByRef

- Defining methods

- Responding to Initialize and Terminate events

- Documenting properties and methods by defining procedure attributes

- Adding documents to your project

- Using the Object Browser
- Understanding type libraries
- Generating a Visual Basic project workspace file

Steps to Creating a Class

No matter how complex the class, the basic steps for creating it are the same. Each time you create a class, you need to follow these steps:

1. Insert a class module.

2. Define the properties for the class.

3. Create the methods for the class.

4. Respond to class events.

   This refers to responding to the Initialize and Terminate events. Adding your own events to the class is presented later in this chapter.

5. Document the class.

   Including documentation for the class directly in the class module provides an easy mechanism for entering, maintaining, and viewing this documentation.

   These steps are detailed in the topics that follow.

Inserting a Class Module

The class module will contain the properties, methods, and events for the class. To begin a new application and insert a new class module:

1. Start a new Standard EXE project in Visual Basic.

2. From the Project menu, choose Add Class Module and add a new class module.

3. If the Properties window is not open, choose Properties Window from the View menu to open it.

   The Properties window shows the properties of the new class module.

4. In the Properties window, set the Name property.

   For the Task class example, set the Name property to "CTask." Note the "C" prefix used to identify this as a class.

5. In the Code window, type your module header above the Option Explicit statement.

Here is the module header for this sample Task class:

```
' Class Name:     CTask
' Author:         Deborah Kurata, InStep Technologies
' Date:           1/6/97
' Description:    Defines a task with a description,
'                 priority, and due time.
' Revisions:
Option Explicit
```

If Option Explicit does not appear in the Code window for your class module, type it in. Then modify your Visual Basic options to automatically add the Option Explicit statement to all new modules you insert in any project. Using Option Explicit ensures that all variables in your application are declared. This helps you develop solid code by preventing typographical errors in your variables.

To set Option Explicit in all new modules:

1. From the Tools menu, choose Options.

   The Options dialog box will appear.

2. Select the Editor tab.

3. Check the Require Variable Declaration check box, as shown in Figure 10.1.

4. Click on OK to close the Options dialog box.

When Require Variable Declaration is set, the Option Explicit statement will be inserted automatically into all new forms, modules, or class modules you create. It will not, however, insert this statement into any existing code. To add Option Explicit to an existing module, type the Option Explicit statement at the top of the module.

Tech Note. *The Option Explicit statement does nothing but ensure that variables are declared. Using Option Explicit does not affect how variable data types are coerced into other data types.*

Defining the Properties

Class properties define the attributes of all objects created from a class. Each object created from the class has a specific value for each property. For example, the TextBox class has properties such as Name, Text, Top, and so on. A text box added to a form is created from that class and has values for each of the properties: Name is txtDescription, Text is blank, and Top is 60 twips. A second text box would usually have different values for the Name, Text, and Top properties.

Figure 10.1

Check Require Variable
Declarations to ensure
that all variables in your
application are declared.

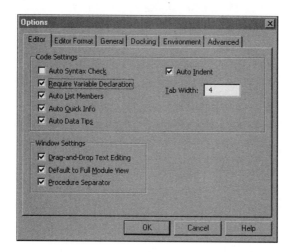

As another example, if you create three tasks from the Task class, each will have its own values for the priority, description, and time due. Changing the priority for one task has no effect on the other tasks' properties.

To create a property:

1. Declare a public variable.

   This variable will represent a property of the class and will contain the value of the property. The property can be a simple data type, such as an Integer or String, or an abstract type, such as an object variable.

Tech Note. *User-defined types (UDTs) cannot be defined as Public in a class module or form.*

OR

1. Declare a private variable.

   This variable will contain the value of the property.

2. Create Property procedures to expose the property.

   Public Property procedures provide a mechanism for exposing the property so it can be accessed from outside the class. A property defined by a Property procedure can be a simple data type, such as an Integer or String, or an abstract type, such as an object variable or user-defined type.

Tech Note.   *A UDT can only be passed to Property procedures declared to be Private or Friend. See the section "Ten Most Common Class Questions" later in this chapter for more information on UDTs.*

OR

3. Create Property procedures to expose the property.

    Property procedures can expose properties that are derived and have no single associated variable to retain a value. For example, an Area property could return the product of the object's height and width and not retain that calculated value.

Declaring a Public Variable

The simplest way to define a property in a class is to declare a public variable in the class module. This only requires one line of code per property. For example, you could define a Description property in a class as follows:

```
Public Description as String
```

Declare the public variable in the Declarations section at the top of the class module. Be sure to provide the data type, such as String. Any variable declared without a data type will be defined as a Variant.

Keynote

Even though this is the easiest way to define properties in a class, it is not the recommended way because there are many dangers to using public variables. Remember the discussion comparing public variables to billboards in Chapter 9, "Strategies for Construction"? Declaring a public variable makes the variable, well, public. Any part of any application that can access the object can manipulate or destroy the property value at will.

Declaring a Private Variable

Keynote

To avoid the hazards of public variables, you can declare private variables for the properties. Private variables can be declared in a class module and used to contain the value of an object's properties. Each object created from a class can have a different set of values for these properties.

Declare a private variable in the Declarations section at the top of the class module. This gives the variable a module-level scope. Be sure to follow your naming and coding conventions in the declaration. (See Chapter 9 for sample naming and coding conventions.) This book uses a prefix of "m_" followed by a data type abbreviation and the property name. The "m_" identifies these variables as module-level variables. The coding conventions used in this example call for the declarations to be alphabetized by property name, ignoring the data type, and for the Property procedures to be listed alphabetically with the Get preceding the associated Let/Set for each property.

The Task class example has properties for task description, priority, and time due. It also tracks the date that the task was created.

```
' PRIVATE: ****************************************
' Private data members

Private m_dtCreated As Date
Private m_sDescription As String
Private m_sDue As String
Private m_iPriority As Integer
```

Notice that the Private keyword is used to declare the variables instead of the familiar Dim statement. Using Private hides these data members and prevents other parts of the application from referencing them. Only procedures within the class module containing the declarations can modify the value of these variables.

Creating Property Procedures

Keynote

If the variables containing the property values are private, what good are they? What is the point of having a protected employee Name property if it cannot be accessed from anywhere? This is where Property procedures come in. *Property procedures* allow properties in a class to be declared as private variables and then exposed through public procedures. Property procedures are similar to Sub and Function procedures, but their primary purpose is to expose the desired properties of the class to the rest of the application.

Create Property procedures for each property of the object that can be accessed by another part of the application. Property procedures normally have logical, user-friendly names such as Description or Priority instead of technical names like m_sDescription or m_iPriority. Using friendly names makes your class properties consistent with classes provided by Visual Basic, such as App.Title, and makes it easier for other developers to use the properties without knowing the naming conventions used.

There are three types of Property procedures:

- **Property Get.** This type of procedure allows other parts of the application to get, or read, the value of a property. The code in the Property Get procedure will return the value of the desired property. Any other code—such as calculations, data conversion or formatting—can be included in the Property Get procedure.

- **Property Let.** This type of procedure allows other parts of the application to set the value of a property that is a String, Integer, or other simple data type. Any other code can be included in the Property Let procedure, such as data validation, conversion, or formatting.

- **Property Set.** This is, essentially, a special case of the Property Let procedure. You use it in place of a Property Let when assigning a variable with an object data type.

In most cases, each property of a class will have a pair of Property procedures: Property Get/Property Let for most data types or Property Get/Property Set for object data types. To define a property that can be retrieved or modified, create a set of Property procedures. For example:

```
' Description of the task
Public Property Get Description() As String
    Description = m_sDescription
End Property
Public Property Let Description(sDescription As String)
    m_sDescription = sDescription
End Property
```

The Property Get procedure syntax is similar to a Function statement with the type of return value identified after the parameter list. The Property Get will be called whenever the Description property of a Task object is requested. It will return the string contained in the m_sDescription private variable. For example, a statement such as

```
Text1.Text = x.Description
```

will call the Property Get procedure, which returns the current value of the private m_sDescription variable.

The Property Let procedure will be called whenever a value is assigned to the Description property. The value assigned to the property is passed to the Property procedure as the last parameter in the parameter list. The code in this Property procedure then assigns the value it is passed to the private variable. For example, a statement such as

```
x.Description = "test"
```

will call the Property Let procedure and pass "test" as the sDescription parameter.

Tech Note. *It is easier to see the Property Get/Let or Get/Set pairs if you are viewing your Code window in Full Module View instead of Procedure View. Full Module View displays all of your code for your module in the Code window with optional line separators between routines, enabling you to scroll through all of the code in the module. Procedure View only displays one procedure at a time in the Code window, requiring you to use the Page Up and Page Down keys to move between procedures. You can set the view by using the buttons in the lower-left corner of the Code window or by setting the Window Settings options using the Options dialog box, as shown in Figure 10.1.*

If necessary, you can restrict a property to read-only by using only the Property Get or modify-only by using only the Property Let or Property Set. For example:

```
' Read-only creation date
Public Property Get Created() As Date
    Created = m_dtCreated
End Property
```

Whenever the Created property of a Task object is requested, this Property Get procedure will be called. The Property Get will retrieve the value of the private m_dtCreated variable and return it as a date.

The data types of the pair of Property procedures must match. For example, the Property Let procedure for the Due property accepts a String as the parameter, so the Property Get procedure must return a String.

```
' Time the task is due
Public Property Get Due() As String
    Due = m_sDue
End Property
Public Property Let Due(sDue As String)
    m_sDue = sDue
End Property
```

Property procedures can also include validation, formatting, or any other processing. The Priority Property procedure ensures that the priority is between zero and four. In this implementation, invalid priority values are changed to 0. Alternatively, the Property procedure could raise an error, as described later in this chapter.

```
' Priority of the task
Public Property Get Priority() As Integer
    Priority = m_iPriority
End Property
Public Property Let Priority(iPriority As Integer)
    ' Prevent invalid values
    If iPriority < 0 or iPriority > 4 Then
        iPriority = 0
    End If
    m_iPriority = iPriority
End Property
```

Creating Property Procedures: A Short Cut

Creating a large number of Property Get and Property Let/Set procedure pairs requires a lot of typing. Visual Basic 5 provides some tools to help you with this process.

To create the template for the Property procedures:

1. Open the class module that is to contain the property.

2. Choose Add Procedure from the Tools menu.
   The Add Procedure dialog box will appear.

3. Enter the property name in the Name text box.

4. Select the Property radio button to define a Property type procedure. When you are finished, the Add Procedure dialog box should look like the one shown in Figure 10.2.

Figure 10.2

You use the Add Procedure option from the Tools menu to insert a template for Property procedures into your application.

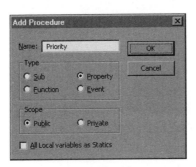

5. Click on OK.

VB5 will generate a prototype definition of the Property Get and Let procedures that looks something like:

```
Public Property Get Priority() As Variant

End Property

Public Property Let Priority(ByVal vNewValue As Variant)

End Property
```

Notice that the data types default to Variant. Variant is generally slower and takes more memory than other data types, so you should change the data types to the correct type for the specific property. You can then add the desired code.

Passing Parameters ByVal or ByRef

There are two ways to pass data to any procedure: ByVal and ByRef. ByVal is short for "by value" and means that the value of the argument will be determined, and a copy of the value will be created and passed to the procedure. Changes made within the procedure to an argument passed by value are not reflected in the calling procedure. ByRef is short for "by reference" and means that a reference to the argument is passed to the procedure, rather than the value itself. Changes made within the procedure to an argument passed by reference will be reflected in the calling procedure. So ByRef is used when the procedure needs to pass values back to the calling procedure.

Keynote

By default, arguments in procedures are passed ByRef. In general, arguments passed ByVal are more efficient than arguments passed ByRef. However, large strings and Variant arrays should be passed using ByRef because it is more efficient to pass the pointer to the string or array than to make a copy of the data and pass the copy. In the case of ActiveX EXEs, there are exceptions to these recommendations, as described in Chapter 13, "Building ActiveX Components."

Public Variables Versus Property Procedures

Using public variables may appear to be more efficient than coding a private declaration and two Property procedures for each property of a class, especially in situations as simple as this Task example class. There are many benefits to using Property procedures, however:

- **Encapsulation.** f the property requires formatting, data validation, or other processing, the code can be encapsulated in the Property procedure. For example, instead of adding code to each routine that uses a creation date property, the Property Get procedure can properly format the date and return it. If the date format needed to be changed, for the year 2000 for example, the code would only need to be modified in one place and all code that used the creation date property would reflect the change.

- **Read-only property.** You can define read-only properties easily by implementing the Property Get with no associated Property Let or Property Set. Or the Property Get can be public and the Property Let can be private to achieve the same read-only result.

- **Maintenance.** You can modify the code for a Property procedure without modifying any of the code using that property. For example, if you formatted a percentage to two decimal places, and then needed to format it for three, you could change the formatting in the Property procedure and the new format would be provided to any code referencing the property. If you had instead used a public variable, you would need to find all places that used it and modify the formatting.

- **No performance penalty.** There is no performance penalty for using Property procedures over public variables. Behind the scenes, Visual Basic implements all public variables as pairs of Property procedures.

Creating the Methods

Class methods define the behaviors of all objects created from the class. Each object can then perform these behaviors. For example, the TextBox class has a Move method so a text box object on a form can be moved by calling the Move method for the object. Just as the actual implementation of the Move method is hidden, the implementation of the methods you create for the class will be hidden from the other parts of the application. This encapsulates the implementation of the class, yet provides the functionality to any part of the application.

To create a method:

1. Determine whether the method will be public or private.

    Only those methods that will be accessed from outside of this class should be declared as Public. All others should be Private.

2. Determine whether the method will return a value.

    If a method needs to return a value, it must be defined as a Function procedure; otherwise it can be a Sub procedure.

3. Write the code for the method.

    The methods for a class are implemented as normal Sub or Function procedures. You can use the Add Procedures dialog box (see Figure 10.2) to add the prototypes for the Sub or Function procedures, but it is usually easier to type the Sub or Function statement manually.

The following code is for a public Clear method in the example Task class. This code clears the properties of the class.

```
' Clear the task
Public Sub Clear()
    Description = ""
    Priority = 0
    Due = ""
End Sub
```

Keynote

Notice that the property names are used instead of the internal private variable names. This will cause the Property Let procedure to be called for each assignment. Even though code in the module has access to the private module-level variables, it is often useful to use the Property procedures. This will ensure that the code in the Property procedure is executed for data conversion, formatting, or raising events.

Responding to Class Events

Class modules can respond to two built-in events: Initialize and Terminate. The Initialize event provides an opportunity to perform initialization of the objects created from the class. The Terminate event provides a place to perform any cleanup processing.

Initialize Event

When an object is created from a class, the Initialize event is generated. Any code in the event procedure for that event is then executed. This will be the first code executed for the object, before any properties are set or any methods are executed.

You could add code in the Initialize event for creating other objects associated with this object or for any other processing that should occur as the object is created.

Tech Note.   *If you have used other object-oriented programming languages, you may recognize the Initialize event as similar to a class constructor. Unlike a constructor, however, the Initialize event cannot be passed any arguments.*

To create an Initialize event procedure:

1. In the Code window's Object box for the class module, select the Class object.

2. In the Procedure box of the Code window, select the Initialize event.

   The Initialize event may have been selected automatically when the Class object was selected. The declaration for the Initialize event procedure is then added to the Code window.

3. Write the code for the event procedure.

The following code uses the system time to set the creation date for the object in the Initialize event.

```
' Initialize event
Private Sub Class_Initialize()
    ' Set the creation date
    m_dtCreated = Now

    ' Display this in a message box
    MsgBox "Task created: " & Created
End Sub
```

The assignment statement in the preceding code uses the private variable m_dtCreated instead of a Property procedure name. This was necessary because the Created property is read-only and has no Property Let procedure. Alternatively, a private Property Let procedure could have been defined. That would ensure that the property was read-only, but allow use of the Property Let within the class containing the property definition. The Msg-Box statement in the code references the Created property, which calls the Property Get to retrieve the property value.

You can handle errors in the Initialize event. If an unhandled error is generated in the Initialize event, the error is raised to the code that created the object. There is more information on error handling later in this chapter.

Tech Note. *The Initialize event should not contain message boxes. The message box was added in this example to demonstrate when the Initialize event occurs. This is very helpful when learning about classes and when debugging them. You should remove this code after you're done experimenting, or replace it with Debug.Print statements to print to the Immediate window.*

Terminate Event

When all references to an object have been released, the Terminate event is generated for the object and any code in the Terminate event procedure for that object is executed. You would add cleanup code to the Terminate event to release dependent objects associated with this object or for any other processing that should occur as the object is destroyed.

To create a Terminate event procedure:

1. In the Code window's Object box for the class module, select the Class object.

2. In the Procedure box of the Code window, select the Terminate event. The declaration for the Terminate event procedure is then added to the Code window.

3. Write the code for the event procedure.

The following code displays the description and priority of the entered task for testing purposes. It displays a second message with the creation date of the task.

```
' Terminate event
Private Sub Class_Terminate()
    ' Display this in a message box
    MsgBox "Task was: " & Description _
        & " Priority: " & Priority
    MsgBox "Task: " & Created & " is now terminated."
End Sub'
```

In this example, the Property Get procedures for Description, Priority, and Created will be called. To see this, work through the next section to learn how to create objects from this class and then use the F8 key to step through this event procedure. You will see the code execute each of the appropriate Property Get statements.

You can handle errors in the Terminate event. If an unhandled error is generated in the Terminate event, the error will be fatal to the application. The error cannot be raised because no code generated the Terminate event. Code that sets an object variable to Nothing simply releases the reference. Visual Basic generates the Terminate event when there are no more references so there is no application code to which the error can be raised. Again, there's more information on error handling later in this chapter.

Tech Note.   *The Terminate event should not contain message boxes. The message box was added in this example to demonstrate when the Terminate event occurs. This is very helpful when learning about classes and when debugging them. You should remove this code after you're done experimenting, or replace it with Debug.Print statements to print to the Immediate window.*

Documenting the Class

Visual Basic 5 provides several easy ways to document your classes within the Visual Basic project. When the documentation is in the project rather than in a separate document file, it's easier to find and reference, and more likely to be kept up to date.

To document the properties or methods for a class:

1. Open the class module to document in the Code window.

2. From the Tools menu, choose Procedure Attributes.
    The Procedure Attribute dialog box will appear, as shown in Figure 10.3.

3. Select the property or method to document in the Name combo box.

Tech Note.   *You can also document events by selecting the event in the Name box. Events are discussed later in this chapter.*

4. Enter the description of the property or method in the Description text box.

5. When desired descriptions have been entered, click on OK.

If you have a help file defined for the project, the help file name will appear in the Project Help File field of the Procedure Attributes screen. You can then associate a Help Context ID with the method or property using the Procedure Attributes dialog box. The defined help topic will appear when the user selects the method or property and then clicks on the question mark in the Object Browser.

If you want more documentation for the project, you can add a Microsoft Word or other document file to the project.

To add a related document to a project:

1. From the Project menu, choose Add File.
    The Add File dialog box will appear.

Figure 10.3

You can use the
Procedure Attributes
dialog box to document
the properties and
methods of your classes.

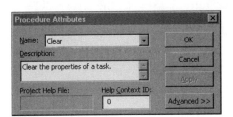

2. Locate the file to add to the project.

   The file must already exist, so if you want a new document you must create it first and then add it to the project.

3. Check the Add as Related Document check box and click on OK.

   If you forget to check the Add as Related Document check box, the file will be added to the project as a standard module. If the file has an extension with a defined association, you can edit this file by double-clicking on it in the Project window. So, you can develop detailed documentation, charts, object models, or any other type of file and maintain it with the other project components directly in the project. The project files included in the CD-ROM use this technique to include a Readme.txt file in each project.

Using the Object Browser

Visual Basic 5 comes with a new and improved Object Browser. The Object Browser provides a list of all classes in all libraries and components referenced by the project. For each class, it lists the public properties, methods, events, and constants. The Object Browser also lists all properties, methods, events and public constants in all modules in the current project. When a property, method, or event from the current project is select, the documentation defined in the Procedure Attributes for that property, method, or event is displayed at the bottom of the Object Browser window.

The Object Browser provides tools for finding classes, properties, methods, events, or constants. It also provides a quick way to navigate to the code for properties, methods, events, or constants.

To work with the Object Browser:

1. From the View menu, choose Object Browser or press the F2 key.
   The Object Browser window appears, as shown in Figure 10.4.

Figure 10.4

The Object Browser lists
all classes, properties,
methods, events, and
constants in your project.

2. Select your project, a library, or <All Libraries> from the Project/
   Library box.

   The Project/Library combo box displays the name of the current
   project along with all referenced libraries for the current project.
   To display other libraries, right-click in the Object Browser, select
   the References option, and check the library you wish to see in the
   Object Browser.

3. Select the class or module from the Classes list.

   The "Members of" list then fills with all properties, methods, events, and
   constants for the selected class.

4. Click on an entry in the "Members of" list.

   The documentation for that member will appear in the Details pane.
   Double-click on the member or click on the View Definition button to
   go to the code for the member.

The Object Browser also allows you to browse object libraries. The Visual Basic (VB) objects and procedures and Visual Basic for Applications (VBA) object libraries are included, so you have a quick reference to all classes, methods, and properties available in Visual Basic. For example, Figure 10.5 describes the Show method for the Form class in the VB object library.

Figure 10.5

The Object Browser also lists the properties, methods, events, and constants for any referenced library, including the standard Visual Basic libraries.

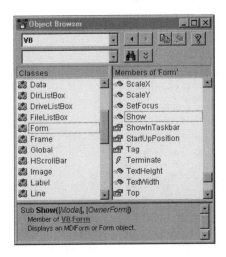

A Word About Type Libraries

What you are really browsing in the Object Browser are type libraries. A *type library* contains the definition of all the classes in a component, including the list of all public methods, properties, events, and constants.

Type libraries can reside in .tlb or .olb files, or within a component in the executable (.exe) or dynamic link library (.dll) file. The name of the type library for a component is shown at the bottom of the Object Browser. For example, the Microsoft Excel 5.0 type library is Xl5en32.olb and the Visual Basic for Applications (VBA) type library is in Vba5.dll.

Even if your project does not yet contain a type library, it will be included in the Object Browser for the project. The Object Browser will always include the list of classes from the current project. For your project to appear in the Object Browser within other projects, it must have a type library. One way to create a type library for a project is to change the project to an ActiveX component and compile the application. The type library is then automatically created within the executable or DLL. See Chapter 13, "Building ActiveX Components," for more information.

What Did This Cover?

This section detailed the steps for creating a class. It described how to insert a class module and add properties and methods for the class. It discussed the difference between the Public and Private keywords and the ByRef and ByVal keywords. It demonstrated how to handle the Initialize and Terminate events. It also explained how to use the Object Browser to review the properties and methods in your class or in object libraries such as Visual Basic (VB) objects and procedures and Visual Basic for Applications (VBA).

If you try to run the example code that you have created so far, you will find that it does not run. Code in a class module will not execute until an object is created from the class, as described in the next section. Save your project because you will use it again.

When you save the sample project, you will find that Visual Basic saved a form, class module, project file, and a file with a .vbw extension. The file with the .vbw extension is the Visual Basic project workspace file. It contains information such as the last size and location of the Code windows for your project.

■ Using an Instance of a Class

A class by itself does not do anything. If you tried to call a class method or set a class property in your code, you would get an error. You first need to create an *instance* of the class, called an *object*. Each object will have its own data values and can execute the Property, Sub, and Function procedures in the class module.

To think about this, let's look again at the cookie cutter metaphor described in Chapter 1. You can think of a class as a cookie cutter; it defines the properties of the cookies, such as height, width, shape, and so on. You can create cookie objects from that cookie cutter class. These cookies are instances of the cookie cutter class, and each has its own values for the cookie properties. After several cookies are created from the class, you can change the shape property of one cookie without affecting the shape properties of the others and you can execute the Eat method on any cookie. Again, you must first create the cookies from the cookie cutter class and then perform the Eat method. You don't perform the Eat method on the cookie cutter class!

The same applies to properties and methods in your class modules. Even though you define the code for the method in the class module, you don't execute the method for the class. Instead, you create an object from the class and then set the properties and call the methods for the object. Setting a property for the object will execute the Property procedures in the class and calling a method will execute the Sub or Function procedures in the class.

When you create an object, you have a reference to it. This reference, or pointer to the object, is stored in an *object variable*. The object variable is then used to refer to the object and to set the object's properties or perform its methods. When you are finished with the object variable, you can release it to ensure that it releases its resources.

A common place to use an object is on a form. An example Task form, shown in Figure 10.6, can create an object from the Task class that was described earlier in this chapter.

Figure 10.6

A simple Task form will demonstrate the techniques for using an object from the Task class.

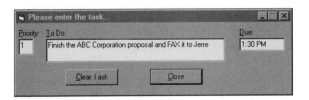

What Will This Cover?

This section will cover the following Visual Basic features:

- Using object variables

- Understanding the difference between early binding and late binding

- Using the TypeName function

- Creating an object from a class

- Accessing an object's properties and methods

- Using the Nothing keyword to release references to objects

Steps to Creating and Using an Instance of a Class

Once you have defined a class, you will want to use the class somewhere in your application. You use a class by creating an object, which is an instance of the class. Any code in a form, standard module, or class module (or even the Immediate window) can create an object from a class. The properties of the object can be set or retrieved and the object can be manipulated by calling the methods. When the object is no longer needed, the instance can be terminated.

Each time you want to use a new object of a class, you need to do the following:

1. Declare the object variable.

2. Create the object.

3. Use the object's properties and methods.

4. Release the reference to the object.

These steps are detailed in the topics that follow.

Tech Note.   *There is an exception to the rule that requires creating an object before using properties and methods for the object. If a class is an ActiveX component defined to be a global class, you can use properties and methods of the object without creating an object. See Chapter 15, "Putting the Pieces Together," for more information on global objects.*

Declaring the Object Variable

Before an object can be created, an object variable must be declared to store the reference to the object. This object variable is then used whenever referring to the object.

There are several options for declaring an object variable:

- Declare a Private variable with the data type defined to be the class of the object.

  For example, a Task form wants to use the capabilities of a Task class. The object variable could be declared in the Declarations section of the Task form as follows:

  ```
  Private m_Task As CTask
  ```

  The m_Task object variable will represent a reference to an object of the CTask class.

Tech Note.   *Declaring the object variable using the class name allows Visual Basic to bind the variable to the object at compile time. This is called* early binding. *Each property or method call that uses an early bound object variable can locate the property or method for the object at compile time and store a reference to it. At run time, the property or method call can use the reference to invoke the property or method immediately, without having to search for the code. Therefore, using early binding improves the performance of the application.*

- Declare a Private variable using the New keyword and with the data type defined to be the class of the object.

  For the Task class example, you could declare the object variable in the Declarations section of the Task form as follows:

  ```
  Private m_Task As New CTask
  ```

  The m_Task object variable will represent a reference to an object of the CTask class. The first time the m_Task variable is used, an object from the CTask class will be automatically created.

Tech Note. *Using object variables declared using the New keyword can affect the performance of your application because each time a statement that uses the object variable is executed, Visual Basic has to determine whether an object has been created. In addition, if you terminate the object and then make another reference to it, a new instance of that class will be created. This may have an unintended effect on your code if you expected to have the property values from the destroyed instance.*

- Declare a Private variable with the data type defined to be Object.

  For the Task class example, you could declare the object variable in the Declarations section of the Task form as follows:

  ```
  Private m_Task As Object
  ```

  The m_Task object variable will represent a reference to any type of object.

Tech Note. *Declaring object variables as Object instead of using the class name can affect the performance of your application because the object variable cannot be bound to the object until run time. This is called* late binding. *Each property or method call that uses a late bound object variable must locate the property or method for the object at run time and then invoke it. Late binding should only be used if the class of the object cannot be known until run time.*

Once you have defined an object variable, you can determine if the object variable references an object by using the TypeName function:

```
TypeName(m_Task)
```

This function will return "Nothing" if the object variable does not reference an object; otherwise it will return the name of the class referenced by the object variable.

Creating the Object

Once an object variable is declared, the object must be created before it can be used. This can be done anywhere in the module that declared the object variable, as long as it occurs before the object is used. For objects that will be used by a form, the object is often created in the Load event for the form. If an object is used by another object, it is normally created in the Initialize event for the other object. Objects used by a single procedure can be declared and created within that procedure. Alternatively, an object can be created automatically the first time it is used.

There are several techniques for creating an object:

- Create the object explicitly by using the Set statement with the New keyword.

    If the object variable was declared without the New keyword, you must use the Set statement as follows:

    ```
    Set m_Task = New CTask
    ```

    When this line of code is executed, an object from the CTask class is created, the CTask class Initialize event is generated, and a reference to the object is stored in m_Task.

    This Set syntax is the preferred technique for creating objects in most cases because the application will know when the object is expected to be created. This allows you to add the necessary error handling or other code.

Tech Note. *When creating objects in the Immediate window, you don't need to declare an object variable, even if you have Option Explicit set, but you must create the object using the Set syntax. Actually, you* can't *declare object variables, or any other variables, in the Immediate window.*

- Create the object implicitly by using it.

    You can only do this if the object variable was declared with the New keyword. For example:

    ```
    m_Task.Clear
    ```

    When this line of code is executed, the application determines whether m_Task currently references an object. If so, it calls the Clear method. If not, a new instance of the CTask class is created, the CTask class Initialize event is generated, a reference to the object is stored in m_Task, and then the Clear method is executed.

    With this technique, the object will be created automatically when it is referenced, which could be in any number of places in the application. This technique is useful for object variables that are defined to be local to a particular routine or for objects that should not be created until they are needed.

Tech Note. *You cannot use the CreateObject function to create an object from a private class. You can use the CreateObject function to create objects from public classes. See Chapter 13, "Building ActiveX Components," for more information on the CreateObject function.*

In the Task class example, a Task form uses an object from the Task class. The object variable was declared without the New syntax as a module-level variable, so the object must be created explicitly. In this case, the object is created during the form's Load event.

```
Private Sub Form_Load()
    ' Create the object
    Set m_Task = New CTask
End Sub
```

When this code is executed, the object is created. Any desired error handling for errors in the initialization process would follow the Set statement.

Setting/Getting Object Properties

Once the object is created, the properties for that object can be retrieved or changed. Properties declared as public variables can be retrieved or changed. A property with a public Property Get procedure can be retrieved and a property with a public Property Let or Property Set procedure can be changed. If a property's Get procedure is private, the property can not be read by the application. Similarly, a property with a private Property Let or Set procedure cannot be changed.

In the Task class example, the user can enter a description of a task in a text box on a form. When the user moves off the text box, the text box's Lost-Focus event is generated. Code in this event can assign the text entered into the text box to the Description property of the task.

```
' Set the text property after entry
Private Sub txtDescription_LostFocus()
    ' Set the property for this task.
    m_Task.Description = txtDescription.Text
End Sub
```

When this code is executed, the Property Let procedure for the Description property is executed for the object referenced by m_Task. The text entered into the text box by the user is passed into the Property Let procedure and assigned to an internal module-level variable. See "Defining the Properties" in the previous section for the Property Let procedure code. Similar LostFocus event procedure code could be created for the Due and Priority properties.

Calling Object Methods

Methods are the actions that can be performed by the object. Any public method can be executed for a particular object. Private methods can only be called from within the class module containing the method.

In the Task class example, the user can click on the Clear Task button, shown in Figure 10.6, to clear the properties of the task. Code in the Click event for that button calls the Clear method of the task.

```
' Clear the task
Private Sub cmdClear_Click()
    ' Clear the task
    m_Task.Clear

    ' Clear the fields on the form
    txtPriority.Text = ""
    txtDescription.Text = ""
    txtDue.Text = ""
End Sub
```

Keynote

When this code is executed, the Clear method is invoked for the task. The text boxes on the form are also cleared in this event procedure. Notice that the code to clear the text boxes is not in the Clear method because the Task class should be completely independent from any user interface for the class. This is true in most cases when creating a class unless the purpose of the class is to provide a specific user interface.

Releasing the Reference to the Object

Objects use memory and system resources. When the object variable is no longer needed it should be disassociated from the object. When an object has no references, the Terminate event will be generated for the object and the resources used by the object will be released automatically.

To release an object variable from an object, use the following syntax:

```
Set objectVar = Nothing
```

An object variable will also be released from an object if the object variable goes out of scope. For example, if the object variable is declared as a local variable, it will be released at the end of the local routine.

In the Task class example, a form uses an object from the Task class. The object was created and the m_Task object variable was associated with the object during the Load event for the form. The object variable can then be released from the object in the Unload event for the form.

```
Private Sub Form_Unload(Cancel As Integer)
    ' Clear all of our object references
    Set m_Task = Nothing
    Set frmTask = Nothing
    End
End Sub
```

The statement that sets m_Task to Nothing removes the reference to the object. If there are no other references to the object, the Terminate event is generated in the CTask class, the object is destroyed, and the resources used by that object are freed. See the section "Working with Forms as Classes" in Chapter 11 for a discussion of the statement that sets frmTask to Nothing.

Tech Note. *The End statement in Visual Basic ends the application. When this statement is executed, the application, well, ends—immediately. The sample code earlier sets m_Task object variable to Nothing, thereby generating the Terminate event. Any code in this event is executed then. If the object variable had not been set to Nothing, it would go out of scope and the Terminate event would be generated. Unfortunately, the End statement would end the application immediately, before any code in the Terminate event could be executed.*

To try this out, use this Task class example and try commenting out the Set statements. Notice that the message boxes in the Terminate events are not displayed.

What Did This Cover?

This section detailed the steps for creating an object from a class and executing code in the class by accessing the properties and methods of the object. It described how to declare and reference object variables, create objects, and use object variables to set the properties and methods for an object. It also provided the correct syntax for releasing the object variable.

You can now run the sample Task class application and it will maintain a single task. With the message boxes in the class, you can see when the object is created and when it is terminated. Note, however, that because the data in the object is not stored anywhere, the data will be lost when you exit the application. The next chapter, "Building Classes: Additional Techniques," discusses how to store the object data.

■ Defining Constants in a Class

Variables in an application provide a mechanism to store values. Those values can be changed simply by assigning a different value to the variable. There are some variables that should not be changed, such as value of *pi*. To define a variable that cannot be changed, you can use a *constant*.

There are also situations in which specific *magic numbers* have specific meanings. For example, the statement

```
frmTask.Show 1
```

calls the Show method of the form and passes a 1 to request a modal type of form. The form is then displayed modally. This is not obvious from simply reading the code. It would be more obvious to use a constant in place of the magic number. The syntax would then be:

```
frmTask.Show vbModal
```

Using a constant instead of a variable ensures values are not inadvertently changed. Using a constant instead of a magic number makes the code easier to read and maintain.

One of the primary benefits of classes is encapsulation. All of the constants associated with a class should be encapsulated within the class. But Visual Basic does not allow a constant to be declared as Public in a form or class module. Visual Basic 5 introduces a new feature to solve this problem: enumeration.

What Will This Cover?

This section will cover the following Visual Basic features:

- Avoiding "magic numbers"

- Defining local constants

- Using the new Enum statement

- Defining global long integer constants

- Defining string constants

Declaring Constants

Visual Basic includes predefined constants such as vbCrLf, for the commonly used carriage return/line feed combination, and vbModal, to represent the value required to show a form as a modal dialog box, as illustrated at the beginning of this section. The Object Browser provides the list of predefined constants for each library.

You can create your own constants by using the Const statement in the Declarations section of a form, module, or class module. For example:

```
Const iWin  = 1
Const iLose = 2
```

To appreciate the benefits of constants, review the following piece of code:

```
Function CalculateScore(i As Integer, iScore As Integer) As Integer
Static iTotal
    Select Case i
        Case 1
            iTotal = iTotal + iScore
        Case 2
            iTotal = iTotal - iScore
    End Select
    CalculateScore = iTotal
End Function
```

The 1 and 2 are sometimes referred to as *magic numbers* because their purpose is unclear from the code. Now compare the preceding code with the following code, which uses constants:

```
Function CalculateScore(i As Integer, iScore As Integer) as Integer
Static iTotal
    Select Case i
        Case iWin
            iTotal = iTotal + iScore
        Case iLose
            iTotal = iTotal - iScore
    End Select
    CalculateScore = iTotal
End Function
```

This code is much easier to read and will therefore be easier to enhance and maintain.

Encapsulating Constants in an Enumeration

Let's expand the previous CalculateScore example. Assume the constants were declared in the Declarations section of the class and the CalculateScore routine was a public method in a class. A form uses an object from the class to calculate the score. To call this method, the form would need code such as:

```
iScore = m_Calc.CalculateScore(1,120)
```

Notice that you have to use the magic number 1 or 2 as the first parameter to the function call. You can't use the constants defined in the class because you cannot declare constants in a form or class to be Public. You could copy the declarations of the constants to the form so you can reuse them, but then you would have to ensure that the constants in the form module were in synch with the constants in the class module. You could also make the constants public in a standard module, but then the class is not encapsulated. Instead, you can use the new enumeration feature in Visual Basic 5.

An *enumeration* is a set of named long integer constants. You can define an enumeration to expose a set of constants required for a class. This set of constants can include the error numbers raised from the class, magic numbers needed as parameters or property values for the class, or any other class constants.

You can declare an enumeration using the Enum keyword in the Declarations section of a form, module, or class module. You can declare an enumeration as Public to expose the constant values and use them anywhere in the application. You can view enumerations in the Object Browser for the project, as shown in Figure 10.7.

Keynote

Tech Note. *Any public enumeration is added to the type library for the application. It will become part of the global name space and can be viewed from the <globals> section of the Object Browser, as shown in Figure 10.7.*

Figure 10.7

Enumerations, listed in the <globals> section of the Object Browser, provide the list of public constants for a class.

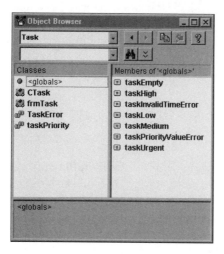

In the CalculateScore example, the Const statements could be replaced with a simple enumeration as follows:

```
Public Enum Winner
        iWin = 1
        iLose = 2
End Enum
```

Any expression that evaluates to a positive or negative long integer value can be assigned to an enumerated constant. If the value of the first constant is not specified, it is given a value of 0. If the value of any other constant is not specified, it is given a value of 1 more than the preceding constant. The following code example provides the same constant values of 1 and 2:

```
Public Enum Winner
        iWin = 5 - 4
        iLose
End Enum
```

This example shows what you could do with an enumeration. However, you would not want to have an enumeration that was so obtuse. You would want to ensure that the values of your enumeration were clear for easier understanding and maintenance.

Now that we have gone through the basics of using an enumeration, let's look again at the Task class example. For the example, a predefined range of valid values was defined for the Priority property. One way to do this is to define a set of enumerated constants for the Priority property.

```
' Define priority values
Public Enum taskPriority
    taskEmpty = 0
    taskUrgent = 1
    taskHigh = 2
    taskMedium = 3
    taskLow = 4
End Enum
```

Keynote

Notice that the name of the enumeration and each enumerated constant is prefixed with the word "task." This follows a recommended naming convention of prefixing an enumeration with a three- or four-character abbreviation of the class containing the enumeration. Because many enumerations are public, this reduces the chance of duplicating names in other classes. Notice also that values were assigned to the enumerated constants instead of using their defaults. It is good programming practice to specify the values instead of using the defaults to ward off problems that might result from any potential future changes in default behavior.

This taskPriority enumeration can be used as the data type of the Priority property. For example:

```
' Priority of the task
Public Property Get Priority() As taskPriority
    Priority = m_iPriority
End Property

Public Property Let Priority(ByVal iPriority As taskPriority)
' Prevent invalid values
    If iPriority < taskEmpty Or iPriority > taskLow Then
        iPriority = taskEmpty
    End If
    m_iPriority = iPriority
End Property
```

The return type of the Property Get procedure and the data type of the Property Let parameter are both of type taskPriority, which is the name of the enumeration. Visual Basic will not restrict the values of variables declared as an enumerated data type to the valid values in an enumeration. Rather, any long integer will be valid.

Notice that the Property Let code now uses the enumerated constants instead of using magic numbers to validate the priority value. These constants provide greater readability, and if other values are added between taskEmpty and taskLow, this code will not need to be changed.

Tech Note. *Enumerations only provide global long integer constants. To define string constants, create a new project, define the strings with public*

Property Get procedures in a class, set the Instancing property of the class to GlobalMultiUse, and compile the class. In any project that needs the string constants, set a reference to the class. The constants will then be available and will appear in the Object Browser. You don't need to create an instance of the class to use the constants since the class is global. See Chapter 15, "Putting the Pieces Together," for more information on global objects.

What Did This Cover?

This section presented techniques for declaring constants in an application. It then demonstrated how to replace long integer constant declarations with an enumeration to make the constants public. It also mentioned how to expose a public set of string constants.

The changes to the Task class application made here will not be apparent when running the application, but they will make the code easier to understand and therefore easier to maintain.

■ Handling Errors

Each class you create should trap its own errors. The coding standards to follow in handling an error in a class, or any routine in the application, should have been defined during the application's design phase as suggested in Chapter 9, "Strategies for Construction." As you develop each routine in an application, you should handle the errors for that routine according to your defined error handling standards.

What Will This Cover?

This section will cover the following Visual Basic features:

- Using the Err object
- Adding error numbers to vbObjectError
- Raising errors
- Using the Error Trapping options

Steps to Handling Errors

To incorporate error handling in a routine:

1. Determine which errors to handle.
2. Define error numbers.
3. Return or resolve the error.

These three steps can be repeated for each routine in the application. The steps are detailed in the topics that follow.

Determining Which Errors to Handle

After developing a routine, evaluate what type of errors the routine can generate. If the routine simply assigns values to variables, it has a minimal chance of generating errors and no error routine may be necessary. If the routine opens a file, a large number of errors could be generated.

Data validations should also be considered, as defined by the business rules. If the value of a property must be between 0 and 4, for example, a value outside of that range is an error. No Visual Basic error will be generated, but this is a validation error and should be handled in the routine.

In the Task class example, the Priority property has a predefined set of values. Instead of just changing the invalid value to something valid, it would be more appropriate to notify the calling routine of the error and allow the calling routine to handle the error.

Defining Error Numbers

If a routine can manage an error internally, no error number needs to be defined. For example, if a routine will generate an error if a file is not found, the routine can create the file and resume without notifying the calling routine that an error occurred. In most cases, however, the error cannot be handled completely within the routine and the calling routine must be notified of the error.

Keynote

Each error that you will raise to the calling routine should have a unique error number. Visual Basic uses error numbers up to vbObjectError + 512. To define an error number that won't conflict with Visual Basic error numbers, select numbers from vbObjectError + 513 to vbObjectError + 65535. To simplify the definition and use of these error numbers, declare them as an enumeration in the module in which the errors could be generated.

For the Task class example, the Priority property error was defined using a public enumeration as follows:

```
' Define error values
Public Enum TaskError
    taskPriorityValueError = vbObjectError + 512 + 2
    taskInvalidTimeError = vbObjectError + 512 + 3
End Enum
```

Alternatively, if your coding standard requires that errors be passed back from routines as part of a function return value or as an event, the error numbers can be any defined values and are not limited to the vbObjectError range.

Returning or Resolving the Error

The last step in handling an error is to return or resolve it. This may be as simple as passing the error up to the calling routine, it may require displaying a message box to the user if the error is generated in the user interface of the application, or it may involve shutting down the application if the error is fatal.

You can pass an error back to the calling routine by using the Raise method of the Err object. This will generate a Visual Basic error that can then be trapped by the calling routine. This technique is particularly useful because it provides a standard mechanism for handling errors generated by Visual Basic and by your code.

Keynote

The Raise method in a routine will be affected by the error trap that is set in that routine. If you have an On Error Resume Next statement in your routine, the Raise method will generate the error and will then resume at the next line in your routine. If you have an On Error GoTo statement in your routine, the Raise method will go to the defined line label in your routine. In either case, it will not raise the error to the calling routine and you may not get the behavior you expected. To ensure that the Raise method raises the error to the calling routine, turn off the error trap with On Error GoTo 0 before raising the error, don't use an error trap in the routine containing the Raise method, or use the On Error GoTo statement and raise the error again from within the error handler.

In the Task class example, the Priority Property Let routine would be as follows:

```
Public Property Let Priority(ByVal iPriority As taskPriority)
    ' Prevent invalid values
    If iPriority < taskEmpty Or iPriority > taskLow Then
        Err.Raise taskPriorityValueError, "CTask::Priority", _
            "Priority value out of range."
    End If

    m_iPriority = iPriority
End Property
```

This routine validates that the priority is between the lowest valid priority value and the highest valid priority value based on the taskPriority enumeration. If the value is out of range, an error is raised. The first parameter of the Raise method is the error number. The second parameter is the source of the error. I like to include both the class name and the routine name to aid in debugging. The last parameter is the error description. These parameters become the values for the Err object's Number, Source, and Description properties.

Alternatively, you could develop this routine with an error trap as follows:

```
Public Property Let Priority(ByVal iPriority As taskPriority)
On Error GoTo ERR_ROUTINE
    ' Prevent invalid values
    If iPriority < taskEmpty Or iPriority > taskLow Then
        Err.Raise taskPriorityValueError, "CTask::Priority", _
            "Priority value out of range."
    End If
    m_iPriority = iPriority
Exit Property
ERR_ROUTINE:
        Err.Raise Err.Number, Err.Source, Err.Description
End Property
```

In this code, the first Err object Raise method will raise the error, and the On Error GoTo error trap will catch the error and resume to the ERR_ROUTINE line label. The Raise method in the ERR_ROUTINE will then raise the error up the call stack to the calling routine.

Tech Note. *Line labels can be any combination of characters that starts with a letter in the first column and ends with a colon (:). By convention I use the same label, ERR_ROUTINE, to label the error handler in every procedure.*

If your coding standard requires the use of function return values for error handling, you can pass the error back to the calling routine by returning the defined error number. However, this is not always possible. For example, Property procedures cannot return values beyond the properties themselves. The error would need to be passed back as a parameter to the Property procedure, which can result in confusing looking code. Instead, the Err object can be used to generate the error.

Another option for returning an error is to pass the error back as a parameter to an error event. Events are described in the section "Generating and Responding to Events" later in this chapter.

Keynote

If an error is passed back to the calling routine, the set of steps for handling the error needs to be repeated in the calling routine. The list of errors to handle is determined, the error numbers are defined (or reused from the routine that generated the error), and the error is passed further up the call stack or resolved. If this step is missed, the result is errors that are handed back up to the calling routine, but not handled when they are received by that routine.

In the Task class example, a Task form uses the Task class. The Task form sets the Priority property of the m_Task object when the text box for entry of the priority loses focus. If the entered value is out of range, an error will be generated within the Priority Property procedure and raised to the LostFocus event procedure, as shown in the previous code. The code in the LostFocus event for the text box needs an appropriate error routine to trap the error raised from the class.

The code in the Task form to trap the error raised from the Priority property in the Task class is as follows:

```
Private Sub txtPriority_LostFocus()
On Error GoTo ERR_ROUTINE
    ' Set the property for this task
    m_Task.Priority = Val(txtPriority.Text)
Exit Sub
ERR_ROUTINE:
    If Err.Number = taskPriorityValueError Then
        MsgBox "Please enter a valid priority value. " _
            & "Valid values range from: " _
            & taskUrgent & " to " & taskLow
    Else
        ' If it was some other error, display a message
        MsgBox "There was an undefined error in the application: " _
                        & Err.Description
    End If
End Sub
```

This code sets an error trap with the On Error GoTo syntax. If the setting of the Priority property generates an error, processing jumps to the ERR_ROUTINE line label to execute the error handler. The code in the error handler uses the Number property of the Err object to determine the error number. The public enumeration in the Task class provides the valid error number constants. If the error is because of an invalid property value, a message box is displayed to notify the user. Otherwise, a generic error message is displayed.

In a production-quality application, a more user-friendly message would be displayed to the user, the real error would be logged, and the application would be terminated gracefully. See Chapter 15, "Putting the Pieces Together," for a discussion of a standard Error handling class that logs errors to a file or the Windows NT event log.

As another example, the Due property can be checked to ensure that it is a valid date:

```
Public Property Let Due(ByVal sDue As String)
    If sDue<>"" And Not (IsDate(sDue)) Then
        Err.Raise taskInvalidTimeError, "CTask::Due", _
        "Invalid date in time due property."
    End If

    m_sDue = sDue
End Property
```

The code in the Task form to trap the error raised from the Due property in the Task class is as follows:

```
Private Sub txtDue_LostFocus()
On Error GoTo ERR_ROUTINE
    ' Set the property for this task
    m_Task.Due = txtDue.Text
Exit Sub

ERR_ROUTINE:
    If Err.Number = taskInvalidTimeError Then
        MsgBox "Please enter a valid value " _
            & "for the time this task is due."
```

```
        Else
            ' If it was some other error, display it
            MsgBox "There was an undefined error in the application: " _
                            & Err.Description
        End If
End Sub
```

When testing error handling in an application using the development environment, watch your Error Trapping setting. This setting is defined in the General tab of the Options dialog box accessed from the Tools menu and shown in Figure 10.8. If Error Trapping is set to Break on All Errors, Visual Basic will enter break mode when any error occurs in the application, ignoring all error handling. This is a good way to turn off error handling if needed for testing or debugging.

If Error Trapping is set to Break in Class Module, Visual Basic will enter break mode when an unhandled error occurs in a class instead of raising the error to the calling routine. This behavior makes it appear that your error is not properly handled by the calling routine, but in reality Visual Basic is just stopping execution to notify you of the error. You can then use Alt+F8 to step into the calling routine's error handler or Alt+F5 to continue.

Keynote

Figure 10.8

Watch your Error Trapping setting. It may cause unexpected results in your error handling while you are testing the application in the IDE.

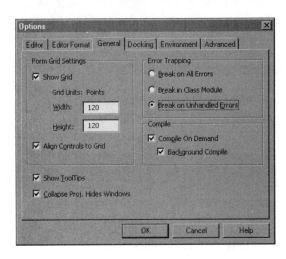

If the Error Trapping setting is Break on Unhandled Errors, Visual Basic will only enter break mode if an error is not handled in the application. Note, however, that with this setting unhandled errors in class procedures will enter break mode on the line that invoked the procedure, not on the line that generated the error in the class module. This can make it harder to track down the source of the error when you're debugging the application.

What Did This Cover?

This section detailed the steps for incorporating error handling into any routine in an application. It discussed how to define which errors to handle, how to use vbObjectError to generate an error number, and how to use the Raise method of the Err object to raise an error.

The Task class example should now generate a message if the priority entered into the Priority text box on the form is not between 0 and 4. If Visual Basic goes into break mode instead of displaying your message box, check the Error Trapping setting, as explained in the previous topic.

If you are working through the examples in this book, be sure to save your project at this point. You will reuse it in the next chapter.

■ Generating and Responding to Events

Keynote

Classes can generate or respond to events. An *event* is basically a message that an object can broadcast at any time. The object that generates the event, called the *event source*, knows when to broadcast the message. An object that can respond to a message is called an *event sink*. Code in the event sink is executed when the event is received.

For example, a button on a form knows that if it receives a mouse click within its displayable area, it should broadcast a Click event. The form is the event sink. But defining an object as an event sink, able to respond to an event, is not enough. If you add a button to a form and click on the button, what happens? Nothing. Nothing will ever happen until you write code to respond to the Click event. You don't write this code into the class that generated the event (you couldn't write code into the button class even if you wanted to). Instead, you write the code in a Click event procedure within the form that is using the button. Code in the Click event procedure is then executed in response to the Click event.

As another example, you can define a PayCalculated event in a TimeSheet object (the event source) and broadcast the PayCalculated message when the object is finished calculating the pay. A Payroll object (the event sink) would contain the code to respond to the TimeSheet object's PayCalculated event and begin generation of the pay checks.

To demonstrate how events can be used in a class, an alarm feature will be added to the Task class example. Recall that the Task class manages information about a task. One of the properties of the task is the time the task is due. The Task class (the event source) can generate an Alarm event when the task due time is reached. A Task form (the event sink) uses an object from the Task class. When the Alarm event is generated by the Task class, the form will respond to the event and notify the user that the task is now due.

For this example, a button will be added to the Task form that will set the alarm and minimize the Task form. The revised Task form is shown in Figure 10.9. With this enhancement, the Task application is starting to become useful. It could be used as a reminder for meetings, conference calls, or a lunch date.

Figure 10.9

A revised Task form will be used to demonstrate events. When the alarm is set, the Task form is minimized and when the task due time is reached, the Task class generates an Alarm event and the form appears to indicate that the task is now due.

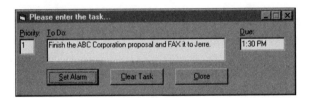

If you are working through the examples in this book, be sure to save your project before adding events as described in this section. The project, without the events, will be reused in Chapter 11, "Building Classes: Additional Techniques."

What Will This Cover?

This section will cover the following Visual Basic features:

- Declaring an event in a class

- Using the RaiseEvent statement

- Declaring objects using WithEvents

- Responding to events

- Responding to events generated by a form or control within a class

Steps to Generating an Event

Any class defined in a class module or form can generate an event. Normally, a class will generate an event if it performs some action and other objects must be notified of the action.

To add an event to a class:

1. Declare the event.

2. Raise the event.

Each of these steps is detailed in the topics that follow.

Declaring an Event

Use the Event statement to declare the event in the Declarations section of a form or class module. The declaration of the event defines the name and parameter list for the event. Once declared, the event will appear in the Object Browser for the class.

Tech Note. *The parameter list for an event can contain the same type parameters as defined for a Property procedure. However, events cannot have named, optional, or ParamArray arguments. Also, events cannot return values.*

For the Task class example, the Task class will generate an Alarm event when the task's due time arrives. The following code declares the event in the Declarations section of the Task class:

```
' Generate an event when alarm goes off
Public Event Alarm()
```

Raising an Event

Use the RaiseEvent statement to generate the event. Only the class or form containing the event declaration can raise the event.

In the Task class example, the Alarm event should be raised when the current time is greater than or equal to the time the task is due. This is shown in the following code:

```
If TimeValue(Now) >= TimeValue(m_sDue) Then
    ' Generate the alarm
    RaiseEvent Alarm
End If
```

Later in this section we'll identify where this code belongs in the Task class.

Tech Note. *When an object raises an event, all of the client applications that have a reference to the object "WithEvents" will handle the event before the object can continue processing.*

Steps to Responding to Events

Any class defined in a class module or form can respond to events. A class can only respond to events from an object if it has a reference to the object.

To respond to an event:

1. Declare the object variable using WithEvents.

2. Set the object variable to an object.

3. Code the event procedures.

4. Release the reference to the object.

Each of these steps is detailed in the topics that follow.

Declaring an Object Variable Using WithEvents

Keynote

To use an object, you must declare an object variable. If an object has events, the form or class that uses the object can chose to respond to the events, but it does not have to. To respond to events generated by the object, the declaration of the object variable must include the WithEvents keyword. Without the WithEvents keyword on the declaration, any events generated by the object will be ignored.

Tech Note.   *Standard modules can not respond to events from objects. Using the WithEvents keyword in a standard module generates a compile-time error.*

For the Task class example, you would need to change the declaration for the Task object in the Task form to the following:

```
' Define this instance of the task class
Private WithEvents mw_Task As CTask
```

Notice the change in the object variable name. The "mw_" convention identifies the object variable as a module-level variable that uses the object with its events.

Tech Note.   *The object variable must be declared as a module-level variable with a specific class name and cannot be declared with the New keyword.*

Setting the Object Variable to an Object

Before using an object from the class or responding to an object's events, the object must be created. As before, you do this with the Set statement using the New keyword. Because the New keyword is not allowed on the declaration of the object variable declared WithEvents, you must create the object with the Set statement.

If an object already exists, the object variable declared WithEvents can be set to the object to begin receiving events from the object.

The Task form in the Task class example already included the code for creating the object when the form is loaded:

```
Private Sub Form_Load()
    ' Create the object
    Set mw_Task = New CTask
End Sub
```

The only change from the original Load event is the name of the Task class object variable, which was changed to conform to the "mw_" naming convention.

Coding the Event Procedures

As soon as you declare the object variable using the WithEvents keyword, the object variable name will appear in the Object box in the upper-left corner of the Code window. When you select this object, the events for the object will appear in the Procedures/Events box in the upper-right corner of the Code window. All events declared in the object's class will appear in the list.

The form or class module using the object does not need to respond to all of the events an object can generate. You can select each event to respond to from the Procedures/Events box and the template of the event procedure will be inserted into the Code window, as shown in Figure 10.10. Any code added to this template will be executed when the event is generated by the object.

Figure 10.10

If a form or class module uses an object with its events, event procedures can be inserted into the form or class module to respond to any of the object's events.

As you can see, this process is very similar to adding event procedures for controls on a form. You just have the additional step of declaring the object variable.

In the Task class example, the Alarm event will be handled in the Task form. When this event occurs, the form will be returned to normal size (it was minimized when the alarm was set) and the form will beep to notify the user that the task is now due. Here is the code for this:

```
Private Sub mw_Task_Alarm()
    ' Ensure the form is not minimized
    If Me.WindowState = vbMinimized Then
        Me.WindowState = vbNormal
    End If

    ' Then beep
    Beep
End Sub
```

Releasing the Reference to the Object

As always, the reference to the object should be disassociated from the object when the object variable is no longer needed. You do this by setting the object variable to Nothing.

The Task class example should already have the following code:

```
Private Sub Form_Unload(Cancel As Integer)
    ' Clear all of our object references
    Set mw_Task = Nothing
    Set frmTask = Nothing
    End
End Sub
```

Notice that you don't need to do anything new to stop events from an object. Simply set the object variable to Nothing.

Responding to Form or Control Events in a Class

One thing is missing from this Task class example. The code to raise the event, presented in the earlier topic "Raising an Event," checks the current time against the time due and raises the event if the current time is greater than or equal to the time due. But where should this code be? You could add the code to a routine that is called when the alarm is set, but that will only check the time once. For this class to work properly, the current time needs to be checked against the time due on a recurring basis until the event is raised. To do this, the project will need a timer.

There are two basic ways to use a timer in Visual Basic. One is to use the Timer control on a form and the other is to use the system timer. An example of using the system timer is presented in the sample code provided with the Professional and Enterprise editions of Visual Basic.

Keynote

Tech Note. *As of this writing, this sample application was in VB/samples/ CompTool/ActvComp/coffee/XTimers.vbp.*

For simplicity, the Task class example will use the Timer control. You could put the Timer control directly on the Task form. However, to follow the three-tiered architecture approach, you should not tie the Task class to the specific user interface of the Task form. Instead, you can insert a new form in the project (named frmTimer) and add a Timer control to that form (named tmrAlarm). Then the Task class, with the Timer form, can be reused with any user interface.

The Task class will encapsulate the processing of the Timer control by intercepting the Timer events directly from the Timer control on the form, so no code is required in the Timer form. The Task class can intercept the Timer events using the same four steps for responding to an event discussed earlier: an object variable of type Timer is declared using the WithEvents keyword, the object variable is assigned to the Timer on the form, Timer event procedures are coded, and the object variable is released when the Task class is terminated. The code for these steps is detailed next.

In the Task class, declare an object variable for the form containing the Timer. This allows each instance of the Task class to own its own form and hence have independent Timers.

```
' Allow response to events from a Timer
Private frmTimer As New frmTimer
Private WithEvents mw_tmrAlarm As Timer
```

Also declare an object variable for the Timer itself. The Timer object variable is declared using WithEvents to intercept the Timer events. Any events generated by the Timer object referenced by this object variable will be received by this Task class. Note that the name of the object variable follows the naming convention of using "mw_" for module-level object variables that will respond to events.

The second step is to set the object variable to an object. You do this in the Initialize event for the Task class:

```
' Initialize event
Private Sub Class_Initialize()
    ' Set the creation date
    m_dtCreated = Now

    ' Set our Timer object variable to the Timer on the form
    Set mw_tmrAlarm = frmTimer.tmrAlarm
End Sub
```

This code sets the module-level object variable for the Timer to the Timer object on the Timer form. This causes all events generated by the control on the form to be raised to the Task class.

For the third step, you can add code to respond to the Timer event. This is where the time will be checked:

```
' When the timer goes off on the form, check the time
Private Sub mw_tmrAlarm_Timer()
    ' Note: This assumes no change in date
    If TimeValue(Now) >= TimeValue(m_sDue) Then
        ' Generate the alarm
        RaiseEvent Alarm
        ' Turn off the timer on the form
        mw_tmrAlarm.Enabled = False
```

```
        End If
End Sub
```

This code receives each Timer event and checks the current time against the time the task is due. If the task is due, the Alarm event is raised. Because the Timer on the form is no longer required, the Enabled property of the Timer is set to False. The Enabled property of the Timer can be set to True again in the SetAlarm method of the Task class.

```
' Start the timer
Public Sub SetAlarm()
    ' Turn on the timer on the form
    If Due = "" Then
        Err.Raise taskInvalidTimeError, "CTask::SetAlarm", _
            "The time due must be set prior to setting the alarm."
    Else
        mw_tmrAlarm.Enabled = True
    End If
End Sub
```

This method is called from the Click event for the Set Timer button on the form. If the Due time is empty, this code raises an error; otherwise it enables the alarm so the Task class will begin receiving Timer events.

When the Task class terminates, you can release the object variables from the objects:

```
' Terminate event
Private Sub Class_Terminate()
    ' Unload the timer and form
    Set mw_tmrAlarm = Nothing
    Unload frmTimer
    Set frmTimer = Nothing
End Sub
```

What Did This Cover?

This section detailed the steps for defining an event in a class and raising the event for an object from the class. Raising the event broadcasts the message. This section also illustrated how to respond to an event. If the object variable was declared using the WithEvents keyword, the class containing the object variable can respond to the event. You can use these techniques to generate your own events from a class module or form.

The example presented in this section demonstrated how a class can intercept events from a form or control on a form. This allows for encapsulation of operations that require form components.

Before the sample Task class application that was modified in this section will work appropriately, you need to finish a few details. First, you need to put code in the Set Alarm button to call the SetAlarm method in the Task class and to minimize the Task form. Then, you need to modify the properties of the Timer object on the Timer form. Set the Enabled property to False so the

Timer won't be enabled until the user selects the Set Alarm button. You may also want to increase the Timer interval to 1000 milliseconds or more.

You can use the resulting Task application to track a meeting or conference call. One additional note: If you enter times in the afternoon, don't forget to include the PM indicator. The default is AM.

■ Compiling the Project

Keynote

Once you have finished and tested a project, you should compile it. In addition to the p-code compiling that Visual Basic has always provided, you can now perform native compilation.

What Will This Cover?

This section will cover the following Visual Basic features:

- Setting project properties

- Compiling to p-code

- Compiling to native code

Steps to Compiling a Project

To compile a project:

1. Set the project properties.

2. Compile the project.

Each of these steps is detailed in the topics that follow.

Setting Project Properties

The project properties are accessed from the Properties option in the Project menu. Project properties are divided into four sections: General, Make, Compile, and Component. These properties identify information specific to the project and should be set prior to compiling the project. Note that the Make and Compile tabs are also available from the Options button on the Make Project dialog box.

General Properties

The General properties include the following:

- **Project Type.** This identifies the project as a standard project or a type of ActiveX component. You can change the type at any time, so you can create a standard project and later convert it to an ActiveX component. See Chapter 13, "Building an ActiveX Component," for more information.

- **Startup Object.** This identifies the first object that will be executed in an application. For most standard projects, it should be set to Sub Main, as discussed in Chapter 7, "Implementation-Centered Design". In ActiveX components, it can be set to None if no startup processing is required for the component.

- **Project Name.** This name appears in the Object Browser for the application and should be clear and descriptive.

- **Help File Name and Project Help Context ID.** These fields allow you to define a help system for the application.

- **Project Description.** This should include a clear description of the application. This description will appear for the component in the References dialog box. Because the References dialog box presents the components alphabetically, pay attention to the first word in the description and start with a word that other developers would think to use to find your application.

Make Properties

The Make properties include the following:

- **Version Number.** You can identify a major and minor version number and a revision number. If you check the Auto Increment check box, the Revision number will be incremented each time you Make the project.

Tech Note.   *The Visual Basic Setup Wizard will not overwrite a new version of your application with one with an equal or lesser version number. If you don't modify the version number of your application, the Setup Wizard will not install the new copy.*

- **Application.** The Application Title is the name you give to the application. You can use any name. This is also the default name for all message boxes in your application. In the Application Icon list, the forms in the application are listed. You can select which form's icon should be used as the application icon.

- **Version Information.** The Type box lists the available version resources. To set a string for the version resource, select the resource in the Type box and then enter the string in the Value box.

- **Command Line Arguments.** These arguments are used when you select Run from the menu. They are treated as if they were entered on the command line. This allows you to test command-line arguments without having to compile and launch the executable from the command line.

- **Conditional Compilation Arguments.** You can define conditional compilation constants in this field. Conditional compilation is discussed in Chapter 11, "Building Classes: Additional Techniques."

Compile Properties

The Compile properties include the following:

- **Compile to P-Code.** This causes the application to be compiled as it always has been—that is, into pseudo code.

- **Compile to Native Code.** This causes the application to be compiled into native code. For many applications, compiling into native code will result in a faster executable. See the Visual Basic documentation for a description of the native code compilation flags and their effect on the performance of your application.

Tech Note.   *Native code does not mean that the application will run without some associated libraries. A user will still need the Visual Basic DLLs to run your application. Use Setup Wizard to determine this list of required distribution files.*

Component Properties

The Component properties are for use only with ActiveX components. They include the following:

- **Start Mode.** This allows you to test your ActiveX component as a stand-alone application or as an object server. This does not affect how the application will run after it is compiled. See Chapter 13, "Building ActiveX Components," for more information.

- **Remote Server.** This field is shown if you have the Enterprise Edition of Visual Basic. It creates a file with a .vbr extension that is required to set up the registry to run an ActiveX component on a remote computer.

- **Version Compatibility.** This replaces the Compatible OLE Server field defined in Visual Basic 4. It defines whether a component is compatible with prior versions of the components. See Chapter 13, "Building ActiveX Components," for more information.

Compiling the Project

After setting the project properties, compile the application by choosing Make from the File menu. The application will be compiled according to the specifications identified in the project properties.

Tech Note.   *You can reduce the time it takes to compile your project by removing any components and references that the project doesn't need. Do* *this by using the Components option from the Project menu and unchecking any components that your project does not need. Then use the References option from the Project menu and uncheck any unnecessary references.*

What Did This Cover?

This section described the many different project properties and explained how to compile the application.

At this point, you should be able to define the properties for the Task class sample application and compile it. You can try different compilation options to check for any differences in performance. With the limited operations of this example, you will probably not see a difference.

■ Ten Most Common Class Questions

When you're working with a new tool, you'll often have new questions. Here are ten of the most common questions about the class tools, with their answers.

1. How do I know whether to use a standard module, form, or class module? There are three types of modules in Visual Basic:

   • **Standard Module.** A standard module is the module with the .bas extension that can contain Sub and Function procedures. You should use standard modules whenever you need to write code that is not associated with a class, although some may argue that all code should be associated with a class.

   Minimally, you will want a standard module in your standard projects for your Sub Main procedure to start the application with code rather than with a form. This standard module could also include any global declarations.

   • **Form.** A form is a class with a user interface. Forms are used for all user interface components of the application. Most of the techniques you can use with class modules—such as exposing properties with Property procedures and raising or responding to events—can also be used in forms. See Chapter 11, "Building Classes: Additional Techniques," for more information.

   • **Class Module.** A class module defines the properties, methods, and events for all objects created from the class. You can use class modules any time you want to gain the benefits of object-oriented programming. You can encapsulate all of the properties and methods for a class in a class module. You can also generate and respond to events. A standard module cannot generate or respond to events.

Tech Note. *One important difference between a standard module and a class module is that there is one set of data in a standard module and it exists for the life of your application. For class modules, there is an instance of your class module data for each object created from the class and that data is destroyed when the object is terminated. Forms, like class modules, also have an instance of the module-level data for each form and that data is destroyed when the form is terminated, not when it is unloaded.*

2. How do I know whether to use a property or a method?

   Basically, you should use a property to define the attributes of an object (nouns) and a method to define its behavior (verbs). The line between what is an attribute and what is a behavior is not always that clear.

   For example, look at the Visual Basic Top and Left properties and the Move method. The Top and Left properties are indeed attributes of an object, but setting them actually performs an action. The Move method moves the object, but also sets the Top and Left properties of that object.

   When working with remote components, you may want to have one method with a parameter for each property or a ParamArray instead of setting each property individually. That way, there is one call across the network containing all of the property values instead of one call per property.

   Examine the requirements of the project to determine whether to use a property, a method, or both in any particular situation.

3. When is the New keyword required?

   Before an object variable can be used, the object must be created. This is done using the New keyword on the declaration of the object variable or in the Set statement assigning the object variable.

   If you use New in the declaration, the object is not actually created until the object variable, m_Task in this case, is first used. If the object is terminated and then referenced again, a new object is created. For example:

```
Dim m_Task As New CTask

' This creates the object
m_Task.Description = "Finish time sheet"
```

   If you don't use the New keyword in the declaration, the object is created when the Set statement is executed. The Set statement uses the New keyword to request a new object. For example:

```
Dim m_Task As CTask

' This creates the object
Set m_Task = New CTask
```

This is often the preferred method because it provides tighter control over when the Initialize event will occur. In the first example, the Initialize event for the object could occur anywhere in the code. A minor modification to the code could easily shift the location of the initialization. In the second example, the Initialize event will occur when the Sct statement is executed.

4. When do I need to use the Set statement?

The Set statement assigns an object variable to reference an object. This is different from assigning values to other data types such as Strings and Integers. When using a String variable, the variable's value is a string; for Integer variables, the value is an integer.

```
Dim sDescription As String
Dim iPriority As Integer

sDescription = "Finish time sheet"
iPriority = 2
```

In this example, the variable sDescription has a value of "Finish time sheet" and variable iPriority has a value of 2. An object variable does not have a value; it has a reference to an object. For example, the variable thisTask does not have a value but is a reference to a Task object. Because object variables are references rather than values, you use a slightly different syntax when assigning object variables.

```
Dim m_Task As CTask
Dim thisTask As CTask

Set thisTask = New CTask
Set m_Task = thisTask
```

The first Set statement includes the New keyword, so it creates a new instance from the CTask class and stores the reference to that object in thisTask. The second Set Statement does not make a copy of the object referenced by thisTask. Instead, it creates another reference to the object. Both the m_Task and thisTask object variables now refer to the same object, so if the properties of thisTask are changed, the change will be seen in m_Task. For instance, you can call your dog "Charlie" sometimes and "Chuck" other times but it is still the same dog. If you feed Charlie, Chuck is fed.

5. Why can't my application find one of my class's methods?

There are several reasons your application may not be able to find a specific method in a class.

- If a method is private and you access the method from outside the class, you will get the error "Method or data member not found."

By default, Sub and Function procedures you create are public, while event procedures are private. Explicitly defining public Sub and Function procedures as Public ensures that they will be available to other parts of your application. For example:

```
' Clear the task
Public Sub Clear()
    Description = ""
    Priority = 0
    Due = ""
End Sub
```

- If you reference the method without the class name, you will get the error "Variable not defined" or "Sub or Function not defined."

  You need to preface the method with the object reference. For example, in the following code, the Clear method call is prefixed with the object variable:

```
' Clear the task
Private Sub cmdClear_Click()
    ' Clear the task
    m_Task.Clear
End Sub
```

6. Why am I getting the error "Object variable or With block variable not set"?

   The most common reason for this is that the object variable has not been initialized.

   If you reference a new object without having declared or set the object with the New keyword, you will get this error. If you comment out the Set statement in the Task class sample code as shown here, you will generate this error.

```
Private Sub Form_Load()
    ' Create the object
    'Set m_Task = New CTask
End Sub
```

   The error is generated because you have not instantiated the object. Make sure the New keyword is included in the object variable declaration or the Set statement is used to create the object.

7. Why did the object I just created terminate?

   Object variables have a scope just like the other variables in your application. If you define a variable in a procedure, the variable is no longer valid when the procedure is complete. If you define an object variable in a procedure, that object reference is released when that procedure is complete.

The following code is an example of an object that will disappear when the procedure is complete:

```
Private Sub CreateTask( )
    ' This is a local object variable
    Dim taskTemp As New CTask

    ' This creates the temporary object
    taskTemp.Description = txtToDo(0).text
End Sub
```

Add message boxes or Debug.Print statements in the Initialize and Terminate events during debugging to help you find these types of errors.

8. When is my object actually created?

An object is created from a class module when:

- A reference to the object is set, as in:

```
Set m_task = New CTask
```

- The object variable was declared with Dim As New and any property or method of the object is referenced, as in:

```
Dim m_Task As New CTask

m_Task.Description = "Finish the paperwork for Admin"
```

Note that Dim as New does not create the object.

- The object is passed as an argument to a procedure.

A form object is created when:

- A reference to the form is set, as in:

```
Set myForm = New Form1
```

- Any property or method of the form is referenced.
- The form is passed as an argument to a procedure.
- The form is loaded.

The form is loaded when:

- The Load statement is used.
- One of the intrinsic properties (like Caption) or methods (like Move) is referenced. The form does not load on referencing any properties or methods you define.
- A control or control array on the form is referenced.

9. Why didn't the object's Terminate event get generated?

The Terminate event will not be executed for an object if you have any remaining references to the object. The Terminate event will not be executed for a form until all references to the form are released, all references to all controls on the form are released, and the form is unloaded.

In the following code, the Terminate event for the object from the CTask class will not be generated because thisTask still has a reference to a Task class object.

```
Dim m_Task As New CTask
Dim thisTask As CTask

Set thisTask = m_Task
Set m_Task = Nothing
```

The code would also need to set the thisTask object variable to Nothing before the Terminate event for that object would be executed.

When you close an application that uses objects, be sure to set all object references to Nothing and unload all of the forms before executing the End statement. Unloading the forms and freeing the references will ensure that any Terminate events get processed.

10. How can I pass my user-defined type (UDT) to a class?

You cannot pass a user-defined type as a parameter to a public procedure in a class module. You can, however, pass UDTs to private procedures or procedures declared with the Friend keyword. Friend, which is new in Visual Basic 5, allows a class to be public to other code in an application, yet private to other external components. See Chapter 13, "Building ActiveX Components," for more information on the Friend keyword.

A standard module could include the following code:

```
Public Type TaskUDT
    Description As String
    Priority As Integer
End Type
Private TaskData As TaskUDT
Private m_Task As New CTask

Private Sub Main()
    ' Set the values into the UDT
    TaskData.Description = "Finish the on-line help"
    TaskData.Priority = 5

    ' Pass them to the object
    m_Task.SetData TaskData
End Sub
```

The Public declaration of the UDT must be in a standard module. You cannot declare Public UDTs in forms or class modules. The UDT can be passed to the class module's SetData method, as shown in the following code:

```
Private m_sDescription As String
Private m_iPriority As Integer

Friend Sub SetData(tUDT As TaskUDT)
    m_sDescription = tUDT.Description
    m_iPriority = tUDT.Priority
    MsgBox m_sDescription & " " & m_iPriority
End Sub
```

Notice the Friend keyword on the declaration of the Sub procedure. This technique does not work if the Sub procedure is declared as Public or Private.

■ Summary

- Classes are a key component of object-oriented programming (OOP).

- Class modules allow you to define the properties, methods, and events for a class.

- You can declare the properties of a class to be private to protect data from direct, uncontrolled changes by other parts of the application.

- Property procedures are a mechanism for exposing the properties of a class to other parts of the application. These Property procedures can provide read-only, write-only, or read/write access to the properties.

- You can create methods of a class by inserting Sub or Function procedures in the class.

- Initialize and Terminate events for the class module allow for any necessary processing as an object is created and destroyed.

- You can document the class within the project using the Procedure Attributes option.

- You can use the Object Browser to quickly navigate to the components of your project. The Object Browser also supplies a quick reference to all of the classes, methods, and properties in the Visual Basic object libraries.

- You can create an instance of a class in any code module. This instance is an object.

- An object variable contains a reference to an object and the TypeName function can be used to determine the class name of the object that the object variable references.

- You can terminate an object by setting all of its references to Nothing.

- You can encapsulate public constants in a class using an enumeration.

- You should implement error handling in all routines that might generate errors or need to handle data validation.

- Programmer-defined events can be raised by an object.

- Any form or class module can respond to events raised by other forms and classes.

- You should set appropriate project properties to describe project attributes and define the compilation options before compiling the project.

- Applications can now be compiled as p-code or as native code.

■ Additional Reading

Jauch, Alex and Kaufman, Dylan, "VB4's Got Pointers," *Visual Basic Programmer's Journal*, Programming with Class column. Vol. 7, No 1, January 1997.

VB4 has pointers, so does VB5. This article describes how you can use that fact to implement dynamic data structures, such as generic queues and binary trees.

■ Think It Over

To supplement and review the information in this chapter, think about the following:

1. Try working through the Task class example presented in the book. When the code presented in the first two sections of this chapter is in place, step through it using the F8 key. This will help you see the order of execution within the application.

2. Look around you and think about real-world objects and how you would write and use them in object-oriented notation. Have fun with it.

   When I was on a trip with my young daughters, we had to change planes in Chicago. When one of my daughters asked "Mommy, is this the same plane we were just on," I said "No, Jessica, it is just another instance of the same class."

The following is slightly modified version of a message from Gregg Irwin, a Visual Basic developer, on the birth of his new daughter:

```
Dim Baby As New Person
Baby.Name = "KatherineGrace"
Baby.Sex = Female
Baby.DueDate = DateValue("4/17/95")
Baby.DateOfBirth = DateValue("4/23/95")
Baby.TimeOfBirth = TimeValue("11:32 AM")
Baby.Weight = 8.69        '-- 8 Lbs 11 oz
Baby.Length = 28800       '-- twips (= 20 inches)
Baby.Mother = "Stacy"
Baby.Father = "Gregg"
```

11

Building Classes:
Additional Techniques

Nobody wants to remain a beginner.

—Alan Cooper

Once you know the basics, you are ready to move from the bunny slope to the intermediate runs. That's where you can really have fun!

This chapter presents several additional techniques to help you create more complex and useful classes. It illustrates how to create a class to manage a set of objects using a collection. It describes how to create a class for storing your object data in a file and then retrieve that data. It demonstrates how to use class techniques with forms. Finally, it discusses several useful debugging techniques.

■ Defining Collections

So far the examples in this book have used only one instance of a class—only one Task object was created. In most applications, you will want to track a set of objects. This can be done using a *collection*, which is an ordered group of items that can be processed as a set. The items in a collection can be any data type, including any type of object.

A collection is basically a cross between an array and a list box. It is like an array because it can contain a set of items. It is like a list box because it provides a predefined set of methods such as Add, Remove, and Item to process the list and it handles shifting the items automatically when an item is added or removed from the list.

A collection itself is an object, so it can be created and referenced anywhere in the application just like any other object. To ensure encapsulation, however, a collection is normally created in a class defined specifically for managing the collection, called a *collection class*.

Keynote

Defining a collection within a collection class encapsulates the collection and keeps the collection private, so no other code can modify it unintentionally or incorrectly. If the collection is private, though, how can objects be added to it? Just as Property procedures provide public exposure to private properties, public *wrapper* methods can provide public exposure to a private collection. Wrapper methods get their name because they provide a public wrapper around the private collection's methods. When an application needs to access a collection, the application can't use the collection's Add, Remove, and Item methods directly; rather the application uses the Add, Remove, and Item wrapper methods provided in the collection class. These wrapper methods in the collection class then call the collection's methods.

Think of the collection class as a place to manage your own private collection. Suppose you have a collection of Star Trek action figures at home. If I want to add an action figure to your collection, I have to give the object to you and you add it to your collection. If I want to take an action figure from your collection, you have to allow me to do it. If I want to use one of your action figures, I have to request it from you.

The Task class example (without the events) from Chapter 10, "Building Your First Class," will be used to demonstrate the techniques for building a collection class. Recall that this example included a Task class with properties and methods to manage a single task. It also included a Task form that used an object from the Task class to manage the information about a single task. For this chapter, the Task form will be replaced with a To Do List form. This new form, shown in Figure 11.1, will allow the creation of a set of tasks that will be managed by the collection.

Figure 11.1

The To Do List form displays a set of tasks that are maintained in a collection.

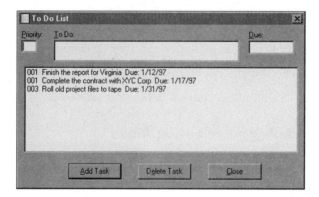

What Will This Cover?

This section will cover the following key Visual Basic features:

- Using a collection object
- Creating a collection class
- Working with the collection methods Add, Item, Remove
- Using the With…End With statements
- Creating unique IDs for objects
- Defining write-once properties
- Defining a default property or method
- Using the For Each…Next statements with the collection class
- Using the Class Builder utility

Steps to Creating a Collection Class

You can add a collection class to a project whenever the project needs to manage a collection of objects. The collection can manage a set of objects from the same class or different types of objects. For example, you could define a collection of tasks to define the items on a to do list. Or, you could define a collection to track all open child forms in an MDI application. You could also define a "dirty objects" collection to hold any object that was changed by the user.

The steps for creating a collection class are

1. Define the collection class.

2. Add properties and methods to the collection class.

3. Set the Item method as the default method.

4. Enable the For Each…Next syntax.

Each of these steps is detailed in the topics that follow.

Defining a Collection Class

Before developing a collection class, you need to define what the collection class will contain. Determine what type of objects will be stored in the collection and whether the collection will be limited to objects of a specific type, or objects of any type.

Once you know what will be in the collection, you can start the code for the collection class. A collection class is implemented using a class module.

To create a collection class:

1. Open the desired project or a new project.

2. From the Project menu, choose Add Class Module and add a new class module.

3. In the Properties window, set the Name property.

   Name the class module with the plural form of the objects that will be contained within it. For example, a collection class for a set of tasks would be named "CTasks." If there is no plural form of the objects, append the word "Collection" to the object name form the collection class name, as in CInventoryCollection.

4. Declare an object variable for the Collection object.

   The object variable can be declared with or without the New keyword. Using the New keyword on the declaration can add a small amount of overhead to all procedure calls invoked on the Collection object.

The Declarations section for the Tasks class is shown here:

```
' Class Name:    CTasks
' Author:        Deborah Kurata
' Date:          1/9/97
' Description:   Maintains the collection of CTask objects.
'

Option Explicit

' Define the collection of tasks
Private m_colTasks As Collection

' Define error values
Public Enum TasksError
    tasksInvalidIndexError = vbObjectError + 512 + 10
End Enum
```

The enumeration is used for handling errors in the collection. In a production-quality application, you may need to handle additional errors.

5. Create the instance of the collection object.

   If the New keyword was used on the declaration of the collection, an instance of the collection will be created automatically when the collection is first used. Otherwise, the instance must be created using the Set statement.

   For the Tasks class, this was done in the Initialize event:

```
' Initialize event
Private Sub Class_Initialize()
    ' Create the collection object
    Set m_colTasks = New Collection
End Sub
```

6. Release the object variable.

   When the collection object variable is no longer needed, it should be disassociated with the collection. When no object variables reference the collection, the collection will be destroyed. Each object referenced in the collection will also be destroyed if there are no other references to the object.

   For the Tasks class, the object variable is freed in the Terminate event for the class:

```
' Terminate event
Private Sub Class_Terminate()
    ' Clear the reference
    Set m_colTasks = Nothing
End Sub
```

You now have a class that will create and destroy a private collection. That is not very useful. This class needs to allow items to be added to the collection or removed from the collection. It should also provide access to an item in the collection when requested.

Adding Properties and Methods to the Collection Class

Minimally, a collection class needs to provide the functionality to add and remove items from the collection and to reference a specific item in the collection. A collection class may also provide a Count property to expose the number of objects in the collection. If the objects don't have a unique key, a method in the collection class can assign unique keys. Any other properties or methods needed to work with the collection can also be added to the collection class.

Be sure to document each method you add to the collection class using the Procedure Attributes, as described in Chapter 10, "Building your First Class."

Developing an Add Wrapper

Because the collection in the collection class is declared to be private, objects can only be added to the collection from within the collection class. To allow other parts of the application to add objects to a collection, a public Add wrapper method is defined in the collection class using a public Function procedure. Instead of allowing an object to be created and passed into this function, the function receives the properties of the object and creates the object itself. This gives the collection class tighter control over the objects that are added to the collection.

Keynote

Well, an object is not *really* added to a collection. Rather, a reference to the object is added to the collection. A collection containing a set of objects really contains a set of object references. These references are stored as Variants in the collection. This book will often refer to "items in a collection," but when referring to objects, you need to translate this into "references to items in a collection."

Items in a collection can be accessed by index position or by a unique key. The index is defined automatically when the object is inserted into the collection. If the Before and After qualifiers are not used when calling the Add method, an object is added to the end of the collection and is given a sequentially higher index number.

Keynote

To make the best use of collections, each object can be assigned a unique string key when it is added to the collection. The unique key provides a quick lookup to the item in the collection. You can use an existing property of the object for the key, if the property will have a unique value for each object. For example, Product objects could use the unique product name as the key. Employee objects would not use the last name as the key because it may not be unique. Objects associated with a record from a table could use the record ID as the key but, depending on the project, this could cause problems with objects associated with a record that has not yet been added to the table and therefore has no record ID.

Tech Note.   *The key assigned to an item in a collection cannot be changed. If the property used as the key for the item is changed and that change needs to be reflected in the key, the item needs to be removed from the collection using the original key (or the index) and then added back to the collection using the new key value.*

If there is no obvious property of the object that could be used as a key, you need to generate a unique key. This can be done in a method of the collection. A method for defining unique keys is discussed under "Developing a Method to Assign Unique Keys" later in this chapter.

Keynote

The defined unique key is assigned as the key for the object in the collection. The collection knows how to use the key to find an object in the collection, but the object itself is not aware of the collection's key. Therefore, you cannot ask an object in a collection for the key used when the object was added to the collection. Rather, if you want the object to know the value of the assigned collection key, you need to store the key as a property of the object.

If an existing property was used as the key, there is no problem. There would already be appropriate Property procedures to Get/Let the value of the property from the object. If a unique key is generated for the object, the object will not know the key value. To solve this dilemma, you can add a property to the object for the storage of the key.

In the Task class example, an ID property was added to the Task class to store the unique ID that was assigned to the object in the collection. The code added to the Declarations section of the Task class for this new property is as follows. Note that this code is added to the Task class, not the Tasks collection class.

```
Private m_sID As String
```

A set of Property procedures can then get or set the ID:

```
' ID within the collection
' NOTE: it must be a unique string that is only set once
Public Property Let ID(sID As String)
Static bAlreadySet As Boolean

    If Not bAlreadySet Then
        m_sID = sID
        bAlreadySet = True
    End If
End Property

Public Property Get ID() As String
    ID = m_sID
End Property
```

Code in the Add method of the collection class, shown next, will set the ID to a unique value generated when the object is added to the collection. This ID will then be assigned as the key for the object in the collection. As mentioned earlier, the unique key used when adding an object to a collection cannot be changed. Code can be added to the Property Let procedure to ensure that nothing changes the ID once the collection class sets it. This is called a write-once property because the value of the property cannot be set a second time. Instead of simply ignoring the attempt to change the value a second time, as done in this code, the Property Let procedure could raise an error to notify the calling routine of the problem.

Tech Note. *If this class were developed as part of an ActiveX component, the ID Property Let procedure would be declared using Friend instead of Public. This would allow the collection class to set the ID but would prevent other applications from setting this property. See Chapter 13, "Building ActiveX Components," for more information on using the Friend keyword.*

Now that the object has a property for storing the unique key assigned to the object in the collection, you are ready to develop the Add method in the collection class. For the Task class example, the Tasks collection class will need the priority, description, and time due for a task. Because the tasks don't have any logical identifier to use as the collection key, the collection class can generate a unique ID. A private NextID method, discussed later in this chapter, is used for this purpose. The collection class creates a new Task object, sets the properties to the appropriate values, and adds the object to the collection using the unique ID as the collection key.

The code for the Add wrapper method in the Tasks collection class is as follows:

```
' Add a task to the collection
' Parameters:
'   iPriority        priority of the task
'   sDescription     string description of the task
'   sDue             time the task is due
' Returns:
'   Task             task object
Public Function Add(ByVal iPriority As Integer, _
                    ByVal sDescription As String, _
                    ByVal sDue As String) As CTask
On Error GoTo ERR_ROUTINE
Dim newTask As CTask

    ' Create the instance
    Set newTask = New CTask

    With newTask
        ' Set a unique ID
        .ID = NextID

        ' Set the properties
        .Priority = iPriority
        .Description = sDescription
        .Due = sDue

        ' Add the member to the collection
        m_colTasks.Add newTask, .ID
    End With
```

```
        ' Return the one that was added
        Set Add = newTask
Exit Function

ERR_ROUTINE:
        ' Pass any error up to the calling class from the lower level object
        Err.Raise Err.Number, Err.Source, Err.Description
End Function
```

The first thing to notice about this routine is the With...End With construct used in this example. The With statement provides a shortcut for referencing the object. It is also more efficient because the application only needs to resolve the reference once. Without this construct, the object reference in this example would need to be repeated five times and be resolved five times. (Can you find the five? If not, they are .ID, .Priority, .Description, .Due, and the .ID in the m_colTasks.Add statement.)

A second thing to notice about this routine is that it is responsible for creating the Task objects and adding them to the private collection. This routine, then, establishes the relationship between the Tasks class and the Task class, as shown in the object hierarchy in Figure 7.9.

If any errors were generated in this routine, the error is raised to the calling routine. For example, if the priority value passed into this routine is out of the valid range, the statement that assigns the value to the Priority property will generate an error. This error is then returned to the calling routine so the user can be notified of the error.

The Add method is implemented as a function that returns a reference to the newly created object to the calling routine. This allows the calling routine to access the object, if necessary. Because the function returns an object reference, a Set statement must be used if the returned value of the function is assigned to an object variable in the calling routine.

If the objects in the collection need to be in a specific order, you can create an ordered collection by defining an additional parameter on the Add method of the collection. The following example would add the new task before the first item.

```
m_colTasks.Add newTask, .ID, m_colTasks.Item(1).ID
```

Tech Note. *Using the Before or After parameters of the Add method can have a negative impact on performance.*

Developing a Remove Wrapper

Because the collection in the collection class is private, objects can only be removed from the collection within the collection class. To expose this functionality, a public Remove wrapper method is defined in a public Sub procedure in the collection class.

Keynote

The parameter of the Sub procedure is a Variant to allow passing in an integer or a string. If the value of the Variant passed to this method is evaluated to be an integer, the value is treated as an index and the object in the collection at the position identified by the index is removed. An index number larger than the number of objects in the collection will generate an error. One thing to note when using the index to access an object is that objects will not necessarily always be in the same position. If objects are explicitly added between other objects or if objects are removed, the index numbers are adjusted automatically.

If the value of the Variant passed to this method is evaluated to be a string, the string is treated as a key and the object that had been added to the collection with the defined collection key is removed from this collection. If the key is not found in the collection, an error is generated.

Tech Note. *A number used as a key and passed to the Remove method will be evaluated as an integer and treated as an index instead of as a key.*

For the Task class example, the Tasks collection class removes the defined object from the collection. If the index is out of range or the key is not valid, the error trap will catch the error and return it to the calling routine.

```
' Remove the member from the collection.
' Parameters:
'    vkey         key or index of member to delete
Public Sub Remove(ByVal vKey As Variant)
On Error GoTo ERR_ROUTINE

    ' Remove the member from the collection
    m_colTasks.Remove vKey

Exit Sub
ERR_ROUTINE:
    Err.Raise tasksInvalidIndexError, "CTasks::Remove", _
        "Collection key or index is invalid"
End Sub
```

This error routine could be enhanced to distinguish problems with the key or index from other errors, such as an error with the m_colTasks object variable. You could do this simply by adding the actual error message to the error description or by logging the actual error message using an Error class, as described in Chapter 15, "Putting the Pieces Together."

Developing an Item Wrapper

An application may want to access the properties and methods of an object in a collection. For example, a To Do List form wants to display the priority, description, and time due for each object in the collection. But, again, the collection is private. A wrapper method in the collection class can be created to provide the reference to a specific item in the collection.

A public Item method can be defined in the collection class using a public Function procedure. The parameter of this Function procedure is a Variant to find the object by index or key as described earlier in the Remove wrapper. The function returns a reference to an object in the collection, so the return data type of this function is the class of the objects within the collection. It must be set to Object if the collection contains objects from different classes. Because the function returns an object reference, a Set statement must be used if the returned value is assigned to an object variable in the calling routine.

For the Task class example, the Tasks collection class will provide a reference to any Task object in the collection. Notice that the Function procedure return value is declared as CTask. This returns the reference to the requested object to the calling routine.

```
' Displays the defined member
' Parameters:
'     vkey          key or index of member to get
Public Function Item(ByVal vKey As Variant) As CTask
On Error GoTo ERR_ROUTINE
    Set Item = m_colTasks.Item(vKey)

Exit Function
ERR_ROUTINE:
    Err.Raise tasksInvalidIndexError, "CTasks::Item", _
        "Collection key or index is invalid"
End Function
```

If the argument passed to the Item method is an index value that is out of range or an invalid string key, the error trap will catch the error and return it to the calling routine.

Developing a Count Wrapper

A collection has one intrinsic property called Count. Count provides the number of objects in the collection. To expose this property for the collection, a Public Property Get procedure is defined. This will return the count from the collection.

For the Task class example, the Tasks class Property Get procedure appears as follows:

```
' Provide the count of the number in the collection
Public Property Get Count() As Long
    Count = m_colTasks.Count
End Property
```

This is a read-only property, so the Property Let procedure is not implemented.

Developing a Clear Method

A collection does not have a Clear method. Other parts of the application can remove objects from the collection by using the public Remove method or by setting the object variable reference to the collection class to Nothing. Setting the collection to Nothing will release the collection and any objects in the collection that are not referenced by any other object variables.

To provide other parts of the application with a simple mechanism for clearing all objects from the collection, you can add a Clear method to the collection class.

For the Task class example, the Tasks class Clear method is as follows:

```
' Clear the collection
Public Sub Clear()
    Set m_colTasks = New Collection
End Sub
```

You can use this Clear method to clear the contents of the collection at any time without destroying the collection class itself.

Developing a Method to Assign Unique Keys

Some objects have a property that can be used as the unique key value for a collection. A social security number, a product identifier, or a record ID all make good unique keys for their particular object. There are other objects, like the tasks in the Task class example, that don't have a property appropriate for use as a unique key. If you want to reference these objects in the collection by key, you have to create a unique key. One way to create a unique key is to develop a key generation routine that declares a static variable and increments it for each object created from the class.

Tech Note. *A static variable is one that retains its value between calls to the routine in which it is defined. If you declare an integer variable x in a procedure and call the procedure, the initial value of x is 0. Say the procedure sets x to 10 and exits. If the variable is not declared with the Static keyword, when the procedure is called again the value of x is again 0 because it is initialized each time the procedure is executed. If the variable is declared as static, when the procedure is called a second time the value of x is 10 because the value is retained.*

It would seem appropriate to implement this key generation routine in the object's class so each object can create its own unique key. However, this technique won't work if the routine is implemented in the object's class because a static variable in a class is independent for each object instance created from the class. So if you set a static variable in a routine for one object to 10 and call that routine again for that object it will still be 10. But if you create a new object and execute the same routine, the static variable value will be 0 because you are creating a new object that is a different instance of the class. The new object will not know about the prior value from the other object. This is just like setting the text property of text boxes. Setting the text for the first text box does not affect any of the other text boxes.

To resolve this issue, you can give the collection class the responsibility for defining unique keys. The collection class knows about all of the objects in the collection, so it can ensure that each object has a unique key. Because there is only one instance of the collection class, a defined static value will be retained appropriately each time the routine is called.

In the Task class example, the NextID method in the Tasks class creates a unique ID by incrementing a static ID variable. This routine is called before an object is added to the collection.

```
' Provides the next available ID
' Returns:
'    NextID        Next unique Task ID
Private Function NextID() As String
Static iID As Integer

    iID = iID + 1
    NextID = "T" & Format$(iID, "00000")
End Function
```

At this point, the collection class wrapper properties and methods are in place and the collection class can be used. There are a few things that you can do, however, to give the Tasks class more default behavior. You can define the Item method as a default method and enable the For Each...Next syntax for the private collection. These techniques are described in the following topics.

Setting a Default Property or Method

Many Visual Basic objects have default properties or methods. For example, the Text property is the default property of a TextBox object, so this code:

```
txtDescription = "Finish this report"
```

is a shorthand version of:

```
txtDescription.Text = "Finish this report"
```

Keynote

Visual Basic 5 provides this feature for the classes you create. You can identify one property or method of a class to be the default property or method. Normally, this should be the property or method used most frequently. Code that uses a default property or method can become more difficult to read because it is not obvious which property or method is being invoked. To minimize the possibility of confusion, the default property or method selected for an object should be the most obvious choice. If there is no obvious choice for a particular class, don't create a default!

For the collection class, the property or method used most frequently is usually the Item method. Each time you need to access a property or method of an object in a collection, you need to retrieve the reference to the object from the collection with the Item method and then invoke the object's property or method. This can be done with code such as:

```
m_Tasks.Item(1).Description
```

This code retrieves the description from the first object in the Tasks collection. If the Item method is defined as the default method, the following code becomes equivalent:

```
m_Tasks(1).Description
```

In the case of the Item method, using a default method can make the code more readable because it makes the m_Tasks collection class appear as an array. This makes the Item method a good choice for the default method. In many other cases, using a default property or method can make the code less readable so default properties and methods should be used with care.

To set a property or method as the default method, ensure that the class module containing the property or method is open in the active Code window. Choose Procedure Attributes from the Tool menu and click on the Advanced button. The Procedure Attributes dialog box will appear, as shown in Figure 11.2.

In the Properties Attributes dialog box, select the name of the procedure that will be the default property or method and then select (Default) as the Procedure ID.

Tech Note. *Only one property or method for a class can be defined as the default. If a default exists and another property or method is selected as the default, the Procedure Attributes dialog box will notify you and void the original default setting.*

Enabling For Each...Next for a Collection Class

The For Each...Next syntax is an efficient mechanism for navigating through a collection. Normally this syntax can only be used within the collection class since the collection is private within the collection class. This means that all collection processing would have to be moved to methods within the collection class or the standard For...Next syntax would have to be used instead, as shown here:

```
Dim i As Integer
    For i = 1 To m_Tasks.Count
        MsgBox "Task was: " & m_Tasks(i).Description
    Next i
```

Figure 11.2

Use the Procedure
Attributes dialog box to
set a default property or
method for a class. A
class can have only one
property or method set
as the default.

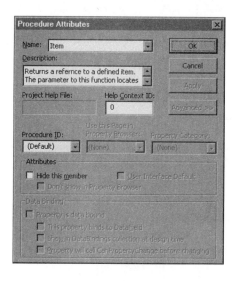

Keynote

However, with Visual Basic 5, there is a trick to exposing the enumerator for the collection in the collection class so any code in the application can iterate through the collection using the For Each...Next syntax. This trick involves adding a NewEnum method to the collection class. The NewEnum method exposes the enumerator used to iterate through the collection. The NewEnum method is as follows:

```
' Exposes the enumeration object
' to allow the For Each...Next syntax
Public Function NewEnum() As IUnknown
    Set NewEnum = m_colTasks.[_NewEnum]
End Function
```

This NewEnum method is a wrapper around the _NewEnum hidden collection method. It returns the collection's enumerator. More precisely, it returns the IUnknown interface of an enumerator object. This enumerator can then navigate through the objects referred to in the collection.

Tech Note. *By convention, the underscore on the _NewEnum method of the collection in the preceding code sample indicates that the method is hidden in the type library. You won't see it listed as a method of the Collection object in the Object Browser. The square brackets around the _NewEnum are required because the underscore is not a valid character in a method name.*

Tech Note. *If you receive a "User-defined type not defined" error on the NewEnum declaration when you run this code, check the project references and make sure you have a reference set to OLE Automation (StdOle2.tlb). This is required when using the IUnknown interface.*

The next step in the trick is magic…. Set the Procedure ID of this NewEnum method to -4 (yes, a negative four) and check the Hide this Member attribute in the Procedure Attributes dialog, as shown in Figure 11.3. Not very obvious, but so obscure that it is actually easy to remember!

Figure 11.3

A Procedure ID of -4 for the NewEnum method exposes the For Each…Next syntax for collections that are private within a collection class. Although this technique is obscure, having For Each…Next syntax for private collections is a very useful feature.

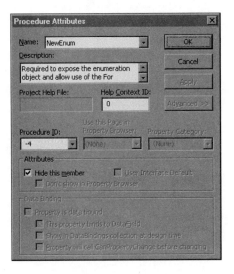

Once the NewEnum method is defined in the collection class, any code that references the collection class can use the For Each…Next syntax. For the Task class example, each task in the collection can be displayed when the form is closed (not a good design for the users, but helpful during testing). Instead of the For…Next syntax shown earlier, the code would be

```
Private Sub cmdClose_Click()
    ' Display the list of tasks
    ' Primarily here to show For Each...Next syntax!
    Dim tempTask As CTask
    For Each tempTask In m_Tasks
        MsgBox "Task was: " & tempTask.Description
    Next

    ' Unload the form
```

```
        Unload Me
End Sub
```

This syntax is more efficient than iterating through the collection using the For...Next syntax.

Collaborating with the Form

After the collection class is complete, it can be used by any part of the application that needs to manage a collection of items. In the Task class example, the To Do List form shown in Figure 11.1 will use the collection class to manage a collection of tasks.

To use the collection class, the form must first declare an object variable for the reference to the collection class object:

```
' Define the instance of the collection class
Private m_Tasks As CTasks
```

The object variable was declared without the New syntax as a module-level variable, so the object must be created explicitly. In this case, the object is created during the form's Load event.

```
Private Sub Form_Load()
    ' Create the object
    Set m_Tasks = New CTasks
End Sub
```

The Click event for the Add button will then invoke the Add method for the collection class to add a task to the collection based on data entered by the user in the text boxes on the form.

```
' Add the defined task to the collection and to the list box
Private Sub cmdAdd_Click()
Dim index As Integer
On Error GoTo ERR_ROUTINE

    ' Add the task to the collection
    m_Tasks.Add Val(txtPriority.Text), txtDescription.Text, txtDue.Text

    ' Add the task to the list box
    lstTasks.AddItem Format$(txtPriority.Text, "000") _
        & Space(2) & txtDescription.Text _
        & Space(2) & "Due: " & txtDue.Text

    ' Clear the fields on the form for entry of another task
    txtPriority.Text = ""
    txtDescription.Text = ""
    txtDue.Text = ""
    txtPriority.SetFocus
Exit Sub

ERR_ROUTINE:
    Select Case Err.Number
        Case taskPriorityValueError
            MsgBox "Please enter a valid priority value. " _
                & "Valid values range from: " _
```

```
            & taskUrgent & " to " & taskLow
        txtPriority.SetFocus

    Case taskInvalidTimeError
        MsgBox "Please enter a time defining when the task is due."
        txtDue.SetFocus

    Case Else
        ' If it was some other error, display it
        MsgBox "Error in application: " _
            & Err.Description
    End Select
End Sub
```

Notice the expanded error handler. Because the Add method of the collection class assigns all of the property values, the error handler has to be prepared to handle any property error.

When the form is unloaded, the object variable can be released:

```
Private Sub Form_Unload(Cancel As Integer)
    ' Clear all of our object references
    Set m_Tasks = Nothing
    Set frmToDo = Nothing
    End
End Sub
```

At this point, you should have an operational To Do List application.

A Shortcut for Creating a Collection Class

Visual Basic Professional and Enterprise Editions come with a VB Class Builder utility. This utility is an add-in that allows you to define a class by defining the properties and methods using a set of dialog boxes. It then generates the code for the defined classes. If you are working through the Task class example, you may want to save your work and start a new project before trying the Class Builder utility.

To use the Class Builder utility to build a collection class:

1. Choose Add-In Manager from the Add-Ins menu and check VB Class Builder Utility.

   This enables the Class Builder Utility add-in. The Class Builder will now appear in the Add-Ins menu.

Tech Note. *Once an add-in is enabled, it will be loaded. If you exit Visual Basic, your add-in selections are saved. The next time you launch Visual Basic, all selected add-ins are loaded. For best performance when entering and exiting Visual Basic, be sure to uncheck any add-ins that you don't need.*

2. Choose Class Builder Utility from the Add-Ins menu.

   The Class Builder dialog box will appear.

3. Add a class using the Add New Class button on the toolbar.

A Class Module Builder dialog box is displayed. Enter the name and other attributes of the class. You can re-create the Task class here, if desired.

4. Add properties and methods to the class.

Use the buttons in the Class Builder dialog box toolbar to add properties, methods, and events. The results for the Task class would appear similar to Figure 11.4.

Tech Note.   *Figure 11.4 actually displays the CTask class created without using the Class Builder. Note that the data types for ID and Priority appear in the Class Builder as Variants instead of their correct Long data type. I have to assume this was a bug in the beta software.*

Figure 11.4

The Task class could have been created with the Class Builder utility.

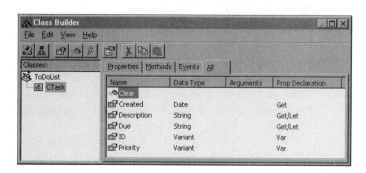

5. Select the project in the Class Builder dialog box and add a collection class to the project using the Add New Collection button on the toolbar.

A Collection Builder dialog box appears. Enter the name and other attributes of the collection class. Be sure to identify it as a collection of objects from the class created in step 3.

6. Add properties and methods to the collection class.

Because you identified the class as a collection class, the Add, Remove, Item, Count, and NewEnum wrapper properties and methods are already defined for you. Use the buttons in the Class Builder dialog box toolbar to add any additional properties, methods, and events. The results for the Tasks collection class are shown in Figure 11.5.

7. Choose Update Project from the File menu to generate the code.

After the last step, Visual Basic will generate the entire framework of your object hierarchy. You may find it interesting to compare the code generated by the Class Builder utility with the code you built throughout this section.

Figure 11.5

The Tasks collection
class could also be
created with the Class
Builder utility.

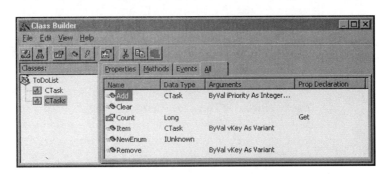

What Did This Cover?

This section defined how to develop a collection class. It included details on declaring a private Collection object and developing wrappers for the collection properties and methods. It also presented how to set a default property or method and a trick for exposing the For Each…Next syntax to work with a private collection in a collection class. Finally, it demonstrated how to define your class hierarchy and generate the basic code for your classes using the VB Class Builder utility.

At this point, you should have an operational application that will track an entire list of tasks. For a greater challenge, add the Alarm event back into the project. Be sure to add it to the collection class and not to the entity class so there is only one Timer form generating Timer events.

■ Storing Class Data in a File

As you noticed when running any of the examples up to this point, the property data for an object is not persistent. When the object is terminated, the data is gone. In some cases this may be appropriate, but in other cases this data must be saved. This involves writing each object's data to a file. Writing the data to a database is discussed in Chapter 14, "Doing Database Objects."

To follow along with the example presented in this section, use the Tasks collection class project from the prior section of this chapter. This section will walk through how to add a file processing class to the project. It will detail how to implement the procedures in the Tasks collection class to read and write the objects from the collection and how to develop the procedures in the Task class to read and write the property values for each object. Figure 11.6 shows the relationships between the Tasks collection class, Task class, and file processing class.

Figure 11.6

The Tasks collection class calls the file processing class to read the data from a file. The file processing class calls the Tasks collection class back to iterate through each task in the collection. For each task, a method in the Task class is called to read the task property values from the file using a method in the file processing class.

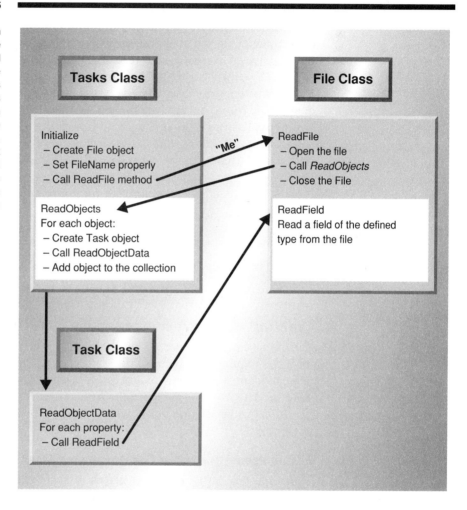

What Will This Cover?

This section will cover the following key Visual Basic features:

- Creating a file processing class
- Writing data from an object into a file
- Reading data from a file to an object
- Using the Me keyword
- Performing callbacks

Steps to Storing and Retrieving Data

To store data in a file, your application will need to open the file, write each data element to it, and then close the file. To retrieve data from a file, your application will need to open the file, read each data element from it in the same order, and close the file. This processing can be done using a file processing class.

Keynote

For the file processing class to be generic it cannot know the data elements to be stored or retrieved for each object. Each object should know how to read and write its own data. So generic opening and closing of the file and reading and writing data to the file is encapsulated in the file processing class, but information about what data to read or write to the file is encapsulated in the objects themselves.

The steps required to develop code for storing and retrieving object data are

1. Create a generic class for file processing.

2. Add code in the collection class to read and write the collection.

3. Add code in each class to read and write the object properties.

These steps are detailed in the topics which follow.

Creating a File Processing Class

The purpose of the file processing class is to handle interaction with a file. To meet this requirement, the file processing class will need a property for a file name to identify the file to be processed. Methods in the file processing class will read data from the file and write data to the file.

To begin, insert a new class into a project and set the name of the class to CFile.

Adding Properties to the File Processing Class

The properties for the file processing class include the file name and an internal integer for storing the file number after the file has been opened. This is the number used to refer to the file when storing or retrieving data in the file. The declarations for the file processing class are as follows:

```
' Class Name:    CFile
' Author:        Deborah Kurata, InStep Technologies
' Date:          1/25/97
' Description:   Generic file processing class.
' Revisions:

Option Explicit

' Path and name of the file to open
Private m_sFileName As String

' File number opened
Private m_iFileNumber As Integer
```

```
' Error constants
Enum FileError
    fileOpenError = vbObjectError + 512 + 2
    fileEOFError = vbObjectError + 512 + 3
    fileReadError = vbObjectError + 512 + 4
    fileWriteError = vbObjectError + 512 + 5
End Enum
```

Because the file processing class works with files, there are many opportunities for it to generate errors: expected errors such as reaching the end of the file, and unexpected errors such as running out of disk space. All of the errors that are to be handled in the file processing class can be defined using an enumeration. The enumeration in this example exposes several possible file errors. You may define more as required by your application.

The Property procedures for the file processing class allow for getting and setting the file name. There are no Property procedures for the file number because it is only used within this class and therefore needs no public interface.

```
Property Get FileName() As String
    FileName = m_sFileName
End Property

Property Let FileName(sFileName As String)
    ' Should validate path here
    m_sFileName = sFileName
End Property
```

To make this class more solid, the Property Let procedure should be modified to validate the data and ensure that the string represents a valid path and file name.

Adding Methods for Writing Data

One of the methods defined for the file processing class is a WriteFile method. This method will write all of the pertinent property values for an object to a file. It handles the opening and closing of the file, but delegates the definition of the data elements to write to the object passed in as a parameter. This allows the file processing class to be generic and not have knowledge of the object's actual data. Because the object should not know how to write its data to the file, the object will call the file processing class back to execute the WritcFicld method.

Keynote

When an object, called a parent object, passes a reference to itself to a method for another object, a *callback* mechanism is established. This simply means that the other object has a reference to the parent object and can call back to any of its properties or methods.

The WriteFile method begins by enabling the error handler with On Error and specifies Resume Next to resume processing with the next statement if an error occurs. This simplifies the error handling in this routine because the error can be handled immediately after the line that generated the error. If a single error handler were defined at the end of the routine, it would need to determine which line generated the error.

After the error trap is set, the WriteFile method deletes any existing file using the Kill statement. If an error occurs on the Kill statement, the error handler simply resumes execution on the next statement and clears the error. This assumes there may be valid situations when no original file existed. This is the case the first time through the application. In a production-quality application, you may want to rename the file to a backup file before killing it. This would allow you to restore to that backup file if there was an error writing the new file.

The FreeFile function is used to retrieve a file number. That file number must be used when referencing the file. The Open statement opens the file for binary operations. If an error occurs upon opening the file, the Raise method of the Err object is used to raise the error to the calling routine. Notice that the error trap is first turned off using On Error Goto 0; otherwise the On Error Resume Next error trap would resume execution of the next line when the error was raised instead of raising the error to the calling routine.

```
' Writes all objects to the file.
' Parameters:
'    obj          Object
Public Sub WriteFile(obj As Object)
' Enable error handling
On Error Resume Next

    ' Kill the existing file
    Kill m_sFileName
    Err.Clear

    ' Get the file number
    m_iFileNumber = FreeFile

    ' Open the file and trap any errors
    Open m_sFileName For Binary As #m_iFileNumber
    Select Case Err.Number
        Case Ø   ' No error
            ' Write the data
            obj.WriteObjects

        Case Else
            ' Turn off error handling here
            On Error GoTo Ø
            ' Pass the error out
            Err.Raise fileOpenError, "CFile::WriteFile", _
                "Error opening file: " & Err.Description
    End Select

    ' Close the file
    Close #m_iFileNumber
End Sub
```

If the file was opened successfully, the WriteObjects method is called for the object using the callback technique. This method writes the appropriate objects to the file. The WriteObjects method is described later in this section. After the file processing is complete, the file is closed.

Because an object does not know how to write to a file, a method in the object's class will call the WriteField method to actually write the data elements to the file. In a binary file, the application is responsible for tracking where each field is stored. This requires reading the data in the same order in which it was written.

The WriteField method has a Variant argument to allow passing in of any data type.

```
' Write a field to the file
' Parameters:
'   vField        field to write to the file
Public Sub WriteField(ByVal vField As Variant)
' Set the error handler
On Error GoTo ERR_HANDLER

    Put #m_iFileNumber, , vField

Exit Sub
ERR_HANDLER:
    Err.Raise fileWriteError, "CFile::WriteField", _
        "Write Error: " & Err.Descpription
End Sub
```

If an error is generated during this writing, an error is raised to the calling routine.

Adding Methods for Reading Data

Once data exists in a file, you will want to be able to read it back out of the file. The ReadFile method reads all of the data from a file into an object. It handles the opening and closing of the file, but delegates the actual reading of the data elements to the object passed in as a parameter. As with the WriteFile method, this allows the file processing class to be generic and not have knowledge of the object's actual data.

The ReadFile method begins by enabling the error handler. It then uses the FreeFile function to retrieve a file number and opens the file. If an error occurs on opening the file, the Raise method of the Err object raises the error to the calling routine. Again the error handler is turned off before raising the error to ensure that the error is raised to the calling routine.

```
' Reads all objects from a file into the defined object
' Parameters:
'   obj           Object to read
Public Sub ReadFile(obj As Object)
' Enable error handling
On Error Resume Next

    ' Get the file number
    m_iFileNumber = FreeFile

    ' Open the file and trap any errors
    Open m_sFileName For Binary Access Read As #m_iFileNumber
    Select Case Err.Number
        Case 0  ' No error
            ' Get the data
```

```
            obj.ReadObjects

        Case 53     ' File not found
            ' Do nothing

        Case Else
            ' Turn off error handling here
            On Error GoTo 0

            ' Pass the error out
            Err.Raise fileOpenError, "CFile::ReadFile", "Error opening file."
    End Select

    ' Close the file
    Close #m_iFileNumber
End Sub
```

If the file was opened successfully, the ReadObjects method of the collection class is called to retrieve objects from the file. The ReadObjects method is described later in this section. After the file processing is complete, the file is closed.

Notice the additional Case statement checking for an error value of 53. This is a file not found error. If the file is not found, no error is generated and no read operation is performed. If the calling routine needed information that no file was found, an error could be raised. For good coding practice, a constant should have been defined for the 53 instead of using this "magic number."

Because an object does not know how to read from a file, a method in the object's class will call the ReadField method to actually read the data elements from the file. The ReadField method has a Variant argument to allow reading of any data type. To retrieve the data correctly, the file processing class must retrieve the data exactly as it was written to the file.

Each value retrieved is passed back as the parameter to the ReadField routine. This is why you cannot use the ByVal keyword in the parameter for this routine.

```
' Reads a field from the file
' Parameters:
'     vField        field read from the file
Public Sub ReadField(vField As Variant)
    ' Set the error handler
    On Error GoTo ERR_HANDLER

    Get #m_iFileNumber, , vField

    If EOF(m_iFileNumber) Then
        ' Reached end of file
        Err.Raise fileEOFError
    End If
Exit Sub

ERR_HANDLER:
    ' Pass the error out
    If Err.Number = fileEOFError Then
        Err.Raise Err.Number, "CFile::ReadField", "EOF"
    Else
        Err.Raise fileReadError, "CFile::ReadField", Err.Description
    End If
End Sub
```

For binary files, the application is not notified of an end of file until after an attempt to get data past the end of the file. Therefore, each routine that reads data from the file needs to check for an end of file. If the end of file was reached, an error is raised.

At this point, the code for a basic file processing class is complete.

Reading and Writing a Collection

Using the file processing class, any object can store data in a file simply by calling the WriteFile method and read data from the file by calling the Read-File method. Before an object can call these methods, however, it needs to implement the WriteObjects method to define the objects to write and the ReadObjects method to define the objects to read.

For the Tasks collection class, the data is read from the file upon initialization of the Tasks collection class object and written to the file when the Tasks object is terminated. The first thing the Tasks collection class needs is a reference to the file processing class. You do this by first defining an object variable in the Declarations section of the Tasks class.

```
' Reference to the file processing class
Private m_File As CFile
```

The file processing object is then created in the Initialize event for the Tasks collection class. After the file processing object is created, its FileName property is set to the defined file in the application's path. In a production-quality application, you may want the user to be able to define the location of the file during the installation of the application, so the path could be read from the registry or an .ini file. Alternately, the location of the file can be selected by the user at run time using the File Open common dialog box.

```
' Initialize event
Private Sub Class_Initialize()
    ' Create the collection object
    Set m_colTasks = New Collection

    ' Read any existing data from the file
    Set m_File = New CFile
    m_File.FileName = App.Path & "\task.bin"
    m_File.ReadFile Me
End Sub
```

The ReadFile method of the file processing object is called to read in any existing data. This lets the application "remember" the last entered task information. Notice the Me keyword passed to the ReadFile method. This establishes the callback mechanism by passing the current object's reference to the ReadFile method. When executed, the file processing class will then have a reference to the current Tasks collection class object.

For the callback to work correctly, the Tasks collection class must implement a ReadObjects method. This method will read the data for all of the objects.

```
' Read the data from the file
Public Sub ReadObjects()
Dim newTask As CTask

    ' Read in the object
    Do Until Err.Number <> 0
        Set newTask = New CTask
        newTask.ReadObjectData m_File

        If Err.Number = 0 Then
            ' Set a unique ID
            newTask.ID = NextID

            ' Add the member to the collection
            m_colTasks.Add newTask, newTask.ID
        End If
    Loop
End Sub
```

Until reaching the end of the file, this routine creates a new object, reads the object data from the file, assigns a unique ID to the object, and adds the object to the collection. Because the collection class does not own the object data, it calls the object's ReadObjectData method to read the object data from the file. This method uses a reference to the file processing class to call the ReadField method and read each property from the file.

When the Tasks collection class is terminated, the data is written back to the file. In this example, the WriteFile method will be called regardless of whether any data was changed. This Tasks class could be modified to include a bIsDirty flag to define when task data was changed, so the WriteFile method would only be called if necessary.

Notice the error handling in the following routine. Because the call to WriteFile is in the Terminate event for the class, errors that occur in the WriteFile method cannot be raised. Instead they can be logged, as shown in Chapter 15, "Putting the Pieces Together." A error handler is used to catch any errors, preventing untrapped VB errors, and resume to attempt any remaining terminate processing.

```
' Terminate event
Private Sub Class_Terminate()
On Error GoTo ERR_ROUTINE
    ' Save the data
    m_File.WriteFile Me

    ' Clear the reference
    Set m_colTasks = Nothing

Exit Sub
ERR_ROUTINE:
    ' Cannot raise errors from
    ' the Terminate event
    ' so do logging here
    Resume Next
End Sub
```

The Tasks class writes the data back to the file by calling the WriteFile method of the file processing class and passing it a reference to itself to establish a callback. For the callback to work correctly, the Tasks collection class must implement a WriteObjects method. This method will write data for all of the objects. Because the collection does not own the object data, it calls a WriteObjectData method for each object in the collection. This method uses a reference to the file processing class to call the WriteFields method and write the object data to the file.

```
' Write the data to a file
Public Sub WriteObjects()
Dim tmpTask As CTask

    ' Write each object's properties
    For Each tmpTask In m_colTasks
        tmpTask.WriteObjectData m_File
    Next
End Sub
```

The ReadObjects and WriteObjects methods must be defined in any class wanting to store data using the file processing class. However, the implementation of those methods may vary significantly from class to class. For example, the Tasks class implementation of these methods called each Task object to write the priority, description, and time due, while a Person class implementation may read and write the name, address, and phone number.

Tech Note. *To ensure that each class implements the correct ReadObjects and WriteObjects methods, you could define and implement a File interface in each class. See Chapter 12, "Interfaces, Polymorphism, and Inheritance" for more information.*

Reading and Writing an Object's Properties

The final piece of the puzzle is in the class for the individual objects. This is the only class that knows about the data to be written to the file. A ReadObjectData method in the class calls the ReadField method in the file processing class to read each property for the object and a WriteObjectData method in the class calls the WriteField method in the file processing class to write each property for the object.

For the Task class, the properties include a priority, description, and time due. The ReadObjectData method in the Task class uses the ReadField method from the file processing class to read each property from the file.

```
' Read the data from the file
Public Sub ReadObjectData(File As CFile)
Dim lInt As Long
Dim sStr As String
    On Error GoTo ERR_ROUTINE

    ' Retrieve the priority
```

```
        File.ReadField lInt
        Priority = lInt

        ' Retrieve the description
        File.ReadField sStr
        Description = sStr

        ' Retrieve the time due
        File.ReadField sStr
        Due = sStr
Exit Sub

ERR_ROUTINE:
        Err.Raise Err.Number, Err.Source, Err.Description

End Sub
```

Each property is retrieved from the file and assigned to the appropriate Property procedure. The order in which the properties are retrieved from the file must match the order in which the properties were written to the file in the WriteObjectData method; otherwise, the data will not be read in the order in which it was written and the properties will not be correctly retrieved.

The WriteObjectData method calls the WriteField method of the file processing class to write each property to the file.

```
' Write the data to a file
Public Sub WriteObjectData(File As CFile)

        File.WriteField Priority
        File.WriteField Description
        File.WriteField Due
End Sub
```

Collaborating with the Form

The form does not need to handle any reading and writing of the data, because the file processing is all handled when the Tasks collection class is initialized and terminated. However, it would be useful for the form to display the information read from the file when the form is loaded.

The Tasks collection class created a collection of objects to store all of the data it read from the file, so the form only needs to iterate through the collection to display the data.

```
Private Sub Form_Load()
Dim tempTask As CTask

        ' Create the instance of the collection class
        Set m_Tasks = New CTasks

        ' Fill the list box with the items from the collection
        ' Shows the For Each...Next syntax!
        For Each tempTask In m_Tasks
            lstTasks.AddItem Format$(tempTask.Priority, "000") _
                & Space(2) & tempTask.Description _
                & Space(2) & "Due: " & tempTask.Due
        Next
End Sub
```

In the Load event for the form, the Tasks collection class is initialized and the file is opened and read as part of that initialization. The For Each…Next syntax can then be used to access each entry in the Tasks collection and add the priority, description, and time due to the list box on the form, as shown in Figure 11.1.

What Did This Cover?

Encapsulating all file processing code in one class allows you to change the type of file or file processing without affecting the code in the individual classes. For example, you could change the file from a binary file to a sequential file that can be read with a text editor simply by changing the implementation of the file processing class. No code that uses the file processing class would need to be modified.

In this section you learned how to create a generic file processing class. The file processing class used a callback mechanism to call the object back to ask it about the information to read or write to the file. In this example, the object was a collection of objects, so it looped through each object in the collection and called a method in the object to read or write the object's property values.

If you created the file processing class and made the changes to the Tasks and Task classes and the To Do List form detailed in this section, you now have a very useful application. It will actually remember the tasks that you created. The next time you execute the application, it will retrieve the tasks from the file and display them in the To Do List form.

■ Working with Forms as Classes

So far we have discussed implementing classes using class modules. It is also possible to implement classes in forms. Just about anything you can do in a class module you can do in a form, including defining properties, methods, and events.

For example, you can define a login class and implement it entirely within a form. You can add properties to a modal dialog box to retain the entered values after the modal form is unloaded. You can add events to a parent form so it can notify a child form when the parent form changes. This last option may need a more specific illustration. Suppose you have an Employee form and a Tasks form. When an employee is selected from the Employee form, the employee's tasks should appear in the Tasks form. If another employee is selected, the Tasks form should change appropriately. By defining an event in the Employee form, the Tasks form can be notified that the Employee form has changed and it can be adjusted accordingly.

Most of the techniques in this section are not new. You have already seen them in Chapter 10 and earlier in this chapter. This section presents a different application of these techniques to demonstrate forms as classes.

What Will This Cover?

This section will cover the following key Visual Basic features:

- Understanding form events

- Adding a property to a form

- Adding a method to a form

- Using a control array on a form

Forms Under the Hood

Keynote

A form is just a class with a user interface. However, there are some special considerations when working with forms. To understand these considerations, you need to understand how forms work under the hood.

First, let's clarify what a form is. When you are building a form in the IDE, the form is a class with a user interface. You can think of the form class in this context as a cookie cutter. It provides the definition of what the form object will be. You can add properties, methods, and events to a form just as you do in a class module. When you run an application, the form that is displayed to the user is a form object created from the form class. The form object has property values that define its appearance, methods that define its behavior, and events that define its interaction with the user. You can think of the form at design time as a form class and at run time as a form object; however, both the form class and form object are normally just called "the form."

As described in Chapter 10, "Building Your First Class," you create an object by declaring an object variable and setting that object variable to a new instance of the class. You can do this with your forms as well, but you don't have to. To keep things easier, Visual Basic automatically defines an object variable with the same name as the form class. This object variable is called a *hidden global form variable*. Visual Basic sets this hidden global form variable to a new instance of the form class at run time the first time the form is referenced. This is one of the differences between a form and a class module.

Let's walk through an example. Suppose you develop a form class called frmTask and somewhere in a project you show the form as follows:

```
frmTask.Show
```

When this statement is executed, Visual Basic defines a hidden global form variable called frmTask, creates a form object using the definition from the form class, and associates the form object with the frmTask form variable. The Initialize event is generated for the frmTask form and any code in that event is executed. The load process then begins: The form object is added to the Visual Basic Forms collection, the Load event for the form is generated and code in the Load event is executed. Because the Show method of the form was invoked, the form is then displayed.

The frmTask form variable provides a reference to the form that can be used to invoke the properties and methods of the form. To disassociate the form variable from the form object, you need to set the form variable to Nothing. If there are no other object variables referencing the form, the Terminate event is generated for the form object and the resources used by the form are freed.

Add the following code to a form class in a test project to try this out:

```
Private Sub Form_Initialize()
    MsgBox "In init: " & Forms.Count
    'MsgBox "In init: " & Form1.Caption
End Sub

Private Sub Form_Load()
    MsgBox "In load: " & Forms.Count
    MsgBox "In load: " & Form1.Caption
End Sub
```

Step through this test project using the F8 key. The first procedure to execute will be the Initialize event procedure. The message box will display "0" because the form has not yet been added to the Forms collection. After the Initialize event code has been executed, the form is loaded and the Load event is generated. At this point, the form is added to the Forms collection, so the count is "1" in the message box displayed from the Load event.

Now remove the comment mark in front of the second message box statement in the Initialize event. Step through this test project again using the F8 key. The first line of code to execute will be the Initialize. The message box will display "0" because the form has not yet been added to the Forms collection. When the second MsgBox statement is executed, the Load event procedure code is called. This is because the Form1.Caption statement is referencing a visual form element that requires loading of the form. At this point, the form is added to the Forms collection, so the count is "1" in the message box displayed from the Load event. Try rearranging the MsgBox statements. Notice how the order of the statements affects the order of execution.

Suppose you want to reference a property on the form *before* loading and showing the form. For example, you want to define the ID of a record whose data is to be displayed on the form. You cannot pass this ID to the Load event, but you can define a property and set the property on the form before loading the form:

```
frmTask.ID = 52
```

When this statement is executed, Visual Basic defines a hidden global form variable called frmTask, creates a form object using the definition from the form class, and associates the form object with the frmTask form variable. The Initialize event is generated for the frmTask form and any code in that event is executed. The value of the ID property is set and the Property Let statement for the ID is executed in the form if one is defined. The form is not loaded.

A form is not loaded unless a control on the form is referenced; one of the intrinsic properties of the form, such as the form caption, is referenced; or the form is explicitly loaded or shown.

When a form is unloaded, Visual Basic removes it from the Forms collection. If there are no other references to the form, the form will be destroyed and its memory and resources will be reclaimed. If there is a remaining reference to the form, such as the hidden global form variable, the form will unload but the form object will still exist. This leaves the form with no user interface but still holding on to resources, memory, and all of the property values. To ensure that this reference is released, be sure to set the hidden global form variable to Nothing as follows:

```
Set frmTask = Nothing
```

Working with Modal Dialog Boxes

A *modal form* is a form that prevents the user from accessing any other application feature until the form is dismissed by the user. The user normally does this by clicking one of two buttons such as OK or Cancel. Code that displays a modal form stops execution and waits for the user to dismiss the dialog box. This behavior is perfect for a login form, like the one shown in Figure 11.7, because you want to prevent the user from performing any other action until the application receives an authorized user ID and password.

Figure 11.7

A login screen provides
a level of security
for an application.

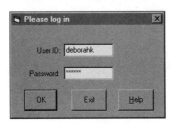

When developing a modal dialog box, in many cases you need to determine which button the user selected. Was it OK or Cancel? Should the application continue, or abort? It may seem difficult to determine the button selection because you could not request that value from any control on the form. However, forms can have public properties and methods, so the selected button, or any property, can be retrieved from the form using Property procedures. No need for hidden labels or global variables to determine which button a user selected!

The code for the login form begins with a standard header. Three properties are defined: user ID, password, and a Boolean property to define whether the user selected the Cancel button.

```
' Form Name:     frmLogin
' Author:        Deborah Kurata, InStep Technologies
' Date:          1/10/97
' Description:   Requests user ID and password.
'
' Revisions:
'
Option Explicit

   ' Store entered user Name and password
Private m_sPassword As String
Private m_sUserName As String
   ' Store status of button click
Private m_bWasCanceled As Boolean
```

The Property procedures for the Login class use only the Get procedures to make the properties read-only. This is desired because the values of the properties are set in the modal dialog box. Any other part of the application can then reference the user ID, password, or user-selected button, even if this form is unloaded!

```
' Read-only procedure for the button status
Public Property Get Canceled() As Boolean
    Canceled = m_bWasCanceled
End Property

' Read-only property for password
Public Property Get Password() As String
    Password = m_sPassword
End Property

' Read-only property for the user name
Public Property Get UserName() As String
    UserName = m_sUserName
End Property
```

A Display method is defined in the login form to provide a common public interface. Every form in your application could have a Display method, or something similar. All code that requests the display of a form could call the Display method rather than the form's intrinsic Show method. Because Display is a method and not an event procedure as is the form's Show method, you can pass parameters to it. This means that you can initialize an Employee form, for example, with the data from a record number passed in to the Display method.

The Display method can also provide other processing such as security checking before displaying the form. This is very useful if your application has secured screens. It also keeps the display type (modal versus nonmodal) encapsulated in the class. In this example, the Display method shows the login form as a modal form so the user cannot continue the application until responding appropriately to the dialog box prompts.

```
Public Sub Display()
    Me.Show vbModal
End Sub
```

To make the coding easier, you can define all of the buttons on form as a control array. A *control array* is a set of controls of the same type and with the same name. Each control in the control array is uniquely identified by an index number. Because the controls all have the same name, they will execute the same event procedure. You identify which control in the control array generated the event with the Index argument passed to the event procedure. The Index can then be used in a Select…Case statement to proceed based on the current control.

Tech Note.   *The easiest way to create a control array is to create your first control, set the name of the control to the desired name, copy the control, and paste it the desired number of times.*

In the login form example, the OK, Exit, and Help buttons were defined as a control array. To make it easier to determine which control array element was which button, constants were defined for the control array index numbers using an enumeration. The declarations for the constants are defined in the Declarations section of the form. For the login form, these declarations are:

```
' Define constants for the buttons
Private Enum LoginButtonIndex
    loginOKButton = 0
    loginExitButton = 1
    loginHelpButton = 2
End Enum
```

When the user clicks on the OK button, the user ID and password are stored in the properties. The button state is set and the form is unloaded. If the user clicks on the Cancel button, the button state is set and the form is unloaded. This is shown in the following code:

```
' Proceed based on the user selection
Private Sub cmdLogin_Click(Index As Integer)

Select Case Index
```

```
        Case loginOKButton
            m_sUserName = txtLogin(loginUserIDText).Text
            m_sPassword = txtLogin(loginPasswordText).Text
            m_bWasCanceled = False
            Unload Me

        Case loginExitButton
            ' Set the Canceled flag
            m_bWasCanceled = True
            Unload Me

        Case loginHelpButton
            ' *** Display the help for this window

    End Select
End Sub
```

When the form is unloaded the Form_Unload event is generated. This is normally where the cleanup is done. Code in prior examples recommended that the hidden global form variable be set to Nothing in the Unload event, as shown in this code:

```
Private Sub Form_Unload(Cancel As Integer)
    ' Do NOT set frmLogin = Nothing here
    ' Set frmLogin = Nothing
End Sub
```

Keynote

But wait! The Set statement in the preceding code is commented out. Why? Because the calling routine wants to retrieve properties from the form. If you set the hidden global form variable to Nothing in the Unload event, the code calling the routine will not be able to reference the properties or methods of the form. In many cases, once a form is unloaded you don't need to access its properties or methods so the Set statement is appropriate. In other cases, such as this modal dialog box example, you don't want to set the hidden global form variable to Nothing at this point so you can check the Canceled property after the form is unloaded.

Tech Note.   *Be careful when you choose not to set the hidden global form variable to Nothing, as you may get unexpected results. For example, a form requests information from the user and stores it in properties of the form. The form is then unloaded, but not set to Nothing. When the form is loaded again, the properties will have their prior values instead of being initialized as you may expect.*

The code that displayed the login form should check the value of the Canceled property to determine whether processing should continue or the user chose to Exit. For this login form example, the display of the form and the property value check are done in a standard module:

```
' Class Name:    MMain
' Author:        Deborah Kurata, InStep Technologies
' Date:          1/10/97
' Description:   Main routine for the application.
```

```
' Revisions:
Option Explicit

Sub Main()
    ' Display the modal login form
    frmLogin.Display

    ' Check the property
    If frmLogin.Canceled Then
        MsgBox "User clicked on Exit - so exit"
    Else
        MsgBox "User clicked on OK - so validate ID and password."
    End If
    Set frmLogin = Nothing
End Sub
```

At some point, the user ID and password require validation. Where you do the validation depends on how your system is designed. The login form could be responsible for handling the validation or the calling routine can check the button status and, if not canceled, retrieve the properties and perform the validation. Alternatively, you could create a Validation class to handle the display of the login form and all user ID and password validation.

What Did This Cover?

This section described how form objects are created from form classes. It detailed the order of the events executed when a form is shown, and compared those to the events that are executed when referencing a property of a form without loading the form.

A login form example illustrated techniques for working with modal dialog boxes. Primarily, the example demonstrated how to use a property to determine which button a user selected on a modal form.

To try this login form example, be sure to set your Startup Object to "Sub Main" in the Project Properties. You should then be able to run the project. If you click on a button, you should get the appropriate message box.

Tech Note. *Visual Basic now comes with a login form template. To insert this login form into your application, choose Add Form from the Project menu and select the Log In Dialog in the New tab of the Add Form dialog box.*

■ Debugging Techniques

The more complex the application, the more important good debugging techniques become. This section provides an overview of some of the most useful or newest techniques available for debugging Visual Basic applications.

What Will This Cover?

This section will cover the following key Visual Basic features:

- Navigating through the code

- Setting bookmarks in the code

- Customizing the menu bar in the IDE

- Using the Run menu options

- Understanding compiling as you run in the IDE

- Using the Immediate window

- Using the Debug object

- Asserting on invalid values

- Using the cool new Instant Watch feature

- Using the new Comment Block feature

- Using conditional compilation

Navigating through the Code

To debug a piece of code, you need to find the code in the project. There are many techniques for finding a particular property or method in the source code of your application. These are listed and described briefly here.

- **Browse through the Code window.** This technique works well if you know basically where to find the property or method. This technique is accomplished more easily if you are using Full Module View. You can set the view by using the buttons in the lower-left corner of the Code window or by setting the Window Settings options using the Options dialog box as shown in Figure 10.1.

- **Use the Object and Procedures/Events boxes at the top of the Code window.** You can select the object from the Object box and then select the procedure or event you want to view from the Procedures/Events box. If the procedure is not associated with a particular object, it will be listed under "(General)." The select procedure or event is then displayed in the Code window.

- **Use the Object Browser.** The Object Browser is shown in Figure 11.8. Select your project in the Library box, and then select the class and member you wish to view. Click on the View Definition button to display the code for that property or method.

- **Use the Find option from the Edit menu.** The Find option allows you to find any text within any component of the project.

Figure 11.8

The Object Browser allows you to browse the current project and then jump to the Code window to view the definition of any property or method in the project.

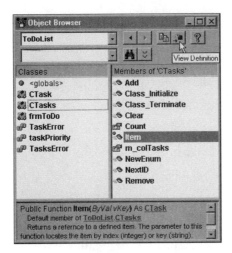

- **Jump with Shift+F2, Ctrl+Shift+F2.** Move the cursor to an identifier and press Shift+F2. If the identifier is a variable, procedure, user-defined type, or enumeration, the code defining the identifier is displayed; otherwise, the Object Browser is displayed for the selected identifier. For example, a Shift+F2 on a call to a Save method will jump to the code for the Save method, even if it is in a different module. A Shift+F2 on Text1.Text will display the Text member of the TextBox class in the Object Browser.

  If you're using Shift+F2 to move through the code, press Ctrl+Shift+F2 to move back to your original location in the code. This feature uses a stack, so pressing Shift+F2 will move you down a set of calls and pressing Ctrl+Shift+F2 will move you back up. Ctrl+Shift+F2 does not move you back to the code from the Object Browser.

- **Set Bookmarks.** Bookmarks are new in Visual Basic 5. They provide a mechanism for setting a placeholder at a particular location in the code and then easily returning to that location. To set a bookmark, choose Bookmark from the Edit menu or right-click on the gray area to the left of the Code window and choose Toggle and Bookmark. A bookmark will appear as a margin indicator. To navigate to a bookmark, choose one of the Bookmarks options from the Edit menu. (You cannot name a bookmark, so if you set a number of bookmarks you have to proceed through them sequentially to find the one you want.)

You may find the bookmark options so useful that you'll wish there was a shortcut key for toggling bookmarks. You can, however, customize your menu bar to provide this feature. To add Alt+B as a shortcut key to toggle bookmarks:

1. Right-click on an empty portion of the menu bar.

    A context menu will appear.

2. Choose Customize from the menu and select the Commands tab.

    The Customize dialog box will appear, as shown in Figure 11.9. The Commands tab displays the menu categories and commands and allows you to customize them.

Figure 11.9

The Customize dialog box allows you to customize the toolbars, menu commands, and options in the IDE.

3. Select Edit from the Categories list and find Toggle Bookmark in the Commands list.

4. Drag the Toggle Bookmark command to an empty portion of the menu bar.

    The Toggle Bookmark icon will appear in the menu bar.

5. Right-click on the Toggle Bookmark icon in the menu bar.

    A special context menu will appear. This context menu will only appear if the Customize dialog box is open.

6. Set the Name to Toggle &Bookmark and the style either to Text Only (Always) or to Image and Text.

This adds Toggle <u>B</u>ookmark to the menu bar, thereby enabling Alt+B as the shortcut key.

7. Close the Customize dialog box.

Whenever you want to toggle a bookmark, you can now use Alt+B.

Running the Application

One way to find which pieces of code need to be debugged is to run the application. You can also step through sections of code that are not executing as expected to watch each line of code as it is executing. Here are several tips for running an application:

- **Run with full compile.** When you are ready to test a set of code, start by running with a full compile. This will flag any syntax errors before beginning the execution of the application. Running without a full compile will only perform syntax checking on code when the code is about to be executed.

Tech Note. *How the project is compiled when you run it in the IDE is determined by the Compile options set on the General tab of the Options dialog box. Selecting Compile on Demand will compile only those portions of the project that are executed. If this option is not selected, the project will be compiled fully before it is run, making it a little slower to start, especially for large projects. If Compile on Demand is set, Background Compile can be set to allow VB to finish compiling the project in the background while you are running it.*

- **Step through problem sections.** If a portion of the code is not executing properly, you can use the F8 key (or the Step Into option from the Debug menu) to execute one statement at a time. You can then follow code execution, using Step Over and Step Out as desired.

Tech Note. *Stepping through the code can sometimes affect how the code is executed. Stepping should not be used to debug mouse, keyboard, or drag events. Nor should it be used when debugging application focus. In those cases, try a different technique such as displaying information to the Immediate window.*

- **Use the Immediate window.** The Immediate window is a window in the IDE that can be used to run portions of your application. With Visual Basic 5, you can call routines, execute code, or create objects from classes without first running and pausing the project. Simply type the statements into the Immediate window. Try it using the first project from this chapter and the text from Figure 11.10.

Figure 11.10

Use the Immediate
window to test the
creation of your classes.

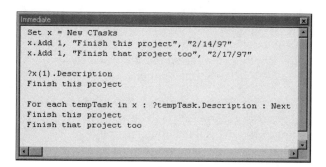

```
Immediate                                                    x
Set x = New CTasks
x.Add 1, "Finish this project", "2/14/97"
x.Add 1, "Finish that project too", "2/17/97"

?x(1).Description
Finish this project

For each tempTask in x : ?tempTask.Description : Next
Finish this project
Finish that project too
```

You can also use the Immediate window to display or set variable values and to review the results of Debug.Print statements in the application.

Each time you press the Enter key on a line in the Immediate window, the line is executed. To execute a loop, enter all of the statements on one line separated with colons (:)— For example, For j = 0 to 7 : myArray(j).Add : Next j can be executed in the Immediate window if you enter it all on one line.

- **Instant Watch.** Instant Watch is a new feature in Visual Basic 5. When a project is running and in break mode, you can move the cursor over a variable and the value is displayed in a ToolTip. This makes it easy to move the cursor in the Code window and view the values of all of the variables.

- **Setting Watch points.** You can set watch points and cause Visual Basic to stop execution when the value of an expression is true or when the expression value changes.

- **Setting Break points.** With Visual Basic 5, break points are shown with margin indicators. You can set a break point anywhere in the application and Visual Basic will break at that point when running the application in design mode.

- **Setting the next statement.** When in break mode, the current statement is shown with a margin indicator. You can set the next statement to any statement within the routine by simply dragging the margin indicator to the new location. The indicated line will be the next line executed when the application resumes running.

Adding Debug Code

Some debugging situations require the addition or removal of debug code from the application. This debug code could be as simple as the display of an "In Init now" message or as complex as the display of all elements in a collection. Depending on the situation, Visual Basic provides several features for adding debug code to the application:

- **Message Boxes.** Message boxes are one of the easiest mechanisms for debugging an application. You can add a message box anywhere in an application to display debug information. You can add messages to Initialize and Terminate events to determine when they are occurring, or to any routine in an application to display state information. There are a few downsides to using message boxes as a debugging tool. First, they can affect the execution of the application. For example, using a message box to debug mouse events, timers, or focus can cause inaccurate results. Also, message boxes containing debug code must be removed from the application before delivery.

- **Debug.Print.** The Print method of the Debug object displays debug information in the Immediate window. Use this method to print any information to the Immediate window. Debug.Print is preferable to message boxes in that the Print method will not stop execution, will not affect events or focus, and will not be compiled into an application.

Tech Note.   *Try typing **Debug.?** into your project.*

- **Debug.Assert.** The Assert method of the Debug object is new in Visual Basic 5. It provides a mechanism for checking the value of a variable. If the assertion is false, the project will go into break mode. For example:

```
x=6
Debug.Assert x = 7
```

Since x is 6 and not 7, the application will go into break mode when the Debug.Assert statement is executed. Debug.Assert statements are not compiled into the application.

- **Comment Block/Uncomment Block.** The Comment Block/Uncomment Block feature is new in Visual Basic 5. The Comment Block option allows you to select a block of code and add comment marks to the beginning of each line in the block. The Uncomment Block option removes the comment markers.

    Comment Block and Uncomment Block are only available from the Edit toolbar. To see this option, right-click on the toolbar and check Edit. The Comment Block and Uncomment Block options appear on this toolbox. You can add accelerator keys for these features using the Customize dialog box discussed under bookmarks earlier in this section.

- **Conditional compilation.** Conditional compilation allows you to selectively mark code to be included or excluded from a compilation. It is basically an If statement that is executed when the application is compiled. A # symbol distinguishes it from a regular If statement. When the condition in the #If statement is true, the code within the #If block is compiled. Otherwise the code within the #Else block is compiled.

  For example, you can define a debug conditional compilation constant and then add code such as the following:

  ```
  #If debugMode Then
       MsgBox "It got here"
  #End If
  ```

  You can set your debugMode conditional compilation constant to True when testing the application and to False before the final compilation. This is also useful if there is a bug on a machine other than the development machine or a bug in the executable that is not seen in the development environment.

  There are several ways to set the value of conditional compiler constants. You can use the Conditional Compilation Arguments text box in the Make tab of the Project Properties dialog box. For example, you could specify debugMode = –1 in the text box to define the value of a debugMode conditional compiler constant. You can specify multiple constants in the text box by separating the values with colons (:)—for example, debugMode = -1 : ABCProject = -1. Values set using this technique are global.

  You could instead use the #Const directive in the code to set the value of a conditional compilation constant, as in

  ```
  #Const debugMode = -1
  ```

  If you want to recompile the application without entering the IDE, you can recompile with different values of the compilation constants by using the /D command line switch. For example, VB /Make/D debugMode = 0 MyApp.vbp. Values set on the command line override any values set with the project properties or Const directive.

What Did This Cover?

This section covered some tips and tricks for debugging applications. This included information on navigating within the code of a project, running a project, and adding debugging information to a project. It also described the many cool new Visual Basic 5 features to aid in debugging. You can try any or all of these techniques using the Task class example created earlier in this chapter.

■ Top Ten Class Techniques Questions

As you move on to more advanced techniques, more advanced questions can arise. Ten of the most common questions about the techniques described in this chapter are summarized here, with their answers.

1. How do I store my object's data into a database instead of a file?

   Refer to Chapter 14, "Doing Database Objects."

2. Why do I need a collection class?

   A collection class ensures that only appropriate objects are added to the collection. It can also encapsulate other collection processing, such as the reading and writing of collection data to a file.

3. Why do I get an error when referencing the 0 element of my collection?

   Predefined collections, such as the Forms collection and the Fields collection, are 0-based. That is, the first element in the collection is element 0. The user-defined collections are 1-based. That is, the first element in the collection is element 1. You cannot use an Option Base statement because a collection is an object, not an array.   '

   The following example will generate an error:

   ```
   ' Define the collection of tasks
   Private m_colTasks As New Collection
   Private m_Task as CTask

   Set m_Task = New CTask
   m_colTasks.Add m_Task
   Set m_Task = m_colTasks.Item(0)
   ```

   When the 0 element is referenced, a "Subscript out of range" error is generated.

4. I put an element into the fifth position of a collection and now it is not there. Where did it go?

   The position of an object in a collection can change whenever an object is added to or removed from the collection. Therefore, the position of any specific object in the collection may vary.

   This works like a list box. Say a particular value is in the fifth element of a list box. If the first element of the list box is then deleted, the desired value becomes the fourth element in the list.

   This is especially important to consider when removing objects from a collection. The following code will generate a "Subscript out of range" error:

   ```
   ' Delete the members from the collection
   For j = 1 to m_colTasks.Count
       m_colTasks.Remove j
   Next j
   ```

Suppose there are only two entries, so m_colTasks.Count is 2. When the first object is removed, the second object is automatically shifted to position 1. When the application attempts to remove the object in position 2, the error occurs. The correct code is

```
' Delete the members from the collection
For j = 1 to m_colTasks.Count
    m_colTasks.Remove 1
Next j
```

This will delete the first element the correct number of times to ensure that all elements are deleted. Or better yet, to remove all elements simply set the collection to Nothing or reinitialize it to a new collection:

```
Set m_colTasks = New Collection
```

5. I added two object elements to a collection and when I displayed them, they were both the same! Why?

Let's look at an example of this:

```
' Define the collection of tasks
Private m_colTasks As New Collection
Private thisTask As New CTask

Private Sub Form_Load()
Dim i As Integer         ' Counter for keys.
Dim sMsg As String       ' Variable to hold prompt string.
Dim sDesc As String      ' Task description.
Dim sTaskList As String  ' List of tasks

    Do
        i= i + 1
        sMsg = "Please enter a name and click OK." & vbCrLf _
        & "Press Cancel to see names in the collection."
        sDesc = InputBox(sMsg, "Name the Collection Items")

        ' If user entered a task, add it to the collection.
        If Len(sDesc) <> Ø Then
            thisTask.Description = sDesc

            ' Add the object to the collection.
            m_colTasks.Add thisTask, CStr(i)
        End If

        ' Clear current reference.
        ' Set thisTask = Nothing
    Loop Until Len(sDesc) = Ø

    For Each thisTask In m_colTasks
        sTaskList = sTaskList & thisTask.Description & _
            vbCrLf
    Next thisTask

    ' Display the list of names in a message box.
    MsgBox sTaskList, , "Tasks In Tasks Collection"

End Sub
```

You can try out this code by running it. Enter a task name and click on OK, enter a second task name and click on OK, and then click on Cancel. The names of your tasks should appear on the list, but they don't. Rather, the last entered name appears twice. What's going on here? This code only creates one instance of the Task class. It sets the description of this task to the name you entered and places a reference to the task in the collection. It then changes the name of the task to the second name you entered and places a second reference to the same task in the collection. So the collection contains two references to the same Task object, with the last name you entered.

To correct this problem, remove the comment from the Set thisTask = Nothing line in the preceding example. This ensures that a new instance of the Task class is generated for each new entry. Using a message box in the Initialize and Terminate events during debugging will help you catch these types of errors.

6. Why am I getting a Type Mismatch error when I try to add a member to a collection?

The ID for the object must be a string. The following code will generate the error:

```
' Define the collection of tasks
Private m_colTasks As New Collection

Public Function Add(iPriority As Integer, sDescription As String) As CTask
Dim taskNew As New CTask
Static iID As Integer

    With taskNew
        ' Set a unique ID
        iID = iID + 1

        ' Set the properties
        .Priority = iPriority
        .Description = sDescription

        ' Add the member to the collection
        ' This line will generate an error
        m_colTasks.Add taskNew, iID
    End With

    ' Return the one that was added
    Set Add = taskNew
End Function
```

You need to convert the integer into a string before using it as the key of a collection:

```
m_colTasks.Add taskNew, CStr(iID)
```

7. Why wasn't the Terminate event generated when the object reference was released?

   If you terminate an object, it will not generate the Terminate event unless there are no other references to the object. For example, in the following code, there are two references to the Task object:

```
Private Task1 As CTask
Private Task2 As CTask

Private Sub Form_Load()
    Set Task1 = New CTask
    Set Task2 = Task1

    Set Task1 = Nothing
End Sub
```

   This code creates one new Task object and sets a reference to it called Task1. It then creates a second reference to the object called Task2. When it sets Task1 = Nothing, the Task1 reference is freed, but the Task2 reference still exists. To correct this problem in the preceding example, set Task2 = Nothing as well.

8. Why wasn't the Terminate event generated when the object reference was released (Part 2)?

   There is another possible cause of this problem. In the code shown next, the Task object variable is defined in the Declarations section. When this form is unloaded, the object variable goes out of scope. Assuming there are no other references to the Task object, the Terminate event will be generated. But before the Terminate event code can be executed, the application abruptly ends when it executes the End statement.

```
Private m_Task as CTask

Private Sub Form_Load()
    Set m_Task = New CTask
End Sub

Private Sub Form_Unload(Cancel As Integer)
    End
End Sub
```

   It is good programming practice always to end your application with an End statement. This ensures that the application does indeed terminate, even if there is a hidden form loaded. You do need to be careful to set your object variables to Nothing before executing the End command.

Tech Note. *If you are creating an ActiveX component, you should not use the End statement.*

   The best way to find the source of these types of problems is to include a message box in both the Initialize and Terminate events during testing of the application.

9. Why did my Property procedure execute when my Initialize event generated an error?

When you use the "Private x as New Class" style to declare an object, the object is instantiated the first time it is referenced, usually by calling a Property procedure or method. If an error occurs in the Initialize event, the error will not stop execution of the Property procedure or method.

To try this, create a Class1 with the following code:

```
Option Explicit

Private Sub Class_Initialize()
    On Error Resume Next

    Open "a.txt" For Input As #1
    Err.Raise Err.Number
End Sub

Public Property Get TotalCount() As Integer
    TotalCount = 7
End Property
```

Assuming you don't have a file called a.txt in your directory, this class will generate an error. Reference this class in a form using the following code:

```
Option Explicit

Private obj As New Class1

Private Sub Form_Load()
On Error Resume Next
    MsgBox obj.TotalCount
    If Err.Number <> 0 Then
        MsgBox "Error!"
    End If
End Sub
```

This declares the object and then creates the instance of the object when the TotalCount Property procedure is called. When you run this example, the obj object will be initialized, the error will be generated, and the TotalCount Property procedure will be executed. Upon return to the form code, the error is still set and will display the "Error!" message box. Even though this is not a big problem with this particular example, if the method or Property procedure called depended on a valid Initialize, it too will generate an error.

The best way to prevent this situation is to use the alternative method of declaring the object without the New keyword and then to explicitly instantiate the object using a Set statement.

10. When should I use the CreateObject syntax?

All objects used in the examples in Chapters 10 and 11 have been created using one of the following sets of syntax:

```
Private m_Task as New CTask
```

OR

```
Private m_Task as CTask
Set m_Task = New CTask
```

There is actually another choice. If your project is an ActiveX component, as described in Chapter 13, "Building ActiveX Components," you can use the following syntax to create an object from a public class:

```
Private m_Task as CTask
Set m_Task = CreateObject("Task.CTask")
```

The CreateObject syntax is most commonly used when creating an object from another application, such as Excel. The syntax to create an Excel object is

```
Dim xlApp As Excel.Application
Set xlApp = CreateObject("Excel.Application")
```

This will create a reference to the Excel Application object.

■ Summary

- Collections contain a set of items of any type.

- Collections do not contain objects, but rather contain references to objects.

- A collection class has a private collection of objects and encapsulates the collection operations in the class.

- A collection class includes wrapper methods to add, remove, and obtain a reference to items in the collection.

- Create a generic file processing class to store and retrieve object data.

- A file processing class handles the general opening, closing, reading from, and writing to the file.

- Implement the ReadObjects and WriteObjects routines in each class that will use the file processing class to read or write object data to a file.

- The form you develop in the IDE is a class. You can add properties, methods, and events to forms.

- When a form is referenced at run time, Visual Basic creates a form object from the form class.

- To define the button the user selected in a modal dialog box, define a property in the modal dialog box form.

- Visual Basic provides a wide range of tools to help you debug your applications.

■ Additional Reading

Kurata, Deborah, "Test Objects in the Debug Window," *Visual Basic Programmer's Journal*, Programming with Class column. Vol. 6, No 7, June 1996.

This article describes how to use the Visual Basic 4 Debug window to create an object and test the properties and methods for the object. Although the Debug window is now called the Immediate window, the techniques described in this article are the same for Visual Basic 5.

■ Think It Over

To supplement and review the information in this chapter, think about the following:

1. Add a Done flag property to the To Do List example to allow defining a task as completed. What impact does this have on the collection class? On the file processing class?

2. Think about how you could use a collection to provide a multiple-level undo feature.

3. Now that you know forms are classes, can you think of some ways you can simplify how you are working with forms? How about managing child forms for an MDI application?

12

Interfaces, Polymorphism, and Inheritance

These interfaces are, literally, different ways of communicationg with

an object—that is, accessing its functionality and its information.

—Kraig Brockschmidt

So far, each object created in the examples in this book had one interface—that is, one way to access the object's functionality and information. That interface was the set of properties and methods for the object as defined in the class module. Visual Basic 5 extends this concept and provides for the development of additional interfaces. The functionality of an object can be accessed through the default interface defined in the class module, or through an alternate interface. This is one of those concepts that is a lot easier to understand through examples than through words.

This chapter uses examples to define interfaces, polymorphism, and inheritance. It then demonstrates how to build an interface with a class module and implement that interface in another class. Multiple classes can implement the same interface, making it easier to support polymorphism. Finally, this chapter presents a technique for using interfaces and delegation to achieve implementation inheritance.

■ What Does It All Mean?

Interfaces? Poly-what? Inheritance? What does all of this mean? Visual Basic 5 provides some cool new object-oriented features, but to make the best use of them you need to understand what they are. After this basic introduction of terms, the remaining sections in this chapter will demonstrate these new features.

Interfaces: Sets of Properties and Methods

I am a Person object. You can have a simple face-to-face conversation with me through my default interface using my Talk and Listen methods. There are also many other ways to communicate with me; that is, there are alternative interfaces. You could invoke a Call method on the phone interface to ring my phone. Or, you could invoke the Transmit method of the fax interface to transmit a document to me. You can invoke the Send method of the e-mail interface to send me an e-mail message. Figure 12.1 illustrates these interfaces.

Each of these interfaces has a particular purpose and is described by a set of properties and methods. For example, the purpose of the e-mail interface is to provide a method for sending electronic mail messages. It has properties such as SendTo, SendFrom, and MessageText and methods such as Send and Delete.

A single class module could define public properties and methods to support all of the functionality defined in Figure 12.1, but this makes the class module very complex. It would be difficult to tell which properties and methods belong to which functionality. For example, a routine could set the SendTo property of the e-mail interface and accidentally call the Transmit

Figure 12.1

The circles protruding from the left side of the diagram depict the interfaces of the object. Because of their shape, the interfaces are often referred to as lollipops.

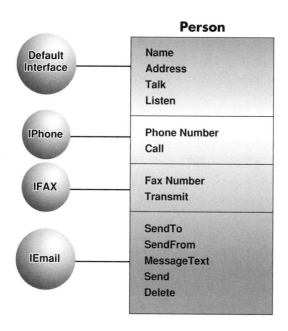

Person

Default Interface
- Name
- Address
- Talk
- Listen

IPhone
- Phone Number
- Call

IFAX
- Fax Number
- Transmit

IEmail
- SendTo
- SendFrom
- MessageText
- Send
- Delete

Keynote

method of the fax interface instead of the Send method of the e-mail interface to attempt to send a message.

Defining all of the properties and methods in a single class also makes it more difficult to reuse an individual interface. There would be no easy way to define another class and reuse the e-mail interface. You would have to figure out which properties and methods in the class were applicable to the e-mail interface and copy and paste them to the new class.

With Visual Basic 5, you can divide an object's functionality into logical sets, called *interfaces*, as shown with the lollipops in Figure 12.1. In that Figure, it is easy to see which properties and methods belong to which interface. A routine can then use an interface and be assured that it can only use the correct properties and methods for that interface.

How do you create these interfaces? When you create a class module, you define the set of properties and methods for a class. These properties and methods are the *default interface* for each object created from the class. You created several default interfaces as you worked through Chapter 10, "Building Your First Class," and Chapter 11, "Building Classes: Additional Techniques." The default interface for the Person object shown in Figure 12.1 includes Name and Address properties and Talk and Listen methods.

You can create an alternate interface by declaring the properties and methods for the interface in a separate class module. The interface does not include any variable declarations or code for the properties and methods, just the procedure declarations. By convention, the name of a class module that contains the definition of an alternate interface is prefixed with an "I" to indicate that it is an interface. The IEmail interface in Figure 12.1 has SendTo, SendFrom, and MessageText properties and Send and Delete methods. The steps for defining an interface are detailed in the section "Creating and Implementing an Interface" later in this chapter.

Keynote

A class can use any number of alternate interfaces. For example, the Person object can use the IPhone, IFAX and IEmail interfaces, as shown in Figure 12.1. To use an interface, the Person class implements the interface. The code required to implement an alternate interface is described under "Creating and Implementing an Interface."

Tech Note.   *The ability of an object to use multiple interfaces is provided through the Component Object Model (COM). For more information about COM, see the books mentioned in the "Additional Reading" section at the end of this chapter.*

Keynote

The bottom line is that an interface documents the list of properties and methods required to provide particular functionality in a class. It leaves the implementation of the functionality to the class. This arrangement makes it easy for multiple classes to support the same interface but have entirely different implementations of the interface. For example, a Person class may implement an e-mail system one way (using AOL at home) while an Employee class would implement it in another (using an intranet with a firewall).

Tech Note.   *The ability of multiple classes to implement the same interface is called* interface inheritance. *The interface is provided automatically in any class referencing the interface. However, unlike implementation inheritance, no code is shared. See "Inheritance: Reusing Functionality" later in this section for more information.*

You can communicate with an object through its default interface by referencing a property or invoking a method defined in the object's class, as you saw in the examples in Chapters 10 and 11. You can also communicate with an object through any of its alternate implemented interfaces by referencing a property or invoking a method defined in the interface. In either case, if you know what interfaces an object supports you can communicate with the object through any of the interfaces without knowing how the interface is implemented for the object.

Let's look at an example more appropriate to your applications. Suppose you are designing an application and find that many classes support the same set of properties and methods. For example, most classes in the application support save functionality. You can group that set of properties and methods into a Save interface, or ISave as is the convention. To keep the example simple, the ISave interface will include an IsDirty property to identify whether the object's property values have been changed and a Save method to perform the save operation on the object. Most interfaces you define will have more than one property and one method.

Any class can implement the ISave interface. Any object created from the class can then be accessed through this interface to perform the save operations. The interface does not provide the save functionality; it does not actually know how to save any particular type of object. It only knows that the object has a property named IsDirty and a method called Save. To implement the ISave interface, the class has to provide the code for the IsDirty property and Save method.

Now the question is "why?" Why would you want to define an interface? There are several benefits to using an interface:

Keynote

- **Simplified development.** In a large application, a class can have many different properties and methods to provide specific types of functionality. The development of the class is simplified if the properties and methods are grouped into interfaces. The process of grouping properties and methods into interfaces is called *factoring*.

- **Standard functionality in a set of classes.** An interface provides a predefined set of properties and methods. If a class implements the interface, it must include each of the properties and methods of the interface. For example, each primary class in your application needs an IsDirty property and Save method. You can define an interface with the required properties and methods. Implementing this interface in each of the classes ensures that each of the properties and methods of the interface is defined in each class.

- **Simplified reuse.** You can implement an interface in any number of classes. If you later want to define that same set of properties and methods in a different class, you can reuse the interface by implementing it in the other class.

- **Addition of new functionality without affecting the existing interfaces.** Looking back at the person example, if you need some new functionality such as cellular phone service, you could modify an existing interface to obtain that functionality. You could add a parameter to the Call method of the phone interface to provide for a cellular phone. But modifying the Call method will break any code that uses the existing Call method.

  Instead, you could add support for new functionality simply by adding another interface. If you need cellular phone service, you can implement a cellular phone interface without any impact on the other interfaces. That is, you can simply add an ICellularPhone interface to the class without affecting the existing IPhone, IEmail, and IFAX interfaces.

  This capability adds to the concept of Visual Basic as a rapid application development (RAD) tool. You can define an initial set of functionality

Keynote

for a class and implement it as a set of interfaces. You can add new functionality later by adding additional interfaces. This incremental development technique lets you add enhancements without worrying about breaking existing code.

This is especially true when you're working with shared components. If a shared component provides a defined set of functionality and later needs more functionality, you can enhance it with additional interfaces. If you don't change the original interfaces, the existing client components don't need to be replaced or recompiled; they can simply use the revised shared component. Only the client components that require the new functionality need be changed. This topic is discussed further in Chapter 13, "Building ActiveX Components."

- **Improved polymorphism.** Multiple classes that implement the same interface can be accessed generically through that interface using polymorphism. This is discussed in detail in a moment under "Polymorphism: Many Forms of Implementation."

- **Achieve implementation inheritance.** If a set of classes share a set of common code, you don't want to repeat the code in each class. Rather, you can develop the common code in a single class, called a *base class*. You can use the base class in any number of classes by referencing the interface of the base class in each class. Each class can then call to the base class to execute the common code. True implementation inheritance would perform this call to the base class automatically. More on this in a moment under "Inheritance: Reusing Functionality."

Polymorphism: Many Forms of Implementation

Polymorphism means "many forms." Basically, polymorphism provides for multiple implementations of the same functionality. For example, Save functionality can have many forms—that is to say that it can be implemented differently for different classes. Visual Basic 4 provided a mechanism for polymorphism in that classes or forms could contain like-named properties or methods. Visual Basic 5 enhances that capability with interfaces.

Suppose your order entry application has a Save option that will save changes made to customers, inventory, or purchase orders. You could write a Save method with a Select...Case structure as follows:

```
Sub Save(iWhat As Integer)
    Select Case iWhat
    Case iCUSTOMER
        SaveCust
    Case iINVENTORY
        SaveInv
        Case iPO
            SavePO
    End Select
End Sub
```

The SaveCust, SaveInv, and SavePO subroutines provide the code required to save the specific type of data. This technique would have been your best choice in Visual Basic 3.

With the introduction of classes in Visual Basic 4, you could create a Customer class, Inventory class, and PO class and leverage polymorphism by adding a Save method to each class. Because the objects have a like-named Save method, you can reduce the eight-line Select...Case structure above into a one-line routine:

```
Private Sub Save(oWhat as Object)
    oWhat.Save
End Sub
```

If the objects were stored in a collection, called m_colObjects in the example, you could use polymorphism to implement "save all" functionality as follows:

```
Private Sub SaveAll( )
Dim obj as Object
    For each obj In m_colObjects
        obj.Save
    Next
End Sub
```

These examples call the Save method without knowing the specific type of object to be saved. Visual Basic would determine the type of object and call the Save method in the appropriate class.

However, there was a downside to polymorphism in Visual Basic 4. Look again at the Save and SaveAll methods just shown. Notice that the oWhat and obj object variables are declared as Object. The object variable could not be declared with the specific type because it was not known at design time whether the object would be a Customer, Inventory, or PO object. By declaring these object variables as Object, the calls to the object's properties and methods are late bound and are therefore slower. (See Chapter 10, "Building your First Class," for more information on late versus early binding.)

Keynote

By implementing interfaces, polymorphism becomes even more powerful. An interface can be defined for a set of functionality, such as the Save functionality in this example. The Customer, Inventory, and PO classes can then implement the ISave interface. Because any object from either of the three classes would support the ISave interface, the object variable can be declared using the interface as the data type. This provides for polymorphism without sacrificing early binding.

You can revise the Save and SaveAll code examples shown earlier to use an ISave interface:

```
Private Sub Save(oWhat as ISave)
    oWhat.Save
End Sub

Private Sub SaveAll( )
Dim obj As ISave
    For Each obj In m_colObjects
        obj.Save
    Next
End Sub
```

The code looks basically the same, only the object variable data types are different. The change will have a potentially significant impact on performance because all calls in the routine will then be early bound instead of late bound.

Keynote

In summary, polymorphism provides the ability to communicate with objects from different classes through a common interface. Defining a common interface for a set of objects simplifies polymorphism because you know all objects support the standard properties and methods in the interface. Interfaces also provide for early binding when using polymorphism because, even though you may not know the type of object until run time, the interface is known at compile time.

Inheritance: Reusing Functionality

Inheritance is the ability of an object to inherit or obtain functionality from another object. For example, a Customer class and a Prospect class have similar functionality, such as Name, Address, and Phone Number properties and a SendFollowUp method for sending follow-up materials. Instead of writing the code to support these properties and methods in both the Customer and Prospect classes, you could add this common code to a *base class*, also called a *parent class*. In this case, the base class would be a Person class and would include the code for the common functionality. The Customer and Prospect classes include only their unique properties and methods; the common properties and methods are inherited from the Person class. The Customer and Prospect classes are then called *subclasses* or *derived classes* of the Person class.

With standard *implementation inheritance*, calling a SendFollowUp method for a Customer object would call the code in the Person base class automatically if the Customer object did not have a SendFollowUp method. This allows the subclasses to inherit all of the implementation—that is, the code—of the base class. Visual Basic does not provide implementation inheritance.

That's right. Visual Basic does not provide standard inheritance. It is important to get over this point. Interfaces can be used to help achieve implementation inheritance, but it is still code intensive. Just because interfaces are a poor substitute for inheritance does *not* mean that interfaces are bad. Interfaces are very useful for dividing functionality into discrete units as discussed earlier in the chapter under "Interfaces: Sets of Properties and Methods."

With that said, you can achieve implementation inheritance using interfaces and delegation. *Delegation* is simply passing a call to another routine. Any time you call a subroutine you are performing delegation. For a complete discussion of delegation, see the references in the "Additional Reading" section at the end of this chapter.

To provide inheritance for the Customer and Prospect classes in our example, you could create a Person interface with the common properties and methods. You could then use the IPerson interface in the Customer and Prospect classes. That would ensure that both the Customer and Prospect classes had the correct set of common properties and methods, but would require both classes to implement the code for the common properties and methods. This solution does not provide for reuse of the code, only for reuse of the interface—that is, the list of properties and methods.

Another solution is to create a Person class, instead of a Person interface. The Person class would define the list of common properties and methods as well as the code for those properties and methods. You could then implement the Person class in the Customer and Prospect classes because Visual Basic 5 allows you to define a class as an alternate interface to another class!

Simply implementing the Person class within the Customer and Prospect classes alone won't provide any more reuse than implementing a Person interface. The code within the Person class will be ignored. To achieve implementation inheritance, you can add code to the Customer and Prospect classes to call the Person class to execute the common code defined in the Person class. For example, when the SendFollowUp method is invoked on a Customer object, the code in the SendFollowUp method of the Customer object calls the SendFollowUp method in the Person class to execute the method. This is shown in Figure 12.2. The code for this technique is presented later in this chapter.

In summary, Visual Basic 5 does not provide implementation inheritance. Instead, you can achieve implementation inheritance by implementing the interface of a base class in a subclass and then delegating from the subclass to the base class.

Looking at this another way, the interface feature of Visual Basic 5 provides an alternative to inheritance for reuse of class functionality. Some may say that the interface technique is more powerful than inheritance because of the complexities of defining correct and solid inheritance hierarchies.

Figure 12.2

Achieve implementation inheritance by implementing the interface of a class and then delegating to the class.

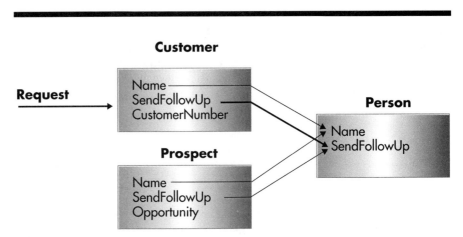

Others may say that the object-oriented features of Visual Basic are not complete without implementation inheritance. The debate on implementation inheritance versus interface inheritance is beyond the scope of this book and will be left to newsgroups and magazine articles. However, it would be nice to have the choice.

■ Creating and Implementing an Interface

As stated in Kraig Brockschmidt's quote at the beginning of this chapter, an interface is simply a mechanism for communicating with an object. You already defined an interface, the *default interface*, when you added properties and methods to a class module. Each object created from the class can be accessed through the default interface by using the properties or calling the methods of the object.

Tech Note. *The name of the default interface is the name of the class prefixed with an underscore. For example, the default interface for a Person class would be _Person. The underscore indicates that the name is hidden in the type library, so you won't see it in the Object Browser.*

Visual Basic 5 provides support for implementing additional interfaces for an object. You can use existing interfaces or create your own interfaces by creating a class module and defining the interface properties and methods in that class module. The interface does not include any module-level variable declarations or code for the properties and methods.

Tech Note. *You can also define an interface by creating a type library and then compiling the type library using the Make Type Library (MkTypLib) utility provided in the Tool directory of Visual Basic Professional or Enterprise Edition.*

Once an interface is created, you can implement the interface in any class by:

1. Declaring the interface with the Implements keyword.
2. Adding code to provide functionality for the interface.

Each object created from the class can then be accessed through its default interface or this alternate interface.

Tech Note. *The keyword used to declare an interface is "Implements," the process of adding code is often referred to as "implementing the code," and the process of declaring an interface and adding the code to support the interface is referred to as "implementing the interface." So it would be accurate, although confusing, to say "Once an interface is created, any class can implement the interface by using Implements and then implementing the code for the interface." Watch out for this terminology when reading the VB documentation and help system.*

The examples earlier in this book were leading to the creation of a contact management system. So far, you have created a fully functional to do list component that can be included in the contact management system to maintain the list of follow-up tasks. In this section, the examples present code to manage the list of customers and prospects for the contact management system.

You may recall from the design chapters of this book that the contact management system design team decided to combine the Customer class and Prospect class into one Person class. This chapter will ignore that design decision for a while to demonstrate how these could be developed as separate classes. In this section, an ISave interface will be created with an IsDirty property that will be set when object properties have been changed and a Save method called to save the class properties. This ISave interface is then implemented in the Customer class.

What Will This Cover?

This section will cover the following key Visual Basic features:

- Creating an interface using Visual Basic
- Using the new Implements keyword
- Implementing an interface
- Using alternate interfaces

Steps to Creating and Implementing an Interface

The steps required for creating and implementing an interface are

1. Design the interface.

2. Create the interface in a new class module.

3. Implement the interface in a class.

4. Use the implemented interface.

    These steps are detailed in the topics that follow.

Designing the Interface

It is important that you carefully consider the properties and methods to be included in each interface you create. Grouping properties and methods into an interface is called factoring and is done as part of the design process. See Chapter 7, "Implementation-Centered Design," for information on the factoring process.

Keynote

    An interface is like a contract. Once you have defined an interface and other classes have implemented the interface, it cannot be changed. Doing so would break the contract you have made with the classes that use the interface. So don't forget the design step.

Creating the Interface

The easiest way to create an interface is to declare the properties and methods of the interface in a class module. No module-level variable declarations or procedure code is required, just the Property, Sub, or Function procedure declarations.

Tech Note. *A class created for the sole purpose of defining an interface has no code beyond the procedure declarations, and objects are usually not created from this class. A class that has no objects created from it is referred to as an* abstract class. *Technically, classes you create with Visual Basic are not abstract classes because an object could be created from the class.*

    To create an interface:

1. Open the desired project or a new project.

    If the interface is to be local to a project, it can be included within the project. If the interface is to be included in many different projects, it should be created as a new ActiveX component, as described in Chapter 13, "Building ActiveX Components."

2. From the Project menu, choose Add Class Module and add a new class module.

This class module will contain the definition of the interface.

3. In the Properties window, set the Name property.

   Use the interface name as the name of the class module. The standard convention is to include an "I" prefix in the interface name. For example, an interface that defines save functionality would be named "ISave."

4. Declare the properties and methods.

   Declare public variables or Property, Sub, or Function procedures in the class module. Be sure to identify any parameters or return values of the procedures with the correct data types. These declarations provide the templates for the properties and methods for the interface. No module-level variable declarations or procedure code is necessary.

Tech Note. *Code in a class module used as an interface, including defined private variables and events, will be ignored when the interface is implemented.*

For the example ISave interface, an IsDirty property is defined that will track whether data has been changed. A Save method is included to perform the save operation. Here is the code for the ISave interface:

```
' Class Name:    ISave
' Author:        Deborah Kurata, InStep Technologies
' Date:          1/11/97
' Description:   Provides an interface for Save functionality
' Revisions:

Option Explicit

' Define a flag to indicate if the properties
' have changed and need to be saved
Public Property Get IsDirty() As Boolean

End Property
Public Property Let IsDirty(bool As Boolean)

End Property

' Define a method to save the property values
Public Sub Save()

End Sub
```

You now have a interface! That wasn't so hard!

Implementing the Interface

Once you have defined an interface, you can implement it in any class module or form. The same interface can be implemented in any number of forms or class modules in an application, and a form or class module can implement any number of interfaces.

Tech Note. *Interfaces cannot be implemented in a standard module.*

To implement an interface:

1. Open the class module or form that will implement the interface, or add a new class module or form.

   In this example, a Customer class will implement the ISave interface.

Tech Note.   *If the interface is defined in an ActiveX component and not as a class module within the current project, you need to set a reference to the ActiveX component before implementing the interface. You do this using the References option from the Project menu, as described in Chapter 13, "Building ActiveX Components."*

2. Declare the interface.

   Visual Basic 5 provides a new keyword, Implements, for implementing an interface within a form or class module. Just add the Implements statement to the Declarations section of the form or class module. For the ISave interface, the code is as follows:

```
Implements ISave
```

   The ISave object will then be added to the Object box in the upper-left area of the Code window and the properties and methods defined in the ISave interface will appear in the Procedures/Events box in the upper-right area of the Code window.

Tech Note.   *If you declared a property in the interface as a public variable, rather than with Property procedures, the property will appear as Property Get and Property Let statements in the Procedures/Events box.*

3. Select the interface from the Object box and select each property and method from the Procedure/Events box.

   The Property, Sub, or Function procedure template for each property and method will be added to the class module or form. Each template will have a procedure name with a prefix defining the interface and the appropriate arguments and data types as defined in the interface.

Tech Note.   *If a class implements an interface, it must implement every property and method in that interface. You must add the procedure template of every property and method here; otherwise the application will not compile. If you don't want to implement a particular property or method in the interface, add the procedure template and raise an error (Const E_NOTIMPL = &H80004001 is the standard error number to use) so the calling code knows that the property or method is not implemented.*

   In the Customer example, the resulting property and method procedure templates will appear in the Customer class as follows:

```
Private Property Let ISave_IsDirty(RHS As Boolean)
```

```
End Property

Private Property Get ISave_IsDirty() As Boolean

End Property

Private Sub ISave_Save()

End Sub
```

Notice that the name of the property or method is prefixed with the name of the interface.

Tech Note.   *The RHS in the Property Let procedure is short for "right-hand side." This will be the value passed in from the right-hand side of an assignment to the property. After the template code is pasted into your class, you can change this variable name to follow your naming conventions.*

4. Add code to implement the interface.

The interface is simply the list of properties and methods and contains no code. The code to implement the interface belongs instead in the class or form that implements the interface. This allows multiple classes to implement the same interface, but have different implementations of the interface.

For properties, this may mean declaring a private variable in the class to maintain the value of the property, code in the Property Get to format and return the property value, and code in the Property Let to validate and set the property value. For methods, you must develop the code to perform the operation.

The Customer class in this example has a default interface that includes a Name, Company and CustomerNumber. These properties are defined in the Declarations section of the Customer class as follows:

```
' Class Name:    CCustomer
' Author:        Deborah Kurata, InStep Technologies
' Date:          1/11/97
' Description:   Provides customer properties and methods
' Revisions:

Option Explicit

Private m_sCustomerNumber As String
Private m_sCompany As String
Private m_sName As String
```

To implement the ISave interface, the Declarations section of the Customer class must also include the Implements statement:

```
Implements ISave
```

A private local variable is declared in the Declarations section of the Customer class to store the IsDirty property defined by the ISave interface and the Property procedure code assigns and returns the value. The resulting code in the Customer class appears as follows:

```
Private m_bIsDirty As Boolean

Private Property Let ISave_IsDirty(RHS As Boolean)
    m_bIsDirty = RHS
End Property
Private Property Get ISave_IsDirty() As Boolean
    ISave_IsDirty = m_bIsDirty
End Property
```

The other Property procedures in the Customer class expose the properties of the default interface:

```
Public Property Get CustomerNumber() As String
    CustomerNumber = m_sCustomerNumber
End Property
Public Property Let CustomerNumber(ByVal sAcct As String)
    If m_sCustomerNumber <> sAcct Then
        m_sCustomerNumber = sAcct
        m_bIsDirty = True
    End If
Fnd Property

Public Property Get Company() As String
    Company = m_sCompany
End Property
Public Property Let Company(ByVal sCompany As String)
    If m_sCompany <> sCompany Then
        m_sCompany = sCompany
        m_bIsDirty = True
    End If
End Property

Public Property Get Name() As String
    Name = m_sName
End Property
Public Property Let Name(ByVal sName As String)
    If m_sName <> sName Then
        m_sName = sName
        m_bIsDirty = True
    End If
End Property
```

The private dirty flag is set to True if any of the Customer object properties are changed.

The Save method from the ISave interface can then be implemented to save the customer data. This type of functionality is presented in Chapter 14, "Doing Database Objects." For this example, a message box is used to confirm that the method was executed:

```
Private Sub ISave_Save()
    MsgBox "Saved the Customer: " & Name
End Sub
```

Keynote

In summary, any class module or form can implement an interface. This means that the interface must be declared and every property and method in that interface must be implemented in each class that uses the interface. This ensures that the interface itself is separate from the implementation of that interface so the interface can be reused in many different classes. The interface can then be used to access an object without knowing how an object will implement that interface.

Using an Implemented Interface

If you look again carefully at the procedure templates generated when you implemented an interface, you will see that the properties and methods of the interface are all private. If these procedures were public, they would be part of the Customer object's default interface. Because the procedures are private, you cannot access them using an object created from the class.

How, then, do you use the new interface? You use the interface itself to access the properties and methods of the interface for an object that implements the interface. To illustrate this concept, let's go back to the person example from the beginning of this chapter. If you want to communicate with a Person object by causing a ring on that person's phone, you can not cause the ring to happen directly. You need to go through the phone interface to generate the ring. Using the Customer example, you cannot invoke a Customer object's Save method directly. You need to invoke the Save method using the ISave interface as shown in Figure 12.3.

Figure 12.3

The properties and methods defined in the ISave interface can only be accessed through that interface.

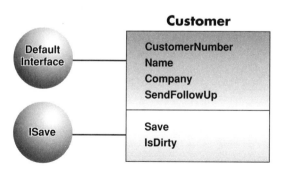

There are two techniques for accessing the properties and methods of an implemented interface for an object:

- **Assign the object to a variable of the interface type.** This technique requires declaring a variable of the interface type and then assigning the object to that variable. This basically points the interface to the object.

You can then invoke the properties or methods of the interface by using the interface variable.

- **Declare a procedure with an argument of the interface type.** This method requires creating a procedure with an argument declared of the interface type. The object can then be passed to this procedure and you can invoke the properties or methods of the interface by using the argument variable.

Although both of these techniques sound complex, they really aren't. The following topics describe these techniques in detail.

Assigning the Object to the Interface

To call a property or method using the default interface of an object, you simply declare an object variable for the object, create the object, and call the property or method using the object variable. This is what you did throughout Chapter 10, "Building Your First Class," and Chapter 11, "Building Classes: Additional Techniques."

Now that you know how to create an alternate interface, you will want to call a property or method using an alternate interface for an object. You can do this by declaring an object variable for the object and a variable for the interface. You then create the object, assign it to the interface, and call the property or method using the interface variable.

Let's take this step by step:

1. Open the form, class module, or standard module that will use a property or method from an interface.

    This example uses a standard module, but you can use this technique in any form, module, or class module.

2. Declare an object variable for the object.

    The object variable provides the reference to the object and can be used to access any properties and methods defined in the default interface in the object's class.

    For the Customer example, the object variable declaration is:

    ```
    Private m_Customer As CCustomer
    ```

3. Declare a variable of the interface type.

    This variable provides a references to the interface. For the Customer example, the interface variable declaration is:

    ```
    Private m_ISave As ISave
    ```

Tech Note. *Using this technique, you will not be creating objects from the interface, so do not use the New keyword on the declaration of the* *interface. You can, of course, use the New keyword when declaring any other object variable.*

4. Set the interface variable to the object variable.

   You can create the object first, and then set the reference to the interface object variable:

   ```
   Set m_Customer = New CCustomer
   Set m_ISave = m_Customer
   ```

   Alternatively, if you don't need to use the m_Customer object variable to reference the default interface of the object, you can create the object when setting it to the interface object variable by using the New keyword on the Set statement:

   ```
   Set m_ISave = New CCustomer
   ```

Tech Note.   *You do not create an instance of the interface.*

5. Invoke the properties or methods using the interface variable.

   The Customer example demonstrates this with the following line of code:

   ```
   m_ISave.Save
   ```

   The statement calls the Save method to execute the code in the private Save method of the ISave interface implemented in the Customer class.

Tech Note.   *Even though the interface is defined in the class module, an interface will not behave like a class. Code added to the interface class module will not be executed. You can try this yourself by adding code to the Save method in the interface and then using the F8 key to walk through the code. Only the code in the Save method of the Customer class will be executed.*

The following code is the Declarations section of the standard module for the Customer example:

```
' Module Name:   MMain
' Author:        Deborah Kurata, InStep Technologies
' Date:          1/11/97
' Description:   Startup object for this application
'                Contains code to demonstrate
'                interfaces
' Revisions:

Option Explicit
Private m_Customer As CCustomer
Private m_ISave As ISave
```

In this example, the m_Customer object variable is declared to be an object from the CCustomer class and the m_ISave variable is declared to be the interface variable.

```
Sub Main()
    Set m_Customer = New CCustomer
    m_Customer.Name = "John Smith"
    m_Customer.Company = "Acme"
    m_Customer.CustomerNumber = "S10102"

    Set m_ISave = m_Customer
    m_ISave.Save
End Sub
```

This routine creates a new customer object and accesses the object through its default interface to set its Name, Company, and CustomerNumber properties. It then sets the object variable to the interface variable to access the object through the ISave interface. When that Set statement executes, Visual Basic asks the m_Customer object if it supports the ISave interface. If it does not, an error is generated.

At this point, you can access any properties and methods of the object. You can use the m_Customer object variable to invoke properties or methods from the default interface. You can use the m_ISave object variable to invoke properties and methods from the ISave interface.

Tech Note. *Regardless of the interface used to communicate with the object, you are still working with the object. You can check this using the TypeName function. Both TypeName(m_Customer) and TypeName(m_ISave) will return CCustomer.*

Declaring a Procedure with an Argument for the Interface

The technique just shown provides access to both interfaces of the object, but if the object had more than two interfaces or if more than one object implemented the interfaces, this technique could be a little clunky.

To make the code a little cleaner, you can create a routine and pass the object to the routine. This technique does not require a declared variable for the interface, nor does it require the object to be assigned to the interface. Rather, the object is passed to the routine in an argument declared with the interface as the data type.

The steps for this technique are:

1. Open the form, class module, or standard module that will use a property or method from an interface.

    This example uses a standard module, but you can use this technique in any form, module, or class module.

2. Declare an object variable for the object.

    The object variable provides the reference to the object and can be used to access any properties and methods defined in the default interface in the object's class. Notice that you don't need a variable for the interface.

    For the Customer example, the object variable declaration is

```
Private m_Customer As CCustomer
```

3. Create a routine to perform the operation.

The object must be passed to that routine as an argument defined with the interface data type.

For example, a Save routine would take an object as a parameter:

```
' Save routine to test the Save methods of the classes
Public Sub Save(obj As ISave)
    If obj.IsDirty Then
        obj.Save
    End If
End Sub
```

This routine accepts an object that has the ISave interface. If the object passed to this method does not support the ISave interface, an error will be generated. The code in this routine checks the IsDirty property and calls the Save method from the ISave interface.

Tech Note. *Regardless of the interface used to communicate with the object, you are still working with the object. Therefore, in this example the function TypeName(obj) will return CCustomer.*

4. Call the routine and pass the object as the argument.

The Customer example code can be modified for this technique as follows:

```
' Module Name:   MMain
' Author:        Deborah Kurata, InStep Technologies
' Date:          1/11/97
' Description:   Startup object for this application
'                Contains code to demonstrate
'                interfaces
' Revisions:

Option Explicit
Private m_Customer As CCustomer
```

For this technique, the m_Customer object variable is declared to be an object from the CCustomer class and there is no interface variable declared.

```
Sub Main()
    Set m_Customer = New CCustomer
    m_Customer.Name = "John Smith"
    m_Customer.Company = "Acme"
    m_Customer.CustomerNumber = "S10102"

    ' Save the customer using the ISave interface
    Save m_Customer
End Sub
```

This routine creates a new customer object and accesses the object through its default interface to set its properties. It then calls the Save routine and passes the Customer object. If the Customer object supports the ISave interface, the Save routine will be executed; otherwise an error will be generated.

What Did This Cover?

This section defined a default interface and described how to develop an alternate interface within a Visual Basic class module. It included details on implementing the interface in another class. It also described two techniques for accessing an object through an alternative interface.

At this point, you should be able to test the Customer example. Be sure Sub Main is defined as the startup object for the application and then run it. If you are still a little fuzzy on interfaces, that's OK. There is more to come in the next section.

■ Polymorphism and Interfaces

Polymorphism is the ability to communicate with objects from different classes through a common interface. This allows you to call a property or method from an interface without knowing the type of object. See the section "Polymorphism: Many Forms of Implementation" at the beginning of this chapter for a detailed description of polymorphism.

To illustrate polymorphism, a Prospect class will be added to the Customer example. This class will track information about a prospective customer. To prepare the Prospect class for this demonstration, define a default interface for the Prospect class to include a Name, Company, and Opportunity, which will describe the sales opportunity with this prospect. Then implement the ISave interface in the Prospect class as described in the previous section.

What Will This Cover?

This section will cover the following key Visual Basic features:

* Using polymorphism

* Using polymorphism with objects in a collection

Implementing Polymorphism

Multiple classes can implement the same interface. The properties and methods defined in the interface can then be invoked against any object created from a class that implemented the interface.

If a Customer and Prospect class both implement an ISave interface, you can use the interface to save the data as shown in the following example:

```
' Module Name:   MMain
' Author:        Deborah Kurata, InStep Technologies
' Date:          1/11/97
' Description:   Startup object for this application
'                Contains code to demonstrate
```

```
'                   interfaces
' Revisions:

Option Explicit
Private m_Customer As CCustomer
Private m_Prospect As CProspect
```

Object variables are first declared for both the Customer and Prospect objects. A Customer object is created and the default properties and methods of the object can be accessed using the object variable. The Save method is called to save the Customer object properties.

The Prospect object is then created and the default properties and methods of the Prospect object can be accessed using the appropriate object variable. The Save method is also called to save the Prospect object properties.

```
Sub Main()
    Set m_Customer = New CCustomer
    m_Customer.Name = "John Smith"
    m_Customer.Company = "Acme"
    m_Customer.CustomerNumber = "S10102"

    ' Save the customer using the ISave interface
    Save m_Customer

    Set m_Prospect = New CProspect
    m_Prospect.Name = "Jessica Jones"
    m_Prospect.Company = "ABC Inc"
    m_Prospect.Opportunity = "May purchase 10,000 widgets"

    ' Save the prospect using the ISave interface
    Save m_Prospect
End Sub
```

The Save method is used to save either type of object. Notice that the object was passed to the Save method using the interface as the data type. This makes each call to a property or method of the interface early bound because the interface is known at compile time. Early binding provides better performance for every property or method invoked on the interface. If any object passed to this method does not implement the ISave interface, an error will be generated.

```
' Save routine to test the Save methods of the classes
Sub Save(obj As ISave)
    If obj.IsDirty Then
        obj.Save
    End If
End Sub
```

The Save method demonstrates polymorphism by retrieving the IsDirty property and calling the Save method on the object without knowing what the object is or how the property or method is implemented. Visual Basic knows which IsDirty Property procedure to execute and which Save method to invoke based on the type of object.

Polymorphism and Collections

You can use polymorphism in combination with a collection to invoke a property or a method for all objects in the collection. You can add any objects that implement the same interface to a collection and then cycle through the collection calling a property or method in the implemented interface.

For example, suppose you had a collection of Customer and Prospect objects. You could go through the collection and execute the Save method on all of them as follows:

```
Dim obj As ISave
    For Each obj In m_colObjects
        If obj.IsDirty Then
            obj.Save
        End If
    Next
```

If you later added a Vendor object to track vendors separately from customers and prospects, you could implement the ISave interface in the Vendor class as well. If Vendor objects were also added to the collection shown in the preceding code, the vendor data would be saved as well as data for customers and prospects in the collection. The preceding routine then just knows how save the vendor—no code changes required!

What Did This Cover?

This section defined polymorphism and demonstrated how to use polymorphism to call properties and methods without knowing the type of object. This functionality was available in Visual Basic 4, but it required all polymorphic calls to be late bound. Using interfaces lets you implement polymorphism without sacrificing early binding.

The Customer example should now display a save message box for both customers and prospects. Use the F8 key to run the example and watch the code as it executes.

■ Inheritance and Interfaces

Inheritance is the ability to reuse functionality in a class. A *base class* defines the common functionality. *Subclasses* inherit that functionality and add functionality as required. Inheritance is a useful feature if objects share common code, and need to extend that common code with unique properties and behaviors.

In the Customer example, a Person base class could be defined to include the common Name and Company properties and a SendFollowUp method for sending follow-up materials. The Customer class would be a subclass of the Person class and would only require the unique properties and methods. In this example it is simply a customer number. The Prospect class would also be a subclass of the Person class and would only need its unique properties and methods. In this example it is a description of the opportunity with the prospect.

Keynote

If Visual Basic supported implementation inheritance, a call to the Send-FollowUp method for the Customer object would automatically call the SendFollowUp method code in the Person class. You can achieve this behavior with Visual Basic by implementing the base class as an interface in the subclasses and then delegating properties and methods from the subclasses to the base class.

This section demonstrates the reuse of functionality through interfaces to achieve inheritance. This technique implements the interface of a class and then delegates to properties and methods in that class. To prepare the Customer and Prospect classes for this demonstration, remove the code for the Name and Company properties.

What Will This Cover?

This section will cover the following key Visual Basic features:

- Implementing a class as an interface

- Using delegation to achieve inheritance

Steps to Achieving Inheritance through Interfaces

The steps required for achieving inheritance through interfaces are

1. Create the base class.

2. Implement the base class in the subclass(es).

3. Declare an object variable for the base class in the subclass(es).

4. Create an object from the base class.

5. Delegate to the base class.

These steps are detailed in the topics that follow.

Creating the Base Class

The base class will provide the functionality that is common to all of the subclasses. This base class would contain the definition of the properties and methods along with the common code for the properties and methods.

To create the base class:

1. From the Project menu, choose Add Class Module and add a new class module.

2. In the Properties window, set the Name property.

   Use the class name as the name of the class module. Even though this class will be implemented as an interface, objects will be created from this class so it will be given a "C" prefix instead of an "I" prefix. For example, the Person base class will be named "CPerson."

3. Declare the properties and methods.

   Declare public variables or Property, Sub, or Function procedures in the class module. Be sure to identify any parameters or return values of the procedures with the correct data types. These declarations provide the templates for the properties and methods for the interface.

4. Add common code.

   The properties or methods in the base class that have similar code in at least some of the subclasses can be implemented in the base class. All subclasses can then share this code.

In the Customer example, the Person base class maintains the person's name and company name. It also provides the code for sending follow-up materials to the person. The code for the Person base class is shown here:

```
' Class Name:    CPerson
' Author:        Deborah Kurata, InStep Technologies
' Date:          1/11/97
' Description:   Provides an interface and implementation
'                for standard person properties and methods
' Revisions:

Option Explicit

Private m_sCompany As String
Private m_sName As String

Public Property Get Company() As String
    Company = m_sCompany
End Property
Public Property Let Company(ByVal sCompany As String)
    m_sCompany = sCompany
End Property

Public Property Get Name() As String
    Name = m_sName
End Property
Public Property Let Name(ByVal sName As String)
    m_sName = sName
End Property

Public Function SendFollowUp() As Boolean
    MsgBox "Follow up sent to: " & Name _
               & " at: " & Company
    ' Successful send
    SendFollowUp = True
End Function
```

In an actual application the SendFollowUp code would include code to print forms, fax messages, or e-mail information to a person. This example simply displays a message box.

Implementing the Base Class

The code in the preceding topic defines a base class. To reuse the code in the base class, you can have each subclass implement the interface of the base class. All this does is add the procedure template for each property and method from the base class to the subclass. The code in the base class is ignored.

To implement the base class in a subclass:

1. Open the class module or form for the subclass.

    In this example, Customer and Prospect subclasses will implement the Person base class.

2. Declare the interface using the Implements keyword.

    Both the Customer and Prospect subclasses will include the following line:

    ```
    Implements CPerson
    ```

    The CPerson class will then be added to the Object box in the upper-left area of the Code window and the properties and methods defined in the CPerson class will appear in the Procedures/Events box in the upper-right area of the Code window.

3. Select the interface from the Object box and select each property and method from the Procedure/Events box.

    The Property, Sub, or Function procedure template for each property and method will be added to the class module or form. Each template will have a procedure name with a prefix defining the interface and the appropriate arguments and data types as defined in the interface.

    In the Customer and Prospect classes, the resulting property and method procedure templates will appear in the class as follows:

    ```
    Private Property Get CPerson_Company() As String

    End Property
    Private Property Let CPerson_Company(ByVal RHS As String)

    End Property

    Private Property Get CPerson_Name() As String

    End Property
    Private Property Let CPerson_Name(ByVal RHS As String)

    End Property

    Private Function CPerson_SendFollowUp() As Boolean

    End Function
    ```

The Customer and Prospect classes now implement three interfaces: the default interface, the ISave interface defined in the prior section, and the interface of the CPerson class. Figure 12.4 shows a Customer object and its three interfaces.

Figure 12.4

The Customer object can be accessed through its default interface or through the ISave or CPerson interface.

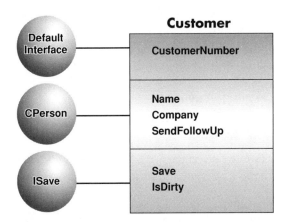

Declaring an Object Variable for the Base Class

Before you can delegate to the base class, you need an object variable to reference the base class. Create the object variable by declaring a private variable of the base class type in the Declarations section of the subclass.

The Customer example defines an object variable for the Person class in both the Customer and Prospect classes as follows:

```
' Declare an instance for delegation
Private m_Person As CPerson
```

Creating an Object from the Base Class

Before an object variable can be used, the object must be created. This happens automatically if you add the New keyword to the declaration shown earlier. Otherwise, you must create the object using a Set statement.

Classes that use other objects frequently create the object in the Initialize event. This ensures that any support objects are created when the primary object is created. Alternatively, the object can be created in the routine in which it is needed.

The code in the Initialize event for both the Customer and Prospect classes creates the base class object, as shown here:

```
Private Sub Class_Initialize()
    Set m_Person = New CPerson
End Sub
```

Any class that sets an object variable to an object should also release the object variable from the object. This is frequently done in the Terminate event for the class. The code in the Terminate event for both the Customer and Prospect classes releases the base class object variable, as shown here:

```
Private Sub Class_Terminate()
    Set m_Person = Nothing
End Sub
```

Delegating to the Base Class

Because the base class is implemented in each subclass, all properties and methods of the base class must be included in the subclass(es). Then you can write code in each subclass to implement the property or method. The base class already has some of the code for this implementation, so instead of repeating this code in each subclass, you can have the subclass call the property or method in the base class. Calling another routine to perform an operation is called *delegation*. Just as you can delegate responsibility for coding part of an application to a coworker, your object can delegate responsibility for an operation to another object.

Keynote

You can be selective about which properties and methods will be delegated to the base class and which will be handled by the subclass. You can allow some subclasses to delegate and others to handle all of the processing themselves. In addition, you can add code to the subclasses to process information before or after the delegation. This allows for processing such as security checking, translations, validation, or other manipulation.

In the Customer example, the Company property is delegated from the subclasses to the base class as follows:

```
Private Property Get CPerson_Company() As String
    CPerson_Company = m_Person.Company
End Property

Private Property Let CPerson_Company(ByVal RHS As String)
    If m_Person.Company <> RHS Then
        m_Person.Company = RHS
        m_bIsDirty = True
    End If
End Property
```

When the Company property is accessed through the CPerson interface, the subclass calls the Person object to retrieve the Company name. When the Company property is assigned through the CPerson interface, the subclass checks the current value against the new value. If the value is changed, it calls the Person object to set the new value. The subclass then sets its own dirty flag. The code for delegating the Name property is done similarly.

The SendFollowUp method can be delegated to the base class as follows:

```
' Send follow-up materials
Private Function CPerson_SendFollowUp() As Boolean
    CPerson_SendFollowUp = m_Person.SendFollowUp
End Function
```

When the SendFollowUp method is called through the CPerson interface, the subclass calls the Person object's SendFollowUp method, as shown in Figure 12.2. That's all there is to delegation!

Using the Base Class Interface

One of the down sides of using an interface approach rather than inheritance is that the client application must know about the base class. In implementation inheritance, the client can know only about the subclass. When using an interface to share common code, the client must use the interface to access the object.

Using the Customer example, the Sub Main procedure would need to be changed to recognize the additional interface. You do this using the techniques defined in the section "Using an Implemented Interface" earlier in this chapter. Here is the resulting Sub Main procedure:

```
' Object variable for the Customer subclass
Private m_Customer As CCustomer
' Object variable for the Prospect subclass
Private m_Prospect As CProspect
 ' Variable for the CPerson interface
Private m_IPerson As CPerson

Sub Main()
    Set m_Customer = New CCustomer
    m_Customer.CustomerNumber = "S10102"

    Set m_IPerson = m_Customer
    m_IPerson.Name = "John Smith"
    m_IPerson.Company = "Acme"
    m_IPerson.SendFollowUp

    ' Save the customer using the ISave interface
    Save m_Customer

    Set m_Prospect = New CProspect
    m_Prospect.Opportunity = "May purchase 10,000 widgets"

    Set m_IPerson = m_Prospect
    m_IPerson.Name = "Jessica Jones"
    m_IPerson.Company = "ABC Inc"
    m_IPerson.SendFollowUp

    ' Save the prospect using the ISave interface
    Save m_Prospect
End Sub
```

This code creates the Customer object and uses the default interface to set the Customer Number property. The Customer Number is the only property left in the default interface for the Customer class, as shown in Figure 12.4. The sample code then sets the Customer object to the CPerson interface. Note the naming convention of including the "I" in m_IPerson to indicate that it is used as an interface. The Name and Company properties can be set using the CPerson interface. The SendFollowUp method can also be called using that interface.

If you step through this code with the F8 key, you will see that the code in the SendFollowUp method of the Customer object executes first, and then calls the code in the SendFollowUp method of the Person object. Because you are treating the Person object as an interface, the code in the Person object is only executing because you are specifically delegating to it within the Customer object code.

The Save routine, shown previously, is then called to save the customer using the ISave interface. This processing is repeated for the Prospect object.

What Did This Cover?

This section defined how to achieve implementation inheritance by creating a base class, implementing the base class in one or more subclasses, and then delegating from the subclass to the base class. This technique is similar to implementing an interface, but provides the additional benefit of code reuse.

At this point, you have a test application that demonstrates two uses of interfaces. The ISave interface illustrates implementation of an interface and polymorphism. The Person class presents a technique for achieving inheritance by implementing a base class as an interface and then using delegation.

■ Summary

- Interfaces provide a mechanism for communicating with objects.

- An object's default interface is defined by the public properties and methods in the object's class module.

- An alternative interface can be defined in a class module or directly into a type library.

- Define an interface in a new class module by declaring the Property, Sub, or Function procedures. No code is required in the interface beyond the declarations.

- Implement an interface in any form or class module by declaring the interface with the Implements keyword and adding code to provide the functionality as defined by the interface.

- Implementing an interface in a form or class module ensures that each property or method in the interface is implemented in the form or class module.

- Polymorphism is the ability to call a property or method for an object without knowing its type or implementation.

- Implement the same interface in several forms and/or class modules to provide for polymorphism.

- Using an interface to support polymorphism makes the properties and methods early bound because the interface is known at compile time.

- Inheritance is the ability of an object to obtain functionality from another object. This promotes reusability.

- Achieve code reuse by implementing the interface of a class and then delegating to the class.

- Provide future functionality by implementing new interfaces instead of modifying existing ones.

■ Additional Reading

Brockschmidt, Kraig, *Inside OLE 2*. Redmond, Washington: Microsoft Press, 1995.

This book provides a detailed description of interfaces and polymorphism with respect to the implementation of OLE (now called ActiveX technologies). The discussions are supported with C++, code examples.

The quote at the beginning of this chapter was from Page 4 of the 1994 edition.

Chappell, David. *Understanding ActiveX and OLE*. Redmond, Washington: Microsoft Press, 1996.

This book provides an excellent and up-to-date summary of the ActiveX technologies. The many graphics help you visualize interfaces and ActiveX components. If you ever wondered what really happens when an object is created from a class, this book will provide the answers.

Kurata, Deborah, "Too Many Tasks? Pass Them On," *Visual Basic Programmer's Journal*, Vol. 6, No 12, October 1996.

This article discusses delegation. It demonstrates delegation to a generic user interface class to provide common user interface behavior throughout an application. Although the article refers to Visual Basic 4, the techniques are similar to those needed for Visual Basic 5.

■ Think It Over

To supplement and review the information in this chapter, think about the following:

1. Think about other real-world examples of interfaces. For example, you may have a spouse interface, parent interface, and worker interface. The spouse interface has an anniversary date property, the parent interface has a pay allowance method, and the worker interface has a salary property. Depending on the situation, you are executing properties and methods from different interfaces.

2. Think about when you could use an interface in an application. Have you developed any classes or forms that seem to have the same or similar routines as other classes or forms?

3. Try creating a simple interface and implement it in a simple class. If you can't think of anything, try an IFile interface using the file processing routines defined in the previous chapter.

4. Try implementing that same interface with a second class. Can you see some ways you may be able to use polymorphism?

5. Think about benefits of code reuse through interfaces versus code reuse through inheritance. If Visual Basic supported both, when would you use interfaces and when inheritance?

- *What Is ActiveX?*

- *Building an ActiveX Code Component*

- *Calling Your ActiveX Component from Excel*

- *Building an ActiveX Control*

- *Building an ActiveX Document Server*

- *ActiveX Do's and Don'ts*

- *Summary*

- *Additional Reading*

- *Think It Over*

13

Building ActiveX Components

No fear.

—Popular T-shirt slogan

Building ActiveX EXEs. Building ActiveX DLLs. Building ActiveX controls. Building ActiveX document servers. Sounds scary, doesn't it? If you have ever done ActiveX/OLE programming (or heard about it), horrible visions of IDispatch and IUnknown may come to mind. But, no fear! With Visual Basic, building an ActiveX component is nothing to be afraid of.

This chapter describes ActiveX and the ActiveX components: ActiveX DLLs (axDLL), ActiveX EXEs (axEXE), ActiveX controls (axControl), and ActiveX documents (axDoc). It also defines the purpose of the Distributed Component Object Model (DCOM) and Remote Automation (RA). After these definitions, this chapter demonstrates how to build an axDLL and axEXE and how to use those code components in Visual Basic applications and in Microsoft Excel. Finally, this chapter presents techniques for creating a simple axControl and details the steps for creating an ActiveX document server to display Visual Basic forms in a Web browser.

■ What Is ActiveX?

Software development has become more and more complex. The users expect more features and more flexibility, the business rules are changing faster than they can be implemented, and projects are getting bigger and bigger. How can this complexity be managed? The answer can be found in *component-based development.*

Every application can be divided into its primary components and each component can be built as a separately compiled unit or reused as an existing component. This simplifies the development, enhancement, and maintenance of the application. Component-based development helps you to manage the ever-increasing complexity of software development by allowing you to focus on one component at a time.

Keynote

These components work together to provide all of the functionality required for an application through the Component Object Model (COM). COM defines how one component can access the services provided by another component. ActiveX technologies are built on COM and allow a component to provide services through one or more interfaces. These interfaces are the public properties and methods exposed by the component, as discussed in Chapter 12, "Interfaces, Polymorphism, and Inheritance."

ActiveX is the new name for the technologies that were called OLE. ActiveX has a lot of new features, like ActiveX documents, thrown in. The term "OLE" has gone back to its original meaning, simply object linking and embedding. Object linking provides for a reference to an OLE object in an OLE container. Object embedding allows a copy of an OLE object to be embedded in an OLE container. The components described in this chapter are not OLE components but rather are ActiveX components.

Tech Note. *For references to more technical information on ActiveX, COM, or OLE, see the "Additional Reading" section at the end of this chapter.*

A component that provides a service is normally called a *server* and a component that uses the services is normally called a *client*. Figure 13.1 depicts the relationship between client applications and a server. A client application requests an object from one of the server's classes. The server is started, a new instance of the class is created, and a reference to the default interface of the object is passed back to the client application. The interfaces are shown in the figure as circles. To manipulate an object, the client application calls methods and sets or retrieves properties using one of the object's interfaces.

Because any one component can both provide services and use services, the distinction between client and server is often blurred. So the term "ActiveX server" is often replaced with "ActiveX component."

Figure 13.1

The first client application has created two objects from Class A and one object from Class B. The second client has created one object from Class B and one object from Class C.

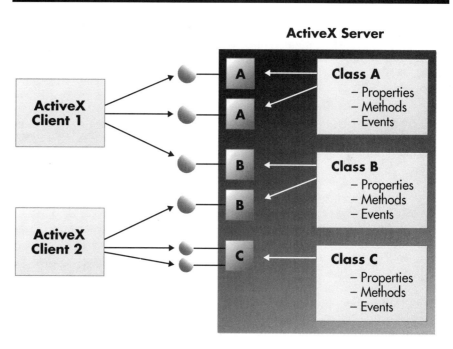

You can develop ActiveX components with many different tools, including Visual Basic. You can use these components in applications developed with Visual Basic, Java, Borland's Delphi, Microsoft Excel, Microsoft Access, Microsoft Visual C++, or Microsoft SQL Server 6.5. More and more products are adding support for ActiveX components.

Keynote

Building ActiveX components has many advantages. You can define business logic and hide the implementation details in an ActiveX component. You can share common code without providing source code by compiling the common code into an ActiveX component. You can develop your own visual components by building your own ActiveX controls. You can leverage your Visual Basic experience by building ActiveX documents for the Web. You can develop standardized components with ActiveX technologies for use in every application in the enterprise, providing truly reusable components. Using ActiveX technologies, you can reduce development and testing costs and increase system reliability.

For example, you can build a Task class and use it in a contact management system and then use the same class in a Web-based project scheduling application. You can build a class to implement complex business rules, such as calculating paychecks, and reuse it in the payroll application and in the contractor tracking application. You can package common functionality in classes—like a file processing class and Login class—reuse them in any application.

Using DCOM and Remote Automation (which will be discussed in a moment), components can then be deployed on a server computer instead of installed on every user's computer. Components can later be changed and updated on the server machine without having to be redistributed to the users.

What Is an ActiveX DLL?

An *ActiveX DLL (axDLL)* is an ActiveX component that is compiled as a dynamic link library (DLL) rather than an executable. The functionality of the DLL can be accessed only by creating objects from a class contained in the DLL.

Tech Note.   *One key difference between an ActiveX DLL and other DLLs is that an ActiveX DLL exposes COM interfaces rather than entry points. This means that you work with objects from the DLL by invoking properties and methods rather than declaring functions as you do with other DLLs.*

When you run an application, it runs in a process on your computer. An axDLL runs in the same process as the client application, as shown in Figure 13.2. That is why axDLLs are called *in-process servers* or simply "in-proc servers." As you can imagine, accessing a server running in the same process as the client application has many advantages, including high performance.

What Is an ActiveX EXE?

An *ActiveX EXE (axEXE)* is an ActiveX component that is compiled as an executable. The functionality of the axEXE can be accessed by creating objects from a class contained within the EXE. In addition, an axEXE can support stand-alone mode and be launched as a standard executable.

Figure 13.2

An ActiveX DLL runs in
the same process as the
client application.

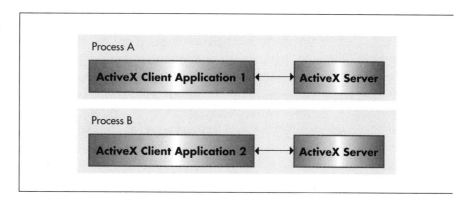

For example, Excel is an ActiveX EXE. You can use Excel as a server to
create and manipulate a spreadsheet object in a Visual Basic application. Alternatively, you can launch Excel and run it as a stand-alone application.

Unlike an axDLL, an axEXE runs in its own process, as shown in Figure
13.3. A client application must communicate with the axEXE across the process
boundaries, so an axEXE is called an *out-of-process* or *cross-process server*.

Figure 13.3

An ActiveX EXE runs in a
separate process, just
like any other executable.

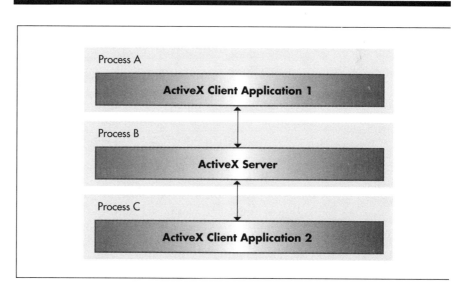

Crossing the process boundary has a performance penalty, but it has
advantages as well. If the server crashes, for example, it won't necessarily
take the client application down with it. You can also access an axEXE from

a 16-bit application. If you need to access a component using DCOM or Remote Automation, the component will need to be an axEXE.

What Is an ActiveX Control?

An *ActiveX control (axControl)* is an interactive object that can reside on any form in any application that supports OCX controls, including Web pages. Any ActiveX control can be added to the Visual Basic toolbox in the IDE and used on any form, on any ActiveX document, or in another ActiveX control. The end user can interact with the control to enter data, make a selection, or display information.

Keynote

One of the many new features of Visual Basic 5 is the ability to create ax-Controls. You can build controls by adding functionality to an existing control, by assembling existing controls into a new control, or by starting from scratch.

AxControls built with Visual Basic can have events, data binding, property pages, and licensing support. They also support asynchronous downloading and hyperlinking, making them great for use on Web pages.

What Is an ActiveX Document?

An *ActiveX document (axDoc)* is a basically a form that can be displayed in an ActiveX document container such as Microsoft Binder 1.0 or Internet Explorer 3.0. Imagine creating a screen with your tried and true Visual Basic tools and then viewing that screen from a Web server using Internet Explorer. With Visual Basic 5, this dream has become a reality.

You can use Visual Basic to create an ActiveX document server. An ActiveX document server is a component that provides an ActiveX document to an ActiveX document container. You define the ActiveX document in the ActiveX document server by adding UserDocuments to a project, much as you add forms and their controls and code. There are a few minor differences between creating forms and creating UserDocuments, as discussed later in this chapter.

What Is DCOM?

Enterprise Edition

The *Distributed Component Object Model (DCOM)* provides for communication among components distributed across a network. It allows an ActiveX component to be accessible to any computer on the network. This feature is available in the Enterprise Edition of Visual Basic.

DCOM is a key feature for implementing a three-tiered architecture as described in Chapter 7, "Implementation-Centered Design." A set of classes can be designed and built to support a specific business process and then compiled into an ActiveX component. The ActiveX component can be installed on a network, where it will be accessible to any application running on any 32-bit computer on that network, including Windows NT and Windows 95 workstations.

Using DCOM allows the ActiveX component to be maintained and controlled on one system, but be accessible from anywhere in the enterprise. This provides for greater reuse of the classes in the ActiveX component because they are available to everyone on the network. The maintenance is simplified because only one copy of the installed component needs to be tracked and upgraded.

An ActiveX component needn't be changed to use DCOM. The only requirement is that the server machine be set up properly for DCOM. The Enterprise Edition provides tools for locating and managing remote objects.

What Is Remote Automation?

**Enterprise
Edition**

Remote Automation is the mechanism for communication between components across a network with Visual Basic 4. It was replaced with DCOM, but is provided in Visual Basic 5 for compatibility and communication with 16-bit client applications.

■ Building an ActiveX Code Component

This section describes issues involved in designing and building ActiveX DLL and ActiveX EXE components, collectively called ActiveX code components. It also describes how to test and distribute the resulting ActiveX code components.

If you want to convert an existing application into an ActiveX component, you can simply change the project type to ActiveX DLL or ActiveX EXE in the Project Properties dialog box, set the class properties for each exposed class, and follow a few rules for the classes as outlined in "ActiveX Do's and Don'ts" later in this chapter.

The final Task class example from Chapter 11, "Building Classes: Additional Techniques," will be converted into an ActiveX DLL and then into an ActiveX EXE to demonstrate the techniques presented in this section. The resulting Task server will provide services for tracking a set of tasks.

What Will This Cover?

This section will cover the following key Visual Basic features:

- Building an ActiveX DLL or ActiveX EXE

- Using Friend properties and methods

- Understanding marshalling

- Implementing unattended execution and multithreading

- Using the Instancing class property

- Defining Global classes

- Using the Start Mode options
- Defining Version Compatibility
- Creating a project group
- Adding a test project to a group
- Setting a startup project for a group
- Setting references to components
- Running two copies of Visual Basic
- Preparing the component for distribution

Steps to Building an ActiveX Code Component

The steps required for building an ActiveX Code Component are

1. Don't forget the design phase.
1. Create a new ActiveX DLL or ActiveX EXE project.
2. Develop the code for the component.
3. Set the class properties for each class.
4. Set the project properties.
5. Test the component.
6. Compile the component.
7. Distribute the component.

These steps are detailed in the topics that follow.

Designing an ActiveX Code Component

You can use the GUIDS methodology to design an axEXE and axDLL just as you design any other component. There are some additional issues to consider, however, as described in the topics that follow.

Designing the Class or Set of Classes

Almost any class or set of classes can be included in an ActiveX code component. To make your components easier to use and maintain, it is best to package similar classes into one component and to define an object hierarchy for that component, as described in Chapter 5, "Goal-Centered Design," and Chapter 7, "Implementation-Centered Design." For example, all of the classes that provide employee services could be in a hierarchy in one employee component while the classes that support accounts payable (AP) could be in another AP component.

Minimizing Cross-Process Communication

An axEXE component runs in a separate process from the client applications that use it, so any communication with the component must cross the process boundary. If you plan to develop an axEXE, you need to design the component to minimize the number of times a client application needs to communicate with the component.

For example, in the first Task class example in Chapter 10, each property of the Task object was set individually; the Priority property was set, then the Description property, and then the Due property, for a total of three separate calls to the component. You can minimize this communication by providing an Add method, as was done in the Tasks class in Chapter 11, to pass all of the properties to the component in one method.

Especially if an object has a large number of properties, using a single method with multiple arguments to pass all of the property values to the component will improve the performance of the axEXE. Defining the arguments of the method as named optional parameters provides flexibility as well.

Displaying Forms from an ActiveX Component

ActiveX code components can display forms. This is especially useful if the component provides user interface features such as a splash screen or login form. These forms should be defined as part of the design process. In addition, you need to consider the effect of the component type on the display of the forms.

An axEXE can display both modal and modeless forms. An axEXE runs its own process, so forms displayed from an axEXE can exhibit unexpected behavior because the form may appear behind the client application. Modal forms that appear behind the client can give the user the impression that the application has "locked up."

An axDLL can also display both modal and modeless forms. Because an axDLL runs in the same process as the client application, modal forms displayed from an axDLL are modal to the client process and exhibit the expected modal form behavior.

Tech Note. *Visual Basic 4 ActiveX DLLs were restricted to displaying modal forms. This restriction no longer applies, but for modeless forms to function properly, the client application must support the display of modeless forms in in-process components. This is true for Visual Basic 5 and Office 97, but not for prior versions of those products. Use the NonModalAllowed property of the App object to determine whether an application supports the display of modeless forms.*

An ActiveX code component should not display forms or have any user interaction if the component is to be executed remotely or if the component will allow multiple threads of execution. See "Developing the Code for the Component" later in this section for more information on multiple threads.

Creating an ActiveX DLL or ActiveX EXE Project

Begin creating an ActiveX code component by starting a new ActiveX DLL or ActiveX EXE project. Or, you can convert an existing project to an ActiveX code component by changing the project type in the Project Properties dialog box, as shown in Figure 13.4.

Figure 13.4

To convert an existing project to an ActiveX component, change the project type.

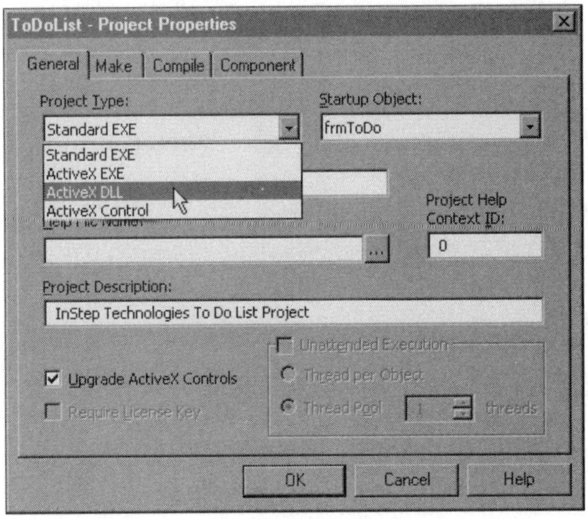

For best performance, use an ActiveX DLL. An ActiveX DLL runs in the same process as the client application, so the performance will be better than with an ActiveX EXE, which runs in its own process. If you will be using DCOM or Remote Automation to communicate with a component on a network, or need to access a component from a 16-bit application, the component will need to be an ActiveX EXE.

To work through this chapter, start an ActiveX DLL project first. After completing all of the steps for building the ActiveX DLL component, you can repeat the steps and build an ActiveX EXE, if you like. Alternatively, you can convert the final Task class example from Chapter 11 into an ActiveX DLL or ActiveX EXE. Just be sure to remove the form from the project.

Developing the Code for the Component

Previous chapters of this book have defined tools and techniques for developing code in classes. This section lists some tips for developing the code for an ActiveX code component.

To try an example Task server component, insert the Tasks, Task, and File classes from the final Chapter 11 example into the new ActiveX EXE or ActiveX DLL project. If you converted the existing Task class example project to an ActiveX EXE or ActiveX DLL, these files will already be in the converted component.

Raising Events

You can declare and raise an event from a class in the component to a client application. This allows you to notify the client application as required. For example, when you're running a long process, you can have a status notification sent to the client application at certain intervals so the client application can display a progress indicator to the user.

Alternatively, you can perform the long process in the background by having the client application call a method in the component that sets a Timer and returns. The client application can then perform other tasks. When the Timer goes off, the component can begin the background process. When the long process is complete, the component can raise an event so the client application can notify the user. This technique provides *asynchronous processing*.

Keynote

Tech Note.   *When an object raises an event, all of the client applications that have a reference to the object "WithEvents" will handle the event before the object can continue processing.*

Defining Friend Properties and Methods

Private properties and methods in a class can only be invoked from within the class in which they are defined. Public properties and methods in a class can be accessed from anywhere in an application that has an instance of the class.

Suppose you create a method in a class and need to make the method public so it can be referenced by another class in the application. To reuse the functionality of the class, you later make the class public and compile the application as an ActiveX component. The public properties and methods in the class have suddenly become even more public. If a class in a component is defined to be public, all of the public properties and methods of the class are exposed to any application that uses the component. As soon as a client application sets a reference to the component, the public properties and methods of all public classes appear in the client application's Object Browser and can be invoked.

Keynote

Wouldn't it be nice if you could somehow make a property or method public for use within an application but private so it could not be used by a client application? Visual Basic 5 introduces the *Friend* keyword for that purpose. You can use Friend instead of Public or Private to expose a property or method in a class for use within an application but hide it from every client application, providing safe internal communication in a component. Because any property or method declared using the Friend keyword is not public, it is not part of the class's public interface.

In the Task server example from Chapter 11, a File Processing class provides read and write operations to store and retrieve task information from a file. These operations call supporting methods in the Tasks and Task classes in the application, so the supporting methods must be declared to be public. When the project is changed to an ActiveX component, the Tasks and Task classes are defined to be public and suddenly all public properties and methods in those classes are exposed to any client application.

However, the Task server does not want to expose the methods used to support the File Processing class. To hide these methods, you can change the function declarations for ReadObjectData and WriteObjectData from Public to Friend. They can then be called from anywhere within the ActiveX component, but will not be exposed to any client application.

Defining a Sub Main

If the component requires some initialization processing, you can add a standard module into the project and define a Sub Main procedure. The Sub Main procedure must be in a standard module and not in a class module. The Sub Main procedure will be executed when the component is loaded, so it should include any code required to initialize the component itself, not the objects instantiated from the component. In many cases, there will be no need for a standard module or Sub Main procedure.

Tech Note. *This is a change from Visual Basic 4, which required a Sub Main procedure as an entry point into the component even if the Sub Main did not contain any code. A Sub Main is no longer required.*

When implementing an object hierarchy in a component, it is normally better to initialize the hierarchy in the Initialize event for the topmost object rather than in Sub Main. Initializing objects and other long processing chores in Sub Main can sometimes cause time-out problems. For example, a client application requests a Task object from the task server. The task server application is then executed and the Sub Main code is run. While Sub Main is running, the client application is impatiently waiting for the creation of the Task object. If the processing takes too long, the client will time out.

Optimizing Marshaling with ByVal and ByRef

An axDLL runs in the same process as its client application so calls to the properties and methods of the axDLL use the client application's stack space to pass arguments. With an axEXE, the arguments must be transferred between the client application's process and the axEXE's process. This transfer mechanism is called *marshaling*. Visual Basic automatically handles all marshaling for your ActiveX components; however, by understanding marshaling and how the use of ByVal or ByRef affect it, you can develop more efficient ActiveX components.

The following list provides tips for passing parameters to ActiveX code components:

- **Pass properties and not an object reference**. Where ever possible, pass a property or set of properties to a component instead of an object reference. Passing simple data types uses less overhead than passing object references.

- **Use ByVal parameters in axDLLs**. A parameter passed ByVal is copied and passed to the component and does not need to be passed back. This is normally the most efficient choice and should be used unless the component must change the value of the parameter.

- **Use ByRef for large strings and Variant arrays in axDLLs**. It is faster to pass a pointer to the large string or Variant array than to make a copy of the string or array and pass a pointer to the copy, as would happen with ByVal. Because the axDLL is in the same process as the client application, the axDLL can use the ByRef pointer to access the string or array elements directly.

- **Use ByVal parameters in axEXEs**. An axEXE cannot use a ByRef pointer directly because the axEXE is in a different process. Instead, a parameter declared ByRef is first copied to the component's address space and then the pointer to the local copy of the data is passed to the component. When the call is complete, the parameter is copied back to the client's address space. So a parameter passed ByRef is copied cross-process twice. When using ByVal, you save the return trip. This technique cannot be used, of course, if the component must change the value of the parameter.

Unattended Execution

An ActiveX component can be built for *unattended execution*. This means that the component will run without user interaction. When a component is marked for unattended execution, no user interface elements will be presented. Messages in message boxes are logged instead of displayed. Unattended execution is useful if the component will be running on a remote system and is required for multithreading.

You can define an ActiveX component for unattended execution by checking the Unattended Execution check box in the Project properties dialog box.

Multithreading

Keynote

In Visual Basic, an application normally has a single thread of execution. Code responds to a request and other requests are blocked and must wait until the code for the first request is complete. When building components, you can define multiple threads of execution to minimize blocking. *Multithreading* allows multiple objects to be run concurrently on separate threads within a single process.

All components in Visual Basic use apartment-model threading to provide thread safety. Each thread is like an apartment and all objects created on the thread, along with their dependent objects, live in the apartment completely unaware of objects in other apartments. Each apartment has its own copy of any global data defined in a component, so objects on different threads cannot share global data—that is, data declared as public in a standard module.

Multiple threads are only available for components that are marked for unattended execution. Any component that displays forms, controls, or ActiveX documents is restricted to a single thread of execution.

If an ActiveX EXE is marked for unattended execution, the threading choices are

- **One thread per object**. Each object is created on a new thread and each thread has a unique copy of all global variables so objects will not know about other objects on other threads.

- **Thread pool**. Each object is created on a thread from the thread pool. If there are fewer objects than threads, each object will run on a separate thread. If more objects are created, they will share a thread from the pool. By sharing a thread, the objects will share global data and can potentially block each other.

  Selecting a thread pool of one causes all objects to run on a single thread. This setting is the default and provides consistent behavior for components created in prior versions of Visual Basic.

Because an ActiveX DLL is in the same process as the client application, the in-process component can only use threads created by the client application. It cannot create any threads of its own, so the threading options are disabled when you create an ActiveX DLL.

You can set the threading options in the Project properties dialog box.

CreateObject versus As New

An ActiveX component can be comprised of several classes with one or more of those classes defined to be externally creatable. When a client application creates an instance of an externally creatable class in the ActiveX component, an object will be created from that class on a new thread, the next thread in the pool, or an existing thread based on the threading selection defined for the component. That object can in turn create other dependent objects. How those dependent objects are created depends on the class Instancing property and on the technique used to create the dependent object.

The following list identifies the choices for defining a dependent object and how the choice affects the creation of the dependent object by another object within the component.

- **Not externally creatable**. You can define a dependent object as not externally creatable by setting the object's class Instancing property to Private or PublicNotCreatable. An object must then create the dependent object using the New keyword because CreateObject can only be used with externally creatable classes. Regardless of the threading selection, the dependent object is created on the same thread as the original object.

    For example: Set m_Task = New CTask

- **Externally creatable and created with New**. You can make a dependent object externally creatable by setting the object's class Instancing property to one of the MultiUse or SingleUse settings. If an object creates the dependent object using the New keyword, the dependent object is created on the same thread as the original object, regardless of the threading selection defined for the component.

    For example: Set m_Task = New CTask

- **Externally creatable and created with CreateObject**. If an object creates the dependent object using the CreateObject function, the dependent object is created as if it were created from a client application. This implies that the dependent object will be created on a new thread, the next thread in the pool, or an existing thread depending on the threading selection defined for the component.

    For example: Set m_Task = CreateObject("Task.CTask")

Tech Note. *If a dependent object is created using the CreateObject function, all property and method calls to that dependent object will be subject to marshaling across the threads similar to cross-process marshaling described previously.*

Setting the Class Properties

There are two properties available for a class in an ActiveX code component: Name and Instancing. You set these in the Properties window for the
class, as shown in Figure 13.5.

Figure 13.5

Use the Properties
window to define the
class Name and
Instancing properties.

Name

This is the name of the class. See Chapter 9, "Strategies for Construction,"
for suggested class naming conventions. The name you define for the class
will appear in the Object Browser. The better the name describes the class,
the easier it is for other applications to use the class.

Instancing

The Instancing property defines whether you can create instances of a public
class from a client application and, if so, how those instances are created. The
setting needed for each class in the component depends on the purpose of
the class. A public class that provides objects to client applications will need
a different setting than a private class that plays a support role within the
component. The settings for this property and the effect of the setting on the
class are described next.

- **Private**. No client application can see any of the interfaces provided by the class nor can any client application create objects from the class. Objects can only be created within the component that contains the class.

  You should use this option for all support classes. This ensures that support objects are only created within the component, making the component encapsulated and more robust.

- **PublicNotCreatable**. Client applications can see the interfaces provided by the class and use them if an existing object reference is exposed. Client applications cannot create objects from the class; objects can only be created within the component that contains the class.

  You should use this option for most dependent classes in the object hierarchy. To allow a client application to navigate through every object in the object hierarchy, all of the objects in the hierarchy must be public and an existing object reference must be exposed via public properties or methods of the class above it in the hierarchy. This is like the Item method in the Tasks class, which provides an object reference to the Task object below it in the hierarchy.

  Saying this another way, to implement an object hierarchy, each object in the hierarchy has an object reference that points to the object or collection of objects at the next lower level in the hierarchy. A client application can navigate through the hierarchy by asking an object for this object reference if the reference is public. The client application can then use this object reference to access the object without needing to create its own object instance.

Keynote

Tech Note.   *When the client application requests the object reference, if you attempt to return a reference to an object from a private class you will generate an error such as "User-defined types and fixed-length strings not allowed as the type of a public member of an object module; private object modules not allowed as the type of a public member of a public object module." The relevant part of that message in this context is the last part describing private object modules. This message means that you need to change the instancing of the Private class to PublicNotCreatable.*

- **SingleUse**. Client applications can create objects from the class, but every request for an object starts another instance of the component. For example, if a client application creates three Tasks objects from the Task server, three instances of the Task server application will be launched and a single object will be provided from each instance.

  This option is recommended for the topmost class in the object hierarchy if the component will require a significant amount of processing time. Using SingleUse ensures that each requested object from a class has its own copy of the component running. Properties and methods can then be invoked for an object from the class without having to wait for any current processing for other objects from the same class.

Dependent objects created from a SingleUse class within the component can have different behavior than objects created from a client application. If you use the New keyword to create dependent objects within the component, as was done in the examples in Chapters 10 and 11, the SingleUse setting is ignored and each object is created from the same instance of the component. However, if you use the CreateObject keyword to create dependent objects within the component, the SingleUse setting is recognized and each object is created from a separate instance of the component. This setting is only available for ActiveX EXEs.

- **GlobalSingleUse**. This setting provides the same type of instancing as SingleUse but makes the class global. This means that properties and methods can be invoked on an object from the class without explicitly creating the object.

  Global classes offer convenience at the price of readability, so GlobalSingleUse is recommended only for objects that provide very global and generic functionality, such as classes that represent libraries of general-purpose functionality or for the top-level application class in a component. This option is ignored when objects are created from within the component. See Chapter 15, "Putting the Pieces Together," for more information on global objects.

- **MultiUse**. Client applications can create objects from the class and the objects will be provided by the same instance of the component. For example, if a client application creates three Tasks objects from the Task sever, only one instance of the Task server application will be launched and all three objects will be provided from that component.

  An ActiveX EXE component can supply multiple objects to multiple client applications. If the component is marked for unattended execution, each object can be created on its own thread. See "Developing the Code for the Component" earlier in this section for more information on unattended execution and multithreading.

  An instance of an ActiveX DLL component will be in the same process as each client application. The ActiveX DLL can then supply multiple objects to the client application in its process. If the component is marked for unattended execution, the ActiveX DLL is thread-safe for use by multithreaded client applications. See "Developing the Code for the Component" earlier in the section for more information on unattended execution and multithreading.

  MultiUse is the recommended setting for the top-most object in an object hierarchy when working with local components or when the server does not require a significant amount of processing time. Using MultiUse is more efficient with memory because it prevents additional copies of the component from being executed.

- **GlobalMultiUse**. This setting provides the same level of instancing as MultiUse but makes the class global. This means that properties and methods can be invoked on an object from the class without explicitly creating the object.

  As with GlobalSingleUse, global classes offer convenience at the price of readability. GlobalMultiUse is recommended only for objects that provide very global and generic functionality, such as classes that represent libraries of general-purpose functionality or for the top-level application class in a component. This option is ignored when objects are created from within the component. See Chapter 15, "Putting the Pieces Together," for more information on global objects.

For the Task server example, the Tasks class is the topmost class in the hierarchy so the Instancing property is set to MultiUse. This allows the component to provide multiple instances of the class. Objects from the Task class are dependent objects, so the Instancing property for the Task class is Public-NotCreatable. This allows the client application to reference information about a Task object in the Tasks collection class but it forces the client to create tasks only through the Tasks collection class. The File class has an Instancing property of Private. This is a support class that should not be accessed from a client application.

Alternatively, the File class could be compiled into its own generic File Processing server component. In that situation, the File class could have the Instancing property set to GlobalMultiUse to allow the properties and methods of the File class to be accessed without creating a File object.

Setting ActiveX EXE and ActiveX DLL Project General Properties

Use the Properties option from the Project menu to define the settings for the component project. Figure 13.6 shows the General tab of the Project Properties dialog box.

Project Type

For an ActiveX code component, this should be set to ActiveX DLL or ActiveX EXE.

Startup Object

Set the Startup Object to None if no startup code is required for your component. Set the Startup Object to Sub Main to start the component

Figure 13.6

Giving the project a
recognizable name and a
clear description makes it
easier for those who use
your component.

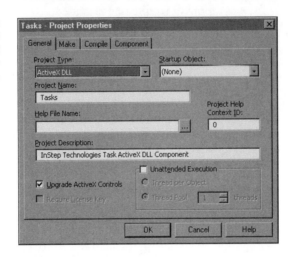

using a Sub Main procedure. See "Developing the Code for the Component" earlier in this section for more information on when to define a Sub Main procedure.

Project Name

The Project Name property defines the name used to identify your ActiveX component. It appears in the Object Browser and in the Windows Registry. Be sure the name is descriptive of the kinds of classes contained within the component. The more descriptive the project name, the less likely the name will be in conflict with another component name.

Tech Note.   *The project name will also be used as the name for the type library for your component.*

Help File Name

You can identify the file containing the help system here. Even if you don't need an end user help system in the component, you can identify a help system to be used by the Object Browser. This is recommended if your class will be used by anyone other than yourself. Even if only you will use your component, adding a help file will help you remember all of the methods and properties you defined and how to use them. See Chapter 15, "Putting the Pieces Together," for more information on help files.

Project Help Context ID

If you created a help file, here is where you should identify the context ID of the help topic containing general component information.

Project Description

The Project Description property should provide a clear description of the component. This description appears in the Object Browser and is listed in the References dialog box. Any client applications that use the component must find the component in the References dialog box by its description.

Unattended Execution

Check the option Unattended Execution if the project can be run without any user interaction. This means that the project will not display any forms or message boxes. Selecting Unattended Execution lets you optionally define multiple threads of execution.

Tech Note. *The Unattended Execution check box is disabled if there are any forms in the component. If a component marked for Unattended Execution attempts to display a message box, the message box is not displayed and the message is instead written to an event log.*

If a component is marked for unattended execution, the component can provide multithreading. An axEXE component can use one thread per object or use a thread pool. An axDLL can only use threads created by the client application. See "Developing the Code for the Component" earlier in this section for more information on unattended execution and multithreading.

Setting ActiveX EXE and ActiveX DLL Project Component Properties

In addition to setting general project options, you can set specialized component options as shown in Figure 13.7 and described next.

StartMode

Set StartMode to Standalone to test the component as a stand-alone executable. Set StartMode to ActiveX Component to test the component as an ActiveX component.

Normally, an ActiveX component terminates if no client application is holding an object reference to any objects from the component. This makes the component more difficult to test at design time because the component will not remain executing to test it. If you set the StartMode to ActiveX Component, the component will remain running at design time so it can be tested.

Figure 13.7

Be sure to set the
Version Compatibility
to prevent missing
references and provide
compatibility with existing
client applications.

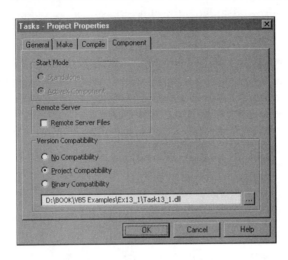

This option is only valid at design time for ActiveX EXEs. This setting is ignored when the component is compiled. The setting is disabled for ActiveX DLLs, as shown in Figure 13.7.

Remote Server

**Enterprise
Edition**

When Remote Server is checked and the component is compiled, a remote registration file (.vbr) is created. This file contains the information the Windows Registry needs to run the component on a remote computer. This option is disabled unless you are using the Enterprise Edition of Visual Basic.

Version Compatibility

Keynote

Version Compatibility is a key feature of components you create with Visual Basic. Suppose you create a component that is used by other programmers throughout your company. You want to modify that component to provide new functionality for one user. The other programmers would be very unhappy if your revision required a recompile of every application that used the component. Instead, you want to make the revised component compatible with the original. Only applications that want to use the new functionality would need to be changed and recompiled. No other client application would be affected.

The compatibility option to select depends on where your component is in its circle of life. When you first create the component, select No Compatibility. This allows you to continue to change and test the component without regard for compatibility with prior versions of the component.

When you first compile the component for use with test client applications, change the Version Compatibility to Project Compatibility. Define the full path to the compiled component in the Version Compatibility text box. This allows you to change the component but keep the reference information the same. This means that you can continue to use the component with a test client application without continuously losing the reference.

Tech Note.   *The Project Compatibility option will generate a new type library each time you compile, so any changes can be made to the component. The type library identifier used when setting the reference is retained so you don't have to update the references in the test client applications each time a change is made to the component. However, depending on the changes made to the component interfaces, the test client application may be incompatible with the component.*

Keynote

Once the component has been published and made public for use by client applications, use the Binary Compatibility option. Define the full path to the published component in the Version Compatibility text box. When you later change the component, the Binary Compatibility option ensures that the revised component is compatible with the component defined in the Version Compatibility text box and all client applications that use the original component will work appropriately with the revised component. If this option is checked, you are notified if you attempt to compile a change to the component that makes it incompatible with the defined component. You can add classes, properties, methods, and events to classes; add interfaces; and change implementation details. Modifying an existing interface causes the component to be incompatible.

Tech Note.   *The Binary Compatibility option will create new class IDs and interface IDs for any new classes and interfaces but will retain the IDs for any existing classes and interfaces.*

If you need to make a change that causes an incompatible component, you should change the project name and file name or at least create a new class name so both the older version and the newest version can be registered and referenced separately. If possible, create a new interface to the class instead of modifying an existing interface in order to maintain compatibility.

Testing the Component

An ActiveX code component provides services to client applications. To test a component, you can create objects and request services from the component using the Immediate window. But this works with the component as if the objects were created from code within the component. To fully test a component, you need to develop a test client application.

When a client application requests an object from a class in an ActiveX code component, the path to the component is found using the Windows Registry, the component is launched, and an object is created. The ActiveX component remains in memory and continues to provide services until all references to objects created from the component classes are released. After the last object reference is released, the ActiveX component terminates.

For the preceding process to work correctly, the ActiveX component must be registered in the Windows Registry and the client application must know how to find it. An ActiveX component is automatically registered when it is compiled. You could recompile the ActiveX component after you completed each change and then run the test application. But using the compiled component prevents you from debugging the component easily, because you cannot step through the component code, set break points, or view internal variable values.

Luckily, Visual Basic provides some features to aid in testing and debugging:

Keynote

- **Immediate window**. The Immediate window can test a component without a client application.

- **Project groups**. To help you debug axDLL components, you can define a project group. A *project group* is a set of two or more projects that can be loaded into the IDE together. To test an axDLL, include the axDLL component to be tested and a test client project in a project group.

- **ActiveX Component Start Mode**. When testing an axEXE component, you can set the Start Mode option for the component to ActiveX Component. This setting allows you to run the project in design mode and set a reference to the running project file from a test client project running in another instance of Visual Basic.

- **Standalone Start Mode**. If an axEXE supports stand-alone mode, you can test that mode by setting the Start Mode option for the component to Standalone. It will then execute as a stand-alone component.

Each of these techniques is detailed in the following paragraphs.

Testing Using the Immediate Window

The Immediate window is a good place for the first test of your axEXE or axDLL. Open the project containing the ActiveX component and use the

View menu to display the Immediate window. Then type statements into the Immediate window to create an object from each class in the component and invoke the properties and methods of each class. Figure 13.8 shows the Immediate window used to test the Task server.

Figure 13.8

Using the Immediate window for testing gives you immediate feedback on correct execution of the code in your classes.

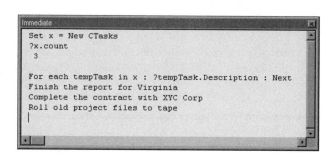

```
Immediate

  Set x = New CTasks
  ?x.count
   3

  For each tempTask in x : ?tempTask.Description : Next
  Finish the report for Virginia
  Complete the contract with XYC Corp
  Roll old project files to tape
```

Tech Note.   *It is interesting to see that creating objects in the Immediate window will not cause the project to go into Run mode. However, break points and other debugging mechanisms are available when testing using the Immediate window.*

Objects in the Immediate window are created as if they were created from the component. This helps you test the execution of the class's properties and methods. However, it does not test how a client application will work with the component. For that test, you need to create a test client application.

Testing with a Client Project in the Project Group

Because axDLLs are run in the same process as a client application, you can test an axDLL using a test client project added to the axDLL project to form a project group. To add a project to a project group and use it to test an axDLL, follow these steps:

1. Use the Add Project option from the File menu to add a client project to the project group.

    You can add an existing project or add a new project. Adding another project to the IDE creates a project group. You can then save the project group so you can reuse the group for debugging the axDLL.

Keynote

Keynote

2. Select the client project in the Project window and set project properties.

   Be sure to select the client project in the Project window first. This sets the context of the Project menu to the client project. Then use the Properties option from the Project menu to define a name, description, and other desired project properties for the test client project.

3. Use the References option from the Project menu for the client project to set the reference to the axDLL.

   The References dialog box will appear, as shown in Figure 13.9. Locate the axDLL project in the References dialog box and check it. The axDLL project will then appear in the Object Browser for the test client application.

Figure 13.9

Set the reference to the ActiveX component in the client project. Notice the path of the component displayed at the bottom of this dialog box.

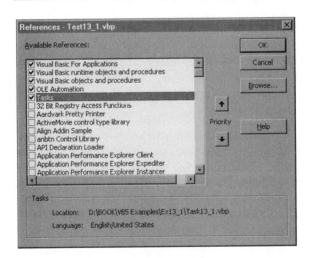

4. Develop the code for the test client application.

   The test client application should create objects from all classes that have the Instancing property set to allow the creation of class instances. For each created object, invoke each public property and method. Then invoke each public property and method of its dependent objects. Use the Object Browser to see the list of objects, properties, and methods provided by the component.

Tech Note. *If you have the ActiveX DLL component project selected in the Project window when you display the Object Browser, the Object Browser will display the public and private members of the component. If you have the test client project selected in the Project window when you display the Object Browser, the Object Browser will only display the public members of the component accessible to the test client application.*

5. Set the test client project as the start up project.

   Right-click on the test client project in the Project window. Then select the Set as Start Up option from the context menu. The project set as the Start Up project will be the project executed when you use the Run menu options. The Start Up project name will then appear boldfaced in the Project window.

6. Run the test client.

   Use the Run menu options to run the test client. Debug and edit the client or axDLL component as necessary.

For the Task server, add a new standard EXE project for use as a test client project. Remove the default Form1 and use the Add Form option from the Project menu to add the To Do List form from the example in Chapter 11, "Building Classes: Additional Techniques" and shown in Figure 11.1. This form will display a set of tasks and allow users to add new tasks and delete tasks. This provides a full-featured test of the Task server component.

Testing with a Client Project using ActiveX Component Start Mode

Because an axEXE component runs in a separate process from the client application, you cannot test an axEXE using a test client project within a project group. Rather, you can run the axEXE in one copy of Visual Basic and a test client project in a second copy of Visual Basic.

To create a test client project and use it to test an axEXE, follow these steps:

1. Compile the axEXE.

   This ensures that the project does not have any compile-time errors and provides a type library and registry entry for the component that can be used to set Version Compatibility.

2. Set project properties for the axEXE.

   Use the Properties option from the Project menu to set the Start Mode. Setting the Start Mode to ActiveX Component keeps the axEXE running so you can test it.

   Set the Version Compatibility to Project Compatibility and select the compiled axEXE in the associated text box. This ensures that the reference to this axEXE will remain valid even if the interface in the axEXE is changed. This simplifies testing of the component.

Keynote

3. Run the axEXE.

   Use the Run menu options to run the axEXE project.

4. Create a new project in a second instance of Visual Basic.

   This will be the test client project.

5. Set project properties for the test client project.

   Use the Properties option from the Project menu to give the test client project a name, description, and other desired properties.

6. Use the References option from the Project menu to set the reference to the axEXE project.

   Check the axEXE component in the References dialog box. Look at the Location displayed for the component at the bottom of the References dialog box and make sure the Reference is set to the axEXE project file (.vbp). The axEXE component will then appear in the Object Browser for the test client application.

Tech Note. *If the axEXE project does not appear in the References dialog box, ensure that it is running as described in Step 3.*

7. Develop the code for the test client application.

   The test client application should create objects from all classes that have the Instancing property set to allow the creation of class instances. For each created object, invoke each public property and method. Then invoke each public property and method of its dependent objects. Use the Object Browser to see the list of objects, properties, and methods provided by the component.

8. Run the test client.

   Use the Run menu options to run the test client. Debug and edit the client application or axEXE component as necessary.

Tech Note. *If you change the axEXE project and rerun the test client, you may receive the error "Connection to type library or object library for remote process has been lost. Press OK for dialog to remove reference." You then need to remove the reference to the axEXE project and reset the reference to the project. To prevent this error, make sure that the Version Compatibility option is set appropriately, as described in Steps 1 and 2.*

For the Task server, create a new standard EXE project in another instance of Visual Basic for use as a test client project. Remove the default Form1 and use the Add Form option from the Project menu to add the To Do List form from the example in Chapter 11 and shown in Figure 11.1. This form displays a set of tasks and allows you to add new tasks or delete tasks. This provides a full-featured test of the Task server component.

Let's look at the code in our test client project and follow what is actually happening. The standard header provides a general description of the client application. A private instance of the collection class is then declared. Since this declaration statement does not contain the New key word, this defines the object variable but does not initialize it.

```
' Form Name:     frmToDo
' Author:        Deborah Kurata, InStep Technologies
' Date:          1/8/97
' Description:   Displays a set of tasks in a to-do list.
' Revisions:
'
Option Explicit

' Define the instance of the collection class
Private m_Tasks As CTasks
```

When the To Do List form loads, it first creates a new object from the Tasks collection class using the Set statement. Visual Basic executes the ActiveX component containing the Tasks class, instantiates an object from the Tasks class in that component, and generates an Initialize event. Code in the Initialize event procedure in the Tasks class opens the file containing the list of tasks, creates an object for each task in the file, and adds the tasks to a private collection. After the Initialize event procedure is executed, the reference to the object created from the Tasks class is stored in the m_Tasks private object variable.

```
Private Sub Form_Load()
Dim tempTask As CTask

    ' Create the instance of the collection class
    Set m_Tasks = New CTasks

    ' Fill the list box with the items from the collection
    ' Shows the For Each...Next syntax!
    For Each tempTask In m_Tasks
        lstTasks.AddItem Format$(tempTask.Priority, "000") _
            & Space(2) & tempTask.Description _
            & Space(2) & "Due: " & tempTask.Due
    Next
End Sub
```

The To Do List form displays a list of the tasks in the collection of tasks, so the form's Load event contains code to fill the list box with the tasks. The For Each...Next syntax uses the NewEnum method of the collection class to enumerate through the collection and display each task in the list box.

When a task is entered into the text boxes at the top of the form and the Add button is clicked, the text box contents is retrieved and passed to the Add method of the collection class. The new task is also added to the list box shown on the form. The text boxes are then cleared for entry of another task.

```
Private Sub cmdAdd_Click()
On Error GoTo ERR_ROUTINE
```

```
            ' Add the task to the collection
            m_Tasks.Add Val(txtPriority.Text), txtDescription.Text, txtDue.Text

            ' Add the task to the list box
            lstTasks.AddItem Format$(txtPriority.Text, "000") _
                & Space(2) & txtDescription.Text _
                & Space(2) & "Due: " & txtDue.Text

            ' Clear the fields on the form for entry of another task
            txtPriority.Text = ""
            txtDescription.Text = ""
            txtDue.Text = ""
            txtPriority.SetFocus
    Exit Sub

ERR_ROUTINE:
        Select Case Err.Number
            Case taskPriorityValueError
                MsgBox "Please enter a valid priority value. " _
                    & "Valid values range from: " _
                    & taskUrgent & " to " & taskLow
                txtPriority.SetFocus
            Case taskInvalidTimeError
                MsgBox "Please enter a time defining when the task is due."
                txtDue.SetFocus
            Case Else
                ' If it was some other error, display it
                MsgBox "Error in application: " _
                    & Err.Description    End Select
    End Sub
```

Error handling in the preceding routine traps for invalid entry errors returned from the Task object. Notice how the error enumerators were used to evaluate the error number. A message box is then displayed to the user to provide notification of the error.

When the To Do List form unloads, the m_Task object variable is set to Nothing to release it from the object. If this were the only object variable referencing the Tasks object, the Tasks object would be terminated. If this were the last instance of any class in the ActiveX component, the component would be shut down and removed from memory. The test client application then releases the form object variable and ends.

```
Private Sub Form_Unload(Cancel As Integer)
    ' Clear all of our object references
    Set m_Tasks = Nothing
    Set frmToDo = Nothing
    End
End Sub
```

Running an ActiveX EXE Standalone

You may design your axEXE component to provide objects to other applications and to run stand-alone. The end user could double-click on the component icon to launch the application or use a client application to request objects from the component. For example, you can use Microsoft Excel by double-clicking on its icon or you can use Visual Basic to request spreadsheet objects from Excel.

To allow your axEXE component to go both ways, you need to add a Sub Main procedure to the axEXE component:

```
Sub Main()
    ' Any required server initialization
    ' code could go here

    ' If the application is launched stand-alone,
    ' display the form.
    If App.StartMode = vbSModeStandalone Then
        frmToDo.Show
    End If
End Sub
```

The StartMode method of the App object and the vbSModeStandalone or vbSModeAutomation constants can be used to check the StartUp mode of the application and proceed accordingly. The Sub Main code will display the To Do List form if this application is run in stand-alone mode but not if it is run as an ActiveX component. You can test the application in both modes simply by adjusting the Start Mode property using the Properties option from the Project menu.

To try running in both modes, add the frmToDo form into the axEXE component you created in the prior example. Add the preceding Sub Main procedure. Then set your Start Mode to the desired mode and run the component.

Compiling the Component

After the component has been fully tested, you should compile it and test it one more time. Before you do this, remove any of the extra message boxes you used to test the application (or use conditioned compilation).

To compile the component, choose Make from the File menu. Visual Basic compiles the component. It also creates a Windows Registry entry and a type library for the component. The type library provides a description of the interfaces the component exposes.

Tech Note. *Each time you generate an executable for your component, Visual Basic creates a set of Globally Unique IDs (GUIDs, pronounced GOO-ids) for the classes and interfaces in the component. If you use the Version Compatibility option, the original GUIDs will be used when you recompile the component, protecting your capability with client applications that use the component. If Version Compatibility is not set, new GUIDs are generated and client applications will generate an error when attempting to use the component.*

To test a compiled axEXE, you can use the same test client application developed to test the axEXE in development mode. You will, however, need to reset the reference from the component project to the compiled component.

Testing a compiled axDLL is somewhat easier. Simply remove the axDLL from the project group, leaving only the test client application. This will display a warning message to let you know that you are removing something the test client application references. After you remove the component project from the project group, Visual Basic will find the associated DLL in the Windows Registry and automatically update the reference. You can then run the test client application and it will correctly reference the compiled DLL.

Distributing the Component

Once you have created the executable, you can distribute it to other programmers or users. Other programmers can then build client applications that use the component. The users can access the component through whatever user interface you provide.

When preparing the files for distribution and then installing the application, you should consider several issues.

Providing Help with Your Component

To help other programmers use the classes in the component, you may want to create a help file for it. The help file would then be available to other programmers through the Object Browser.

Registering Your Component on the Destination Computer

When distributing the component, you need to register it on the destination computer. The easiest way to ensure that the component and all required Visual Basic files are installed and registered on the destination computer is to create an installation program using the Setup Wizard provided with Visual Basic.

Keynote

Even if you don't want to use the Setup Wizard to create an installation program, you can use Setup Wizard to create a dependency file (.dep). This dependency file lists the files required by the component, including version and registry information.

What Did This Cover?

This section detailed the steps required to design, build, test, compile and distribute an ActiveX DLL and ActiveX EXE component. After discussing how to develop the code for the component, this section described how to set the class properties to define instancing and multithreading. It also illustrated how to set the project start mode and define the all-important version compatibility options. It demonstrated techniques for testing the component using a project group for axDLLs and a separate running copy of Visual Basic for axEXEs. Finally, this section provided information on compiling and distributing the ActiveX component.

If you worked through the steps in this chapter, you converted the Tasks class example from Chapter 11 into an ActiveX DLL and/or ActiveX EXE component. You can now call this component from any client application, including Excel.

■ Calling Your ActiveX Component from Excel

Any ActiveX code component you create can be accessed from any client application that understands how to communicate with ActiveX components. For example, you can call your component from Microsoft Excel or Microsoft Access. Imagine developing a standard set of business rules, such as tax calculations or price markups, and having these rules available to end users through Excel. With ActiveX components you can do it!

This section describes how to use an ActiveX component from Excel. For more information on using ActiveX components with Microsoft Office, see *Object Programming with Visual Basic 4,* which is referenced in the "Additional Reading" section at the end of this chapter.

If you don't own Microsoft Excel but have another application that can be used as an ActiveX client application, you can try using your component with that application. If you have no other applications that support ActiveX clients, you will not be able to work through this section, but you are encouraged to read through the example anyway.

Tech Note. *This example was developed and tested using Microsoft Office 95. It was not tested with the recently released Microsoft Office 97.*

Steps to Calling an ActiveX Component from Excel

The steps required for calling an ActiveX component from Microsoft Excel are

1. Insert a new module into Excel by choosing Macro from the Insert menu and then choosing Module.

2. Define a reference to the component using the References option in the Tools menu.

   Use the Browse button to select your component if it does not appear on the list.

3. Display the Object Browser from the View menu to review the class names and objects available in the component.

4. Develop Excel VBA code to create an object from the class and invoke properties and methods for the object.

```
Option Explicit
Sub Main()
    Dim i As Integer
    Dim m_Tasks As CTasks
    Dim m_Task As Object
```

```
' Create an object from your class
Set m_Tasks = CreateObject("Tasks.CTasks")

' Add the column headers
Cells(1, 1).FormulaR1C1 = "Priority"
Cells(1, 2).FormulaR1C1 = "Description"
Cells(1, 3).FormulaR1C1 = "Due"

' Put each task in a new row
i = 1
For Each m_Task In m_Tasks
    i = i + 1
    Cells(i, 1).FormulaR1C1 = m_Task.Priority
    Cells(i, 2).FormulaR1C1 = m_Task.Description
    Cells(i, 3).FormulaR1C1 = m_Task.Due
  Next
End Sub
```

The CreateObject syntax requires the name of the project (Tasks) and name of the class (CTasks) and creates an object from the defined class. The preceding code adds column headers to the active spreadsheet. It then enumerates through the collection and for each task it selects a cell in the first column and displays the priority of the task. It displays the description in the second column and the time due in the third column.

5. Click on a spreadsheet tab and then run the macro by choosing Macro from the Tools menu.

   If you have created and saved any tasks in the earlier examples, each task will appear in a column of the spreadsheet. If you don't see the list of tasks you created, make sure the current directory in Excel is set to the directory containing your task list file.

■ Building an ActiveX Control

An ActiveX control is an interactive object that can reside in any application that supports OCX controls, including Visual Basic 4, Visual Basic 5, and Web pages. Any ActiveX control can be added to the toolbox in the Visual Basic IDE and used on any form. The grid and spinner controls that come with Visual Basic are examples of ActiveX controls.

One of the most exciting features of Visual Basic 5 is its ability to create ActiveX controls. So Visual Basic takes yet another capability that had only been available to C++ developers, and provides it to Visual Basic developers.

Keynote

Even with Visual Basic, creating a full-featured ActiveX control is not easy. There are many details to handle. Visual Basic provides Wizards to help you through this process, but even working through the steps in the Wizards is not trivial.

This section provides an overview of the process of building ActiveX controls. For a complete discussion of the details of creating a full-featured ActiveX control, please refer to the Visual Basic documentation or other books specifically dedicated to the creation of ActiveX controls, as listed in the "Additional Reading" section at the end of this chapter.

What Will This Cover?

This section will cover the following key Visual Basic features:

- Creating a control from existing controls
- Creating an enhanced control
- Creating a user-drawn control
- Using PropertyBags
- Using the ActiveX Control Interface Wizard
- Testing an ActiveX control using a project group

Steps to Building an ActiveX Control

The steps required for building an ActiveX control are

1. Don't forget the design phase.
1. Create an ActiveX control project.
2. Create the user interface of the control.
3. Develop the code for the control.
4. Set the UserControl properties.
5. Set the project properties.
6. Test the control.
7. Compile the control.
8. Distribute the control.

These steps are detailed in the following topics.

Designing an ActiveX Control

You can use the GUIDS methodology to design an ActiveX control. In the case of a control, however, you need to consider three different types of subject matter experts to complete the design.

- **End user**. This is the person who will be using the application containing the ActiveX control. The end user's perspective provides information on how the control should behave when used on a form. For example, how will the control respond when the end user clicks on the control on a form?

- **Developer**. This is the person who will add the ActiveX component to a project and then use the control in one or more forms. This person will be concerned with the available properties, methods, and events provided by the control. The visual view of the control to the end user will also be a concern of the developer who is supporting that user.

- **Implementor**. This is the person who will be building the ActiveX component. This person will be interested in the complexity of the control and the combination of the end user's desired behavior and the developer's requested functionality.

Keynote

You need to consider the control from all three perspectives to make sure it is designed appropriately. Ignoring any aspect can result in a control that does not provide all the necessary functionality. For example, you can create a control that looks nice for an end user, but if the control doesn't support basic events that a developer would require the developer won't use it.

The design process will define the purpose, user interface, and expected behavior of the control. It will also list the properties, methods, and events that the control must provide to the developer. Be sure to use appropriate names for these properties, methods, and events to follow Visual Basic standards. For example, define a property named Foreground instead of Pen-Color to define text color.

Creating an ActiveX Control Project

Begin building an axControl by creating a new ActiveX control project. You can create any number of axControls in this project. To make the axControl file easier to use, you should group related controls in one project. For example, you could have an Address project that contained a control for the street address block, a control to display a city and state based on a zip code, and a control for country codes. All three controls could reside in one axControl file (.ocx). This will be like some third-party controls you may have seen that distribute several controls in one custom control component. When you reference the one custom control component from the vendor, several controls are added to your toolbox.

When you create an ActiveX control project, a default UserControl is displayed. A UserControl is similar to a form; it has a window for the user interface of the control and code for processing control events. If you will define more than one control within the project, use the Add User Control option from the Project menu to add one UserControl for each defined control in a project.

Creating the User Interface of the Control

After you have created an ActiveX control project, the next step in developing an ActiveX control is to create the user interface, as defined during the design phase. There are three basic ways to build the user interface of a control:

- **Combine existing controls.** You can build a control by combining several other controls into a new control. The controls that make up the control are called *constituent controls*. For example, you can build a spinner control using a text box and scroll bar.

- **Enhance an existing control.** You can build an enhanced control by adding properties, methods, and events to an existing control. For example, you could build your own text box control that provides all of the features of a standard text box but only allows the entry of numeric values.

- **Build the control from scratch.** Controls that you create from scratch are called user-drawn controls. You build a control from scratch if it requires a unique interface or has other unique requirements. For example, a combo box with New and Edit buttons at the bottom of the dropped down list will need to be user drawn.

You build the user interface of a control in the UserControl window. You can add or draw controls as required for your new control. You can add any controls to a UserControl except the OLE container control. That control is disabled in the toolbox when a UserControl window is active.

As a very simple example, the priority, description, and due fields on the Task form will be combined into an ActiveX Task control as shown in Figure 13.10. Notice that the upper-left corner of the Task control appears in the upper-left corner of the window. This ensures that extra space does not appear around the control when it is added to a form.

Figure 13.10

The Task control combines three text boxes for the priority, description, and time due.

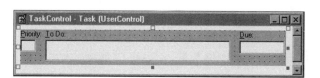

Developing the Code for the Control

A developer using your control will expect that it provides a basic set of functionality. For example, developers will expect to add the control to a form and have it resize as they resize the UserControl window. They will also expect to set properties—such as such as a Name, Index, and Tab Indcx—for the control on a form at design time, and have the values of these properties saved within the form file (.frm).

You can add code to events of the UserControl to provide this desired functionality. For example, you could add code to the Resize event of the UserControl to resize the constituent controls. You can add code to the ReadProperties and WriteProperties events of the UserControl to read and write the control properties to the PropertyBag object and ultimately to the form file.

An end user using your control will expect certain behaviors from it as well. If the control has a button, the end user will expect to be able to click on it. If the control has a text box, the user will expect to be able to enter text box into it.

Keynote

When you consider the large numbers of properties, methods, and events supported by most controls, adding your own code to provide all of this functionality may seem overwhelming. To walk you through this process, Visual Basic provides an ActiveX Control Interface Wizard as an add-in to help you map properties, methods, and events. Simply select the add-in from the Add-In Manager. The Wizard will then appear as an option in the Add-Ins menu.

The ActiveX Control Interface Wizard expects that you have created an ActiveX control project and created the user interface of the control. You can then use the Wizard to help you create all of the code for the control.

Try out the Wizard using the Task control. Define the properties, methods, and events you feel are appropriate for the control.

Setting the UserControl Properties

There are many properties listed in the Properties window for a UserControl. These properties identify visual aspects of the control and general control parameters. One of the most important properties is the Name. The Name property is used to identify the control each time it is used by a developer. It is also the name that appears in the ToolTip for the control in the toolbox.

Setting ActiveX Control Project Properties

Use the Properties option from the Project menu to define the settings for the axControl project. Be sure to provide a clear description and set the Version Compatibility appropriately. See "Setting ActiveX EXE and ActiveX DLL Project General Properties" and "Setting ActiveX EXE and ActiveX DLL Project Component Properties" earlier in this chapter for more information on project properties.

Testing the Control

Keynote

You cannot simply run an ActiveX control project to test it because to test an axControl you must add the control to the Visual Basic toolbox and then place it on a form. You can test the axControl within the axControl project by adding a second project to create a project group and adding the axControl to a form in that second project. This tests how the control will perform for developers. You can then run the second project to test how the control will perform for the end user.

To add a project to a project group and use it to test an ActiveX control, follow these steps:

1. Choose Add Project from the File menu to add a test project to the project group.

   You can add an existing project or a new project. Adding another project to the IDE creates a project group that you can save. You can then open the project group instead of a single project to open both projects in the IDE.

2. Select the test project in the Project window and set project properties.

   Be sure to select the test project in the Project window first. This sets the context of the Project menu to the test project. Then use the Properties option from the Project menu to give the test project a name, description, and other desired properties.

3. Close the ActiveX control project.

Keynote

   Closing the ActiveX control project activates the axControl. You can then see the control in the toolbox and add the control to a form in the test project.

Tech Note. *If you open the axControl project when viewing the test project form that contains the axControl, hash marks will appear through the axControl, which will be inactivated in the test project form. Closing the axControl project will remove the hash marks and activate the axControl.*

4. Add the control to a form in the test project.

   This demonstrates how the control will perform for a developer. For a complete test, be sure to try setting a wide range of design-time properties. Edit and debug the control as needed.

5. Set the test project as the startup project.

   Normally, this happens automatically when a project is added to a project group that contains only a UserControl project. If the test project is not the startup project, right-click on the test project in the Project window and select the Set as Start Up option from the context menu. The project set as the Start Up project will be executed when you use the Run menu options. The Start Up project name will then appear boldfaced in the Project window.

6. Run the test project.

   Use the Run menu options to run the test project. This demonstrates how the control will perform for an end user. Edit and debug the control as needed.

7. Close and reopen the project.

   This tests the saving of the design-time properties. Each property set for the control should be set to the value you defined when testing the control as a developer.

For the Task control, add a test project. Then add the Task control to a form in the test project and try it out.

Compiling the Control

Keynote

If the control will be private to a particular application, you can leave it in the project without compiling it separately. If the control is to be provided to other developers, you need to compile and distribute it.

To compile the control, select the control project in the Project window and choose Make from the File menu. A control file with an .ocx extension will be created. If the control is going to be used on a Web page, you may want to check that the Compile option in the Project Properties dialog box is set to Optimize for Small Code.

Distributing the Control

Once you have compiled the axControl project, you can distribute the axControl to other programmers. Other programmers can then add the control to any form in any application.

When preparing the files for distribution and then installing the control, you should consider several issues, as described in the following topics.

Providing Help with Your Control

To help other programmers use the control, you may want to create a help file for it. Other programmers could then gain access to the help file through the Object Browser.

Registering Your Control on the Destination Computer

When distributing the control, you need to register it on the destination computer. The easiest way to make sure that the control and all required Visual Basic files are installed and registered on the destination computer is to create an installation program using the Setup Wizard provided with Visual Basic.

Keynote

Even if you don't want to use the Setup Wizard to create an installation program, you can use it to create a dependency file (.dep). This dependency file lists the files required by the control, including version and registry information.

Adding the Control to the Toolbox

To add the new control to the toolbox, choose Components from the Project menu. The new control should appear in the list. Once the control is selected in the list, it will appear in the toolbox and in the Object Browser.

Tech Note. *ActiveX controls that you build with Visual Basic 5 also work in Visual Basic 4. However, they will not appear in the Visual Basic 4 Object Browser.*

What Did This Cover?

This section provided a brief overview of control creation. It described the steps for creating a control and some tips for designing, building, testing, compiling, and distributing the control. Please see the "Additional Reading" section at the end of this chapter for references to more information on control creation.

■ Building an ActiveX Document Server

With the current excitement over Web technologies, it is no wonder that Visual Basic has facilities to make it easier to create Web content. You can now use Visual Basic to create an ActiveX document server. An ActiveX document server is a component that can provide ActiveX documents to an ActiveX document container, such as Internet Explorer. ActiveX document server? ActiveX document? ActiveX document container? What does all that mean and how does it relate to Web content?

Keynote

An *ActiveX document (axDoc)* is a specific display of information. It is not necessarily a document at all. An ActiveX document can be a spreadsheet, graph, chart, schedule, or any display of data. An employee data entry screen can be a document in this context, as can an order form. You can create an axDoc by adding a UserDocument to a project. A UserDocument looks just like a form, but instead of appearing as part of an application it appears within another application, called an *ActiveX document container*. Examples of ActiveX document containers are Internet Explorer 3.0 and Office Binder 1.0.

You can only add a UserDocument to an ActiveX EXE or ActiveX DLL type of project. The axEXE or axDLL is the *ActiveX document server* and will provide the axDoc object to an application that requests it, much as other ActiveX servers can provide other types of objects to an application. To be an ActiveX document server, the axEXE or axDLL simply needs to include one or more UserDocuments.

Keynote

To summarize, an ActiveX document is similar to a form. You create it in a project by adding a UserDocument to the project. An ActiveX document server is the ActiveX EXE or ActiveX DLL project containing the UserDocument. The ActiveX document server provides the ActiveX document object to another application. An ActiveX document container can request the ActiveX document object and display it.

Let's clarify this concept with an example. Microsoft Excel is an ActiveX document server. It can provide documents, spreadsheets for example, to an ActiveX document container. Try this: Launch your Web browser and open an Excel spreadsheet. Your Excel spreadsheet will appear in the browser! You can see in Figure 13.11 that Excel's menus are joined, or *negotiated*, with the menu in Internet Explorer.

Figure 13.11

Internet Explorer is an ActiveX document container. It can display any ActiveX document, including an Excel spreadsheet.

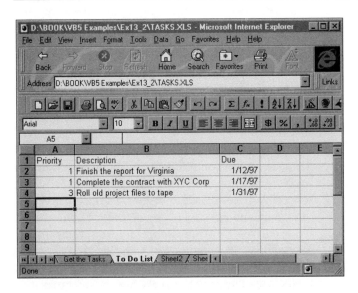

Tech Note. *If you don't have a Web browser that supports ActiveX documents, you can download Internet Explorer from Microsoft's Web site (http://www.microsoft.com/ie/default.asp) to try this.*

If you look at a process list when displaying the Excel spreadsheet in Internet Explorer, you will see that Excel is running. Excel is the ActiveX document server that is providing the ActiveX document, which is the spreadsheet, to the ActiveX document container, in this case Internet Explorer.

Keynote

For something even more fun, try opening the Excel spreadsheet you created in the section "Calling Your ActiveX Component from Excel" from within your Web browser. Use the Excel menu to run the macro and the resulting spreadsheet should appear something like Figure 13.11. The Web browser is displaying an Excel spreadsheet that contains a macro that is calling an ActiveX component that you created in Visual Basic. Imagine the possibilities!

For example, executives can browse corporate information using a Web browser to bring up and perform "what if" analyses using an Excel spreadsheet. The Excel spreadsheet communicates with an ActiveX component that collects the data from a multitude of remote systems. So the executives are using familiar tools, but the power behind those tools has significantly increased.

This section outlines the steps for building an ActiveX document server and displaying an ActiveX document within an ActiveX document container such as Internet Explorer. To demonstrate these techniques, the To Do List form from the ActiveX EXE test client project, detailed under "Building an ActiveX Code Component" earlier in the chapter, will be converted into an ActiveX document and displayed in Internet Explorer.

What Will This Cover?

This section will cover the following key Visual Basic features:

- Creating an ActiveX document server

- Creating an ActiveX document

- Creating a hyperlink in an ActiveX document

- Testing an ActiveX document

- Creating a cabinet file (.cab)

- Building an HTML page to display an ActiveX document

Steps to Building an ActiveX Document Server

The steps required for building an ActiveX document server are

1. Don't forget the design phase.

2. Create an ActiveX Document server project.

3. Build the UserDocuments.

4. Develop the code for the server.

5. Set the UserDocument properties.

6. Set the project properties.

7. Test the ActiveX document.

8. Compile the ActiveX document server.

9. Distribute the ActiveX document and server.

These steps are detailed in the topics that follow.

Designing an ActiveX Document Server

You can use the GUIDS methodology to design an axDoc server just as you design any other component. There are some additional considerations, however, when working with axDoc servers.

- **ActiveX document container**. Some axDoc containers have different behaviors and object models than others. The code you need to move between UserDocuments in Internet Explorer, for example, is different than the code needed for Office Binder. Some containers also provide different support or no support for modeless windows.

Tech Note. *You could support multiple types of browsers with one set of source code using conditional compilation. See Chapter 11, "Building Classes: Additional Techniques," for more information on conditional compilation.*

- **Viewport**. An axDoc will appear within the viewport provided by the AxDoc container. This can be a problem if buttons at the right side of the document provide required functionality and those buttons are not easily seen because of the size of the viewport.

- **Menus**. The menu of your axDoc will be merged with the menu from the axDoc container. You need to consider this when defining your menus.

- **About Box**. Microsoft recommends that you add an About box to each axDoc server. This box is a standard place to provide information about the axDoc server.

- **PropertyBag**. The PropertyBag can be used to store properties from an axDoc. Which properties to store and when to store them should be determined during the design phase.

The design for the axDoc server will include the user interface for the axDoc and any code required to manage that interface. In addition, any other components that are required for the axDoc server need to be designed.

Creating an ActiveX Document Server Project

Begin building an axDoc server by creating a new axDoc server project or by converting an existing project into an axDoc server. This project will contain the ActiveX document(s).

To create an axDoc server project:

1. Start a new ActiveX Document DLL or ActiveX Document EXE project.

   A UserDocument will be inserted into the project as the default module.

OR

1. Start a new ActiveX DLL or ActiveX EXE project.

   A class module will be inserted into the project as the default module.

2. Use the Add User Document option from the Project menu to add a UserDocument.

OR

1. Open an existing project.

   This project will be converted to an axDoc server project.

2. Use the Properties option from the Project menu to change the Project Type to an ActiveX EXE or ActiveX DLL.

3. Choose Add-In Manager from the Add-Ins menu and check the VB ActiveX Document Migration Wizard.

   A menu option for the Wizard is added to the Add-Ins menu.

4. Select ActiveX Document Migration Wizard from the Add-Ins menu.

5. Follow the Wizard's instructions to convert forms in the project to ActiveX documents.

   Regardless of the set of steps you follow, after this process you should have an axDoc server project and at least one UserDocument in that project.

   You can use any of these techniques for the Web-based To Do List example. If you did the ActiveX EXE test project in the "Building an ActiveX Code Component" section earlier in this chapter, you can open that project and convert the To Do List form to an ActiveX document using the ActiveX Document Migration Wizard.

Building the UserDocuments

You can add one or more UserDocuments to an ActiveX document server. Each UserDocument defines the user interface for one ActiveX document. You build a UserDocument just as you do a form; simply add controls to the

Figure 13.12

A UserDocument is similar to a form. It provides the user interface and code for the ActiveX document.

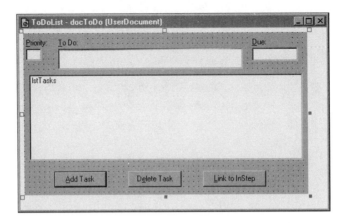

UserDocument. You can add any controls to a UserDocument except the OLE container control.

The UserDocument is saved in a file with a .dob extension. If the User-Document contains graphical data, that data is stored in a .dox file. These two file types are similar to the .frm and .frx files used for forms.

You can add code to the UserDocuments just as you add code to a form. However, there is no load and unload of a UserDocument. Code that would normally be added to the Load or Unload events for a form can instead be added to the Initialize and Terminate events for the UserDocument.

Figure 13.12 shows the UserDocument for the To Do List example. It includes three text boxes, one list box, and three buttons. If you converted the To Do List form to a To Do List UserDocument, be sure to change the Close button to a Link button. An ActiveX document is not normally closed, rather the user navigates to another ActiveX document. If you created the project from scratch, be sure to set a reference to the Tasks ActiveX server since this example uses that server.

Tech Note. *If you want to try this example without referencing the Task server, leave out all of the code from this project and simply display a message box when the buttons are clicked.*

The code for the To Do List UserDocument is almost the same as the code for the To Do List form, detailed in the earlier section "Building an ActiveX Code Component." However, instead of performing initialization in the Load event, you use the Initialize event, as shown here:

```
Private Sub UserDocument_Initialize()
Dim tempTask As CTask
```

```
' Create the instance of the collection class
Set m_Tasks = New CTasks

' Fill the list box with the items from the collection
' Shows the For Each...Next syntax!
For Each tempTask In m_Tasks
    lstTasks.AddItem Format$(tempTask.Priority, "000") _
        & Space(2) & tempTask.Description _
        & Space(2) & "Due: " & tempTask.Due
    Next
End Sub
```

Tech Note. *If you ran the Wizard to convert the To Do List form, you will find that the Wizard simply called your Form_Load code from the UserDocument_Initialize event.*

You need to add the code for cleaning up the objects to the UserDocument Terminate event instead of in the Unload, as follows:

```
Private Sub UserDocument_Terminate()
    ' Clear all of our object references
    Set m_Tasks = Nothing
End Sub
```

The new Link button on the UserDocument will link to another Web page. The code for that is

```
' Links to the InStep Technologies Web page
Private Sub cmdLink_Click()
    UserDocument.Hyperlink.NavigateTo ("http://www.insteptech.com")
End Sub
```

As you would expect, this code could link to any Web page. To link to another ActiveX document, insert the path to the Visual Basic document file (.vbd). Visual Basic document files are described in detail later in this section.

Developing the Code for the ActiveX Document Server

You can add any other forms, class modules, and standard modules to an axDoc server project. These additional modules can provide support functionality for the axDoc.

For the To Do List example, the supporting code is provided by the Task ActiveX component.

Setting the UserDocument Properties

The properties available for a UserDocument are similar to those provided for forms. Two properties available only for UserDocuments are HScrollS-mallChange and VScrollSmallChange. These properties identify the distance the UserDocument will scroll (in twips) when the user scrolls within the ActiveX document container's viewport.

Setting ActiveX Document Server Project Properties

Use the Properties option from the Project menu to define the settings for the axDoc server project. Be sure to provide a clear description and set the Version Compatibility appropriately. See "Setting ActiveX EXE and ActiveX DLL Project General Properties" and "Setting ActiveX EXE and ActiveX DLL Project Component Properties" earlier in this chapter for more information on project properties.

Testing the ActiveX Document

You cannot simply run an ActiveX document server project to test an axDoc because testing an axDoc requires an axDoc container. You can test the axDoc by running an axDoc container application, such as Internet Explorer. The axDoc container application will request the axDoc from the axDoc server. But how do you tell the axDoc container application which axDoc you want displayed?

A Visual Basic document file with a .vbd extension stores the definition of the axDoc and its associated axDoc server. When you open a Visual Basic document file in an axDoc container application, the container application reads the file and determines which axDoc server to execute and which axDoc to request from that server. You can think of the Visual Basic document file as your reference to the appropriate axDoc.

Keynote

Tech Note. *In reality, the Visual Basic document file is a structured storage file. This is the same type of file used to store Word documents and Excel workbooks.*

To test an ActiveX document, follow these steps:

1. Run the axDoc server project.

   If the project does not stay in Run mode, verify that the Start Mode project property is set to ActiveX Component.

   When the project is run, a temporary Visual Basic document file is created in the Visual Basic directory for each axDoc in the project. The Name property of the UserDocument is used as the name of the Visual Basic document file and .vbd is the extension.

Tech Note. *The temporary .vbd files are created in the Visual Basic directory, regardless of where the project was saved. When the project is compiled, .vbd files are created in the directory specified for the compiled project. After the compile, running the project in design mode still causes a set of temporary .vbd files to be created in the Visual Basic directory.*

2. Launch an axDoc container application.

   You can use your Web browser if it supports axDocs.

3. Use the Open feature of your browser to open the .vbd file.

   The .vbd file will reside in the Visual Basic directory. When the file is opened, your axDoc should appear within the browser. Cool!

4. Test the ActiveX document.

   Use the features of your axDoc. Because you are running the project in development mode, you can set break points, watch points, and perform other debugging as you would with any other project.

For the To Do List example, the To Do List axDoc should appear as shown in Figure 13.13. Try adding tasks to the list, removing tasks from the list, or linking to the defined Web page.

Figure 13.13

The ActiveX document you defined in the UserDocument can be displayed in any ActiveX document container, such as Internet Explorer.

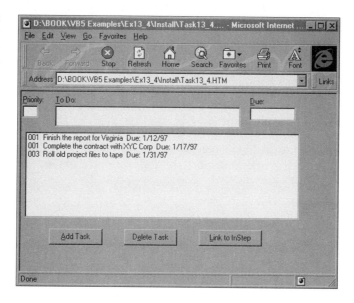

Compiling the ActiveX Document Server

To compile the axDoc server, choose Make from the File menu. Visual Basic will compile the project to an EXE or DLL and create a document file (.vbd) for each UserDocument in the axDoc server. These files are created in the same directory as the compiled axDoc server.

You can rename the Visual Basic document files, giving them any name you like. To test the compiled server, repeat the previous test using the .vbd files created in this step.

Distributing the ActiveX Document and Server

Once you have compiled the axDoc server, you can distribute it or add the files to your Web site. Other users can then view your axDocs from any axDoc container.

If you plan to deploy the axDoc on a Web server, the easiest way for an end user to access your axDoc is through a HyperText Markup Language (HTML) Web page. The Web page can reside on a Web server anywhere on the World Wide Web or on a local intranet.

When a user accesses a Web page, the Internet browser downloads and displays the page. If other components are needed for the Web page, such as your axDoc and axDoc server, the browser will also download the components. Because some of these components, like the axDoc server, can be large, the files should be compressed into a cabinet file (.cab). When a .cab file is downloaded, the browser verifies the file for safety and decompresses it. The browser then registers the decompressed components in the Windows Registry, installs them, and activates them on the user's system.

Building the .cab File

A cabinet file (.cab) contains the set of components needed by a Web page. This file is compressed to minimize the time required to download it. A .cab file will normally contain

- All ActiveX components required for a project. For displayed axDocs, this minimally includes the associated axDoc EXE or axDoc DLL.

- Any other support files required for a project.

- An information file (.inf) that contains references to other required .cab files, called secondary .cab files, and .cab file properties such as safety and registry information. This file also has a location for a digital signature.

Keynote

The easiest way to build a .cab file is to use the Setup Wizard. The Setup Wizard provides the option Create Internet Download Setup. When this option is selected, the Setup Wizard locates all of the files needed by the project and compresses them into the .cab file. It also builds the HTML page, as described in the next topic.

Tech Note. *Setup Wizard allows you to define the location of the secondary .cab files for the generic components, such as Msvbvm50.dll and DAO. You can have these components downloaded automatically for the user from the Microsoft Web site, or from any other location you specify.*

Building an HTML Page

You can create an HTML page to display your axDoc using VBScript. The HTML page must identify the name and class ID (GUID) of the axDoc and the name and version of the .cab file containing the components required by the axDoc. It must then display the axDoc in the frame of the browser.

The following sample is the HTML page to display the docToDo axDoc:

```
<HTML>
<OBJECT ID="docToDo"
CLASSID="CLSID:D738DEF0-7AA7-11D0-BB11-00AA00594B54"
CODEBASE="Task13_4.CAB#version=1,0,0,0">
</OBJECT>

<SCRIPT LANGUAGE="VBScript">
Sub Window_OnLoad
        Document.Open
        Document.Write "<FRAMESET>"
        Document.Write "<FRAME SRC=""docToDo.VBD"">"
        Document.Write "</FRAMESET>"
        Document.Close
End Sub
</SCRIPT>
</HTML>
```

You could build this HTML page but it is much easier if you let Setup Wizard do the work for you. When you select the option Create Internet Download Setup, the Setup Wizard will build the required .cab file and build the HTML page. Once the HTML page is built, you can view your axDoc simply by double-clicking on the HTML file or by opening the HTML page in your Web browser.

Deploying the ActiveX Document to a Web Server

To deploy the axDoc for viewing from your Web site, you need to upload the Visual Basic document file (.vbd), the HTML page (.htm), and the cabinet file (.cab) to your Web server. You can upload these files to any Web server running Internet Information Server (IIS).

Tech Note. *You should also be able to upload your axDoc files to a UNIX-based server. However, at the time of this writing this feature was not working. Watch for an upcoming knowledge base article on this topic.*

Keynote

When a user references the HTML page from your Web site by requesting the page directly or via a hypcrlink to the page, the files for the axDoc are copied down to the user's system, the HTML script is executed, and the axDoc appears in the Web browser.

Considering Safety

Safety is a major concern when downloading files from a Web site. Users want to have confidence that what they are downloading will not damage their other computer files. To help with safety, you can design and built your component to ensure that it has no harmful results on the users' computer.

When using the Setup Wizard, you can mark the component as safe for scripting—that is, it cannot be scripted to cause harm to the user's system. You can also mark a component as safe for initializing, meaning that the component can be initialized with any values without causing harm to the user's system.

Visual Basic also reserves space in the .cab file created by the Setup Wizard for a digital signature to ensure the safety of the component.

Tech Note. *Depending on the security information identified with the component and the security options selected in your Web browser, the sample ActiveX document you developed in this chapter may not download automatically from your Web site. If the document does not download, try adjusting the security settings of your Web browser temporarily to see if that corrects the problem.*

What Did This Cover?

This section described ActiveX documents, ActiveX document servers, and ActiveX document containers. It then illustrated how to create a simple ActiveX document server and an ActiveX document and provided tips for designing, building, testing, compiling, and distributing the ActiveX document. The resulting ActiveX document can be displayed in an ActiveX document container, such as Internet Explorer.

■ ActiveX Do's and Don'ts

There are several do's and don'ts for creating ActiveX components. Several of these items repeat information provided in earlier sections of this chapter. They are restated here to provide you with a thorough checklist of do's and don'ts.

ActiveX Component Do's and Don'ts

The following are recommendations to follow when building or using ActiveX components.

General

- **Do** document the interface for your component using the Procedure Attributes. Optionally, add a help file for the component.

- **Don't** display errors from the component. Instead, return an error code to the client application or raise a run-time error to the client application. Raising errors was discussed in Chapter 10.

- **Do** raise error numbers greater than vbObjectError + 512 and less than vbObjectError + 65535. Values between vbObjectError and vbObjectError + 512 can conflict with other Visual Basic error values.

- **Do** document your error numbers. Define public enumerations for the error numbers and document them in the help file for the component.

- **Don't** use any object in the Visual Basic object library as a parameter or return value for exposed properties or methods in public classes. These objects are not intended to be used from outside a single project and using them in this manner may cause unexpected results. You can review the list of Visual Basic (VB) objects using the Object Browser.

- **Do** set all object variables to Nothing before ending a client application. When the End statement is executed in a client application, the component is shut down and the Terminate events of any objects that have not yet been terminated are not executed.

- **Do** set the Version Compatibility for compatibility between versions of your component.

- **Don't** change the interface of your component once the component has been used by a client application.

User Interface Considerations

- **Don't** return references to Form and Control objects from your component. Rather, provide wrappers for the properties and methods of forms and controls if they must be manipulated by a client application. For example, instead of returning a text box and allowing the client application to manipulate the text box, provide wrapper methods in the component for Move and wrapper properties for Text.

Performance

- **Do** use the most specific object type available. Instead of declaring an object as Object, use the specific object type, such as CTask. This is called early binding and improves performance.

- **Do** use object substitution to substitute a simple name for an extended object reference. Each "." in the syntax represents a lookup, so the fewer times the lookups are performed the better the performance. For example:

```
For i = 1 to 10
    <some code>
    txt(i) = myApp.TimeSheet.Employee.Name
Next i
```

performs better if rewritten using substitution:

```
Dim emp as New Employee

' Create the substitution object variable
Set emp = myApp.TimeSheet.Employee

For i = 1 to 10
    <some code>
    txt(i) = emp.Name
Next i
```

- **Do** use With...End With to minimize the number of repeated lookups for the same reason as the previous recommendation. This has the added advantage of not requiring the temporary substitution object.

- **Do** use in-process servers (ActiveX DLLs) instead of out-of-process servers (ActiveX EXEs) whenever possible to improve performance. Calls to objects within the application's process space, either in the application or in an in-process server, are significantly faster than calls to objects outside the application's process space.

- **Do** pass as much data to and from a component as possible in each call. The data transfer is fast, but the calling is slow, especially with out-of-process servers. For example, you could pass a set of parameters in an array instead of calling the component multiple times.

Testing

- **Do** compile your component (or start with Full Compile) before testing it. This ensures that there are no compile-time errors.

- **Do** test ActiveX DLLs and ActiveX controls by adding a project to the project group containing the component. This greatly simplifies the testing.

Terminating the Component

- **Don't** refer to objects provided by the server as public object variables in standard modules. This causes problems when terminating the component.

- **Do** ensure that all forms are unloaded. If the process closes and there are hidden forms that are still loaded, these forms are not always unloaded correctly.

- **Don't** provide a method that terminates your component. Let the component be automatically terminated when no references to the component exist. If you provide an Exit option in a component that displays a user interface, simply unload the forms the user opened and free all object instances that were created. Don't terminate the component.

- **Don't** include an End statement in a component, because this will prevent the component from correctly terminating. A component will automatically terminate when there are no loaded forms, no references to objects from the component, and there is no code executing in the component.

■ Summary

- Developing applications as sets of components simplifies development and maintenance and leverages reuse.

- Creating and distributing an ActiveX component allows you to provide the functionality of a set of classes without having to provide the source code for the classes. It also allows you to create components that can be reused in other applications without including the component within the application. You can thus create truly reusable components.

- ActiveX code components can be in-process or out-of-process. An out-of-process component is an executable that runs in its own process. An in-process component is a DLL that runs in the same process as the client application. Therefore, in-process servers have better performance.

- Visual Basic 5 supports the creation of ActiveX controls. You can create controls for use in Visual Basic 4, Visual Basic 5, Visual C++, on Web pages, and any other product that supports ActiveX controls.

- You can leverage your knowledge of Visual Basic when creating Web content by creating ActiveX document servers and ActiveX documents.

- DCOM and Remote Automation allow an ActiveX component to be executed over a network. A component can be installed on any machine on the network and any client application can then access it remotely.

- When developing a component, set the Version Compatibility appropriately to ensure that changes to a component will not affect any applications that currently use the component, such as your test client application.

- For a client application to find a component, the component must be registered in the Windows Registry. Visual Basic does this automatically when you run the component in design mode or when you compile the component project.

- Test an ActiveX DLL or ActiveX control by adding a test project to the project group.

- Test an ActiveX EXE by running the component in one copy of Visual Basic and the test client application in another.

- Test an ActiveX document by running the ActiveX document server in Visual Basic and displaying the ActiveX document in an ActiveX document container such as Microsoft Internet Explorer 3.0 or Microsoft Office Binder 1.0.

- When you distribute the component, it will need to be registered on the destination system. This is done automatically if you use the Setup Wizard to install your component. If you don't use the Setup Wizard, you need to register it yourself.

- The components you create can be used from Microsoft Excel, Microsoft Access, and any other application that supports ActiveX.

- Follow the recommended do's and don'ts for creating ActiveX components.

■ Additional Reading

Appleman, Daniel. *Dan Appleman's Developing ActiveX Components with Visual Basic 5.0*. Emeryville CA: Ziff-Davis Press, forthcoming May 1997.

Rather than rehashing the Visual Basic documentation, Appleman cuts to the chase, covering the most essential problems, the undocumented pit-falls and the most efficient ways of creating ActiveX components in Visual Basic.

Brockschmidt, Kraig, *Inside OLE*. Redmond, Washington: Microsoft Press, 1995.

This very thick book provides a detailed description of OLE technologies, before they were renamed ActiveX. It demonstrates how to implement OLE features using C and C++.

Chappell, David. *Understanding ActiveX and OLE*. Redmond, Washington: Microsoft Press, 1996.

This book provides an excellent and up-to-date summary of the ActiveX technologies. The many graphics in this book help you visualize interfaces and ActiveX components. If you ever wondered what really happens when an object is created from a class, this book will provide the answers.

Dehlin, Joel and Curland, Matthew. *Object Programming with Visual Basic 4*. Redmond, Washington: Microsoft Press, 1996.

This book provides an introduction to objects and classes. It then demonstrates how to use Microsoft Excel, Word, and PowerPoint objects.

Goren, Craig. *Visual Basic 5 Enterprise Development*. Indianapolis: Que, 1997.

This book describes how to build three-tier client/server information systems with Visual Basic Enterprise Edition. It describes the user, business, and data service layers of a three-tier application architecture. It also describes in detail creation of ActiveX components, distribution and management of components, security, and error processing.

McManus, Jeffrey P. *How to Program Visual Basic 5.0 Control Creation Edition.* Emeryville CA: Ziff-Davis Press, 1997.

This all-in-one guide uses a unique, full-color format and step-by-step instructions to show how to create ActiveX controls.

Microsoft Press. *OLE 2 Programmer's Reference.* Redmond, Washington: Microsoft Press, 1994.

This two volume set is a reference for C and C++ programmers. Even if you are not interested in accessing OLE with C or C++, this set of documents provides a good overview of OLE including user interface guidelines.

■ Think It Over

To supplement and review the information in this chapter, think about the following:

1. Think about other applications you have written. What benefits would you see if you broke these applications into components?

2. Think about when you would use an in-process server versus an out-of-process server.

3. Try creating a simple class and making it an ActiveX component. Then develop a small test program to use your server.

4. If you are familiar with using VBA in Microsoft Excel, modify the VBA module created in this chapter. Sort the spreadsheet by priority. For a more challenging task, allow the user to edit the task list in Excel and write the modified tasks back to the task file.

5. Try setting up an ActiveX component on a remote computer, if you have Visual Basic, Enterprise Edition, and access to the necessary network facilities.

6. Have you ever wished you could create your own control? What would it look like? How would it perform? Try creating it with Visual Basic.

7. Have you been creating any Web pages? Which of those pages would have been easier to create with a Visual Basic form?

14

Doing Database Objects

Try not! Do, or do not; there is no try.

—Yoda the Jedi Master, *The Empire Strikes Back*

Chapter 11 demonstrated storing and retrieving application objects from data files. In many applications, data files do not provide all of the features needed for data storage, such as sharing data across a network. This is especially true when the application must access data within a business enterprise. The application must then "do" database objects.

This chapter describes several methods of accessing a database. It then demonstrates how to work with the data control using both bound controls and the associated data objects. A more complex example does all of the data processing with data access objects (DAO).

■ Accessing a Database with Visual Basic

Visual Basic has become a very powerful database application development tool. You can connect to most databases, retrieve desired information, display it, modify it, and store it. With that power comes more choices. The method of data access you select will depend on the requirements of your application and on the database(s) you need to access.

The database accessing choices include

- **Data control**. The data control provides a "no code" approach to database accessing. You simply add the data control to a form, set properties to define the recordset associated with the data control, and bind data-aware controls to the data control. That's all it takes to create a database application, if you don't mind the user navigating records with the VCR-like user interface of the data control.

- **Data control with code**. The data control's recordset can be accessed with code in the application. This means you can get the benefits of using the data control yet still have the flexibility of doing some database operations yourself. You can also hide the data control and add your own buttons to provide a more user-friendly mechanism for navigating through the records.

- **Data access objects (DAO)**. The DAO is an object model with properties and methods that can be accessed with code to manipulate the data or structure of the database. This approach provides the maximum flexibility in working with the database; however, it is very code intensive.

Tech Note. *Visual Basic 5 comes with DAO 3.5. This version of DAO supports ODBCDirect, which provides the familiar DAO object model but calls the RDO libraries to access the ODBC for connecting to remote databases. Using ODBCDirect, you can use one object model, the DAO, to develop applications that support an Access database on a laptop when the user is away from the office and a SQL Server or Oracle database when the user is connected at the office. You could do this before Visual Basic 5 but it* *involved using SQL passthrough or attached tables to access the remote database, which had a significant impact on performance.*

Enterprise Edition

- **Remote data control (RDC).** This is similar to the data control but it uses RDO to access the ODBC for connecting to remote databases.

Enterprise Edition

- **Remote data objects (RDO).** RDO is similar to DAO, but with access to the ODBC for connecting to remote databases. Visual Basic 5 supports RDO version 2.0, which provides improved local cursor support, optimistic batch updates, and stand-alone connection and query objects.

- **Active data objects (ADO).** ADO provides a data model for accessing OLE DB data sources. OLE DB is a new specification for a common interface to many different types of data sources on different types of systems. OLE DB allows seamless integration of data from the mainframe, UNIX servers, and Windows workstations. While the ODBC works primarily with relational data, OLE DB provides for alternative data architectures. Maybe an object-oriented database product is not far away?

Tech Note.   *As of this writing, there was no information about ADO or OLE DB in the Visual Basic 5 documentation set, but developers have successfully implemented ADO in both VB4 and VB5 projects. You can find out more about ADO in the materials referenced in the "Additional Reading" section at the end of this chapter or by searching Microsoft's Web site (http://www.microsoft.com).*

Figure 14.1 takes the "under the hood" view of these choices and depicts how each of these database accessing methods fits into the three-tiered architecture of an application. This figure was discussed in detail in Chapter 8, "Data Design." Examples of the first three options are illustrated in this chapter. See the "Additional Reading" section at the end of this chapter for references to more information on ODBCDirect, RDC, RDO, and ADO.

■ The "No Code" Approach: Using the Data Control

The data control is a control in the Visual Basic toolbox that, when added to a form, provides a link from the form to a database. Many of the other Visual Basic controls, such as text boxes and list boxes, are data-aware and can be tied to the data control. You can also create your own data-aware ActiveX controls. Controls tied in this manner are called *bound controls*. As the data control manipulates records in the database, the values of the fields in a record are automatically displayed in the bound controls.

Figure 14.1

Visual Basic provides several choices for transferring data between the user interface tier and the data tier.

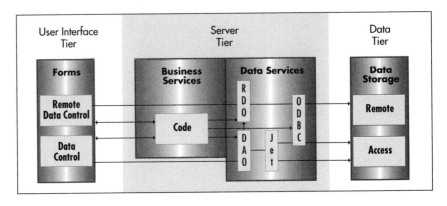

Keynote

Using this approach is very simple and requires no coding. Just add the data control to a form, set the properties to define the set of desired data, add controls to the form, bind the controls to the data control, and that's it. This approach is very good for developing quick prototypes because it requires little or no code.

The example in this section is a contact management system that helps salespeople to track the customers or prospects they have contacted. It allows the salesperson to enter the name, date, and type of contact. It also provides a place for notes about the contact. To work through this example, copy the database from the CD-ROM as described in the Appendix.

What Will This Cover?

This section will cover the following key Visual Basic features:

- Using the data control for automatic database processing
- Using the Categorized tab on the Properties window
- Using the BOFAction and EOFAction properties
- Using the bound grid control
- Binding a list box control
- Using the VB Data Form Wizard

Steps to Creating a Simple Database Application

Creating a very simple database application requires the data control, a few text boxes, and no code. The sample application in this section is a little more challenging. It uses the bound list box and grid controls in addition to the commonly used text boxes.

The basic steps for constructing a simple database application are

1. Create the form.

2. Add a data control and set the properties to bind the data control to the data.

3. Bind the other controls to the data control.

These steps are detailed in the topics that follow. Notice that there is no hint of any coding going on here!

Creating the Form

Assuming you are creating this form as part of a well-designed system, you would already have defined the user interface for the form. For this example, the form is a simplified version of a contact management system form and is shown in Figure 14.2.

Figure 14.2

A bound list box and bound grid come with the Professional and Enterprise Editions of Visual Basic.

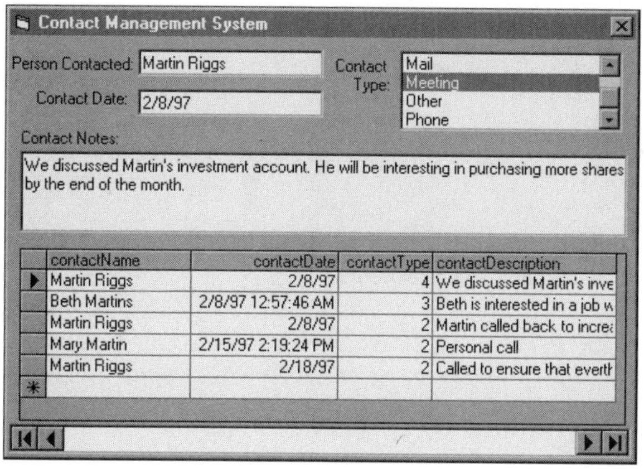

This form uses bound text boxes for the Person Contacted, Contact Date, and Contact Notes fields. A bound list box is used to display the Contact Type choices and a bound grid is used to display all contacts that have been made.

Tech Note.   *If you do not see the bound list box or bound grid in your toolbox, choose Components from the Project menu and then check the Microsoft Data Bound List Controls and Microsoft Data Bound Grid Control. These controls should then appear in your toolbox.*

Setting the Data Control Properties

Set the appropriate properties of the data control to define the desired recordset. The easiest way to define these settings is to use the Categorized tab of the Properties window, as shown in Figure 14.3. All of the properties needed to define the recordset for a data control are grouped in the Data category. The properties in the Data category are

Figure 14.3

The new Categorized tab in the Properties window groups the data control's Data properties together for easier review and modification.

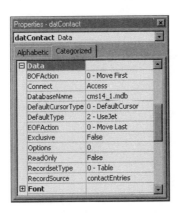

- **BOFAction** defines what the control should do when it hits the logical beginning of the file (BOF). For example, a setting of 0 - Move First will set the current record pointer back to the first record when the BOF is reached.

- **Connect** defines the type of database to be accessed. You may be surprised at the very long list of options. When connecting through ODBC, Connect defines the connection string.

- **DatabaseName** defines the path and file name of the database to be accessed. Even if the code will reset this value, setting it at design time will provide a list of available record sources for the RecordSource property of the data control.

Tech Note.   *The DatabaseName property defines the full path designator to the database. Using this setting will prevent the application from executing properly on any machine that does not have the database in that specific path. You can resolve this issue by writing some code to change the path, as shown in the next section.*

- **DefaultCursorType** defines the type of cursor used on a connection. You can let the ODBC driver select the type of cursor, use the ODBC cursor library, or use server-side cursors. This setting is only used with ODBCDirect.

- **DefaultType** defines the path to the data. You can use the Jet engine or ODBCDirect, which accesses the ODBC through an RDO DLL. The Jet engine is recommended when using the Access database and ODBC-Direct is recommended when using remote databases such as SQL Server or Oracle.

- **EOFAction** defines what the control should do when it hits the logical end of the file (EOF). For example, a setting of 0 - Move Last will set the current record pointer back to the last record when the EOF is reached. This prevents the record pointer from being in an unknown state.

- **Exclusive** indicates whether the database is opened for single-user or multiuser access. Single-user access locks the entire database until it is closed, and provides faster database operations. Multiuser access allows multiple users to open the database. This setting is ignored when using ODBC.

- **Options** allows you to set database options such as forward-only scrolling or SQLPassThrough.

- **ReadOnly** indicates that the user can only read records and cannot update them.

- **RecordsetType** defines the type of recordset to be accessed. You can select Table to build a recordset of all records in a table. Select Dynaset to define a dynamic, updatable, fully scrollable, keyset-type cursor on a set of data optionally joined from several tables. If you can use a read-only, forward-only view of the data from one or more tables, select Snapshot.

Tech Note.   *Setting the RecordsetType to Table provides faster data access and uses less memory than a dynaset; this setting is recommended when data is retrieved from one table. However, table-type recordsets don't work with attached tables.*

- **RecordSource** defines the source of data for the data control. This is the name of the table for table-type recordsets or a query for dynaset- and snapshot-type recordsets.

The property settings for the data control shown in Figure 14.2 are listed in Figure 14.3.

Binding Controls to the Data Control

Defining the database and recordset associated with the data control is only the first step. To view data from the recordset, you need to tie fields in the recordset to controls on the form. When a user moves through records with the data control, these bound controls will automatically display the field values. To bind a control on the form to the data control, set the data properties of the control using the Data category in the Properties window. The Data-Source property of the control must be set to the name of the data control and the DataField property to a specific field within the recordset defined by the data control.

For each of the text boxes on the form in Figure 14.2, the DataSource was set to datContact, the data control bound to the contactEntries table. The DataField properties are set to the fields in the contactEntries table. You may also want to set the MaxLength property for the text boxes to the width of the field in the database. This prevents "data is too long for field" type errors.

In addition to simple text boxes and labels, you can bind list boxes, combo boxes, and even a grid. The grid control maps each record in the data control's recordset to a row in the grid. It lists each field in the record in a column in the grid. Use the grid properties to hide, move, or adjust the columns.

List boxes and combo boxes provide a list of items the user can select, like the Contact Type in Figure 14.2. These controls use the same properties as other bound controls:

- **DataSource** is the name of the data control on the form. It binds this control to the data control.

- **DataField** defines the name of the field in the recordset for the bound data control. It binds this control to the defined field.

The specified DataField links the one value from the current row of the recordset to the control. But for list boxes and combo boxes, you will want to display the list of available choices. In a normalized database, this list of choices is usually in a different table. A second data control can be added to the form and bound to the table containing the list of items to display in the list box or combo box.

In this example, a contactTypes table stores a description and a unique ID for each contact type. This table is bound to a second, hidden data control. Figure 14.4 lists the properties for the hidden data control. The Order By clause defined in the RecordSource property sorts the records by description so they appear sorted in the list.

Figure 14.4

A second, hidden data control provides the link between the list box contents and the associated table.

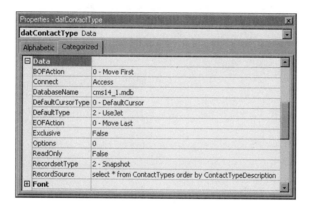

This second data control must be bound to the list portion of the list box or combo box. The properties required to bind the list portion of list boxes and combo boxes are included in the List category in the Properties window and are as follows:

- **BoundColumn** defines the field in the recordset for the list, defined by RowSource, that matches the field identified in the DataField property. When an item is selected from the list, the value of the field identified in this property is assigned to the field identified in the DataField property. This is normally set to the key field of the table containing the list.

- **ListField** defines the field in the recordset for the list, defined by Row-Source, that is used to fill the list. If this field is empty, BoundColumn is used to fill the list.

- **RowSource** defines the name of the data control that identifies the recordset for the list.

By selecting two different fields in the ListField and BoundColumn properties, you can list the description of items in the list box and use an ID value to update the actual bound record. Figure 14.5 shows the property values used for the list box in the contact management system example.

Figure 14.5

A bound list box requires the Data properties to identify the field in the database to store the selection, and the List properties to present the list for selection.

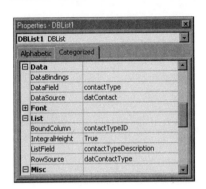

One additional list box and combo box property to note is the MatchEntry property. Selecting Basic Matching will locate the first entry in the list with the letter that the user types. Selecting Extended Matching provides a typematic search—that is, as the user types a character the entry matching the typed string is found in the list box or combo box. For example, if the user types **p** the entry will move to the first "p," if the user then types **h** the entry will move to the first "ph" entry.

Tech Note. *The MatchEntry property does not work if the RecordsetType is set to Table and does not work well unless the list is sorted.*

Using the VB Data Form Wizard

What could be easier than developing a database front-end by putting a data control on a form, adding a few text boxes, and setting a bunch of properties? Having the VB Data Form Wizard develop it for you! You can use the VB Data Form Wizard to generate a form for creating, reviewing, updating, and deleting database information. To use the VB Data Form Wizard to create a form:

1. Choose Add-In Manager from the Add-Ins menu and check the VB Data Form Wizard.

   A menu option for the Wizard will be added to the Add-Ins menu.

2. Chose Data Form Wizard from the Add-Ins menu.

3. Follow the Wizard instructions to identify the fields to be included on the form.

That's all there is to it. In under a minute, the form is finished. Notice that the Data Form Wizard does not provide options for inserting lists or grids onto the form. You would have to do that manually after running the Data Form Wizard. If you look closely at the form generated by the Data Form Wizard, you will see that it generated some code. Using code with the data control is described in the next section.

What Did This Cover?

This section detailed the steps for creating a simple database application. It added data controls to a form and bound the other controls to those data controls. That was it—no coding required. For an even easier method for developing a simple database application, use the Data Form Wizard.

You should now be able to simply run the application. Just ensure that the database paths are set correctly in the DatabaseName properties of the data controls.

You can use the arrows on the user interface of the data control to move through the records. You can update the data in the controls at the top of the screen, or directly in the grid. Any updates you make will automatically be stored. To create a new entry, move to the last entry in the grid and type the new entry.

■ The "I Want It All" Approach: Using the Data Control and Code

One complaint about using the data control is your total loss of control. Visual Basic does everything for you and you can't do much about it. But that's not entirely true; you do have access to the data control's recordset. This means you can get the benefits of the data control and yet still have some control. You can have the best of both worlds.

What Will This Cover?

This section will cover the following key Visual Basic features:

- Using the data control's recordset for manual database processing

- Joining tables to create a dynaset

Adding Code to the Simple Database Application

In the previous section, you saw how quickly and easily you could create a database application. But look at the result. Is it as user-friendly as you would like? Does it provide all the information the user requires? If you want to add functionality to this simple application, you will need to add some code.

First, let's look at the user interface. The data control is arguably not the most user-friendly method of navigating through records in a table. The method of adding records by moving to the last row of the grid is definitely not intuitive. And what does that "3" mean in the contactType column, displayed in Figure 14.2? Figure 14.6 shows a revised and improved user interface.

Figure 14.6

This user interface hides the data control and adds buttons for record processing.

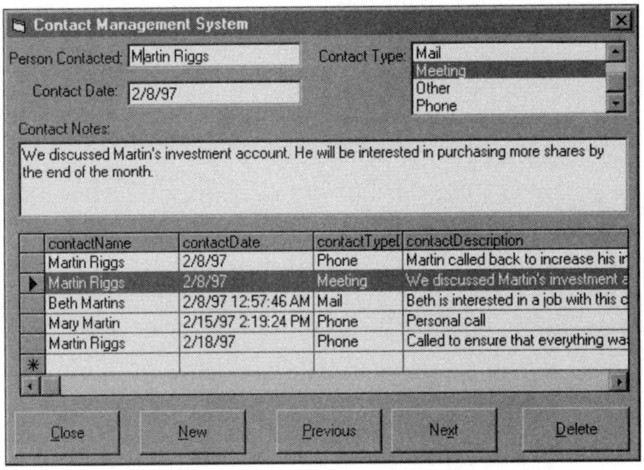

The controls on the form remain bound to the data control to simplify the display of data in the fields. The only changes made to the application are the following:

- **Joined tables**. The primary data control was bound to a dynaset-type recordset. This dynaset contains the data resulting from the join of the contactEntries and contactTypes tables to display the contact type description instead of the ID in the grid.

- **Controlled record processing**. A set of buttons was added to control the record processing, and the data control was hidden. Code was then required to handle the database actions for the buttons.

These changes are discussed in the topics that follow.

Joining Tables

In a normalized database, a logical set of information may span multiple tables. For example, the contactEntries table does not include the text of a contact type description. Rather, it includes a key, called a *foreign key*, into a table that lists the contact type descriptions. When you store the key instead of the string in the contactEntries table, the database uses less space. Furthermore, the string values can be more easily changed (or localized) in the contactTypes table without affecting the actual data in the contactEntries table.

A contact type of "3" is meaningless to users unless they memorize what it means or tape a legend to the monitor. To display the type description instead, you can join the table containing the foreign key and the table containing the descriptions. Then you can display the description instead of the foreign key value.

Keynote

The code to join the tables is frequently included in the Load event for the form:

```
Private Sub Form_Load()
On Error GoTo ERR_ROUTINE
    ' Set the Contact data control
    datContact.DatabaseName = App.Path & "\cms14_2.mdb"
    datContact.RecordSource = "Select * " & _
        "from contactEntries Left Join contactTypes " & _
        "on contactEntries.contactType = contactTypes.contactTypeID " & _
        "order by contactDate"
    ' Open database and recordset
    datContact.Refresh

    ' Set the Contact Type data control
    datContactType.DatabaseName = App.Path & "\cms14_2.mdb"
    datContactType.RecordSource = "Select * " & _
        "from contactTypes " & _
        "order by contactTypeDescription"
    ' Open database and recordset
    datContactType.Refresh
Exit Sub
```

```
ERR_ROUTINE:
    ' Display the error
    MsgBox "Error in application: " _
        & Err.Description
    Unload Me
End Sub
```

This code uses the App.Path property to set the path to the database. This assumes the database will be in the same directory as the application.

Tech Note. *Using App.Path in this fashion will cause an error if the App.Path is in the root directory. For example, if you run this application from a floppy, App.Path is a:\. Appending this value to the file name will result in a DatabaseName of a:\\cms.mdb, which is an invalid path. To prevent this type of error, you can develop a routine to check for the "\" and add one only if it is needed.*

The RecordSource of the Contact data control in the preceding code is set to a Select statement to define the dynaset. A Left Join is used to join every row in the table identified to the left of the Left Join clause (contactEntries) with a matching record from the table to the right of the clause (contactTypes). The Refresh method opens the database and recordset.

Controlling the Record Processing

The user interface shown in Figure 14.6 displays buttons to handle the record processing instead of the data control. Because other controls are still bound to the data control, the data control cannot be removed. You can leave it visible as an alternative navigation method or you can hide it by setting its Visible property to False.

The buttons on the form in Figure 14.6 are defined in a control array so the code for the buttons will be encapsulated in one event procedure. Instead of working with the control array index numbers, which are basically "magic numbers," you can declare a set of constants with an enumeration, as shown here:

```
' Constants instead of magic numbers
Enum contactButton
    contactCloseButton = 0
    contactNewButton = 1
    contactPreviousButton = 2
    contactNextButton = 3
    contactDeleteButton = 4
End Enum
```

Each button must then perform the appropriate action. The Close button simply unloads the form and the data control takes care of saving any changes. The New button calls the AddNew method of the data control's recordset to start a new record. This will clear the fields on the form for entry of new information. The New button code then sets the focus to the first control on the form for easy data entry.

```
' Process the button selection
Private Sub cmdContact_Click(Index As Integer)
On Error GoTo ERR_ROUTINE

    ' Proceed based on selection
    Select Case Index
        Case contactCloseButton
            Unload Me

        Case contactNewButton
            datContact.Recordset.AddNew

            ' Set focus to the first field
            txtContact(0).SetFocus

        Case contactPreviousButton
            datContact.Recordset.MovePrevious

        Case contactNextButton
            datContact.Recordset.MoveNext

        Case contactDeleteButton
            datContact.Recordset.Delete
            datContact.Recordset.MoveNext
    End Select
Exit Sub

ERR_ROUTINE:
    ' Display the error
    MsgBox "Error in application: " _
        & Err.Description
End Sub
```

The Previous and Next buttons perform the associated operations, and the Delete button deletes the record and moves to a valid record position.

Tech Note. *This Delete button code may generate an error if you delete the last record in the recordset.*

Because the code is manipulating the recordset instead of the data control, the BOFAction and EOFAction properties have no effect. To prevent errors when moving past the beginning or end of the file, you can add your own code to handle the BOF and EOF conditions using the Reposition event of the data control.

```
Private Sub datContact_Reposition()
    If datContact.Recordset.BOF Then
        datContact.Recordset.MoveFirst
    End If

    If datContact.Recordset.EOF Then
        datContact.Recordset.MoveLast
    End If
End Sub
```

What Did This Cover?

Using the data control and just a little code, you have a more flexible and user-friendly application. This section demonstrated how to access the data control's recordset from your code to have the benefits and simplicity of bound controls, along with the power and flexibility of coding it yourself.

Be sure to copy the database for this example from the CD-ROM as described in the Appendix. Then run the example in this chapter to process the records with your code. You can still update the data in the controls at the top of the screen, or directly in the grid. Any updates you make will automatically be stored. Compare the code described here with the code generated by the VB Data Form Wizard. You will find that much of the code is the same.

■ The OO Approach: Using Data Access Objects

Visual Basic comes with a set of prebuilt objects for accessing databases. These are called the data access objects (DAO). The data access object model is shown in the *Guide to Data Access Objects* provided with the Professional and Enterprise Editions.

You can work with the DAO objects and collections just as you work with other objects, accessing their properties and performing methods to ma nipulate data or modify the database structure. You can even add your own properties to the DAO objects. Using this object-oriented approach requires more work, but gives you the most control over data access.

The structure of a DAO application includes the following components:

Keynote

- **Form.** The form handles the user interface for the application. Code in the form is responsible for transferring data from the properties of a business object to the controls on the form. If a user modifies any of the displayed information, the form is responsible for copying the changes back from the controls to the properties of the object.

- **Business object class.** This class defines the properties and methods for the business object. Code in this class often includes validation against a set of business rules. This class should not contain any code that refers to any user-interface component. This allows the class to be reused with any user interface.

  For example, the Task class was used in Chapters 10, 11, and 13 with many different types of interfaces. One form displayed only one task, one form displayed multiple tasks, and one form displayed tasks on a Web page!

- **Business object data transfer (BODT) class.** This class is responsible for locating a requested record in the database and copying the fields from that record to properties of an object. If the properties are changed, this class must update the database with the changes.

Keynote

The goal of this architecture is to keep the information about the controls on the form encapsulated in the form, the information about the business object encapsulated in the business object, and the information about the fields in the database encapsulated in the business object data transfer class. This is consistent with the three-tiered architecture approach presented in Chapter 7, "Implementation-Centered Design."

This section will describe how to create each of these components. As an example, an address book application will be developed. This application can be used as part of the contact management system to keep the address and phone information for each contacted person. The user interface for this application is shown in Figure 14.7. To work through this example, copy the database from the CD-ROM as described in the Appendix.

Figure 14.7

The Address Book
form displays all the
information in an address
book record. You could
add a little flair to this
form by including icons
on the buttons.

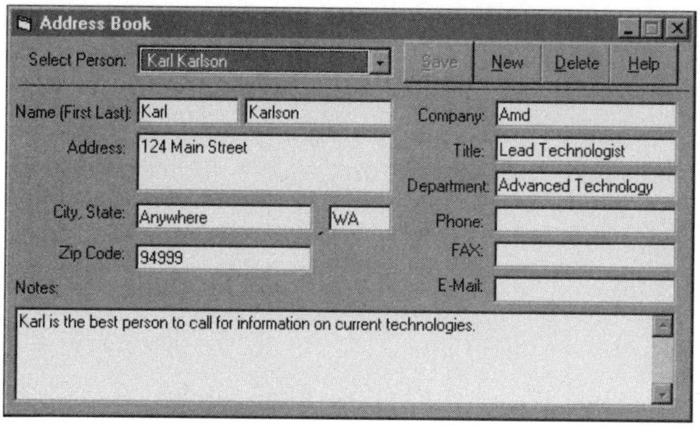

![Address Book form screenshot showing fields: Select Person: Karl Karlson; Name (First Last): Karl, Karlson; Address: 124 Main Street; City, State: Anywhere, WA; Zip Code: 94999; Company: Amd; Title: Lead Technologist; Department: Advanced Technology; Phone; FAX; E-Mail; Notes: Karl is the best person to call for information on current technologies.]

What Will This Cover?

This section will cover the following key Visual Basic features:

- Creating a generic Database class

- Using the Database object

- Using the Recordset object

- Passing an arbitrary number of parameters to a method using the ParamArray keyword

- Defining a Property procedure with a typed optional parameter
- Viewing the Call Stack

Steps to Creating a DAO Application

The basic steps required for building a single form DAO application are

1. Build a generic Database class.

2. Create the business object class.

3. Create the business object data transfer class.

4. Create the form.

5. Create the Sub Main procedure

These steps are detailed in the topics that follow. When building a more complex application, you will have many forms, business objects, and business object data transfer classes. You can repeat steps 2 through 4 as needed to implement all of the required user interface components and business objects.

Keynote

There is not necessarily a one-to-one correspondence between a business object class and a form. That is to say, you may have several forms showing different views of the information provided by a single business object class. You may have a form that includes information provided by several business objects. You should make the decisions about the number of forms and classes during your design.

Building a Generic Database Class

A Database class can encapsulate the functionality required to work with a database. You can get fancy with this class and wrap all of the DAO properties and methods in the Database class. This provides the highest degree of flexibility because you could completely replace the database access technology simply by changing the Database class.

Alternatively, you can create a Database class to simply wrap the opening and closing of the database, maintain a global reference to the database for use throughout the application and encapsulate error handling for those operations. The Database class in this example uses the second approach.

The Database class begins with the appropriate header.

```
' Class Name:    CDatabase
' Author:        Deborah Kurata, InStep Technologies
' Date:          1/22/97
' Description:   Provides database services
' Edit History:
'
Option Explicit
```

The Declarations section contains the declaration of the properties and constants. Properties include the workspace, database, and database name.

```
' Database
Private m_DB As Database
Private m_sDBName As String
Private m_WS As Workspace

' Database error enumeration
Enum dbErrors
    dbOpenDBError = vbObjectError + 512 + 1000
    dbOpenRSError = vbObjectError + 512 + 1001
End Enum
```

An enumeration defines the constants in the application. The dbErrors enumeration would include many more database error constants in a production-quality application.

The Property procedures provide public access to the database name and read-only access to the database reference. This allows other parts of the application to create a recordset using this database reference. You could also expose the workspace if you want to perform transactions.

```
' Provide a pointer to the database
Public Property Get db() As Database
    Set db = m_DB
End Property

' Name of the database file
' When the name is set, the database is opened
Public Property Let dbName(s As String)
    m_sDBName = s

    ' Open the database
    dbOpen
End Property

Public Property Get dbName() As String
    dbName = m_sDBName
End Property
```

The Property procedure for the Name property will open the database as soon as the name of the database is defined. For a production-quality class, this code would close any open database before opening a new one.

When the Database class is initialized, the workspace is defined. A workspace is a database session in which you can manage transactions and define a secure user group. A production-quality application would have error handling here.

```
Private Sub Class_Initialize()
    ' Use the default work space
    Set m_WS = Workspaces(0)
End Sub
```

The only way for this particular Database class to open a database is to pass in a database name. The database is opened in the private Open method of the Database class called from the Property Let procedure for the database name property. Opening a database is frequently a cause of errors, so error trapping is first enabled with the On Error GoTo statement. Then the desired database is opened within the current workspace.

```
Private Sub dbOpen()
On Error GoTo ERR_ROUTINE:
    Set m_DB = m_WS.OpenDatabase(dbName)

Exit Sub

ERR_ROUTINE:
    Err.Raise dbOpenDBError, "CDatabase::dbOpen", _
        "Error opening the database."
End Sub
```

The Terminate event is used to close everything and free the references. If an error occurs in opening the database or recordset, any attempt to close the offending object generates an error, so this code determines whether the object has a value and only closes it if appropriate. It then frees the references to all objects it maintains.

```
Private Sub Class_Terminate()
If Not (m_DB Is Nothing) Then
        m_DB.Close
    End If

    Set m_DB = Nothing
    Set m_WS = Nothing

End Sub
```

The resulting class provides a good start to a product-quality Database class.

Tech Note. *If you receive errors such as "User-defined type not defined" when you attempt to compile this code, you are probably missing the reference to the data access objects. Use the References option from the Project menu and select the Microsoft DAO 3.5 Object Library. If you use these techniques for applications that use an Access 2.0 database, you can select the Microsoft DAO 2.5/3.5 Compatibility Library.*

Creating the Business Object Class

The business object class defines the properties and methods for a business object. It can contain validation of user-entered information against a set of business rules. It can also provide translation or formatting of the business object properties to provide a consistent look for the property throughout the application and code to convert the user-entered value into the correct format for the business object.

The business object class in this sample application is called Person because it tracks information about a person in the address book. This person will have properties and business rules appropriate for an entry in an address book.

The Person class begins with the appropriate header.

```
' Class Name:    CPerson
' Author:        Deborah Kurata, InStep Technologies
' Date:          1/22/97
' Description:   Provides services to maintain person information
'                such as name, address, phone
' Edit History:
'
Option Explicit
```

The member data stores the properties for the class. Notice the large number of fields for data entry in Figure 14.7. Each field has a property in the Person class. By convention they are listed alphabetically, ignoring the prefix.

```
' Person data elements
Private m_sAddress As String
Private m_sCity As String
Private m_sCompany As String
Private m_sDepartment As String
Private m_sEmail As String
Private m_sFAX As String
Private m_sFirstName As String
Private m_lID As Long
Private m_sLastName As String
Private m_sNote As String
Private m_sPersonType As String
Private m_sPhone As String
Private m_sState As String
Private m_sTitle As String
Private m_sZipCode As String
```

There are two Property procedures for each property in the Person class. The Property procedures provide a mechanism for validating the data from the form prior to adding it to the database, and for formatting the data from the database before showing it on the form.

```
' PUBLIC: ****************************************
' Public property procedures

Public Property Get Address() As String
    Address = m_sAddress
End Property
Public Property Let Address(ByVal sAddress As String)
    m_sAddress = StrConv(Trim(sAddress), vbProperCase)
End Property

Public Property Get City() As String
    City = m_sCity
End Property
Public Property Let City(ByVal sCity As String)
    m_sCity = StrConv(Trim(sCity), vbProperCase)
End Property
```

```
Public Property Get Company() As String
    Company = m_sCompany
End Property
Public Property Let Company(ByVal sCompany As String)
    m_sCompany = StrConv(Trim(sCompany), vbProperCase)
End Property

Public Property Get Department() As String
    Department = m_sDepartment
End Property
Public Property Let Department(ByVal sDepartment As String)
    m_sDepartment = sDepartment
End Property

Public Property Get EMail() As String
    EMail = m_sEmail
End Property
Public Property Let EMail(ByVal sEMail As String)
    m_sEmail = sEMail
End Property

Public Property Get FAX() As String
    FAX = m_sFAX
End Property
Public Property Let FAX(ByVal sFAX As String)
    m_sFAX = sFAX
End Property

Public Property Get FirstName() As String
    FirstName = m_sFirstName
End Property
Public Property Let FirstName(ByVal sName As String)
    m_sFirstName = StrConv(Trim(sName), vbProperCase)
End Property

Public Property Get ID() As Long
    ID = m_lID
End Property
Public Property Let ID(ByVal lID As Long)
    m_lID = lID
End Property

Public Property Get LastName() As String
    LastName = m_sLastName
End Property
Public Property Let LastName(ByVal sName As String)
    m_sLastName = StrConv(Trim(sName), vbProperCase)
End Property

Public Property Get Notes() As String
    Notes = m_sNote
End Property
Public Property Let Notes(ByVal sNotes As String)
    m_sNote = sNotes
End Property

Public Property Get Phone() As String
    Phone = m_sPhone
End Property
Public Property Let Phone(ByVal sPhone As String)
    m_sPhone = sPhone
End Property

Public Property Get State() As String
    State = m_sState
End Property
```

```
Public Property Let State(ByVal sState As String)
    m_sState = StrConv(Trim(sState), vbUpperCase)
End Property

Public Property Get Title() As String
    Title = m_sTitle
End Property
Public Property Let Title(sTitle As String)
    m_sTitle = sTitle
End Property

Public Property Get ZipCode() As String
    ZipCode = m_sZipCode
End Property
Public Property Let ZipCode(ByVal sZip As String)
    m_sZipCode = sZip
End Property
```

Keynote

This is frequently what a business object will look like: private variables to store the in-memory copies of the data from the database for each property; two public Property procedures for each property; and any business rules, validation, formatting, or conversion required when assigning or reading the properties.

In addition to the standard set of Property procedures for each property, you can add other Property, Sub, or Function procedures to the business object. For example, a Name Property procedure can provide an alternative wrapper around the last name and first name.

```
' Concatenated version of name
Public Property Get Name(Optional LastNameFirst As Boolean = False) As String
    If LastNameFirst Then
        Name = LastName & ", " & FirstName
    Else
        Name = FirstName & " " & LastName
    End If
End Property
```

Notice that this Property procedure demonstrates the use of a typed optional parameter with a default value. Defining the parameter as optional and then identifying a default allows the property to be retrieved without providing the parameter. The following code retrieves the name in first name/last name order:

```
m_Person.Name
```

The code retrieves the name with the last name first:

```
m_Person.Name(True)
```

Creating the Business Object Data Transfer Class

The purpose of the business object data transfer (BODT) class is to provide a mechanism for transferring data between the database and the properties of the business object. Just as the form transfers data between the form and the object properties (tiers one and two), the BODT class transfers data between the object properties and the database (tiers two and three). This is the only class that should know about the database structure and table and field names.

There are several ways to implement this BODT class. The approach you select will depend on the requirements of the project and the defined system architecture as described in Chapter 7, "Implementation-Centered Design."

- **Data control management**. The BODT class can manage the recordset associated with the data control. This provides the easy development techniques associated with the data control with some encapsulation on working with the data control recordset.

  This approach is often used for prototypes and for very simple applications that manage data from a simple database schema.

- **Collection management**. The BODT can be a collection class that is responsible for maintaining the collection of objects. A routine in this class retrieves the records for the collection, creates an object for each record, and adds the object to the collection.

  A collection class is a good technique for data transfer when working with data files or when working with a recordset that has a small number of records. For example, all of the line items on an invoice could be retrieved from the database and kept in a collection.

  Collection classes may not be the best choice when working with recordsets with a large number of records. Remember the example from Chapter 7? Imagine a customer table with 10,000 records. An application moves through each record, creates an object, transfers the data from the record to the object properties, adds the object to the collection, and repeats this 10,000 times. Five minutes later, the processing is complete! (OK that may be an exaggeration, but you get the point.)

- **Recordset management**. The BODT class can simply manage the recordset, because the recordset is already a logical set of data retrieved from a database. In many cases, it seems unnecessary to move the rows from the recordset into another collection of data. The BODT would provide the list of logical row keys, such as last name, that could be displayed to the user in a list. The user selects a row and the BODT is responsible for finding the row in the recordset and transferring the data for the row from the recordset fields into the object properties. Because the user normally views only one record of data at a time, a single object can be reused to display the data for the current row.

  This approach works well when there is a reasonable number of records that can be collected into a recordset and the records will be accessed using DAO. This approach does not work as well using RDO because RDO has no feature for finding a row in a resultset. Nor does it work well when the number of records gets too large to easily manage in a single recordset.

With a large recordset or RDO, this BODT class could provide a list of logical row keys by defining a read-only, forward-only scrolling cursor. This list is displayed to the user for selection. The user selects a row and the BODT is responsible for finding the row in the database using SQL or a stored procedure. With this minor modification to this technique, it provides better support of large recordsets and remote data.

- **Array management**. The BODT can manage a set of data in an array. Data can be transferred from a recordset to a two-dimensional array using the GetRows method that is available for DAO and RDO.

This approach works well in a distributed environment. A BODT class resides in a component either on the same computer as the database or on another computer. It is responsible for creating the recordset (or resultset) using SQL or as the result of a stored procedure. It then copies the data from the recordset to an array using the GetRows method and ships the array across the network to the client application. If the data is changed, the BODT class receives an array of information across the network from the client application and creates the correct SQL or calls the appropriate methods to store the data back in the database.

Tech Note.   *The GetRows method returns data in a Variant array. You can combine data from different sources and pass it across the network in one array by creating a Variant array of Variant arrays. See the article by Bill Storage referenced in the "Additional Reading" section at the end of this chapter for details on working with Variant arrays.*

An optional second BODT component on the user's workstation, or another computer, accepts the array and copies the data from the array into the properties of the business object. It also bundles the properties of the object into an array to pass back to the first BODT for an update. Using a second BODT eliminates the need for the user interface to understand, manipulate, or return the array created by the first BODT.

Keynote

You may use several approaches for the BODT classes in your application. For example, an invoicing application may use the data control management approach for the customer maintenance portion of the application, a recordset management approach for the set of invoices, a collection approach for the set of line items on an invoice, and the array management approach for the product information transferred from a distributed system.

For the address book application, the recordset management approach will be used for the BODT. This class is called Persons because it tracks a set of records for the Person business class.

The code begins with the standard header:

```
' Class Name:    CPersons
' Author:        Deborah Kurata, InStep Technologies
' Date:          1/25/97
' Description:   Provides services to interface to
'                the data for all persons
' Edit History:
'
Option Explicit
```

The BODT class manages the recordset and copies the data for the current row in the recordset to the business object. This requires that the BODT class have a variable for the recordset. The recordset variable represents the logical set of data from the database that will be processed. The recordset can be a single table in the database or a set of records resulting from an SQL statement, QueryDef, or stored procedure.

The properties also include a reference to the Person object for the current record and a Boolean flag tracking the status of the current record. If the record has been changed and needs to be updated in the database, it is considered to be "dirty."

```
' Recordset
Private m_rs As Recordset

' Reference to a person object
Private m_Person As CPerson

' Dirty flag
Private m_bIsDirty As Boolean
```

Errors raised from the Persons class are defined in an enumeration. In a production-quality application, more errors would be defined here.

```
' Error constants
Enum persError
    persInitError = vbObjectError + 512 + 2000
End Enum
```

Property procedures are provided to expose needed private variables. The IsDirty Property procedures allow other parts of the code to set or retrieve the dirty state of the current record. The Person Property procedure returns the reference to the Person business object. This property is exposed to allow navigation down from the Persons class to the Person class. By convention, a Property procedure that returns the reference to another object is named using the class name, without the "C" prefix.

```
Public Property Get IsDirty() As Boolean
    IsDirty = m_bIsDirty
End Property
Public Property Let IsDirty(bIsDirty As Boolean)
    m_bIsDirty = bIsDirty
End Property
```

```
Public Property Get Person() As CPerson
    Set Person = m_Person
End Property
```

When this BODT class is initialized, the required recordset is opened. This code uses a dynaset-type recordset and opens the recordset based on a defined SQL statement. If the recordset only references one table, you could use a table-type recordset for performance reasons. Notice that the database object used when opening the recordset is the one defined in the Database class.

```
Private Sub Class_Initialize()
Dim sSQL As String
Dim sErr As String
On Error Resume Next

    ' Set the SQL statement
    sSQL = "select * from Person"

    ' Open the recordset
    Set m_rs = g_DB.db.OpenRecordset(sSQL, dbOpenDynaset)
    If Err.Number <> 0 Then
        sErr = Err.Description
        On Error GoTo 0
        Err.Raise dbOpenRSError, "CPersons::Initialize", _
            sErr
    End If

    ' Create the reference to a Person object
    Set m_Person = New CPerson
    If Err.Number <> 0 Then
        sErr = Err.Description
        On Error GoTo 0
        Err.Raise persInitError, "CPerson::Initialize", _
            sErr
    End If
End Sub
```

The last step in the initialization process is to create the reference to the Person class. The Persons class uses one Person class object to track the current record's data.

Both opening a recordset and instancing a Person object could cause an error, so error trapping is enabled with the On Error Resume Next statement. This allows specific error handling after each line that can cause an error. Note that an On Error GoTo 0 is required to turn off the error trap before using the Err.Raise method or the error trap will trap the raised error and resume at the next statement instead of raising the error to the calling routine. Because the On Error GoTo 0 statement clears the Err object values, the Err.Description is stored before clearing the error handler.

Many of the routines in this example do not include the error handling in order to keep the examples focused on the data transfer techniques. For your BODT class to be production-quality, all of the methods in the class need error handling implemented.

The Terminate event is used to close everything and free the references. If an error occurs in opening the recordset, any attempt to close the recordset generates another error. This code determines whether the recordset is open and only closes it if appropriate. It then frees the references to all objects it maintains.

```
Private Sub Class_Terminate()
On Error Resume Next
    ' Close the recordset and database
    If Not (m_rs Is Nothing) Then
        m_rs.Close
    End If

    ' Clear the references
    Set m_rs = Nothing
    Set m_Person = Nothing

End Sub
```

The Add method performs the required initialization for creating a new record. It first calls the Save method to save data for the current record. This provides the automatic saving facility. It then reinitializes the Person object. This is a quick way to clear all of the properties for the object.

```
' Add a new record
Public Sub Add()
    ' If the person object is dirty, save it
    Save

    ' Reinitialize
    Set m_Person = New CPerson
End Sub
```

Notice that this does not call the AddNew method on the recordset. This allows the user to cancel the creation of a new record at any point without concern for canceling the add. The AddNew method will be called when the new record is saved.

The Delete method deletes the current record from the database. It then executes the MoveFirst method on the recordset to move to a valid record position.

```
' Delete the current record
Public Sub Delete()
    m_rs.Delete
    m_rs.MoveFirst
End Sub
```

In some cases, you may need to keep track of deleted records for an audit trail or for historical review. You can track deleted records by modifying the Delete method to add the deleted record to a deleted record table before deleting it. Alternatively, you can retain the deleted record in the same table and prevent the record from being used as an active record by assigning a record status code. Instead of deleting the record, you could set the record status code to "D." When a recordset is created for the table, the statement

```
Where recStatus <> 'D'
```

could be used to collect only the active records. This Delete method could be modified to set that action code instead of performing the delete.

Keynote

This illustrates one of the benefits of using a class to encapsulate this functionality. The decision to use a record status code or deleted record table can be made at any point in a project, including a future revision, without affecting any of the modules or applications that use this class.

The FillPersonList method in the Persons class fills any list box or combo box with all of the entries from this recordset. This calls a generic FillList routine to fill the provided list.

```
' Fill any list with Person list data
Public Sub FillPersonList(lst As Control)
    FillList lst, "personID", "FirstName", "LastName"
End Sub
```

Tech Note. *This method and the FillList method described later make the assumption that this BODT class is in the same project as the form using the BODT. If the BODT class is in a separately compiled ActiveX component, you need to use a different technique for these methods because objects such as forms and controls should not be passed to ActiveX components. The FillPersonList and FillList routines could instead provide an array of the desired elements and the user interface component could load the control from the array.*

The FillList method fills any list box or combo box with all the records from a recordset. Because the number of fields to display in the list is not predefined, the last parameter in this method uses the ParamArray keyword to allow an undefined number of parameters. Each additional parameter passed to this method is passed into the sColumns array.

Tech Note. *This FillList method provides a generic method for a common requirement, so it is best added as a Public method in a generic data access class.*

The FillList method begins by saving the current location in the recordset using the recordset's Bookmark property. It resets the recordset pointer to the first record using MoveFirst and then processes each record in the recordset. It locates each of the fields passed into the sColumns array, concatenates them, and then adds the entry to the list box or combo box. The record ID is stored in the Item Data property to provide access to the record.

```
' Fill any list with the data from the recordset
' Parameters:
'    cbo         list type control to fill
'    sIDColumn   name of the column containing the record ID
'    sColumns    name of the columns of data to display
Private Sub FillList(cbo As Control, sIDColumn As String, ParamArray sColumns() As Variant)
Dim sData As String
Dim i As Integer
Dim bmCurrentPos As Variant
```

```
' Save the current position
bmCurrentPos = m_rs.Bookmark

' Clear the list
cbo.Clear

' Move to the first record
m_rs.MoveFirst

' Add each record until the end of the file
Do Until m_rs.EOF
    ' Concatenate each desired column
    sData = ""
    For i = 0 To UBound(sColumns)
        sData = sData & " " & m_rs(sColumns(i))
    Next i

    ' Add the item to the list
    cbo.AddItem sData
    cbo.ItemData(cbo.NewIndex) = m_rs(sIDColumn)

    ' Move to the next row
    m_rs.MoveNext
Loop

' Return to the current position
m_rs.Bookmark = bmCurrentPos
End Sub
```

When all the records in the recordset have been processed, the position in the recordset is returned to the original position. The control passed to this routine is now populated with the list of keys from the recordset.

Once a user selects a desired record from the list in the user interface of the application, the record ID can be retrieved using the ItemData. The user interface then calls the Find method and passes it the record ID to locate within the recordset. Before the Find method will find the record, it will save the data for the currently displayed record. This provides the automatic saving feature.

```
' Find the defined person record
' Parameters:
'   lID         ID of desired record
Public Sub Find(lID As Long)
Dim vBookmark As Variant

    ' If the person object is dirty, save it
    Save

    ' Find the requested person
    vBookmark = m_rs.Bookmark
    m_rs.FindFirst "personID = " & lID
    If m_rs.NoMatch = True Then
        ' Return to the bookmark
        m_rs.Bookmark = vBookmark
    Else
        UpdateObject
    End IfEnd Sub
```

The Find method stores a bookmark to the current record and then calls the FindFirst method of the recordset to find the ID in the recordset. If it is found, the UpdateObject method updates the object properties with values from the database. If the ID is not found, the recordset returns to the original record position using the bookmark. It could raise an error in this case if it is important for the calling routines to know that it did not find the requested record.

The UpdateObject method transfers the information from the current record to the object's properties. Each field in the record is retrieved using the following syntax:

```
m_rs!LastName
```

The exclamation point (!) denotes a collection lookup. This syntax is a shortcut notation for the following:

```
m_rs.Fields("LastName").Value
```

The recordset has a collection of fields. The Item method for the Fields collection is the default method, so you can access a particular item from the Fields collection by index number or key. In the case of the Fields collection, the key is the name of the field in the database. This syntax is similar to the Tasks collection from Chapter 11, "Building Classes: Additional Techniques." The Value property is the default property of the Field object, so it is not required. The collection lookup simply needs to define the key of the field to look up the value.

Tech Note. *You can also use the collection lookup syntax with your collections. For example, the following syntax*

```
m_colTasks.Item("T00005").Description
```

retrieves the description for the Task object with a key of "T00005." This syntax is equivalent to:

```
m_colTasks!T00005.Description
```

If Description were the default property of the Task object, this syntax would simply be

```
m_colTasks!T0005
```

The UpdateObject method uses the collection lookup syntax to retrieve each field from the table and copy the value of the field to the object's associated property.

```
' Copy the data to the Person object
Private Sub UpdateObject()
    With m_Person
        .LastName = m_rs!LastName & ""
        .FirstName = m_rs!FirstName & ""
```

```
                .Address = m_rs!Address & ""
                .City = m_rs!City & ""
                .State = m_rs!State & ""
                .ZipCode = m_rs!ZipCode & ""
                .Company = m_rs!Company & ""
                .Title = m_rs!Title & ""
                .Department = m_rs!Department & ""
                .Phone = m_rs!Phone & ""
                .FAX = m_rs!FAX & ""
                .EMail = m_rs!EMail & ""
                .Notes = m_rs!Notes & ""
                .ID = m_rs!PersonID
        End With
End Sub
```

Tech Note. *The "" following each entry ensures that a null is not assigned to the object properties.*

This method is private and cannot be called directly from outside of this class. Rather, it is called from the Find method to reset the object's properties to the record found in the recordset. After this method has been executed, the object's properties contain the field values from the current record and the user interface of the application can transfer the data from the object's properties to controls on the form. The user can then review or edit the information.

When the user has finished the required changes, the user interface can copy all of the user-entered values to the properties of the object and then call the Save method to save the changes. The Save method is also called from the Add and Find methods to automatically save current data before adding a new record or finding a different record. The Save method checks the dirty flag to determine whether the properties of the object have been changed. If so, it calls the private UpdateRecord method to update the record with the properties of the object and turns the dirty flag off.

```
' Save the current record
Public Sub Save()
    ' If the person object is dirty, save it
    If m_bIsDirty Then
        UpdateRecord
        ' Turn the dirty flag is off
        m_bIsDirty = False
    End If
End Sub
```

The UpdateRecord method transfers the information from the object's properties to the database. It begins by checking the current ID. If the ID is zero, it assumes there is a new record and performs the AddNew method of the recordset. If there is an existing record, it assumes this is an Edit operation. A record must be in AddNew or Edit mode before the fields can be set or the record updated. The fields are then transferred from the Person object back to the record in the recordset.

```
' Update the record with the current Person
' object properties
Private Sub UpdateRecord()
    ' If the ID is 0, it is a new
    If m_Person.ID = 0 Then
        m_rs.AddNew
    Else
        m_rs.Edit
    End If

    ' Copy the fields
    With m_Person
        m_rs!LastName = .LastName
        m_rs!FirstName = .FirstName
        m_rs!Address = .Address
        m_rs!City = .City
        m_rs!State = .State
        m_rs!ZipCode = .ZipCode
        m_rs!Company = .Company
        m_rs!Title = .Title
        m_rs!Department = .Department
        m_rs!Phone = .Phone
        m_rs!FAX = .FAX
        m_rs!EMail = .EMail
        m_rs!Notes = .Notes
    End With

    ' Do the Update
    m_rs.Update
    m_rs.Bookmark = m_rs.LastModified

    ' Retrieve the (new) ID
    m_Person.ID = m_rs!PersonID
End Sub
```

After the update, the Bookmark property is used to set the recordset position to the updated record. This is especially important for the AddNew operation, which will otherwise return to the location prior to the AddNew. The ID in the Person object is set from the record to ensure that the record has the correct ID. Again, this is most important for the AddNew operation where the ID was 0.

Keynote

When you have completed the BODT class you have the code to transfer property values from an object to a record in the database and from the current database record to the object's properties. This should be the only class that is aware of the database structure and the names of the fields in the recordset. Every other place in the application should reference the object properties.

Creating the Form

The user interface for your form should have been defined as part of the design process. For this example, the form is a simple Address Book, as shown in Figure 14.7.

The form for the address book application demonstrates how error handling can be accomplished. This example traps all errors in event procedures and notifies the user of the error with a message box. If this were a production-quality application, the error messages would be more user-friendly than those shown here, and the actual error information would be written to a log. Errors in other routines are raised to the user interface. This approach assumes that the event procedures will always be at the top of the call stack.

Tech Note. *To view the call stack when running the application, use the Call Stack option from the View menu.*

Because this example demonstrates a pure DAO application, there is no data control on the form and none of the controls on the form are bound. The controls are primarily simple text boxes. The buttons are displayed on the top line—instead of the standard bottom or side—so they are where the user will need them. The user can search for the desired person using the combo box in the upper-left corner. If the person is not found, the New button is easily within reach with only a small mouse movement.

Keynote

The code in the form is responsible for transferring information from the properties of the object to the controls on the form and changed values from the controls to the properties of the object. The form is oblivious as to how the object retrieved the value for the properties or how it will save them. This is the whole idea behind the three-tiered architecture: The user interface does not need to be concerned about how data is retrieved or saved.

The form event procedure that will contain the code to transfer the information entered by the user to the properties of the object will depend on the requirements of the application. Several choices are

- **LostFocus on the control.** One of the most user-friendly choices is to copy the information entered by the user to the appropriate business object property when the user leaves the field. Business rules defined in the Property Let procedure for the property are then executed and the user can get immediate feedback about any problems with the data entry. For example, if a Priority property must be between 0 and 4 and the user enters a 9, the Property Let procedure for the Priority raises an error. The form can handle the error and turn the text box foreground color to red to show the error.

  Tech Note. *In many cases, it is not a good idea to display a message box after every error in data entry. To see how this would be, try turning on your Auto Syntax Check setting by choosing Options from the Tools menu. Every time you make any mistake the IDE shouts at you with a message box. It is much nicer to have this setting off and simply see the errors in red. This same thing holds true for the users of your application.*

- **Click on a button.** A Save or OK button can transfer all of the user-entered information onto the properties of the business object. The user is then not notified of any business rule errors defined in the Property Let procedures until after selecting the button.

- **Click on a list or combo box.** The user-entered information can be transferred from the form to the properties of the business object when the user makes another selection. This provides an auto-saving feature much like that provided by the data control. This would be used in conjunction with the prior entry choice to allow an explicit save in addition to the automatic save.

The address book application uses the second two approaches. It transfers the data from the form to the properties of the object when the user moves off of the displayed record and when the user clicks on the Save button.

The form code begins with the standard header.

```
' Form Name:    frmPerson
' Author:       Deborah Kurata, InStep Technologies
' Date:         1/24/97
' Description:  Displays Address Book information
' Revisions:
'
Option Explicit
```

Because the Persons BODT class controls the Person object, the form will access the Person object properties through the Persons class. To identify that the form will use an object from the Persons class, an object variable is declared in the Declarations section of the form.

```
' Reference to a persons object
Private m_Persons As CPersons
```

As discussed in Chapter 9, "Strategies for Construction," using hard-coded numbers (called "magic numbers") throughout your application can make your code hard to read and maintain. In this example, enumerations were used to define constants for each button and text box on the form.

```
' Buttons
Enum persButton
    persSaveButton = 0
    persNewButton = 1
    persDeleteButton = 2
    persHelpButton = 3
End Enum

' Text boxes
Enum persText
    persFirstNameText = 0
    persLastNameText = 1
    persAddressText = 2
    persCityText = 4
    persStateText = 5
    persZipCodeText = 6
    persCompanyText = 7
    persTitleText = 8
    persDeptText = 9
```

```
        persPhoneText = 10
        persFAXText = 11
        persEMailText = 12
        persNotesText = 13
End Enum
```

When the form is loaded, the Load event is generated. Code in the Load event will create the instance of the Persons class.

```
Private Sub Form_Load()
On Error Resume Next

    ' Create the instance
    Set m_Persons = New CPersons
    If Err.Number <> 0 Then
        ' Display the error
        MsgBox "Error in application: " _
            & Err.Description
        Unload Me
    End If
End Sub
```

When the form is unloaded, any displayed data is saved. The references to the Persons class object and the form are then released.

```
Private Sub Form_Unload(Cancel As Integer)
On Error Resume Next
    ' Save any currently displayed data
    DoSave
    ' Clear the references
    Set m_Persons = Nothing
    Set frmPerson = Nothing
    End
End Sub
```

When the user drops down the combo box on the form, the DropDown event is generated. The code in this event clears the combo box and refills it with the list of person names along with their record IDs. The list is reset each time the combo box is dropped down to ensure that it contains the most up-to-date database information. If the data does not change frequently or if you want to maximize performance, it could be filled in the Load event and on an as-needed basis.

```
Private Sub cboPerson_DropDown()
On Error GoTo ERR_ROUTINE
    ' Clear the combo
    cboPerson.Clear

    ' Fill the combo box with the information from the database
    m_Persons.FillPersonList cboPerson
Exit Sub

ERR_ROUTINE:
    ' Display the error
    MsgBox "Error in application: " _
        & Err.Description
End Sub
```

When the user selects a person's name from the list, the record ID is retrieved from the ItemData property of the combo box and the DoFind method is called to find the ID in the recordset.

```
' When a person is selected, fill the form for this person
Private Sub cboPerson_Click()
On Error GoTo ERR_ROUTINE
    ' If something is selected
    If cboPerson.ListIndex <> -1 Then
        ' Fill the form for the selected person
        DoFind cboPerson.ItemData(cboPerson.ListIndex)
    End If
Exit Sub

ERR_ROUTINE:
    ' Display the error
    MsgBox "Error in application: " _
        & Err.Description
End Sub
```

The DoFind method first calls UpdateObject to copy all of the current values from the controls on the form to the Person object properties. This is necessary for the automatic saving feature. The DoFind method then calls the Find method in the Persons class to find the specified ID in the recordset. Recall that the Find method in the Persons BODT class will automatically save the current Person object properties, find the record with the defined ID in the recordset, and then copy the fields from that record to the Person object properties. The Person object properties are then copied to the controls on the form by calling the UpdateForm method in the DoFind routine.

```
' Do the Find
Private Sub DoFind(lID As Long)
On Error GoTo ERR_ROUTINE
    ' Update the object with current data
    UpdateObject

    ' Find the selected person
    m_Persons.Find lID

    ' Display the selected person in the form
    UpdateForm
Exit Sub

ERR_ROUTINE:
    Err.Raise Err.Number, Err.Source, Err.Description
End Sub
```

The preceding code basically performs the same operations that bound controls perform automatically. The code updates the recordset with the values from the controls on the form, finds the desired record in the recordset, and displays the values for that record in the controls on the form.

The UpdateForm method transfers the data from the Person object properties to controls on the form. This will invoke the Property Get procedure for each property.

Notice the use of the With...End With statements. This provides better efficiency when assigning a set of values for an object. The m_Persons.Person syntax is using the Person property in the Persons class to retrieve a pointer to the Person object.

```
' Update the controls on the form from the object
Private Sub UpdateForm()
On Error GoTo ERR_ROUTINE
    ' Display the selected person in the form
    With m_Persons.Person
        txtPerson(persFirstNameText).Text = .FirstName
        txtPerson(persLastNameText).Text = .LastName
        txtPerson(persAddressText).Text = .Address
        txtPerson(persCityText).Text = .City
        txtPerson(persStateText).Text = .State
        txtPerson(persZipCodeText).Text = .ZipCode
        txtPerson(persCompanyText).Text = .Company
        txtPerson(persTitleText).Text = .Title
        txtPerson(persDeptText).Text = .Department
        txtPerson(persPhoneText).Text = .Phone
        txtPerson(persFAXText).Text = .FAX
        txtPerson(persEMailText).Text = .EMail
        txtPerson(persNotesText).Text = .Notes
    End With

    ' This turned the dirty flag on
    ' Turn it back off
    m_Persons.IsDirty = False

    ' Ensure the correct buttons are enabled/disabled
    cmdPerson(iDELETE_BUTTON).Enabled = True
    cmdPerson(iSAVE_BUTTON).Enabled = False
Exit Sub

ERR_ROUTINE:
    Err.Raise Err.Number, Err.Source, Err.Description
End Sub
```

The Change event for the text box, shown next, sets the dirty flag on if the text box content is changed. This event is fired even if the text box contents are changed by the application, as was done in preceding the code, so that code needs to turn off the dirty flag. To make the application more user-friendly and provide better visual feedback, the previous code disables any buttons on the form that are not appropriate at any particular time. For example, if no changes have been changed, the Save button is disabled.

```
' When data has changed, enable the Save button
Private Sub txtPerson_Change(Index As Integer)
    cmdPerson(iSAVE_BUTTON).Enabled = True
    m_Persons.IsDirty = True
End Sub
```

When the Change event is fired, the Save button is enabled and the dirty flag is set. This flag helps ensure that any changes made by the user are saved to the database.

The command buttons on the form shown in Figure 14.7 were defined as a control array. This causes all events for the command buttons to use one set of event procedures. Constants for the control array indexes were defined at the top of this form module. These constants can be used to provide processing of the command button selection using a Select…Case statement.

If the New button is selected, the DoAdd method is called to add a new record. The Save button calls the DoSave method to save the currently displayed information. The Delete button calls the DoDelete method to delete the current record. The Help button is not implemented in the following code:

```
Private Sub cmdPerson_Click(Index As Integer)
On Error GoTo ERR_ROUTINE
    Select Case Index
        Case persNewButton
            ' Clear the screen for a new entry
            DoAdd

        Case persSaveButton
            ' Put the current data
            ' from the form to the object
            DoSave

        Case persDeleteButton
            ' Delete the current person
            DoDelete

        Case persHelpButton
            ' *** Help file would go here
            MsgBox "This will display help."
    End Select
Exit Sub

ERR_ROUTINE:
    ' Display the error
    MsgBox "Error in application: " _
        & Err.Description
End Sub
```

The DoAdd method calls UpdateObject to transfer the current data from the controls on the form to the properties of the object and then calls the Persons class Add method. The Add method of the Persons class automatically saves the current data, if the data had been changed, and initializes the Person object to clear the properties. After executing the Add, the UpdateForm method is called to copy the empty properties to the controls on the form, basically clearing the form. Clearing the form in this manner ensures that any defaults defined in the Property procedures for the properties will appear on the form correctly. The Delete button is then disabled and the combo box selection is cleared.

```
' Add a new record
Private Sub DoAdd()
On Error GoTo ERR_ROUTINE
    ' Update the object with current data
    UpdateObject
```

```
        ' Add the new record
        m_Persons.Add

        ' Clear the fields
        UpdateForm

        ' Enable/disable the buttons
        cmdPerson(iDELETE_BUTTON).Enabled = False

        ' Clear the combo selection
        cboPerson.ListIndex = -1
Exit Sub

ERR_ROUTINE:
        Err.Raise Err.Number, Err.Source, Err.DescriptionEnd Sub
```

When deleting a record, you need to decide what you will do after the delete. You can't leave the information for the deleted record displayed on the screen or the user will assume that the record wasn't deleted. You could move to the first record and display it, but what are the chances that the user would really want to see that first record? The DoDelete method, shown next, will delete the record and call DoAdd to clear the screen and prepare for entry of a new record.

```
' Delete the displayed record
Private Sub DoDelete()
On Error GoTo ERR_ROUTINE
        ' Delete the current record
        m_Persons.Delete

        ' Do a new so the screen is cleared
        DoAdd
Exit Sub

ERR_ROUTINE:
        Err.Raise Err.Number, Err.Source, Err.Description
End Sub
```

The DoSave method is executed when the user explicitly selects the Save button. If the dirty flag is set, this method calls the UpdateObject method to update the object properties with the values from the controls on the form. It then calls the Save method in the Persons class to save the property values to the database.

```
' Save the current record
Private Sub DoSave()
On Error GoTo ERR_ROUTINE
        If m_Persons.IsDirty Then
                ' Update the object with current data
                UpdateObject

                ' Save the data
                m_Persons.Save

                ' Enable the delete button
                cmdPerson(persDeleteButton).Enabled = True
                ' Disable the save button
                cmdPerson(persSaveButton).Enabled = False
```

```
        End If

Exit Sub
ERR_ROUTINE:
        Err.Raise Err.Number, Err.Source, Err.DescriptionEnd Sub
```

The UpdateObject code will only be executed if the user makes a change to one of the property values, which results in the dirty flag being set. If the dirty flag is set, the value from each text box is transferred to the appropriate object property. This will invoke the Property Let procedure for each property. In most applications, the Property Let procedures contain code for validation and will raise an error if a value is not valid. If the Person object in this example had validation, this routine would need to trap for validation errors and proceed accordingly.

```
' Update object from controls on the form
Private Sub UpdateObject()
On Error GoTo ERR_ROUTINE
        ' If the current information has changed, copy
        ' it back to the person object
        If m_Persons.IsDirty Then
            With m_Persons.Person
                ' Set the values from the form to the class
                .FirstName = txtPerson(persFirstNameText).Text
                .LastName = txtPerson(persLastNameText).Text
                .Address = txtPerson(persAddressText).Text
                .City = txtPerson(persCityText).Text
                .State = txtPerson(persStateText).Text
                .ZipCode = txtPerson(persZipCodeText).Text
                .Company = txtPerson(persCompanyText).Text
                .Title = txtPerson(persTitleText).Text
                .Department = txtPerson(persDeptText).Text
                .Phone = txtPerson(persPhoneText).Text
                .FAX = txtPerson(persFAXText).Text
                .EMail = txtPerson(persEMailText).Text
                .Notes = txtPerson(persNotesText).Text

            End With
        End If
Exit Sub

ERR_ROUTINE:
        Err.Raise Err.Number, Err.Source, Err.Description
End Sub
```

As you can see, the form contains quite a bit of code. Some developers like to keep the code in the form at a minimum to optimize form load time. To meet this goal, you could create a form support class and move a large amount of this code into the form support class.

Creating the Sub Main Procedure

Most applications should start with a Sub Main procedure instead of a startup form. This allows you to run code before displaying any form and to display a set of forms.

The Main module for the address book application starts with a standard header:

```
' Module Name:   MMain
' Author:        Deborah Kurata, InStep Technologies
' Date:          1/24/97
' Description:   Start up module for
'                Address Book application
' Revisions:
'
Option Explicit
```

A public reference to the Database class is defined in this procedure. That makes the Database class, and hence the database, easily accessible to all parts of the application.

```
' Global reference to the database class
Public g_DB As CDatabase
```

The Sub Main procedure in the main module creates the instance of the database class and then sets the dbName property to the name of the database. Looking back to the Property procedures for dbName in the Database class, you will find that the Property Let procedure opens the database when a name is assigned. The last step in the Sub Main is to show the main form. All other processing is handled from that main form.

```
Sub Main()
On Error GoTo ERR_ROUTINE
    ' Create the instance of the database class
    Set g_DB = New CDatabase

    ' Open the database
    g_DB.dbName = App.Path & "\Person.mdb"

    ' Show the main form
    frmPerson.Show
Exit Sub

ERR_ROUTINE:
    MsgBox "This application had an error: " & _
        Err.Description
End Sub
```

When you have finished creating the Sub Main procedure, you have completed the database application. If you have copied the database for the application from the CD-ROM as identified in the Appendix, you should be able to run the application and maintain a set of addresses in your address book.

What Did This Cover?

This section explained how to create a full—albeit small—object-oriented database application using classes and the data access objects (DAO). You can use these techniques to create any database application.

Compare the amount of code required here for working with the DAO to the code that used a data control in the previous section. As you can see, there is a significant amount of code required when working with the DAO.

■ Summary

- You can access databases by using the data control, remote data control, data access objects (DAO), remote data object (RDO), active data objects (ADO), an API or a combination of these.

- You can access remote databases with the data control or DAO 3.5, using ODBCDirect. Or, using the Enterprise Edition of Visual Basic, you can use the remote data control and remote data objects.

- The data control can be bound to a specific set of data from a database. Other controls, such as text boxes, list boxes, grids, and controls you develop can be bound to the data control. This allows development of a database application with no code.

- The recordset created by the data control is available to the application. You can use it to set properties or access methods of the recordset. This lets you retain the benefits of using the data control yet have the flexibility of coding unique requirements.

- The VB Data Form Wizard provides a quick and easy way to create a table maintenance form.

- For complete flexibility, the application can abandon the data control and handle all data processing with the data access objects (DAO).

- A logical three-tiered database application will have forms, business object classes, and business object data transfer (BODT) classes.

- The form handles the transfer of information from the user interface to the business object properties.

- The business object class contains the properties and methods of the business object. It also includes validation of property values and other business rules.

- The BODT class handles transfer of information from the business object properties to the database. This encapsulates all the information about a specific recordset into one class. If the fields in that recordset are later changed, this is the only class that is affected.

- A BODT class can be implemented to manage the recordset for a data control, a collection of business objects, the recordset itself, or an array of data from a recordset.

- You can create a generic Database class to handle the basic database operations such as opening and closing the database.

■ Additional Reading

Jennings, Roger. "Activate Data Objects with OLE DB," *Visual Basic Programmer's Journal*, December 1996

   This article quotes Microsoft to say, "Over time, all our products will standardize on ADO and OLE DB." It then describes the OLE DB object model and how it compares to DAO and RDO.

Jennings, Roger. *Database Developer's Guide with Visual Basic 5*. Indianapolis, Indiana: Sams Publishing, July 1997.

   This book describes how to access data using Visual Basic 5. It includes information on three-tiered architecture and using the data access object (DAO) and remote data objects (RDO).

Storage, Bill. "Taming the Wild Variant," *Visual Basic Programmer's Journal*, Vol. 6, No. 9, August 1996.

   This article describes how to use Variants to create fully dynamic two-dimensional arrays. This technique is useful for passing data between remote components.

Vaughn, William R. *The Hitchhiker's Guide to Visual Basic & SQL Server, Fourth Edition*. Redmond, Washington: Microsoft Press, 1996.

   This book provides details about accessing remote data from Visual Basic, including DAO, RDO, RDC and the ODBC. This book is packed with sample code, and provides must-read information when doing client/server applications.

Guide to Data Access Objects: Professional Features

   The Microsoft Visual Basic documentation for accessing databases is very well written and includes many examples. It is recommended reading if you will be doing database objects.

■ Think It Over

To supplement and review the information in this chapter, think about the following:

1. Think about how you have done data accessing in the past. If you have used data controls, think about how you would make use of the data control's recordset.

2. Create a database and try the three methods of accessing the data: data control, data control with code, and DAO. Notice the time difference required for the development of each of the three methods.

3. Review how the ParamArray keyword was used in the database application. Think about other places you could use this keyword.

4. Consider the different ways to create a business object data transfer (BODT) class, and then pick a past database project you have done and think about how you would implement it using a BODT.

15

Putting the Pieces Together

Ah, to build, to build!

That is the noblest art of all the arts.

Painting and sculpture are but images,

Are merely shadows cast by outward things

On stone or canvas, having in themselves

No separate existence. Architecture,

Existing in itself, and not in seeming

A something it is not, surpasses them

As substance shadow.

—Henry Wadsworth Longfellow (1807–82), U.S. poet

After you have completed the design of the architecture and are familiar with the builder's tools, you are ready to develop something that has its own substance and existence. You are ready to build your application.

The chapters in Parts 1 and 2 of this book provided information to help you design your application. The chapters in Part 3 have shown you how to use the object-oriented tools available in Visual Basic. This chapter will provide information on a few additional tools and techniques and then describe how to put the pieces together to construct a production-quality application.

■ Using a Resource File

A *resource file* is a special type of file that can contain icons, bitmaps, wave files, cursors, strings, and other binary information. This file can be compiled and added to your Visual Basic application.

Keynote

Using a resource file instead of including the resources (strings, icons, and so on) directly in your application has several advantages:

- **Resources are loaded when needed**. The resources from the resource file are loaded when the code loads them. Resources added directly to a form are loaded when the form is loaded, even if it is not visible. When you add the resources to a resource file instead, the form can be loaded more quickly and required resources can be loaded as needed.

- **Localization is easier**. The application can be localized by simply adding the resource strings or bitmaps for the other languages into the resource file. This requires no changes to the software and prevents the translators from needing the source code of the application.

- **Maintenance does not require a programmer**. Another organization can maintain the strings for the application. In some of the applications I have developed for clients, the training organization wanted control of the content for message boxes and screen elements. Resource files make it easy for nonprogrammers to maintain these strings.

Creating a Resource File

Creating a resource file is much like creating a help file—it requires a specific set of steps and some additional tools outside the Visual Basic development environment.

1. Create the individual resource files for each icon, bitmap, wave file, or cursor.

   You can use any tool for this task, such as Microsoft Image Editor or Microsoft Paint.

2. Create a resource definition file listing all of the individual resource files and any string resources.

    You can use any text editor for this job, such as Notepad or WordPad. Only one resource file can be added to a project, so a reference to every icon, bitmap, wave file, or cursor and every resource string in the application can be added to the resource file.

    The file will look like this:

    ```
    //Resource File for the contact management system application
    //Bitmaps
    2     BITMAP MOVEABLE PURE "cms.bmp"

    //String Table
    STRINGTABLE DISCARDABLE
    BEGIN
    2     "Please log in"
    3     "User Name:"
    4     "Password:"
    5     "The User Name and Password entry were not found. Please try again."
    END
    ```

    This resource file defines a sequential set of constants, 2 through 5, for the login screen. All resources added for a particular screen or object should be grouped together in a sequential order in this resource file to make the resources easier to maintain. Skip numbers between groups to simplify later additions.

Tech Note.   *The resource ID of 1 is reserved for the application icon and should not be used.*

3. Compile the resource file using the RC application that comes with the Professional and Enterprise Editions of Visual Basic.

    The command line for this would be similar to the following:

    ```
    C:\DevStudio\VB\Wizards\Rc.exe D:\MyProject\Cms.rc
    ```

    The compiled file will have an .res extension.

Referencing the Resource File

After the resource file is compiled, you can add the file to your application and retrieve resources from the file as they are needed. The steps for working with the resource file are as follows:

1. Choose the Add File option from the File menu and add the compiled .res file to your project.

2. The resources are then available to your application.

3. Define the offset to the group of resources for a particular object or screen.

The resource offset constant for the login screen is as follows:

```
' Resource constants
Const loginResOffset = 2
```

If your application will use resources from the resource file in several places, you may want to make these constants a global enumeration. This makes it easier to track and maintain the resource numbers.

4. Use LoadResPicture to load in bitmaps, icons, and cursors; use LoadResString to load string resources; use LoadResData for any binary information.

The following code retrieves a picture from the resource file and adds it to the picture property of the form. The picture appears in the upper-left corner of the screen, as shown in Figure 15.1. Strings are retrieved from the file for the form caption text and the two field labels. The button captions could have been stored in the resource file as well.

Figure 15.1

The login screen uses a resource file to load the bitmap for the icon in the left corner and the strings for the window caption and labels.

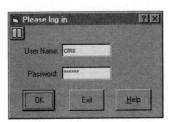

```
' Define constants for the text boxes
Private Enum LoginTextIndex
    loginUserIDText = 1
    loginPasswordText = 2
End Enum

' Resource constants
Const loginResOffset = 2

Private Sub Form_Load()
    ' Load the resources
    Me.Picture = LoadResPicture(loginResOffset, vbResBitmap)
    Me.Caption = LoadResString(loginResOffset)
```

```
        lblLogin(loginUserIDText).Caption = _
            LoadResString(loginUserIDText + loginResOffset)
        lblLogin(loginPasswordText).Caption = _
            LoadResString(loginPasswordText + loginResOffset)
End Sub
```

Notice that the string resources in this example are in the same order as the text box control array. This allows the individual string resource IDs to be defined by adding the login screen resource offset to the control array index. This same constant can be used for the help system. More on that later in this chapter.

Tech Note. *Here's a tip for working with string resources. Set the Caption of the label, or other control, to the correct text prefixed with an "x." This allows you to more easily see which field on a form is which and helps you to ensure that the resource file is correctly setting the Caption. Any Caption with an "x" remaining at run time is not correctly being retrieved from the resource file.*

■ Using the Registry

The Windows *Registry* is a centralized repository for configuration or context information. It offers an alternative to the .ini files used in prior versions of Windows. The Windows Registry was discussed in detail in Chapter 8, "Data Design."

Keynote

There are two basic methods for accessing the registry. You can use either the Windows application programming interface (API) or the SaveSetting, GetSetting, GetAllSettings, and DeleteSetting methods provided in Visual Basic.

In this example, the registry will be used to store the last defined location of the contact management system main window. The code to save the location of the window is in the Unload event for the form. The parameters for the SaveSetting function includes the application name, a section name, a key name, and a key value. In this example, a section called "MainForm" was defined with two keys: Top and Left.

```
Private Sub Form_Unload(Cancel As Integer)

    ' Save the current window location
    SaveSetting App.EXEName, "MainForm", "Top", CStr(Me.Top)
    SaveSetting App.EXEName, "MainForm", "Left", CStr(Me.Left)

    <other Unload code>
    End
End Sub
```

The settings are retrieved from the registry during the Load event. The parameters for the GetSetting function are similar to the SaveSetting function.

```
Private Sub Form_Load()
Dim lTop As Long, lLeft As Long
    <other Load code>
```

```
            lTop = Val(GetSetting(App.EXEName, "MainForm", "Top"))
            lLeft = Val(GetSetting(App.EXEName, "MainForm", "Left"))
            Me.Move lLeft, lTop

            <other Load code>
End Sub
```

These settings are written into the registry under the key HKEY_CURRENT_ USER\ Software\VB and VBA Program Settings\cms15\ MainForm, as shown in Figure 15.2. If you want to store information in some other key, you need to use the API functions RegCloseKey, RegCreateKeyEx, RegDeleteKey, RegOpenKeyEx, RegQueryValueEx, and RegSetValueEx. (Check out the downloads in http://www.citilink.com/~jgarrick/vbasic/ for an example.)

Figure 15.2

Visual Basic provides features to read and write registry settings, but only in a predefined registry location.

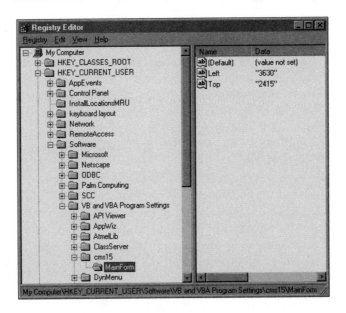

■ Logging Events

In production-quality applications, you will want to log certain events such as application startup, the ID of the user logging in, error information, and application termination. This provides information that the organization can use to determine how an application is being used, who is using it, and important information for tracking down errors. It can also be used within ActiveX components to track how and when the components are being used and to log any component errors.

Keynote

In prior versions of Visual Basic, you had to write your own event logging routine or use the Windows API to access the Windows NT event log. Visual Basic 5 introduces a new set of properties and methods for directly writing to the event log.

To encapsulate event logging, an Error class was developed for the contact management system. The primary routine in that class is as follows:

```
' Standard error routine
' Any error that requires a log entry should call this routine.
' Parameters:
'    sMessage      String message
'    lErrLogType Type of error
Public Sub ErrorLog(sMessage As String, lErrLogType As Long)
Dim sPrintMsg As String

    ' Add the date and time to the message.
    sPrintMsg = Now & Space(5) & sMessage

    ' If it was an error message, append actual error info
    If lErrLogType = vbLogEventTypeError Then
        sPrintMsg = sMessage & vbCrLf & _
            " Error: [" & Err.Number & "]: " & _
            Err.Description & _
            " Error in: " & Err.Source
    End If

    ' Write it in the event log
    App.LogEvent sPrintMsg, lErrLogType

    ' Output the string to the debug window as well
    Debug.Print sPrintMsg

End Sub
```

This routine accepts the message and an event log type. The message can be any text, but the event log type is expected to be one of the predefined event logging constants: vbLogEventTypeError, vbLogEventTypeInformation, or vbLogEventTypeWarning. The ErrorLog routine concatenates the date and time onto the message. If the type indicates that it was an error, the error number, description, and source are appended to the message. The LogEvent method of the App object is then called to write the message as an application event to the event log.

The LogEvent method will, by default, write the message to the Windows NT event log if the user is running Windows NT, and to a file called Vbevents.log in the Windows directory if the user is running Windows 95. You can set a different log file name and additional logging options by using the StartLogging method of the App object.

To prevent event log clutter, events are not logged when running at design time. The code in the ErrorLog method shown previously works around this by writing the messages to the Immediate window when running at design time. If you want to test your error logging, you need to compile the application and run the executable.

Keynote

■ Expanding Visual Basic Functionality with the Windows API

Visual Basic is getting more and more powerful with each release. However, there are still features available in Windows that are not accessible directly from Visual Basic. For example, suppose you want to present a modeless window as a topmost window to create a toolbox or splash screen. If you want to provide this Windows feature in your Visual Basic application, you need to use the Windows application programming interface (API). The Windows API is simply a set of functions provided with Windows. Using the Windows API you can get information about the system, send messages to controls, manage device output, and much more.

This section presents a very brief overview of using the Windows API from Visual Basic. The definitive work on this topic is the book *Dan Appleman's Programmer's Visual Basic 5.0 Guide to the Win32 API*. See the "Additional Reading" section at the end of this chapter for the reference to that work.

What Will This Cover?

This section will cover the following key Visual Basic features:

- Declaring a Windows API function or constant

- Using the API Viewer

- Calling a Windows API function

- Using AddressOf

Each of these features is detailed in the topics that follow.

Declaring a Windows API Function or Constant

To use a Windows API function, you first need to declare the function. This declaration defines the name of the function, the name of the Windows DLL containing the function, and the parameters and return value for the function. This is sometimes called the *function prototype*. If the function requires specific constant values, the constants must also be declared.

If the API function or associated constants must be available to multiple modules in your application, you need to declare them as public in a standard module. These could be added to the same standard module containing the Sub Main. Normally, however, you will want to wrap the API function in a method of a class to provide the functionality of the API call, yet keep the API details encapsulated in one class. You can then declare the function and associated constants as private.

For example, a class module will contain an onTop property that will make a form topmost. The API function call that can set a form as topmost is SetWindowPos. Here are the declarations for that function and its associated constants:

```
'Declare for formSetTopMost
Private Declare Function SetWindowPos Lib "user32" _
 (ByVal hwnd As Long, ByVal hWndInsertAfter As Long, _
 ByVal x As Long, ByVal y As Long, ByVal cx As Long, _
 ByVal cy As Long, ByVal wFlags As Long) As Long

' SetWindowPos hwndInsertAfter values
Const HWND_TOPMOST = -1
Const HWND_NOTOPMOST = -2
' SetWindowPos Flags
Const SWP_NOSIZE = &H1
Const SWP_NOMOVE = &H2
Const SWP_NOACTIVATE = &H10
```

Tech Note. *You may be able to achieve the desired topmost behavior by defining a parent for the form. For example, a toolbox window you create will reside over a main window if the main window is defined to be the parent of the toolbox window. See "Completing User Interface Details" later in this chapter for more information on defining a parent window.*

Using the API Viewer

As shown in the preceding code, the Windows API declarations are often long and complex. Instead of manually typing them, you can add these declarations to your application using the API Viewer (Apiload.exe) that comes with Visual Basic, Professional Edition and Enterprise Edition. This application displays the constants, declarations, and types for API function calls, as shown in Figure 15.3. You can select the desired constants and declaration from the list, copy them to the Clipboard, and paste them directly into your application.

Calling a Windows API Function

After the function and associated constants are declared, you can call the function as you call any other function. However, you need to be aware of differences between the data types used by Visual Basic and the types expected by the Windows API. Refer to Appleman's book for details on the correct Visual Basic data types required for a particular Windows API function call.

The code for the onTop property that uses the SetWindowPos API function declared earlier is shown here:

```
' When this property is set, the window is made top most
Public Property Let OnTop(frmTop As Form, bSetOnTop As Boolean)
    If bSetOnTop = True Then
        ' Set the window to topmost window
        Call SetWindowPos(frmTop.hwnd, HWND_TOPMOST, 0, 0, 0, 0, _
            SWP_NOSIZE Or SWP_NOMOVE Or SWP_NOACTIVATE)
```

Figure 15.3

The API Viewer makes it easier to include the correct API declaration for constants, functions, or types in your application. Add each needed element to the selected items list and then choose Copy to copy the declarations to the Clipboard.

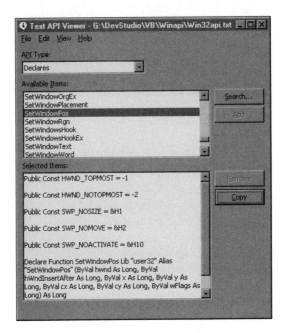

```
      Else
        ' Set the window to not topmost window
        Call SetWindowPos(frmTop.hwnd, HWND_NOTOPMOST, 0, 0, 0, 0, _
                   SWP_NOSIZE Or SWP_NOMOVE Or SWP_NOACTIVATE)
      End If
End Property
```

This Property procedure expects a form and a flag identifying whether to turn the topmost property on or off. The SetWindowPos API function call is then executed. The call expects the window handle of the form, provided by Visual Basic in the hwnd property, a constant defining the placement of the window in the z-order, a set of longs identifying the location and size of the window, and some flags identifying window properties.

Note that API calls normally expect window coordinates in pixels while Visual Basic normally uses twips. Visual Basic provides the two functions TwipPerPixelX and TwipPerPixelY to provide conversion between twips and pixels.

Using AddressOf

Several Windows API calls require the use of callbacks. Callbacks were demonstrated in Chapter 11, "Building Classes: Additional Techniques," where a reference, or pointer, to an object was passed to another object. The second object could then call back the first object because it had its reference. The

Keynote

Windows API does not know about your objects, so it wants a pointer to a function, not a pointer to an object.

A new Visual Basic 5 feature lets you pass a pointer to a function using the AddressOf operator. When you use AddressOf, Visual Basic passes the address of a defined procedure to the Windows API function. The Windows API function can then call back to the defined procedure.

Tech Note.   *You should only use AddressOf in a call to an API procedure. You cannot use AddressOf to call a procedure from another Visual Basic procedure. Instead, use the techniques described in Chapter 11 or use an Event.*

To use the AddressOf operator in an API function, follow these steps:

1. Write the function that will be called back.

   This function must have the correct parameters as expected for the callback. See Dan Appleman's book, listed in the "Additional Reading" section at the end of this chapter, for that information.

   For example:

   ```
   Function MyEnumFontFamProc(lpNLF As LOGFONT, lpNTM As NEWTEXTMETRIC, _
       ByVal FontType As Long, LParam As ListBox) As Long
   Dim sFaceName As String
       sFaceName = StrConv(lpNLF.lfFaceName, vbUnicode)
       LParam.AddItem Left$(sFaceName, InStr(sFaceName, vbNullChar) - 1)
       MyEnumFontFamProc = 1
   End Function
   ```

   Watch out for errors in this function. You cannot raise errors back to the Windows API function. Using an On Error Resume Next will prevent errors from propagating to the Windows API, but can also mask problems with your function.

2. Declare the API function.

   For example:

   ```
   Declare Function EnumFontFamilies Lib "gdi32" Alias _
       "EnumFontFamiliesA" _
       (ByVal hDC As Long, ByVal lpszFamily As String, _
       ByVal lpEnumFontFamProc As Long, LParam As Any) As Long
   ```

3. Call the API function and use the AddressOf operator to pass the name of the function created in Step 1.

   For example:

   ```
   EnumFontFamilies hDC, vbNullString, AddressOf MyEnumFontFamProc, LB
   ```

Tech Note.   *For a complete example of using the EnumFontFamilies function, including the necessary type declarations and constants, see the Visual Basic online help example for AddressOf or consult Dan Appleman's book, which is listed in the "Additional Reading" section at the end of this chapter.*

■ Defining Global Objects

If you have a library of standard functions, basically any set of functions, you can add those functions to a class module and expose them using the Public key word on the function declarations. If you compile the class as an ActiveX component following the steps defined in Chapter 13, "Building ActiveX Components," you can reuse your library in any project and provide the library to any other developer without providing the source code.

For a simple example, a function library that provides mathematical calculations could be implemented as a class in an ActiveX component and used as follows:

```
Private m_Math As CMath

Private Sub Form_Load()
    Set m_Math = New CMath
End Sub

Private Sub cmdAdd_Click()
    m_Math.FirstValue = txtAdd(0).Text
    m_Math.SecondValue = txtAdd(1).Text
    txtAdd(2).Text = m_Math.AddValues
End Sub
```

Keynote

To use your library, developers need to declare an object variable, create an instance of the object, and use the object variable to invoke the properties and methods. Wouldn't it be nice if there were an easier way? Visual Basic 5 allows you to define global objects that don't need to be declared or created. Simply set the Instancing property of the class module to GlobalMultiUse to define a global object. Developers can then use the library without having to declare an object variable or create an instance of the object.

If the CMath class had its Instancing property set to GlobalMultiUse and the application had a reference to the component containing the CMath class, the preceding code would simply be as follows:

```
Private Sub cmdAdd_Click()
    FirstValue = txtAdd(0).Text
    SecondValue = txtAdd(1).Text
    txtAdd(2).Text = AddValues
End Sub
```

Keynote

Using GlobalMultiUse can have a serious affect on readability. The GlobalMultiUse setting is only recommended for truly generic functionality. You must take care in naming properties and methods for the global objects because of the possible conflict with other global names.

Tech Note. *You can use a global object to define global constants when you cannot use an enumeration. An enumeration can only define long integer constants, so you can define string and other constants using a global object.*

■ Completing User Interface Details

The prototype of the user interface of an application is frequently created during the design phase. When you move into the development phase of your project, the user interface needs to be completed. This normally involves polishing the look of the forms, adding forms such as a splash screen and about box, and adding additional user interface details.

Figure 15.4 shows the user interface of the main screen for the contact management system. This screen is used to define each contact made with a particular person. Through the View menu, this screen provides access to the Address Book form and To Do List form developed in previous chapters.

Figure 15.4

The main screen in the contact management system allows the user to define each contact made with a particular person.

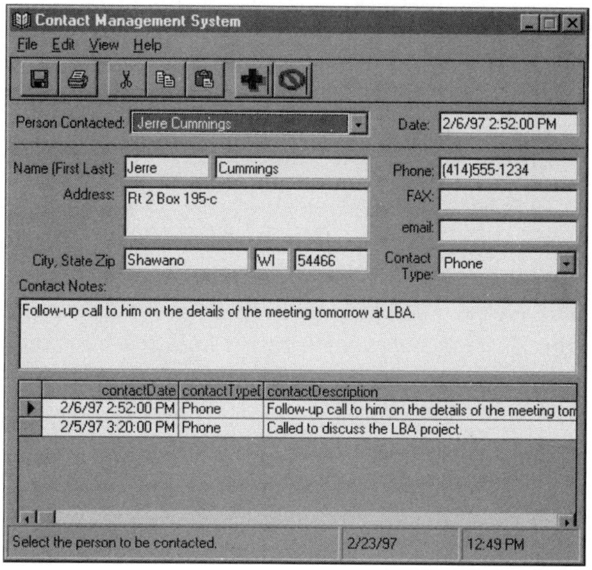

This section describes some tips and techniques for polishing your application's user interface.

What Will This Cover?

This section will cover the following:

- Defining window size and placement

- Implementing drag and drop of text

- Polishing the menu

- Handling a File menu

- Handling an Edit menu

- Building a Window class

- Adding pop-up menus

- Adding a toolbar

- Adding a status bar

- Defining icons for the application

- Providing help in the application

Defining Window Size and Placement

Visual Basic provides several new tools to help you place windows on the user's screen. These tools are

- **Form Designer window**. You may have noticed the window around your forms in the IDE. This is the Form Designer window. It separates the form displayed to the user from the window you use to create the form. Making these two separate windows allows you to adjust the amount of the form you see at design time without affecting the size of the form that will appear to the user.

    Tech Note.   *You may not see the Form Designer window around your forms if you are running using the SDI development environment.*

- **Form Layout window**. Use the Form Layout option from the View menu to display the Form Layout window. This window allows you to visually define at design time where your forms will appear at run time. You can drag the current form to any location on the Form Layout window, including locations outside of the viewable area. To help you size and place the forms, you can set Resolution Guides for 640x480 and 800x600, as shown in Figure 15.5. To turn on the guides, right-click on the Form Layout window and choose Resolution Guides from the context menu.

- **New form properties**. The new StartUpPosition property defines the startup location of a form at run time. You can display the window centered on its parent window, centered on the screen, or allow Windows to place the form in its default location. There is also a new Moveable property that locks a window in place and prevents the user from moving it.

- **Defining a window owner**. A new parameter on the Show method for a form allows you to specify an owner form to establish a parent/child relationship between the owner form and the form being shown. When you define a parent/child relationship, the child form is minimized when the

Figure 15.5

Use the Form Layout
Window to define window
placement at design time.

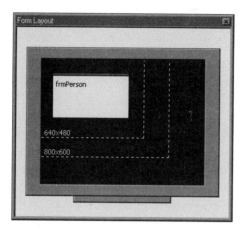

parent is minimized and unloaded when the parent form is unloaded.
Setting a window owner also makes the child window appear in front of
the parent window. Depending on the design of your application, this
may not be a desired behavior.

When you run the completed contact management system, discussed
later in this chapter, you can see this behavior. If you open the Address
Book window it will appear on top of the main window. If you then minimize the main window, the Address Book window will be minimized.

Implementing Drag and Drop of Text

Another new feature in Visual Basic 5 is the ability to drag and drop text or
graphics from one control to another control in your application or in any
other application. This ability, called OLE drag-and-drop, is implemented by
setting the OLEDragMode and OLEDropMode to Automatic for the controls.

Tech Note.   *This feature is different from the standard drag and drop
feature that lets you drag and drop controls. Instead, this feature lets you drag
and drop the contents of controls.*

Keynote

Imagine being able to let a user drag a name and address from an Address Book window into a Word document, or drag some notes from the
Contract Management window into the description of a task on the To
Do List window. This is now as simple as setting two properties for the
controls. For more control, you can also manage the OLE drag-and-drop
operations in code.

When you run the completed contact management system, discussed
later in this chapter, you can try out the drag and drop feature. Open the To

Do List window and drag text from the Contact Notes field in the Contact Management main window to the Description field in the To Do List window. You can also try dragging from the list of tasks in the To Do List window to the notes in the Contact Management main window.

Tech Note. *When you drag text you are removing it from its original location and dropping it to the new location. To instead drop a copy of the text at the new location, hold down the Ctrl key when dropping the text.*

Polishing the Menu

The menu you created for the prototype during the design phase of the project should be polished for use in the production-quality application. Make sure you have shortcut keys and other menu and menu option properties set appropriately and add all of the required code to handle the menus.

Keynote

You can update the menu or set the menu option properties using the Menu Editor. A new VB5 menu editing feature is the ability to update menu properties using the Properties window. Each menu and menu item is listed in the combo box at the top of the Properties window. You can select the menu or menu item and then adjust the properties, as shown in Figure 15.6.

Figure 15.6

The menus and menu options are now listed in the Properties window so you can edit menu properties without opening the Menu Editor.

You add code to handle the menus in the Click event of the menu options. The usual code required for the File and Edit menus is presented in the next topics.

Handling a File Menu

Normally, the File menu in an application allows the users to open new or existing files, save files, print, and exit. The New menu option creates a new file, which is normally specific to an application. The Open, Save As, and Print menu options call routines that access the Open, Save As, or Print common dialog box. However, application-specific code is required to open, save, or print the selected file. The Save menu option saves any changes to the file and Print Preview displays a preview of the file to the screen; both of these are also application-specific. The Exit menu option simply unloads the form. Any specialized code for the unload would be in the QueryUnload or Unload event for the form.

If all of the File menu options are in a control array, they are handled in one event procedure by matching the control array index with the defined menu option constants as shown in the following code:

```
' File menu options
Enum salesFileMenu
    salesFileNew = 0
    salesFileOpen = 1
    salesFileSave = 2
    salesFileSaveAs = 3
    salesFilePrint = 5
    salesFilePrintPreview = 6
    salesFileExit = 8
End Enum

Private Sub mnuFile_Click(index As Integer)
Dim sFileName As String
Dim iNumCopies As Integer

    Select Case index

        Case salesFileNew
            ' Create the new file
            ' *** Code needed here to create a new file
            MsgBox "Code here would create a new file"

        Case salesFileOpen
            ' Use the common dialog to retrieve a file name
            FileOpenDB cdlg, sFileName

            ' If the user did not cancel, open the file
            ' *** Code needed here to open the file
            If Len(sFileName) <> 0 Then
                MsgBox "This would open a file named: " _
                    & sFileName
            End If

        Case salesFileSave
            ' Save the current data on the form
            DoSave
```

```
            Case salesFileSaveAs
                ' Use the common dialog to save to a different
                ' file name
                FileSaveAsDB cdlg, sFileName

                If Len(sFileName) <> Ø Then
                    MsgBox "Code here would save as a file named: " _
                        & sFileName
                End If

            Case salesFilePrint
                ' Use the common dialog to obtain print
                ' specifications
                FilePrintDB cdlg, iNumCopies

                ' *** Code needed here to call a print routine
                MsgBox "Code here would print the information."

            Case salesPrintPreview
                ' *** Code needed for a print preview routine
                MsgBox "This would display a print preview."

            Case salesFileExit
                ' Close the window
                Unload Me
        End Select
End Sub
```

Separate routines are then called for each option's specific processing. For a prototype, temporary message boxes can be added.

The routine to interact with the Open common dialog box displays the dialog box and returns the name of the file selected to open. As shown next, it first sets an error handler to handle any errors. It then sets the properties of the common dialog box. The CancelError property determines whether an error is generated when the user selects the Cancel button from the Open dialog box. The DialogTitle property defines the text for the title bar of the common dialog box. The Filter property sets the types of files to be listed in the common dialog box. The ShowOpen method then displays the Open dialog box.

```
' File Open dialog box processing
' Parameters:
'   cDlg        Common dialog control
'   sFileName   Name of the file selected by the user
'                       (Returned)
Private Sub FileOpenDB(cdlg As Control, sFileName As String)
    ' Set the error handler
    On Error Resume Next

    ' Use the common dialog box
    cdlg.CancelError = True
    cdlg.DialogTitle = "Open the File"
    cdlg.Filter = "All Files (*.*)|*.*|" _
        & "Text Files (*.txt)|*.txt|" _
        & "Log Files (*.log)|*.log"
    cdlg.ShowOpen

    ' Trap error if user cancels
```

```
        If Err.Number = cdlCancel Then
            ' Return an empty file name
            sFileName = ""
        Else
            ' Return the file name
            sFileName = cdlg.filename
        End If
End Sub
```

If the user cancels the common dialog box, the Err.Number will be set. An empty file name can then be returned. Otherwise, the name selected in the common dialog box is returned.

The Save As common dialog box is similar to the Open dialog box.

```
' File Save As dialog box processing
' Parameters:
'    cDlg          Common dialog control
'    sFileName     Name of the file selected by the user
'                  (Returned)
Private Sub FileSaveAsDB(cdlg As Control, sFileName As String)
    ' Set the error handler
    On Error Resume Next

        ' Use the common dialog box
    cdlg.CancelError = True
    cdlg.DialogTitle = "Save the File As"
    cdlg.Filter = "All Files (*.*)|*.*|" _
        & "Text Files (*.txt)|*.txt|" _
        & "Log Files (*.log)|*.log"
    cdlg.ShowSave

        ' Trap error if user cancels
    If Err.Number = cdlCancel Then
        ' Return an empty file name
        sFileName = ""
    Else
            ' Return the file name
        sFileName = cdlg.filename
    End If
End Sub
```

The Printer common dialog box routine begins by setting an error handler to resume to the next statement on an error and then sets the common dialog box properties. The Flags property setting of cdlPDUseDevModeCopies tells the common dialog box to return the number of copies the user selected in the common dialog box. The ShowPrinter method then displays the Printer dialog box.

```
' File Print dialog box processing
' Parameters
'    cDlg          common dialog control
'    iNumCopies    number of copies selected
Private Sub FilePrintDB(cdlg As Control, iNumCopies As Integer)
    ' Set the error handler
    On Error Resume Next

        ' Use the common dialog box
    cdlg.CancelError = True
    cdlg.DialogTitle = "Print"
```

```
cdlg.Flags = cdlPDUseDevModeCopies
cdlg.ShowPrinter

' Trap error if user cancels
If Err.Number = cdlCancel Then
   iNumCopies = 0
Else
   iNumCopies = cdlg.Copies
End If

End Sub
```

Using the common dialog boxes instead of your own unique forms for Open, Save As, and Print simplifies your code and provides a standard interface for these operations.

Handling an Edit Menu

The Edit menu normally contains options to cut, copy, and paste using the Clipboard. It may also provide other editing options. A click on an Edit menu option will generate a Click event for that option. Because the menu options are in a control array, one Click event procedure is used for all of the menu options.

The code for an Edit menu is as follows:

```
' Edit menu options
Enum salesEditMenu
    salesEditCut = 0
    salesEditCopy = 1
    salesEditPaste = 2
End Enum

' Handle the Edit menu options
Private Sub mnuEdit_Click(index As Integer)
Dim Win As New CWindow

    Select Case index
        Case salesEditCut
            Win.EditCut

        Case salesEditCopy
            Win.EditCopy

        Case salesEditPaste
            Win.EditPaste
    End Select
End Sub
```

The constants defined in the enumerations are declared in the Declarations section of the form. A Window class is used to perform the actual editing functions. This Window class is described in the next section.

Following the practice of progressive disclosure described in Chapter 6, "User-Interface Design," menu options that are not applicable in the current context should be disabled. The following code disables all of the Edit menu options and then enables only those that are currently valid. This is done in the Click event for the top-level Edit menu so it will be adjusted each time the user selects the menu.

```
' Enable/disable the appropriate Edit menu options.
Private Sub mnuEditMenu_Click()
    ' Set error handling
    On Error Resume Next

    ' Disable all three
    mnuEdit(salesEditCut).Enabled = False
    mnuEdit(salesEditCopy).Enabled = False
    mnuEdit(salesEditPaste).Enabled = False

    ' Ensure there is an active control
    If Not (Screen.ActiveControl Is Nothing) Then
        ' Check for text boxes or combo boxes
        If TypeOf Screen.ActiveControl Is TextBox _
          Or TypeOf Screen.ActiveControl Is ComboBox Then

            ' If something is selected, enable cut and copy
            If Screen.ActiveControl.SelLength > 0 Then
                If Err.Number = 0 Then
                    mnuEdit(salesEditCut).Enabled = True
                    mnuEdit(salesEditCopy).Enabled = True
                End If
            End If

            ' Something is on the Clipboard, enable paste
            If Clipboard.GetFormat(vbCFText) Then
                mnuEdit(salesEditPaste) = True
            End If

        End If
    End If
End Sub
```

When the user drops down the Edit menu, this code is executed to ensure that only those edit operations that are valid are available.

Building a Window Class

Visual Basic provides many built-in properties and methods for forms. There are a few features, however, that you must code. For example, you must develop the code for the Edit menu Cut, Copy, and Paste options if your application will support the Clipboard. Also, there is no form property to make a window the topmost window. You normally use this property to make a splash screen appear on top while the main form of the application is built behind it. Instead of recoding this functionality for each application, you can code it once in a Window class, and reuse this class in every application that needs it.

Here is the Declarations section of the Window class:

```
' Class Name:    CWindow
' Author:        Deborah Kurata, InStep Technologies
' Date:          1/24/97
' Description:   Generic window class to provide
'                additional form properties and
```

```
'                    Windows methods.
'
' Revisions:
'
Option Explicit

Enum WinError
    winCBClearError = vbObjectError + 512 + 2
    winCBSelectError = vbObjectError + 512 + 3
    winCBGetError = vbObjectError + 512 + 4
End Enum
```

The EditCopy method of the Window class copies the selected text to
the Clipboard. It begins by setting an error handler. It clears the Clipboard,
and then copies the selected text from the active control to the empty Clipboard. If an error occurs with either the clear or the copy, an error is raised
to the calling routine. The calling routine can determine what to do about the
error.

```
' Standard Copy procedure
' This could be enhanced to support alternative Clipboard types
Public Sub EditCopy()
    ' Set the error handler
    On Error Resume Next

    ' Clear the Clipboard
    Clipboard.Clear
    If Err.Number Then
        On Error GoTo Ø
        Err.Raise winCBClearError, "CWindow::EditCopy", _
            "Could not clear Clipboard."
    Else
        ' Place selected text on the clipboard
        Clipboard.SetText Screen.ActiveControl.SelText
        If Err.Number Then
            On Error GoTo Ø
            Err.Raise winCBSelectError, "CWindow::EditCopy", _
                "Could not set text from active control to Clipboard."
        End If
    End If
End Sub
```

A common error that could occur in this EditCopy routine is caused when
no control is active or when the active control does not have a SelText property. When this occurs, the error handler is turned off and the error is raised
so the calling code can handle the raised error. Alternatively, the calling code
can ensure that this routine is not called unless a copy operation is valid.

The EditCut method cuts the selected text from the control and copies it
to the Clipboard. It begins by setting an error handler. It clears the Clipboard, copies the selected text from the active control to the empty Clipboard, and then clears the selected text. If an error occurs in any of these
steps, an error is raised to the calling routine for processing.

```
' Standard Cut procedure
' This could be enhanced to support alternative Clipboard types
Public Sub EditCut()
```

```
' Set the error handler
On Error Resume Next

' Clear the Clipboard
Clipboard.Clear
If Err.Number Then
    On Error GoTo 0
    Err.Raise winCBClearError, "CWindow::EditCut", _
        "Could not clear Clipboard."
Else
    ' Place selected text on the Clipboard
    Clipboard.SetText Screen.ActiveControl.SelText
    Screen.ActiveControl.SelText = ""
    If Err.Number Then
        On Error GoTo 0
        Err.Raise winCBSelectError, "CWindow::EditCut", _
            "Could not set text from active control to Clipboard."
    End If
End If
End Sub
```

The EditPaste method copies the Clipboard text to the current insertion point. It begins by setting an error handler. It gets the text from the Clipboard and inserts it at the selected text location. If an error occurs during this operation, an error is raised to the calling routine.

```
' Standard Paste procedure
' This could be enhanced to support alternative Clipboard types
Public Sub EditPaste()
    ' Set the error handler
    On Error Resume Next

    ' Place the text from the Clipboard
    Screen.ActiveControl.SelText = Clipboard.GetText()
    If Err.Number Then
        On Error GoTo 0
        Err.Raise winCBGetError, "CWindow::EditPaste", _
            "Could not set text from Clipboard to active control."
    End If
End Sub
```

If the Window class will provide the OnTop property, the declarations for the SetWindowPos API function and the OnTop Property procedure code shown in the earlier section "Expanding Visual Basic Functionality with the Windows API" can be included in this Windows class.

If you develop standard routines for windows operations, you can easily reuse them. For example, the Clipboard functions can be called from the menu options, a toolbar, or a pop-up menu.

Keynote

Adding Pop-Up Menus

Pop-up menus are the floating context menus that appear throughout Windows when the user right-clicks on an object. For an example of a pop-up menu, right-click on a file in the Project window of the Visual Basic IDE. The right mouse button works in many places throughout the IDE.

Keynote

Users will be expecting pop-up menus in your applications as well. Visual Basic provides features to help you create pop-up menus for your objects. For example, the pop-up menu shown in Figure 15.7 is displayed automatically when the user clicks on any text box in your application. No code or property settings are required.

Figure 15.7

Pop-up menus provide the users with a convenient method of accessing the most common actions for an object on the screen.

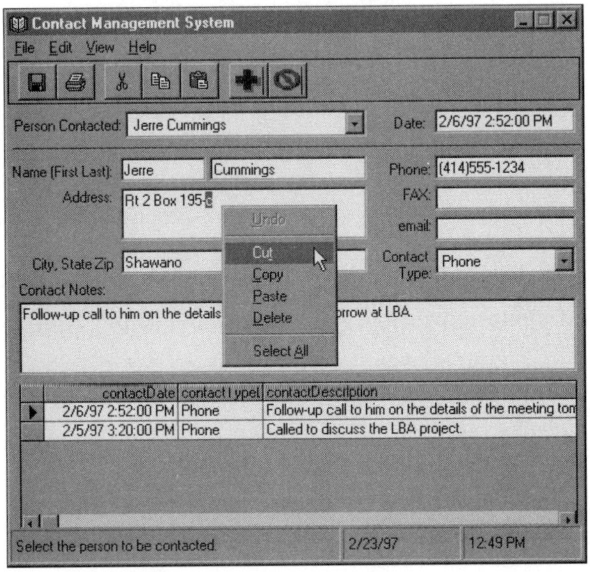

If you want more pop-up menus in your application, follow these steps:

1. For a particular object in your application, determine the most common operations the user would want to perform.

   For example, in the contact management system, the users may want to create a new contact or save the current contact by right-clicking on the form.

2. Create the pop-up menu with the Menu Editor.

   The caption for the pop-up menu's top-level menu will not be seen by the user but will be referenced in your code, so give it an appropriate caption. The options within that menu will be displayed when the user right-clicks.

3. Set the visible property of the pop-up top-level menu to invisible by unchecking the Visible property.

   This ensures that the pop-up menu does not appear in the menu bar at the top of the form.

4. Add the PopupMenu method to your code for the desired object.

   In the following example, a pop-up menu is displayed when the user right-clicks on the form. The name of the top-level menu containing the pop-up menu is defined to be mnuContactPopup. The other parameters of the PopupMenu method specify the pop-up flags, x and y coordinates, and the default menu option to appear in bold. For this example, the mnuContact(1) menu option will appear in bold and will be the default option in the pop-up menu.

```
Private Sub Form_MouseUp(Button As Integer, Shift As Integer, _
    X As Single, Y As Single)
    If Button = vbRightButton Then
        PopupMenu mnuContactPopup, , , , mnuContact(1)
    End If
End Sub
```

   Notice that the MouseUp event is normally used to display pop-up menus.

5. Write the code to perform the operations defined by the pop-up menu options.

   For example, the pop-up menu for the main form in the contact management system will perform New and Save operations. The code for this is shown here:

```
' Popup menu options
Enum salesPopupMenu
    salesPopupNew = 0
    salesPopupSave = 1
End Enum

Private Sub mnuContact_Click(Index As Integer)
    Select Case Index
        Case salesPopupNew
            ' Create a new contact
            DoAdd

        Case salesPopupSave
            ' Save the current contact
            UpdateObject
            m_SalesPerson.Persons.Save
    End Select
End Sub
```

The constants used in the preceding code were defined in the Declarations section of the form.

Adding a Toolbar

Many applications have a toolbar at the top of the form, as shown in Figure 15.7. The toolbar contains buttons for each of the most common operations in an application, providing a shortcut to the operation. For example, many toolbars include cut, copy, and paste buttons for quick access to those editing operations.

You can implement a toolbar using a panel control or the Toolbar control that is provided as one of the Windows Common Controls. The Toolbar control creates the toolbar across the top of the window, complete with buttons. You can define a ToolTip that will appear when the user moves the cursor over a button. You can also specify an image for each button by binding the Toolbar control to an ImageList control, which is also part of the Windows Common Controls.

The ImageList control allows you to create a collection of images in one control. The ImageList does not display the images, but rather provides a repository for images used by other controls or other parts of the application. Each image is then available to the application through a ListImages collection and can be referenced by an index or a key, just like any other collection. Any object with a picture property can use a picture from the ListImages collection.

Tech Note.   *If you do not see the Windows Common Controls in your Visual Basic toolbox, choose Components from the Project menu and check Microsoft Windows Custom Controls.*

If the application will be used by the documentation, testing, usability, or marketing staff while it is being developed, you may want to add code to each button that displays a message box describing the feature accessed by the button. This will provide a stub for each feature until the feature is implemented and connected to the buttons.

To tie code to the buttons on the toolbar, use the Toolbar control's ButtonClick event; it passes in the selected button. If you defined a unique key for each button with Toolbar control properties, you can use the Key property of the button in a Select Case statement. Here is the code for the toolbar in the contact management system:

```
Private Sub Toolbar1_ButtonClick(ByVal Button As Button)
Dim Win As New CWindow
Dim iNumCopies As Integer

    Select Case Button.Key
        Case "SAVE"
            ' Save the current data on the form
            DoSave

        Case "PRINT"
            ' Use the common dialog to obtain print specifications
            FilePrintDB cDlg, iNumCopies

            ' *** Code needed here to call a print routine
            MsgBox "Code here would print the information."

        Case "CUT"
            Win.EditCut

        Case "COPY"
            Win.EditCopy
```

```
        Case "NEW"
            ' Perform the new operation
            DoAdd

            ' Set focus to the notes area
            txtContact(2).SetFocus

        Case "DELETE"
            ' Delete the record
            If Not datContact.Recordset.EOF Then
                datContact.Recordset.Delete
                ' Move to the next valid record
                datContact.Recordset.MoveFirst
            End If
    End Select
End Sub
```

Notice that this reuses the code that handles the common dialog box and Edit menu options.

Adding a Status Bar

Many applications have a status bar at the bottom of the main window as shown in Figure 15.7. The status bar normally provides reference information, such as the date and time or current page number.

The status bar can be implemented using sets of panels, or you can use the StatusBar control that is provided as one of the Windows Common Controls. The StatusBar control creates the status bar at the bottom, including individual panels to separate various bits of information. Predefined panel styles automatically set date, time, or keyboard key states.

Keynote

A few words of caution when working with a status bar: Don't put important information there. People don't normally look at the status bar unless they are looking for specific reference information. For example, in Microsoft Word it is convenient to have the current page number at the bottom, especially when you're trying to hit a certain page count or when you're printing a range of pages. But if you were typing along and a message in the status bar told you to save because of an imminent crash, do you think you would notice it?

Defining Icons for the Application

Windows applications can have a small icon (16x16 pixels) and a large icon (32x32 pixels). The large icon is used to represent the application in shortcuts and when displayed in the large icon file list view. The small icon appears in the title bar and in the small icon file list view. If a small icon is not provided, Windows attempts to make one from the large icon. As you might imagine, the results are not always the best.

Keynote

You can create multiple icons for your Visual Basic application by placing both icons in one .ico file. You can do this using utilities such as Microsoft Image Editor, which comes with Visual Basic. Image Editor is a paint-type application for drawing your icons, bitmaps, or cursors that supports the addition of multiple icons in one .ico file.

Once you've created both sizes of icons in the .ico file, you can assign the icon file to one of the forms in the project. Set one of your form's Icon property to the name of the .ico file. The small version of the icon will immediately appear in the title bar of the form.

The icon file used for the application is by default set to the icon assigned to the main form. However, you can assign any form's icon as the application's icon. This is set in the Make tab of the Project Properties dialog box.

Providing Help in the Application

Applications that interface with users should provide some amount of help to those users. This help can be provided in many ways, some of which are more complex and time-consuming to develop than others.

Improving the User Interface

One method of providing help to the users is to make the application very self explanatory. Add instructions directly to the form. Expand the one or two word field labels to a phrase or sentence to better define what the user should enter into the field. Notice that the title bar in Figure 15.1 does not say "Login Screen," but rather provides instructions as to what the user should do. This is a very simple technique for providing help in your application. However, it may not be enough.

Adding ToolTips

Visual Basic 5 introduced a new ToolTipText property that will automatically display ToolTips for your controls. A *ToolTip* is a word or phrase that appears when the user places the mouse pointer over a control. Now you can set ToolTip text for any control on your form to provide additional help on using the control.

Keynote

Displaying ToolTips is much better than displaying the text in a status bar because the text appears where the user is looking, right below the cursor.

Providing a Help System

To provide more assistance than a ToolTip, you can create a help system for your application. Help systems are usually provided through options in a Help menu. The user can select an option or press the F1 key for context-sensitive help. The Windows Help menu standard defines only one Help menu option for displaying help. The Help screen then displays a set of folders for Contents, Index, and Find options.

Tech Note. *The process of developing the help system is somewhat complex and cannot be done from the Visual Basic development environment. This process involves developing the help topics using a word processor such as Microsoft Word, converting the files to a Rich Text Format, creating a project file using a text editor such as Notepad, and finally compiling them using the help compiler. This set of steps explains the primary reason for the availability of so many third-party help system authoring tools. It is well worth the cost to purchase a third-party tool to automate your help system development process.*

Once the help file is created and compiled, you need to set the help file name in the Project Properties dialog box. The help file itself is not added to the project. Rather, the name of the help file is listed in this dialog box.

If the Help menu options are in a control array, one Help menu Click event procedure will contain all code for all of the menu options. If the Help Topics menu option is selected, the following code retrieves the help file name and uses the common dialog control to display the help system. If the About menu option is selected, the About box is displayed.

```
' Help menu options
Enum salesHelpMenu
    salesHelpTopics = Ø
    salesHelpAbout = 2
End EnumPrivate

' Constant to display the Help
' Topics tabbed dialog box
Private Const cdlHelpFinder = 11

Sub mnuHelp_Click(Index As Integer)
   Select Case Index

     Case salesHelpTopics
       ' Specify the help file to open
       cDlg.HelpFile = App.HelpFile
       cDlg.HelpCommand = cdlHelpFinder
       cDlg.ShowHelp

     Case salesHelpAbout     ' About
       ' Display an about box
       frmAbout.Show
   End Select
End Sub
```

Each form and control on the form can then be given a help context ID number, stored in the HelpContextID property, that identifies the number of the help text for that form or control. When the user presses the F1 key, the help system topic for the active control or form will be displayed.

Implementing What's This Help

What's This Help is the Windows name for field-level help. It aids the user in answering the question "What's this?" for any field on a form. This type of help is frequently provided to the user as a button with a question mark, as shown in Figure 15.8. The user clicks on this button and the cursor becomes an arrow with a question mark. If the user then clicks on a control, the help topic for that control is displayed, as shown by the User Name box in the figure. What's This Help is similar to a ToolTip, but provides more information and optional links to other help topics.

Figure 15.8

The user can select the What's This Help button (the question mark) and then click on a field to get field-level help.

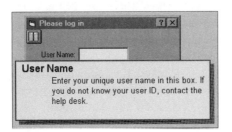

The content of the What's This Help topic comes from the help file, so you must use the technique described in the previous section to develop the help topics. If possible, set the help context IDs for the fields to the same values as the resource IDs. This allows you to create one set of constant identifiers for your fields that can be used for both the help system and the resource file.

Once you've created the help file, implementing What's This Help involves setting the following properties:

- **WhatsThisHelp.** Setting this property for a form defines whether the form provides What's This Help. If this property is set to False, What's This Help is disabled. If it is set to True, What's This Help is available.

   Tech Note. *As of this writing, there is a bug that prevents the F1 key from displaying the help topic defined by the help context ID when the WhatsThisHelp property setting is True.*

- **WhatsThisButton.** Setting this property for a form defines whether the button will appear in the title bar, as shown in Figure 15.8. If this property is set to False, the button will not be displayed. If it is set to True, the button will appear in the title bar. For the button to appear, the form must have a border.

- **WhatsThisHelpID.** Setting this property for a field defines the help context ID number for the field. Note that the form does not have this property. The purpose of What's This Help is to provide field-level help.

With these properties set appropriately, What's This Help will be displayed when the user clicks on the What's This Help button and then on a control on the form. In addition, two methods are available to display the What's This Help from your code:

- **WhatsThisMode.** Calling this method sets What's This Help just as if the user had clicked on the What's This Help button. The cursor changes to an arrow and a question mark and the user can click on a field. This is best used when What's This Help is provided from a toolbar or menu option.

- **ShowWhatsThis**. Calling this method for a control displays What's This Help for that control. This method is not available for forms.

Implementing Tip Wizards

Tip Wizards are dialog boxes that appear during execution of the application and provide additional information on the task the user is performing. For example, when the user manually updates several columns in a Microsoft Project chart, Project displays a Tip Wizard suggesting a shortcut to accomplish the same task.

Presenting intelligent Tip Wizards is somewhat complex in terms of the programming because you must track what the user is doing. This allows the Wizard to know when it is appropriate for the tip to appear. Tip Wizards can add polish to your application and make it very user-friendly.

Tech Note.   *A state machine is a good mechanism for tracking system state to determine when to display a particular Tip Wizard.*

When adding Tip Wizards to your application, don't forget to include a check box at the bottom that says "Don't Show Me This Again." This allows the users to turn off the tips when they are no longer needed or desired. Be sure to provide a mechanism to turn them back on, perhaps through a property page or options screen similar to the tabbed Properties dialog box in the Visual Basic development environment.

■ Reviewing the Development Strategies

Before beginning construction, it is always a good idea to review the architectural design and development plan. To this end, let's review the design and strategies defined by the contact management system team. The user interface for the primary window of the contact management system was designed in Chapter 6, "User-Interface Design," and is shown in Figure 15.4. The final object model for the contact management system was defined in Chapter 7, "Implementation-Centered Design," and displayed in Figure 15.9.

Figure 15.9

The object model for the contact management system provides the blueprint for putting the pieces together.

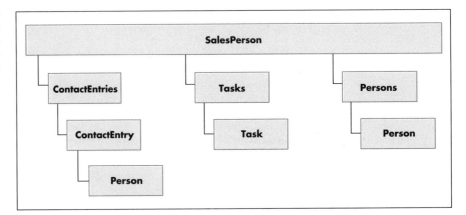

The team made the following design and strategy decisions:

- The data for the contact entries will be stored in a database on the file server. The ContactEntries BODT class will manage the data for the data control. A bound grid and other bound controls will be used to display the contact information, so no class is needed for the ContactEntry objects.

- The data for the tasks will be stored on the local computer. The Task class will provide the properties and methods to retrieve and manipulate a single task and the Tasks class will manage the collection of all tasks.

- The Tasks and Task classes will be developed as an ActiveX component to provide for reuse of these classes in other applications.

- The customer and prospect data will be stored as generic person information in the same database as the contact entries. A Persons BODT class will manage the recordset of data. The Person class will manage the individual data elements for one record.

- The Persons and Person classes will be developed generically. They may be enhanced and made into a remote automation server in the future.

- The basic framework of the application and the Contact Management, Address Book, and To Do List forms and related code will be developed by one programmer.

- The Tasks server will be developed by a second programmer.

- All other classes required by the contact management system will be developed by a third programmer.

- Interim deliverables will be prepared. Each component will be completed independently, using stubs as needed, and provided for testing and documentation before the entire system is complete.

- SourceSafe will be used for source code control. Each interim deliverable will serve as a check point in the source code control system.

Now the developers are ready to begin construction.

■ Creating the Application Framework

Any construction process begins with a solid foundation and framework. All other components are then purchased or built and attached to this framework to complete the construction. For software construction, you build the framework of the application and get it under source code control. The developers can then add the necessary components onto the framework and complete the application.

Application Framework Components

The application framework normally includes files such as:

- **Main module.** This module includes the startup code for the application, declarations and creation of any global object variables, and any global API declarations.

    Tech Note. *Global object variables are object variables declared as Public in a standard module. Don't get these confused with global objects, which were described earlier in this chapter in the section "Defining Global Objects."*

- **Splash form.** The splash form is the first screen that the user sees. Add the form using the Add Form option in the Project menu to display the Add Form dialog box. From here, you can create this form from scratch by selecting Form, or use the template provided by Visual Basic by selecting Splash Screen.

- **Login form.** This form displays the login screen and requires and ID and password before the user can access the application. You can create this form from scratch or use the Log In Dialog template provided by Visual Basic. An example Login form was created in Chapter 11, "Building Classes: Additional Techniques."

- **About box form.** The About box displays information about the application, including the application name, author, and copyright information. You can create this form from scratch or use the About Dialog template provided by Visual Basic.

- **Main form.** This is the main form of the application. It can be presented as an MDI, SDI, or explorer-style window, as discussed in Chapter 6, "User-Interface Design." You can create this form from scratch or use a template provided by Visual Basic.

- **Error Class.** The error class provides generic functionality for processing errors, such as logging the error to a file or to the NT event log. See the "Logging Events" section earlier in this chapter for more information.

- **Window class.** This generic class provides wrappers for Windows functions such as Clipboard support. See the "Completing User Interface Details" section earlier in this chapter for an example of a Windows class.

- **Database class.** A database class can encapsulate access to a database. See Chapter 14, "Doing Database Objects," for details on implementing a Database class.

- **Resource file.** This file contains strings and bitmaps used in the application. See the section "Using a Resource File" at the beginning of this chapter for more information.

- **Help file.** This file contains the help information displayed when the user requests help. The help file can include both field-level help and procedural help. See the section "Completing User Interface Details" earlier in this chapter for more information.

Keynote

You can define standardized components for this framework and reuse them by adding your own templates. You can create templates for any project component such as forms, modules, class modules, and UserControls. Simply add the project component to the appropriate template directory as defined by the path in the Environment tab of the Options dialog box. The project component will then appear in the correct Add dialog box.

For example, if you create a standard login form for your company, you can add the login form to the appropriate template directory. When you use the Add Form option, your form will appear in the Add Form dialog box.

Instead of creating each component for the application framework, you can use the VB Application Wizard provided by Visual Basic to create this framework automatically, as discussed next.

Using the VB Application Wizard

When starting a new application, you can use the VB Application Wizard to insert the application framework into the project automatically. To use the VB Application Wizard to create the framework for a new project:

1. Start a new project and select VB Application Wizard from the New Project dialog box.

2. Follow the Wizard instructions to define the framework of the application.

OR

1. Start a new project.

2. Remove the default form that was added to the project.

3. Choose Add-In Manager from the Add-Ins menu and check the VB Application Wizard.
   A menu option for the Wizard will be added to the Add-Ins menu.

4. Choose Application Wizard from the Add-Ins menu.

5. Follow the Wizard instructions to define the framework of the application.

That's all there is to it. In a minute or two, the application framework is in place. This framework can include a splash screen, login form, main form, data entry screens, a Web browser screen, and so on. You can then add code to this framework as needed to complete your application. For example, you may add code to the splash screen to have it displayed on top of the main form.

■ Building the Application Hierarchy

As shown in Figure 15.9, most applications have an object hierarchy. Each class in the hierarchy is related to the classes below it in the hierarchy. You establish the relationship between the levels in the hierarchy through containment. Each class contains a reference to the lower level classes.

Each class in the contact management system is described here. All of the code for the contact management system is provided as defined in the Appendix.

- **SalesPerson class.** This is the topmost class in the object hierarchy. The object variables for the ContactEntries and Persons classes are declared within this class to establish the hierarchy.

```
' Contact entry recordset class
Private m_Contacts As CContactEntries

' Person recordset class
Private m_Persons As CPersons

' Contacts class
```

```
Property Get Contacts() As CContactEntries
    Set Contacts = m_Contacts
End Property
' Persons class
Property Get Persons() As CPersons
    Set Persons = m_Persons
End Property
```

Property Get procedures are implemented in this class to expose a reference to the ContactEntries and Persons classes. These procedures allow for navigation to the lower levels in the hierarchy. The SalesPerson class also creates the instances, initializes, and finally terminates the Persons and ContactEntries objects.

- **ContactEntries class.** This is a business object data transfer (BODT) class. Because contact entries are handled by a data control, this class is responsible for defining the requirements for the recordset attached to the data control. It keeps the SQL statements outside of the form. This class ensures that only the contact entries for the selected person are included on the screen.

- **Persons class.** This is also a BODT class, however it uses the data access objects (DAO). The code for this class is detailed in Chapter 14, "Doing Database Objects." The code was changed for this application in that the recordset only contains the list of persons for the salesperson that logged in. That way one salesperson cannot see the Address Book for the other salespeople.

- **Person class.** This class identifies the properties for the person currently displayed in the Address Book. The code for this class is detailed in Chapter 14, "Doing Database Objects."

The Tasks and Task classes are not listed here because these classes are not included in the contact management system. Rather, these classes were created in a separate Tasks server component as described in Chapter 13, "Building ActiveX Components." A reference to the Tasks server component is defined in the contact management system to establish the relationship between the components.

Instead of creating the class hierarchy manually, you can use the VB Class Builder Utility as described in Chapter 11, "Building Classes: Additional Techniques."

■ Connecting the Forms to the Hierarchy

The last step in constructing an application is to put the pieces together. You need to connect the user interface to the application hierarchy. Normally, that involves defining a reference in the main form to the topmost class in the hierarchy and then using exposed properties of that topmost class to navigate down to any other class.

For the contact management system, the forms are connected to the hierarchy as follows:

- **frmMain.** This is the main form in the application. It declares an object variable and creates an instance of the SalesPerson class. Because many of the controls on the form are bound, it manages the recordset of the data control by using the exposed ContactEntries property from the SalesPerson class.

  To allow the user to see information about the person contacted, information from the Address Book is also displayed in the main form. This information is retrieved and updated using the exposed Persons property from the SalesPerson class.

  The remainder of the code in this form manages the menu options, pop-up menus, help, and other details, as described in the section "Completing User Interface Details" earlier in this chapter.

- **frmPerson.** This is the Address Book form. The code in this form is almost identical to the code described in Chapter 14, "Doing Database Objects." Two additional features were added for this application. A Display method in this form will allow passing in a reference to a Persons class. This automatically populates the Address Book form with information for a predefined person, so the person shown in the Contact Management window can appear automatically in the Address Book when the form is displayed. For example, the user is looking at Jessica Jones in the Contact Management window and selects the Address Book option from the view menu. Jessica Jones appears in the Address Book. The user can update Jessica Jones or select another person.

  The second new feature is related to the first; it provides updates back to the Contact Management window. For the example, if information for Jessica Jones is updated in the Address Book, when the Address Book is no longer the active form the changes are saved. When the Contact Management window becomes the active form, it retrieves the new values, so the changes to Jessica's information will appear on the Contact Management window.

- **frmTask.** This is the To Do List form. The code for this form was detailed in Chapter 11, "Building Classes, Additional Techniques." This form uses the Task ActiveX component created in Chapter 13, "Building ActiveX Components."

■ Inspecting the Application

As you finish the application components, you should inspect them to make sure they are operational, meet quality standards, and are complete before passing them over the wall to the testing organization.

I hear this now as a joke, but I actually knew programmers who allowed the compiler to inspect the application. If it compiled, it was done. Ship it! How testing is done and how much testing is done depends on the programming environment and should have been defined during the design, as described in Chapter 9, "Strategies for Construction." Regardless of the formality of your development environment, you should perform some minimal amount of inspection before providing the application to the users.

This section supplies some general tips for inspecting your application. It also provides a few tips for optimizing your application.

Tips for Inspection

The inspection process involves running the application to determine whether it executes properly. These tips can help you with that process.

Compiling the Application

Because Visual Basic provides Compile on Demand and Background Compile, it is possible that your application has never been fully compiled. You can either turn off the Compile on Demand and Background compile flags, use the Start with Full Compile option from the Run menu, or use the Make option. Regardless of the method you use, you should fully compile the application before beginning the inspection.

Using Conditional Compilation

With conditional compilation, you can have code in your application that is only compiled when you set a conditional compilation flag. This allows you to add extensive debugging code into the application to aid in inspecting and debugging. More information on conditional compilation is provided in Chapter 11, "Building Classes: Additional Techniques."

Using the Debug Object

You can add Debug.Print statements to the application to display specific values in the Immediate window to monitor how the application is executing. The Debug.Assert method can be used to stop the application if a variable has an unexpected value, which helps in debugging. The compiler will ignore the Debug statements, so you don't need to be concerned about removing them before preparing the application for production. There's more information on the Debug object and Immediate window in Chapter 11, "Building Classes: Additional Techniques."

Running the F5 Test

F5 is the function key equivalent for the Start option from the Run menu. This starts your application running. You can then work through each menu option, dialog box, button, and control to ensure that it functions as expected. This is frequently called *black box testing* because the test evaluates the operation of the system by the inputs and outputs and not by what is going on inside the application.

In a formal process, this type of testing is normally done using a test specification to ensure that all of the features of the application are covered. This could also include automated run sessions, which are available in testing tools such as Microsoft Visual Test.

Running the F8 Test

Once you are assured that the application functions as expected, you can run an F8 test. The F8 key is the function key equivalent for the Step Into option from the Run menu. It executes a single line and stops. This allows you to easily see where the application is going. This is called *white box testing* because the code is visible and inspected throughout the process.

You can use the Set Next statement to force error conditions or other case statements to improve the coverage of your test. Because Visual Basic is event driven, it is always possible for unexpected events to be generated. Running the F8 test will help you find those situations.

Performing the F8 test will help you inspect every line of code. This may seem like a large task, but is quite manageable if done on one component at a time as you finish the component. However, this test only tests how well the current code operates. It does not point out any missing functionality. This is why the F5 test was suggested first.

Tips for Optimization

When you performed the basic inspection you probably found and corrected many errors. Now you are ready to look at the performance of the application. Here are some general tips for optimizing your application.

Understanding the Problem

Keynote

The first step to optimizing the application is to understand the real problem. You could make a particular loop lightning fast, but it will not appear any faster if the system is waiting for the screen to repaint. Your efforts may be better spent improving the screen repainting.

Take a good look at the application and evaluate where the speed problems are. Is the problem the speed of some calculations or the apparent speed of the application due to the screen painting? Spend the time understanding the problem before simply tweaking algorithms.

Profiling the Application

Visual Basic comes with the Microsoft Visual Basic Code Profiler. This tool identifies which parts of your Visual Basic application are used and how long it takes to run parts of the application. You can use it to determine which parts of the application need the most optimization effort.

Tech Note. *As of this writing, there was a Code Profiler provided with Visual Basic 4.0, but no sign of one yet in Visual Basic 5.*

Performing Timing Tests

Write a sample application and compare speeds for alternative operations. For example, the speed for using CInt( ) may be different from Val( ). By performing these comparisons and documenting them for your later use, you can use the most efficient operations. I would bet there will be an article or two and newsgroup discussions on this topic as well.

Improving Apparent Speed

The apparent speed is the speed the user perceives. There are many ways to improve this perceived speed. For example, splash screens give the user something to look at while an application is loading, providing an improved perceived application startup.

Another little trick is showing progress indicators. Giving the user something to watch improves the perceived time. If it looks like it will take a long time, the user can do something in the interim, like get a cup of coffee.

Using a Resource File

Loading resources from a resource file when they are needed decreases the load time of the forms. This improves the perceived overall speed of the application. The techniques for using a resource file are discussed in the "Using a Resource File" section of this chapter.

Limiting the Controls

Ever put 50 controls on a form with frames and other containers and then watch the screen paint? The number of controls on a form directly affects the display speed of the form. If screen painting is a critical issue, you can modify some of the controls to lightweight type controls such as line drawings, images, and labels. Limiting controls will improve speed.

Cleaning Up after Yourself

Free any object variables you are no longer using. When all object variables referencing an object are freed, the object is terminated and the memory for that object is reclaimed. The same is true for other large structures such as arrays.

Requesting Needed Data

Often it seems easier to create a recordset with a simple query, and then wade through that recordset to find needed records. As much as possible, minimize the contents of the recordset to the smallest set possible for better performance.

Trying Various Compilation Options

Visual Basic now has many choices for how the application is compiled. The setting you select could have an impact on the performance of the application.

■ Preparing the Delivery

Your application is done, inspected, and optimized! It is now ready to be delivered, even if it is only to the internal testing organization. You could try to determine all of the components of the application yourself, including all of the components Visual Basic needs, or you can let the Setup Wizard take care of everything for you.

Using the Setup Wizard

The Setup Wizard is an application provided with Visual Basic that creates distribution diskettes. It opens a defined project file and determines all of the files that the project requires. You have the option to add other files, such as a database file or help system. It then compresses the files and copies them onto a disk or to a specific directory. It also creates an installation program and a deinstall program.

An end user of the application can use the resulting installation program to install the application. This will register all required components in the registry and copy the files to the correct directories. It uses the version information in the files to ensure that a newer file is not overwritten by a file with older version information.

The end user can use the uninstall program provided by the Setup Wizard to remove your application and all of its components. This is especially useful during testing to remove the entire application before testing another installation.

Tech Note. *One word of caution on using the Setup Wizard: It will not overwrite a file if it has the same or earlier version information. If you compile the application, perform a test installation, find a problem, fix it, recompile, and rerun the setup, the old version of the application will not be overwritten unless you have incremented the version information or uninstalled the original application.*

■ Summary

- With a design, a good set of tools, and a basic understanding of how to use the tools appropriately, you can build well-constructed applications.

- Resource files are a good place to store the strings, bitmaps, and other binary information for your application. They provide more efficient loading of these resources and editing of the information, making localization easier.

- The registry provides a centralized location for application configuration and context information, such as the last selected window position.

- You can log application events to a log file or to the Windows NT event log directly from Visual Basic.

- You can extend Visual Basic functionality by using the Windows application programming interface (API). The Windows API allows you to include functionality in your Visual Basic application that is available in Windows but is not provided directly by Visual Basic.

- Use the API Viewer provided with Visual Basic to make API declarations easier to insert into your application.

- You can define global objects that don't need to be created by an application. This is useful for libraries of common functions.

- There are many new features available for polishing your user interface. Among other things, you can specify window size and placement, implement drag-and-drop of control text, and set menu properties.

- Pop-up menus are popular in Windows and will be expected in your applications.

- You can use the Toolbar, ImageList, and StatusBar controls provided as part of the Windows Common Controls to give your application a standard look.

- Windows uses two different sized icons for each application. Both icons must be created in the same .ico file and assigned to the Icon property of a form in the application.

- You can provide help to the user by writing more descriptive text on the forms, implementing a traditional help system, including ToolTips, and adding What's This Help to the application.

- You can use the VB Application Wizard to create the application framework for your application in a few minutes.

- Once the framework is in place, you can add code specific to the application.

- The top-level class in the application contains the references to the other primary objects in the application.

- Use the VB Class Builder utility to create the hierarchy of classes in your application.

- You can improve your code inspection techniques by using conditional compilation, the Immediate window, and the F5 and F8 keys.

- Before optimizing your application, use a profiler and inspection to determine what needs the most optimization.

■ Additional Reading

Appleman, Daniel. *Dan Appleman's Visual Basic 5.0 Guide to the Win32 API.* Emeryville, California: Ziff-Davis Press, 1997.

This book is a "must have" if you will be accessing the Win 32 API from Visual Basic.

■ Think It Over

To supplement and review the information in this chapter, think about the following:

1. Why would you use a Resource file? How about the Registry? Event log?

2. Think about how you have put all of the pieces together to build applications in the past. How are the steps suggested here different from what you have done before? How are they easier or harder?

3. Many programmers using Visual Basic 5 have said they now can develop applications much faster and with fewer errors than with prior versions of Visual Basic. Which features of Visual Basic 5 do you think help with this increase in productivity?

4. How much inspection do you normally do with your applications before turning them over to your testers or your users? Do you think it is enough? Too much?

■ Final Thoughts

Well, you've made it. In this book we have covered a lot of ground. You now have an understanding of how to convert an idea into requirements, the requirements into an object-oriented design, and the design into a complete application using Visual Basic. You can apply these techniques to any software development project that comes your way.

I hope you enjoy doing objects with Visual Basic 5.

■ Appendix

■ About the Accompanying CD-ROM

This appendix describes the contents of the CD-ROM provided with this book. This CD-ROM contains the following:

- Source code for the samples demonstrated in this book

- A demo version of Rational Software Corporation's Rational Rose object-oriented analysis and design tool

- The Poet Software's Poet object database management system (ODBMS) with Poet Automation for use with Visual Basic

- Sample chapters of Dan Appleman's *Visual Basic 5.0 Programmer's Guide to the Win32 API*

- An article from Dan Appleman which is based on his upcoming book *Dan Appleman's Developing ActiveX Components with Visual Basic 5.0*

■ Installation

To install the source code from the CD-ROM to your hard disk, simply drag the file folders from the Code directory on the CD-ROM to your hard drive. Since the code on the CD-ROM consists of project files instead of executable applications, no installation program is necessary.

Tech Note. *Files on the CD-ROM are marked as read-only. You must change the read-only attribute after copying the files to your hard disk if you wish to modify the files. This is especially important if you wish to write to any of the database files provided on the CD-ROM.*

To turn off the read-only attribute after you have copied the files to your hard disk, select the desired files using Windows Explorer and choose Properties from the File menu. Then uncheck the read-only attribute in the Properties dialog box.

To install the Rational Rose demo software, use the setup program Setup.exe in the Rational directory of the CD-ROM. This setup program will install the demo Rational Rose software to a directory you define. Documentation for this project is provided in the help files installed with this product.

To install the Poet ODBMS, use the setup program Setup.exe in the Poet directory of the CD-ROM. This setup program will install the Poet ODBMS to a directory you define. Documentation for this product is provided in the Poet\UGuide directory.

Tech Note. *If you use Windows 95, you must reboot after installing Poet to allow the software to work appropriately.*

■ Source Code on the CD-ROM

The project files contained on the CD-ROM provide the source code for the samples used throughout Part 3 of this book. These project files are organized in file folders by chapter. See the associated chapter for more information on each sample project, including a detailed description of most of the source code.

The sample applications on the CD-ROM have been tested using a beta version of Visual Basic, Enterprise Edition running under Windows 95. Since this CD-ROM was made prior to the release of Visual Basic, it could not be tested with the production version.

CHAPTER 10: Building Your First Class

Creating an Object from a Class

Project Name: Task10_1.vbp
File Folder: Ex10_1

This sample project demonstrates building a class in a class module and creating an object from the class. Message boxes are displayed to identify when the object is initialized and terminated.

The resulting application allows you to define a task, which can be any assignment that you don't want to forget. The application can be minimized and then brought back up at any time to review the task. Since the task is not stored, it will not be retained once the application is terminated.

For a challenge, try the following:

- Provide validation on the entered time due.

- Add a category to the application. The user could then select a category for the task such as "personal," "business," "school" and so on. You can implement this as a text box or as a combo box.

Raising Errors from a Class

Project Name: Task10_2.vbp
File Folder: Ex10_2

This sample project demonstrates the use of an enumeration. The valid values for the task priorities are defined in a public enumeration. This project also provides an example of error handling. A public enumeration is used to expose the error numbers that can be raised from the class to the calling routine.

The resulting application validates the priority and time due and raises an error if the values are not valid. The user interface traps the error and presents a message to the user.

For a challenge, try the following:

- Define an enumeration in the class that assigns long integer values to the categories that were identified in the prior challenge.

- Add error handling to validate the category value.

Raising Events from a Class

Project Name: Task10_3.vbp
File Folder: Ex10_3

This sample project demonstrates programmer-defined events. An Alarm event is defined in the Task class and that event is raised to the Task form when the task is due. An event procedure in the Task form responds to the Alarm event. This project also provides an example of capturing events from a control. A Timer control is used to check the time against the time the task is due.

The resulting application allows you to set an Alarm. When you set the Alarm the form is minimized. When the task is due, the form beeps and redisplays. NOTE: The default time is AM, so you must enter PM for afternoon times.

For a challenge, try the following:

- Think of another type of event that this class could generate.

- Define the event and raise it in the class, then respond to the event with an event procedure in the form.

CHAPTER 11: Building Classes: Additional Techniques

Creating a Collection Class

Project Name: Task11_1.vbp
File Folder: Ex11_1

This sample project demonstrates building a collection class. Wrapper methods are created for the Add, Remove, and Item methods of the collection. A NewEnum method is also created to expose the collection's enumeration. This allows you to use the For Each...Next syntax with the collection class. This project also illustrates how to set a default property or method. The Item method is defined as the default method of the collection class.

The resulting application allows you to create a set of tasks for a to do list. You can add or delete items in this list. Since the tasks are not saved, the list is lost when you exit the application.

For a challenge, try the following:

- Implement the code to add a task to the collection with a defined category.

- Add the Alarm event from the prior example to set an alarm for any of the tasks in the list. NOTE: Be sure to define the Timer form in the collection class and not in the Task class so there is only one timer for any number of tasks with alarms.

Saving Objects to a File

Project Name: Task11_2.vbp
File Folder: Ex11_2

This sample project demonstrates a generic file processing class. This class stores any object data to a file. In this example, all of the tasks in the collection are stored in a simple binary file.

The resulting application allows you to define a set of tasks in a to do list and save those tasks. When the application is run again, the tasks will be read from the file and displayed.

For a challenge, try the following:

- Implement the code to add the category to the file.

- Change the file type to write the data to a sequential file that can be opened with a text editor.

Try rewriting the routines in the file processing class such that a callback would not be required. Hint: You will need to separate the method for file opening and file closing.

Using Forms as Classes

Project Name: Login.vbp
File Folder: Ex11_3

This sample project demonstrates how to use class techniques, such as Property procedures, in a form. In this example, a Property procedure is used for a login dialog box to define which button the user selected in the dialog box. This sample also demonstrates how to convert user entry of the Enter key to a Tab.

The resulting application presents a login screen for entry of a user ID and password. Any application could include this login screen and call the Property procedures to determine if the user clicked the OK button or the Exit button.

For a challenge, try the following:

- Add a login screen to the Task11_2 project described above.

- Terminate the Task11_2 project if the user clicked cancel in the login screen and proceeding to the to do list if the user clicked OK in the login screen.

CHAPTER 12: Interfaces, Polymorphism, and Inheritance

Implementing an Interface

Project Name: CMS12_1.vbp
File Folder: Ex12_1

This sample project demonstrates building an interface in a class module. That interface is then implemented in a class by using the Implements keyword and developing the code for every property and method in the interface.

The resulting application uses the default interface to set the properties for a Customer object and then uses an ISave interface to save the properties. This application does not actually save the data, rather it displays a message box.

For a challenge, try the following:

- Define an IFile interface for the file operations defined in the Saving Objects to a File example.

- Implement the IFile interface in the Tasks class defined in the Saving Objects to a File example.

Leveraging Polymorphism

Project Name: CMS12_2.vbp
File Folder: Ex12_2

This sample project demonstrates implementing an interface in two classes and then using the standard interface to leverage polymorphism. An object from either class is passed to a routinc as a parameter that is defined to be the data type of the interface. This allows use of polymorphism without giving up early binding.

The resulting application uses the default interface to set the properties for a Customer object and then passes the object to a Save method to save the properties. This process is then repeated for a Prospect object. This application does not actually save the data, rather it displays message boxes.

For a challenge, try the following:

- Implement the IFile interface in the Customer and Prospect classes to replace the ISave interface.

- Leverage polymorphism to save both the Customer and Prospect object data to a file.

Achieving Inheritance

Project Name: CMS12_3.vbp
File Folder: Ex12_3

This sample project demonstrates how to use interface inheritance and delegation to achieve implementation inheritance. A class is developed to contain the interface and code to define a Person object. The Person class is implemented in a Customer and Prospect class so they can both share the common Person class code. Because Visual Basic does not provide implementation inheritance, each property and method in the Customer and Prospect classes that is part of the Person interface will need to delegate to the Person class.

The resulting application uses the default interface to set the unique properties for a Customer object, uses the Person interface to set the properties and call the methods for a general person, and then passes the object to a Save method to save the properties. This process is then repeated for a Prospect object. This application does not actually send follow-up materials or save the data, rather it displays message boxes.

For a challenge, try the following:

- Add a Person interface to the project defined in the challenge for the prior example.

- Achieve inheritance by implementing the Person interface in both the Customer and Prospect and delegating to the Person interface.

CHAPTER 13: Building ActiveX Components

Building an ActiveX DLL

Group Name: Task13_1.vbg
File Folder: Ex13_1

This example is provided in a project group. The ActiveX DLL project and the sample project to test it are included in the same project group. Open the project group to open both projects.

The sample ActiveX DLL project includes the classes from the Saving Objects to a File example. Class and property settings are defined for the classes, but no changes are required to the code to make these classes a part of the ActiveX component.

The test project is the same To Do List form from the Saving Objects to a File example. This form references the ActiveX component.

To try this example, compile the ActiveX DLL, set the Version Compatibility to Project Compatibility, and define the path to the compiled ActiveX DLL.

The test project uses the ActiveX DLL to retrieve the list of tasks from the file and display them in the test project form.

For a challenge, try the following:

- Create a new project with a new user interface to display tasks. Then reference this ActiveX DLL.

- Compile the IFile interface from the prior example to an ActiveX DLL and reference it in this project.

Building an ActiveX EXE

Project Name: Task13_2.vbp and Test13_2.vbp
File Folder: Ex13_2

This sample ActiveX EXE project includes the classes from the Saving Objects to a File example. Class and property settings are defined for the classes, but no changes are required to the code to make these classes a part of the ActiveX component. The test project is the same To Do List form from the Saving Objects to a File example. This form references the ActiveX component. These projects are not part of a project group because an ActiveX EXE is an out-of-process server and cannot be tested within a project group.

To try this example, compile the ActiveX EXE, set the Version Compatibility to Project Compatibility, and define the path to the compiled ActiveX EXE. Then run the ActiveX EXE project.

In another copy of Visual Basic, open the test project. Set a reference in this project to the ActiveX EXE project that is running, then run the test project. The test project uses the ActiveX EXE to retrieve the list of tasks from the file and display them in the test project form.

For a challenge, try the following:

- Create a new project with a new user interface to display tasks. Then reference this ActiveX EXE.

- Install the ActiveX EXE on a remote computer and use DCOM to access the component. This can only be done if you have the Enterprise Edition and appropriate hardware and network.

Creating an ActiveX Client with Excel

Project Name: Tasks.xls
File Folder: Ex13_2

This project demonstrates using Microsoft Excel as a client application for your server.

The provided Excel macro will display the tasks, created with the user interface in the prior example (see Test13_2.vbp), in an Excel spreadsheet.

If you don't have Microsoft Excel 7.0 or higher on your computer, you will not be able to review this project.

To execute the macro included in this project, follow these steps:

1. Select the Get the Tasks tab to review the code.

2. Select the References option from the Tools menu to define the reference to the ActiveX EXE or ActiveX DLL (see the prior examples).

3. Select the To Do List tab to return to the spreadsheet.

4. Select Macro from the Tools menu to obtain the list of VBA macros.

5. Run the Main macro and the tasks should appear in the spreadsheet.

For a challenge, try the following:

- Add a category column to the spreadsheet.

- Store any revised cells back to the file.

Building an ActiveX Control

Group Name: Task13_3.vbg
File Folder: Ex13_3

This example is provided in a project group. The ActiveX control project and the sample project to test it are included in the same project group. Open the project group to open both projects.

The sample ActiveX control project demonstrates how to create an ActiveX control. The sample control is a set of three text boxes that can be used for entry of task information. The test project is simply a form that will contain the ActiveX control to test it.

To try this example, compile the ActiveX control, set the Version Compatibility to Project Compatibility, and define the path to the compiled ActiveX OCX. Ensure the UserDocument is closed, then open the form in the test project. You should be able to see the control appear in the form. Resizing the control should resize the text boxes within the control. You can also run the test project to view the control as a user would see it.

For a challenge, try the following:

- Use the ActiveX Control Interface Wizard to define the interface (properties, mcthods, and events) for the control.

- Compile and use the control in a Visual Basic 4 project.

Building an ActiveX Document Server

Project Name: Task13_4.vbp
File Folder: Ex13_4

This sample project demonstrates how to create an ActiveX document. The To Do List form from the Building an ActiveX EXE example was included in this project and converted to an ActiveX document using the VB ActiveX Document Migration Wizard. The resulting ActiveX document will use the ActiveX server from the Building an ActiveX EXE example.

To try this example, ensure the ActiveX EXE from the Building an ActiveX EXE example is compiled and the reference to it is set in this project. Then compile this ActiveX document server and exit Visual Basic. Then run the Setup Wizard and select an Internet download setup. After the Setup Wizard is complete double-click on the Task13_4.HTM file that was created in the directory you had defined in the Setup Wizard. If you have Microsoft Explorer 3.0 or later, the To Do List form should be displayed inside Microsoft Explorer.

For a challenge, try the following:

- Create your own ActiveX document within the project.

- Establish a link between the two ActiveX documents.

- Copy the files from the Setup Wizard installation to your Web server (it must be an IIS server as of this beta) and try displaying the HTML page from the Web server.

CHAPTER 14: Doing Database Objects

The "No Code" Approach

Project Name: CMS14_1.vbp
File Folder: Ex14_1

This project demonstrates the development of a database application with no coding. It uses a data control and bound controls to display and edit information from a database.

The resulting application allows you to track your contacts. You can keep a list of all phone calls you make/receive, the e-mail you have sent/received, meetings you have attended, and so on.

If you receive an error that the database is not found, ensure the DatabaseName property of the two data controls are set to the directory of the database (cms14_1.mdb).

For a challenge, try the following:

- Add a "Follow-up Required" field on the form for defining which contacts require some type of follow-up.

- Store this field in the database. Using Access is the easiest way to define the field in the database.

Tech Note.   *You must copy the project files for this project from the CD-ROM to your hard drive before running them because they use an Access database, which attempts to open a lock file in the same directory as the database.*

The "I Want it All" Approach

Project Name: CMS14_2.vbp
File Folder: Ex14_2

This project demonstrates the development of a database application with a minimal amount of code for an improved user interface and correct setting of the database directory.

The resulting application allows you to track your contacts. You can keep a list of all phone calls you make/receive, the e-mail you have sent/received, meetings you have attended, and so on.

Due to the way in which App.Path was used in this project, it will not run from a root directory such as d:\. It will run in d:\Ex14_2.

For a challenge, try the following:

- Add a "Type of Follow-up Required" field on the form for selecting some type of follow-up: "None," "Call," "Sales Literature," and so on.

- Create a table of these follow-up types in the database.

- Store the foreign key to the followUpTypes table in the contactEntries table.

Tech Note.   *You must copy the project files for this project from the CD-ROM to your hard drive before running them because they use an Access database, which attempts to open a lock file in the same directory as the database.*

The OO Approach

Project Name: Per14_3.vbp
File Folder: Ex14_3

This project demonstrates the development of a database application using the data access objects. It also presents how to create a standard Database class for use in any application.

The resulting application allows you to create and maintain an address book. This address book can be used to track contacts or friends.

For a challenge, try the following:

- Add a Person Type field on the form for selection of a person type (customer or prospect).

- Store this field in the database.

- Change the lengths of the fields in the database to provide additional space for entry of information, such as an e-mail address. Using Access is the easiest way to modify the database.

Tech Note.   *You must copy the project files for this project from the CD-ROM to your hard drive before running them because they use an Access database, which attempts to open a lock file in the same directory as the database.*

CHAPTER 15: Putting the Pieces Together

Building a Full-Featured Application

Project Name: CMS15.vbp
File Folder: Ex15_1

This project demonstrates the development of all of the components of an application. This includes using an application framework, building the classes in an object hierarchy, using a resource file, saving settings to the Registry, logging errors to the NT event log or any log file, using the Windows API, adding pop-up menus, using ToolBar and StatusBar controls, implementing What's This help, providing ToolTips and defining icons for the application.

To log into the application, use an ID of "cms" and any password. The resulting application allows you to track your contacts. You can keep a list of all phone calls you make/receive, the e-mail you have sent/received, meetings you have attended, and so on. It also allows you to maintain your address book and keep track of your to do list.

Notice that you must select a person before entering contact information. Otherwise the contact entry will be orphaned. Same is true if the person is deleted. This is because of the master/detail relationship between the person and the contact entries. Since bound controls are used for the detail, it is difficult to correctly maintain these relationships. To solve this problem, you could rewrite the contact entries code to use DAO instead of the data control.

For a challenge, try the following:

- Add the "Type of Follow-up Required" field and associated database changes defined in the challenge from the CMS14_2 project.

- Automatically add a task to the task list when a Follow-up Required selection is set to anything but "None".

- Change the lengths of the fields in the database to provide additional space for entry of information, such as an e-mail address. Using Access is the easiest way to modify the database.

- Put the strings for the labels on the Contact Manager window in the resource file.

- Implement What's This help for the Contact Manager window.

- Allow specification of the contact management system database from the Open common dialog box.

- Store the last selected database to the Registry.

- Default the contact management system database to the entry in the Registry.

- Implement error handling in all routines that could generate an error.

Tech Note.   *You must copy the project files for this project from the CD-ROM to your hard drive before running them because they use an Access database, which attempts to open a lock file in the same directory as the database.*

Using the Files

Ziff-Davis Press, by convention, adds an End-User License Agreement to every book. The following statements provide you additional rights with regard to the project files contained in this Appendix.

You may use, modify, enhance, and distribute these project files as a part of any application that you develop. These files are provided as-is, and no guarantees are made regarding their operation or fitness for any application.

■ Software on the CD-ROM

The CD-ROM contains two software products mentioned in the book that will be of particular interest to Visual Basic programmers: Rational Rose and Poet ODBMS.

Rational Software Corporation's Rational Rose object-oriented analysis and design tool can help you document the objects and model the relationships between the objects. It can then generate the code for those objects. A demo version of this software is included on the CD-ROM. See http://www.rational.com for more information about this product.

The Poet object database management system (ODBMS) from Poet Software provides access to its ODBMS using Automation. A trial copy of this software is included on the CD-ROM. See http://www.poet.com for more information about this product.

■ Bonus Book Chapters on the CD-ROM

In addition to the source code and software, the CD-ROM also contains two chapters from Dan Appleman's book *Dan Appleman's Visual Basic 5.0 Programmer's Guide to the Win32 API*. It also contains an article by Dan Appleman, "The Four Models for Control Creation Using Visual Basic 5.0," which is based on his upcoming book, *Dan Appleman's Developing ActiveX Components with Visual Basic 5.0.*

■ Index

A